Growing Up
in the Middle Ages

ALSO BY PAUL B. NEWMAN

Daily Life in the Middle Ages
(McFarland, 2001)

Growing Up in the Middle Ages

PAUL B. NEWMAN

McFarland & Company, Inc., Publishers
Jefferson, North Carolina, and London

LIBRARY OF CONGRESS CATALOGUING-IN-PUBLICATION DATA

Newman, Paul B., 1961–
Growing up in the Middle Ages / Paul B. Newman
p.   cm.
Includes bibliographical references and index.

ISBN-13: 978-0-7864-3084-0
(softcover : 50# alkaline paper) ∞

1. Children — Europe — History.   2. Civilization, Medieval.
3. Social history — Medieval, 500–1500.
I. Title.
HQ792.E8N49   2007   305.23094'0902 — dc22   2007002650

British Library cataloguing data are available

On the cover: Tree of Consanguinity, France,
1471 (Bibliothèque nationale de France)

Manufactured in the United States of America

McFarland & Company, Inc., Publishers
Box 611, Jefferson, North Carolina 28640
www.mcfarlandpub.com

For Bobby

Acknowledgments

I would like to thank the following institutions who allowed me to use images from their collections: the Walters Art Museum, the North Lincolnshire Museum, the Kunsthistorisches Museum, the Bibliothèque Nationale de France, the British Library, the Bodleian Library, the Morgan Library and Museum, the Wellcome Library, and the Philadelphia Museum of Art. I am particularly grateful for the assistance of Ms. Christianne Henry, head of the library at the Walters Art Museum; Ms. Anna Smith of the Wellcome Library; Dr. Kevin Leahy of the North Lincolnshire Museum and Dr. Sally Crawford for their kind help in providing the photograph of an Anglo-Saxon feeding vessel; and Pierre Terjanian, associate curator of Arms and Armor at the Philadelphia Museum of Art. I also strongly recommend that anyone interested in childhood or, indeed, any other aspect of life in the Middle Ages, visit the Web sites of these libraries and museums, especially since many now offer searchable online databases containing hundreds of full-color photographs of medieval manuscripts with illuminations.

I must also thank John Price, Ana Garcia, and Jane Walker for taking the time to read my manuscript and make suggestions for improvements as well as for their help in paring down the number of my typographical errors.

I also thank my son, Bobby, without whom I would never have become so interested in childhood. Finally and most importantly, I thank my wife Alice for her endless patience and tireless support. Without her, this book would never have been written.

Table of Contents

List of Illustrations

Introduction

When I started writing this book on growing up in medieval Europe, I had little idea how much disagreement and debate there was over the history of childhood. In the 1960s, several historians asserted that childhood as we know it today did not exist during the Middle Ages and was only created within the recent past. Citing examples such as the common use of child labor in Europe and the United States beginning in the late 18th century, some argued that society as a whole did not truly value children and recognize childhood as something worth protecting until the late 19th and early 20th centuries, when measures were enacted to stop such exploitation of children. Admittedly, this is a simplification of these historians' positions, but their main thrust remains that the further back one looks in history, the worse children were treated. As one of these historians expressed it, "the history of childhood is a long nightmare from which we have only begun to awaken. The further back in history one goes, the lower the level of child care and the more likely children are to be killed, abandoned, beaten, terrorized, and sexually abused."* Thus, when one looks as far back as the Middle Ages, the treatment of children must have been horrible beyond belief. (Though if the statement quoted above is true, it seems unlikely that mankind would exist today. After all, if one applies this reasoning to the Paleolithic, no children of early humans could have survived the sheer, unbridled brutality of their parents.)

The decades since the 1960s have witnessed a great increase in our knowledge and understanding of childhood in the Middle Ages. Through the work of numerous historians who have sifted through the archaeological and written records, we can better reconstruct how medieval society viewed children and childhood. Thanks to such scholars as David Herlihy, Shulamith Shahar, Sally Crawford, Barbara Hanawalt, Nicholas Orme, and many others whose names and works can be found in the bibliography of this book, we can see that adults in medieval Europe did recognize childhood as a time in which children learned and developed and that they did not treat children simply as little adults. Certainly, children in the Middle Ages experienced a childhood that was different in many ways from that of children today. However, there are important similarities as well. As we will see, many aspects of childhood are timeless, such as the growth and development of children and their need to play.

I have tried to present a balanced picture of the experiences of children in medieval Europe, both good and bad. There is no denying that some children were abused and

*From chapter one of Lloyd de Mause, ed., The History of Childhood (New York: Psychohistory Press, 1974).

neglected. Further, infant mortality was much higher in the Middle Ages than in Europe today. Simply surviving to adulthood was far more of a challenge then than it is today. On the other hand, many children were nurtured by their parents, who provided them with the best care they could provide. Some still died despite their parents' care but many thrived, learned trades, married, and went on to raise children of their own.

Before we begin examining childhood in medieval Europe, there are a few points I need to clarify about the scope of this book and some of the terms which I have used. As for the time frame of this book, I have tried to provide as much information as possible about childhood in Europe from the beginning of the Middle Ages, when the Roman Empire in western Europe fell in the late 5th century, through its end with the ascendancy of the Renaissance in northern Europe in the 15th century. I have tried to include as much information as possible from sources throughout the period. Unfortunately, there is much less evidence, archaeological, pictorial, and documentary, from the early Middle Ages than there is from the later Middle Ages. As a consequence, most of the evidence presented is drawn from sources in the 13th through 15th centuries.

The geographical scope of this book is western Europe, from Spain and Italy in the south, to England and Scandinavia in the north, and to Poland and lands which are currently part of the Czech Republic in the east. As with the unevenness in the availability of materials over centuries of the Middle Ages, some regions of Europe have yielded more evidence about childhood than others. England, Italy, and, to lesser degrees, France and the modern-day states of Belgium, Luxemburg, and the Netherlands have provided most of the information available about childhood in medieval Europe. Some material is available from other parts of Europe and has been included wherever possible but the preponderance is drawn from the countries listed.

Finally, the nobility and other wealthy families tend to be over-represented when studying life in the Middle Ages because these groups left more physical and documentary evidence than the poor and middling classes who constituted the majority of medieval Europeans. Although this imbalance affects the study of childhood as much as any other area of life in the Middle Ages, there are still accounts of miracles and other records which provide insights into the lives of ordinary families and their children. While there may not be as much evidence about them, the children of peasants, craftsmen, and the others who were neither wealthy nor noble are not forgotten in this text.

I would also like to clarify the meanings of certain terms used in this book. The word "Church" refers to the Christian religion as a whole, with the pope as its leader, while "church" means the building in which Christians worshipped. This use of "Church" is not intended as a slight to any other Christian denominations. It is simply recognizing that this form of Christianity was the dominant religion throughout western Europe for most of the Middle Ages.

Another term which requires clarification is "peasant." I have used this word to mean all men and women who worked the land, grew crops and raised livestock. In fact, this group was far from homogenous and included both freemen and serfs, who were often called *villains* in the Middle Ages. Serfs were subject to various restrictions on their freedom and had to render assorted customary services and payments to their lords. In exchange, the lords allotted land to the serfs for them to cultivate. Freemen, while subject to taxes and the laws of their lords, typically did not owe any services to their lords and had greater protections than serfs under the law. Further, as their title suggests, they enjoyed greater freedoms, both socially and economically, than serfs. Despite these differences among those who worked the land, the term "peasant" is an adequate designation for all these people for the purposes of this book.

With these caveats in mind, we can now proceed to examine the world of children and childhood in medieval Europe. We will start with birth, move on to the care of infants and children, and then look at children at play. Next follows the care and disciplining of children. After that, we will learn about education and career-training for all classes of medieval society. Finally, we will see how children made the transition into adulthood.

1

Birth and Baptism

What was it like being born in the Middle Ages? It was often dangerous and difficult for both the mother and child. While it is never an easy process, giving birth in medieval Europe all too frequently resulted in the death of the mother, the child, or both. Priests routinely encouraged expectant mothers to make their confessions and receive communion before labor began so that their souls would be prepared in case they died during delivery. And midwives were instructed how to perform emergency baptism for sick or dying newborns to save their souls.

While birth remains risky, many of the dangers have been significantly reduced. In the U.S. and other industrialized countries, expectant mothers and their unborn children routinely receive prenatal medical and dietary care that helps ensure that both of them are in the best possible health for delivery. And, while some mothers choose to deliver at home with the help of a midwife, most mothers today give birth in well-equipped hospitals, attended by an obstetrician and a host of other health care professionals trained in the latest techniques and using the most up to date medications. Even mothers who deliver at home are usually only a short ambulance ride from such facilities and help if their deliveries become complicated.

However, such care for pregnant women is a fairly recent development. As with other areas of medicine, the obstetrical care that we expect and enjoy today is largely a product of the advances that began in the 19th century and have been continuously improved through the present. Of course, in many parts of the world, from impoverished countries to slums in even the most wealthy nations, women still give birth without such care, facing many of the same risks experienced by European women in the Middle Ages.

If the baby was born alive and healthy, he then had to face the risks of infancy in an age before vaccinations, safety standards, and scientifically proven nutritional guidance. Obviously, some did not survive but many did. Further, while parents recognized the extreme risks and possible tragedies facing them, many clearly greeted the prospect of a new child with the same mix of joy and trepidation experienced by parents before and since the Middle Ages.

Prenatal Care

Before examining birth, we must take a brief look at the period of life immediately preceding it. The time of pregnancy is critical for both the mother and her child. From the moment of conception, the fetus is wholly dependent upon the health of his mother for his own health and development. For the mother, pregnancy places severe strains on her entire body. Today, we recognize the need for prenatal care for the benefit of both the mother and the child.

In the Middle Ages, prenatal care was extremely limited though some common aspects of pregnancies were already recognized. Morning sickness was understood to be a normal part of pregnancy. There was also a general awareness that expectant women needed to be kept as well fed as possible. Some medical writers recommended that expectant women should eat little but often. Chicken, partridge, and thrushes were considered good foods for pregnant women since these foods were thought to be very nutritious and easy to digest. It was also recognized that pregnant women sometimes have cravings for unusual foods and even for non-food substances like chalk and charcoal.

While the special needs of a developing fetus for certain vitamins and other nutrients were largely unknown until recent times, a few medical men in the Middle Ages did make some connections between diet and the development of the fetus. In addition to recognizing the impact of a mother's diet on her fertility, these physicians recorded that women who had poor diets were more likely to deliver children who were weak or had other birth defects. However, their only solution was to admonish expectant mothers not to eat acorns, wild greens and roots, and other similar foods. For practical purposes, this advice was worthless. Acorns and wild plants were eaten only by people who could not obtain any better foods and were starving. Clearly, only extremely poor women or women caught up in some disaster such as a famine or displacement caused by wars resorted to eating these foods, because they had no other choice. They did not eat these foods because they wanted to. The real problem was dietary deficiencies caused by poverty or disasters.

Some additional instructions on prenatal care were offered as remedies to prevent miscarriages. A 13th century Italian medical writer cautioned women to avoid activities such as sex and taking too many baths, though other experts advised mothers to take daily herbal baths starting two to three weeks before their due dates. Mothers-to-be were also advised to avoid falls and beatings; presumably the latter point was aimed more at their husbands than the women themselves. To lessen physical stress on both them and their unborn children, pregnant women were also often advised not to perform strenuous work. Through priests' sermons, the Church endorsed this recommendation. While this is practical advice, much work performed by women, whether farming or practicing a craft, was physically demanding, and most women had no choice but to continue working to support themselves and their families.

One early medieval text provided some very modern-sounding prenatal advice. It recommended that, to avoid miscarriage, an expectant woman should avoid horseback riding, drinking alcoholic beverages, and eating salty or sweet foods. Foreseeing the harm of the often jarring motions of riding on horseback as well as the risks of simply falling or being thrown from the horse seems fairly obvious, but making a connection between alcohol consumption and its damaging effects on the fetus is surprisingly modern. Even more surprising is the caution against excessive salt intake. High blood pressure is a common problem for some expectant women and salt can worsen it. High blood pressure in pregnancy can harm both the mother and her fetus. For the mother, high blood pressure can damage the kidneys and other organs, especially the liver and brain. If the kidneys are damaged, they are less effective in filtering the mother's blood and allow excessive amounts of protein to remain in the bloodstream. This condition can ultimately lead to the mother suffering seizures and possibly even death. For the fetus, this condition can result in premature birth, low birth weight, and possibly death (stillbirth). Pregnant women under the age of twenty are among the groups identified as having a higher risk of developing these conditions. Since most women in the Middle Ages appear to have started their child-bearing before age twenty, virtually all medieval women were in the high risk group at some point in their lives. Given that the impact of high blood pressure on pregnancy and the role of salt intake in contributing to high blood pressure have only been established scientifically within the past 100 years, it is a mystery as to how an early medieval medical writer made any connection between salt and miscarriage. The fact that medieval medical practitioners did not fully understand this connection is reinforced by some writers who stated that the problem with excess salt was that the child would be born without hair or nails.

In addition to their physical health, expectant women were also advised to care for their mental health during pregnancy. Exposure to situations that triggered strong negative feelings such as anger, fright, or anxiety was to be avoided. While the physical stresses that accompanied these emotions was of some concern, it was commonly believed that that these feelings were passed along and could be deeply imprinted on the character of the developing child in the mother's womb. Thus, a child could grow up to be excessively angry, fearful, or anxious if his mother had suffered these feelings during pregnancy. Conversely, mothers-to-be who thought pleasant thoughts and had happy experiences during pregnancy were believed to instill these feelings in their children's character.

A few people even believed that the mother's state of mind could affect the physical form of her child. Mothers who envisioned beautiful people while awake or dreaming were thought to somehow help shape their developing children into these pleasing forms. On the other hand, ugly children were result of ugly thoughts while pregnant. Thoughts or dreams about animals such as cows or, more exotically, monkeys, especially created the risk that one's child would be born with some resemblance to these creatures.

Returning to more practical physical preparations for delivery, pregnant women were advised not to undergo bleeding. Bleeding was the practice of having a small incision made in a vein, allowing blood to flow out. This practice was also referred to as *venesection*. It was often a routine part of health care regimens and was believed to help balance bodily humors and thus improve health. Expectant women were also counseled to avoid taking any medications because the medications could adversely affect the fetus. Italian medical writers in the 13th century further recommended that pregnant women should practice holding their breath and bearing down to prepare for the physical exertions required for delivery.

Assistants for Delivery

So how did women give birth in the Middle Ages? Certainly the mechanics of the process haven't changed any. And the basic mechanics of delivery were fairly well understood in the Middle Ages. After all, medieval society was agrarian and a far larger percentage of the population was involved in animal husbandry than today, so that many people had assisted or at least witnessed animals such as ewes or cows giving birth. But birth of a human baby was clearly recognized as requiring special skills. Today, most women in industrialized countries routinely consult with their gynecologists and obtain a referral to a trained obstetrician for care once they believe they are pregnant. But this was not an option in the Middle Ages. In medieval Europe, mothers could seek help in delivering their babies from several sources:

Fig. 1. Biographies of Alexander the Great and accounts of his achievements were popular among medieval nobility. This is an illustration of the birth of Alexander from one of those histories. While his birth took place in the 4th century B.C., the artist has depicted the event as a royal birth in the late 15th century A.D. Queen Olympias, Alexander's mother, is shown in bed, recovering from the exertions of childbirth. The infant Alexander is being warmed by the fireside. The basin in which he was washed immediately after birth is on the floor. In keeping with contemporary customs, only women are shown as attending the birth. These women include servants as well as other noblewomen.

physicians, midwives, friends, family, and neighbors, as well as from God. As discussed below, physicians rarely assisted in delivering babies though surgeons sometimes played a role. Midwives are the group most commonly associated with delivering babies in this period. However, it cannot be determined how many deliveries were made by professional midwives as opposed to amateurs, that is, women from among the expectant mother's circle of family, friends, and neighbors who had likely assisted or at least witnessed other births and volunteered to help (figs. 1 and 10). There seems to have been a preference for the professional midwife, likely based on the presumption that she possessed greater expertise, in part because of the sheer numbers of births she had assisted. Lastly, as for God's role, mothers in childbirth and their attendants, regardless of whom they were, always prayed for His assistance.

Physicians

Physicians seldom played a major role in births in medieval Europe. University-trained physicians were very scarce and usually charged fees that only the wealthier could afford. Further, as discussed below, medieval physicians were often poorly trained in obstetrics and gynecology and rarely attended deliveries, even of those patients wealthy enough to afford their services.

In the Middle Ages, virtually all accredited physicians were men. Medieval universities generally limited admissions to Christian men. This restriction was created by several factors. First, the universities were typically founded as places for priests and other members of the clergy to study Christian theology. University officials (who were clerics themselves) saw no point in admitting women since the Church barred women from becoming part of the clergy. This reasoning served to bar Jews from attending as well. This restriction continued to apply long after the universities had added many non-theological courses of study, including medicine. A second factor was that to be admitted to a university one had to have a working knowledge of Latin. Latin was required since the texts and lectures were all in that language. Again, this was a consequence of the original theological education mission of the universities: universities were for advanced education of the clergy and Latin was the language of the Church the clergy served. It was part of the Church's inheritance from the Roman Empire. The Church had its official documents written in Latin and used Latin as the common language to unite its otherwise linguistically diverse flock. Not surprisingly, the only people who typically had sufficient training in Latin were men who usually were either already members of the clergy or were in training to become clergymen. Apart from clerics or clerics-in-training, a small but growing number of laymen from relatively wealthy families also had opportunities for such education and attended universities in increasing number over the course of the Middle Ages. Women, on the other hand, rarely had the opportunity to learn Latin and other subjects required for admission to universities. And even if a woman possessed the requisite knowledge, she would still be denied entrance to a university since she was barred from becoming a member of the clergy. Denied a basic university education, women had few opportunities to study advanced subjects such as medicine. However, a very small number of women, such as daughters of physicians, did practice advanced medicine, including gynecology and other specialties, in many locations throughout medieval Europe. Some of the other women who managed to practice medicine were residents of the kingdom of Naples. Here, in Salerno, women were allowed to practice medicine, primarily gynecology and surgery, after passing an examination given by a group of physicians and surgeons. However, these female practitioners disappeared before the end of the 12th century and formal medical training and the practice of medicine clearly came to be dominated by the universities and their male graduates throughout all of Europe.

This stress on the exclusion of women from medical training and practice is not to suggest that men could not be competent in gynecology and obstetrics. The subsequent history of medicine has proven that men can certainly practice these specialties. But for most of the Middle Ages they were severely handicapped because their education was largely limited to the study of a relatively small number of classical Greek and Roman texts. With one exception, these texts contained only scant information on women's health issues including pregnancy and delivery, and what little information did appear was often based on fantastic theories rather than first-hand observations and reasoned explanations. And none of these texts appear to have provided anything like a "how-to" guide to delivering a baby. Birth, when it was addressed, was described only in vague terms. However, beginning in the mid–13th century, more medical texts became available as translators in Spain provided new texts translated from the Arabic. Some of these texts contained classical Greek and Roman tracts which had been lost to western Europe. Arabic scholars had translated these texts into Arabic from the Greek or Latin in the past, and the translators in Spain translated them into Latin. Most were eventually translated into the various vernacular languages of Europe. Some of the texts included the writings of Islamic medical experts. While these writings were generally influenced by the same classical Greek and Roman theories on health and disease that European scholars followed, the Islamic medical writers added information drawn from their own knowledge and experience. The new and more complete information from the classical world combined with the sum knowledge of several centuries of Islamic medical practice and thought provided an immensely valuable addition to medieval Europe. It spurred developments in the study and practice of medicine, including in the fields of gynecology and obstetrics.

In addition to the new information from external sources, 13th century European authors on natural history created new compendiums containing medical information which added recent theories and practices to traditional body of knowledge. Some of these authors appear to have actually interviewed practicing midwives and included this information in their writings. Some even seem to include information based on their own first-hand experience with deliveries. Thus, for much of the Middle Ages, while university-trained physicians typically had very limited knowledge and skills in gynecology and obstetrics, the practice of medicine in these and others areas did gradually improve over the course of the period.

Though their collective knowledge and experience improved over the centuries, most medical men continued to lack any significant expertise and largely shunned the practice of obstetrics and gynecology. A few surviving tracts indicate that some physicians claimed that they did not practice in these areas because these were distasteful matters or were otherwise work unsuitable for men. However, several prominent medical writers acknowledged that women should assist with deliveries because they were best suited for the job. Regardless of the stated rationales, with the exception of few royal and noble births, physicians very rarely assisted in births and passed the job off to midwives and other women. While physicians were absent from most births, a professional surgeon was sometimes called in when a cesarean section was needed to deliver a baby. These emergency deliveries are discussed more below.

Medieval women do not appear to have been upset by the absence of physicians at their deliveries. Most could not afford their services and thus had no expectation of having a physician in attendance. Of those women whose families could pay to hire a physician, some, perhaps, wished to protect their modesty and so had no desire to have a strange man observing and handling them so intimately. Others may have been repelled by the treatments that physicians were likely to prescribe. While these could include reasonable and inoffensive advice on diet and rest, they could also include less appetizing treatments ranging from drinking wine mixed with dust of frankincense and dust made from a hare's heart to being fumigated with smoke from burning salted fish bones, horses' hooves, or dung of a cat or lamb. However, in general, the lack of attending physicians does not appear to have been a matter of concern and was simply taken for granted.

As for distasteful treatments, physicians were not alone in prescribing them. Women and men practicing healing based on a combination of traditional home remedies and their own ideas and experiences were, by far, the most common medical practitioners in medieval Europe and far outnumbered university-trained physicians. Yet some of the treatments prescribed by these empirical practitioners contained dangerous herbal compounds and various dungs as well and so were often no less offensive or noxious that those of the physicians. Still, women needing medical attention appear to have routinely sought out other women such as these empirical practitioners for health care. Presumably women felt that these female healers would at least have sympathy for and a far better understanding of the pains and conditions they were describing than any male practitioners could have, regardless of their training. Therefore, the most important considerations in selecting delivery attendants were likely that women ordinarily sought out the help of other women with their health problems and, most simply, that giving birth was an exclusively female activity in which only other women traditionally assisted. Thus, women practicing medicine empirically and specializing in childbirth appear to have been the most common attendants at birth. These were the midwives, both professional and amateur.

Midwives

Midwives existed in many societies long before the Middle Ages. Depictions of women assisting in childbirth appear in Egyptian hieroglyphics. Midwives practiced in classical Greece and Rome as well. One of few surviving Roman texts on gynecology includes an outline of qualifications for the ideal midwife. In this text, Soranus of Ephesus (active 98–138 A.D.) wrote that a midwife should be physically robust, disciplined, sympathetic, sober, discreet, and calm with a good memory and knowledge of medicine. She should also have soft hands with long, slim fingers and short nails so that her touch would be delicate when performing her duties.

Besides listing the qualities she should possess, Soranus indicated that the midwife served as an adjunct to the physician. She was to consult with a physician on any difficult matters and follow his directions. Soranus' writings were available in the Middle Ages and were influential in medical courses in medieval universities. His guidance was often repeated in medieval compilations of medical information, though medieval physicians interpreted his writings in their own way. Some physicians in the Middle Ages appear to have interpreted Soranus' writing as supporting their view that the midwife was wholly subordinate and inferior to the physician. But, regardless of the physicians' views, midwives clearly functioned independently of physicians on a routine basis. With first-hand experience that many physicians typically could not match, they were quite capable of acting on their own.

Midwives had no formal medical training but their clients seem to have expected them to have undergone an apprenticeship or similar hands-on training before practicing on their own. For most of the Middle Ages, there was no regulation of the qualifications of midwives or the care they provided. Midwives were never organized in guilds, so there were no formal requirements for an apprenticeship until the later Middle Ages when some cities on the Continent began to regulate midwives to provide some assurance of the quality of their services. By the late 14th century, the cities of Lille in France and Constance in Switzerland were already regulating midwives, and in the 15th century, many other cities, including Frankfurt am Main, Regensburg, Nuremberg, and Munich, also began creating government controls over midwives. These regulations included requiring some basic training through apprenticeship (Nuremberg required a four year apprenticeship) as well as barring unlicensed midwives from practicing. In addition to examining their professional qualifications, officials appointed by the city government also passed judgment on the midwife's character before permitting her to practice. The examinations were often performed by physicians or clergymen but in some instances groups of the city's most respected women performed the examination. These groups also had disciplinary authority and enforced prohibitions against unlicensed practitioners as well as restrictions on the licensed midwives such as prohibitions against their administering "potions" or drugs to any of their patients.

Midwives also frequently had to give oaths assuring that they would perform their duties faithfully. Some cities went further and required midwives to

- report illegitimate births and instances of suspected infanticide;
- be prepared to perform emergency baptisms;
- not try to hasten labor so that they could more quickly move on to another delivery or otherwise take on too many deliveries at once in an effort to collect as many fees as possible; and
- provide services to all citizens, poor and rich, who needed them.

Many cities recognized that it was impractical to rely on the charity of midwives to provide services to all their residents, regardless of their ability to pay. Thus, some municipal governments began employing midwives or at least subsidizing all or part the midwife's fee so that even poor citizens could have professional assistance with their births. The first cities known to have provided this benefit were Frankfurt am Main in 1302 and Bruges in 1312. Other cities on the Continent followed this example. As with regulation of midwives, most of the documented instances are for German cities. It is interesting to note that many of these municipalities appear to have begun employing midwives or otherwise paying for their services *before* they began regulating their practice. Perhaps assuring that the city was getting good services in return for its payments was one of the motives behind imposing regulations.

As for the terms of their employment, Bruges required its municipal midwives to work 270 days a year. Besides regular payments for their work, some cities provided midwives with other compensation such as exemption from the city's taxes and supplies of firewood at the city's expense, which was a significant perk in an age when wood was the primary fuel for cooking and heating homes. Some northern European cities also exempted the midwife's family from the burden of performing the regular rounds of guard duty expected of most citizens.

While many of the larger cities on the Continent provided assistance to their poor pregnant citizens, one notable exception was Paris. Here, for most of the Middle Ages, poor mothers-to-be had to rely on the limited resources available at hospitals such as the Hotel Dieu which provided care for the indigent. By the 15th century, a specialized facility for birth had been established in Paris, but it had only 24 beds. Even though two to three pregnant women were expected to share each bed, this facility certainly did not meet the needs of city with an estimated population of around 100,000. City governments throughout England also appear to have never helped their poorer residents by providing free or subsidized midwifery. The only free professional care available to poor pregnant women in England was in hospitals. These hospitals were operated by clerics and financed by donations from individual citizens. They more often focused on the spiritual rather than physical health of their patients, but these hospitals tried to provide whatever medical care they could. One such hospital was the hospital of St. Mary Spital near Bishopgate in London. Founded in the 12th century, this hospital provided care for a small number of pregnant women as part of its overall medical services for the sick. The care was often very minimal and many hospitals were far from hygienic. The risk of contracting an infection or other disease from one's fellow patients was quite high. And so hospitals were usually a last resort when seeking any health care.

In addition to the poor, hospital patients were usually pilgrims, other travelers, and other persons who had no family in the area to help them. Unwed mothers, particularly in urban areas, often fell into this last category. In the 15th century, Richard Whittington, famed mayor of London, may have had this problem in mind when he endowed St. Thomas's hospital in Southwark with funds for a new building with 8 beds to provide care for unwed mothers. He also stated that these services be "kept secret" so that these women would not suffer public shame and loss of reputation.

However, a few beds in a handful of hospitals could have provided care to only a very limited number of expectant mothers. Further, while London was and would remain the largest city in England, it accounted for only a small percentage of the country's total population. Most of the population was still rural and had no access to hospitals since these were primarily located in larger urban areas. Thus, most poor, pregnant women in England must have relied on any help they could find. The fortunate ones could turn to relatives, neighbors, and friends when giving birth.

For those women who could afford professional help, the selection of a midwife was presumably based on either friends' recommendations or the general public reputation of a midwife. But there is not enough surviving data to determine how much of a choice most women had. Women in cities and larger towns may have had some real choice, but in many cases, especially in rural areas, women likely had to make do with whichever midwife practiced in the vicinity. Only the nobility and other wealthy families could afford to hire midwives of particularly noted skill and have them brought any significant distance to attend a delivery. Records from 14th century England reveal that midwifery could be very profitable for any woman who gained a good reputation among the nobility. By the end of the 15th century, the English royal family paid very substantial sums annually to retain the services of certain preferred midwives.

While the focus has been on professional midwives, it should be noted that full-time, paid midwives may not have constituted the majority of women who served as midwives in Europe over the course of the Middle Ages. For most if not all of the Middle Ages, rural areas and smaller towns likely did not have sufficient populations provide enough work for a woman to make a living solely by being a midwife. Only the larger towns and cities appear to have had enough demand to support paid professionals. For example, Nuremberg in 1417 had an estimated 16 licensed midwives serving a total population of possibly 25,000. Assuming that around half of these citizens were female, there was one midwife for about every 750 females, and this figure must be reduced by the number of females too old or too young to bear children. So, very roughly, there may have been one midwife for every 400 to 500 women of child-bearing age. While this estimate is very speculative, it does suggest the number of women that a midwife could reasonably serve as well as the size of the client base needed for a midwife to make a living. If this is correct, there were many areas in medieval Europe which were too sparsely inhabited to support a full-time midwife. In some towns, part-time professionals might have existed. These women could have supported themselves by farm- or craft-work between deliveries. Yet, how many women were professional midwives, full- or part-time, cannot be established. Further, professional midwives did not have a monopoly on experience in assisting with births. In both the country and the city and towns, female relatives, friends, and neighbors routinely attended births and many appear to have assisted as well. Combining this with the personal experience that many had from giving birth themselves, these women constituted a readily available pool of helpers. Admittedly, the skills and knowledge of this group varied tremendously, but the same can be said of the many unregulated midwives who practiced throughout the Middle Ages. Still, since they were the most accessible, these helpful amateur midwives probably assisted in the majority of deliveries for much of the Middle Ages, apart from deliveries for those women wealthy enough to command professional service. However, since such assistance left no physical evidence and was largely undocumented, we cannot determine the accuracy of this assumption with any reasonable certainty.

Delivery

Most women gave birth in their own homes, in their own beds. As mentioned above, only poor women who had no other options delivered in a hospital. Reclining in a bed is the most common posture shown in medieval illustrations (figs. 1 and 10). Birthing stools had been used in classical Rome. The seat of the stool had a large opening in it, rather like a modern toilet seat. By the late Middle Ages, the stool had evolved into a chair with back and arms. While there is at least one medieval depiction of a woman using a birthing stool, it does not appear to have been widely used. There is also an image of a woman delivering while squatting and supporting herself by holding on to a rope suspended from a beam above. Delivering in a squatting position was and is used in many cultures outside of Europe, but surviving literature and images clearly indicate that reclining in bed was the most common position for giving birth in medieval Europe. Allowing her to lie in a bed was in accord with the general guidance that the mother should be made as comfortable as possible so that she could better endure the exertions of childbirth. The importance of soothing the mother and keeping her calm was well understood.

Once the mother had taken to childbed, midwives and other attendants employed a variety of means to ease the mother's pain and facilitate the birth. One method was to wash the woman's stomach and thighs and apply oils. Often, the birth canal and cervix were oiled as well. Midwives were also advised to oil their hands and insert one into the birth canal if it was necessary to try to widen the opening of the womb. A less drastic measure was to massage the woman's stomach to try to move the baby down into the birth canal. However, some birth attendants must have gotten too forceful at times since late medieval instructions admonished them not to apply too much force in efforts to speed up the delivery. Another technique was to have the mother sneeze to help force the baby out. Several texts advised administering irritating powders such as dried, ground hellebore root to make the mother sneeze violently. Hellebore is poisonous and is very dangerous to ingest, but the small amounts inhaled do not appear to have caused any harm. And, very practically, birth attendants were also to encourage the mother to bear down to help move her child down and out through the birth canal. Some texts even specified that mothers should be told not to bear down until after the cervix was sufficiently dilated. This last advice was to help mothers conserve their strength and not tire themselves out with pointless exertion.

In addition to physical means, mothers and birth attendants sometimes turned to magic. Some of the magic was performed in preparation for the birth. Anglo-Saxons recorded that mothers could prepare for their upcoming delivery by stepping across a grave three times while reciting a chant about the triumph of life over death. Anglo-Saxon mothers were also advised to write a prayer in Latin on wax and then tie this talisman to the bottom of the right foot to help ensure a successful birth. During delivery, other magic was sometimes used. This included placing aetites on the mother's belly or thighs. Aetites are walnut-sized nodules of iron-bearing rock and are often hollow. They were referred to as eaglestones from the belief that eagles collected them in their nests to promote egg laying. The supposed benefits of eaglestones were also recognized in Jewish and Islamic cultures. Jet, a lustrous black stone, was another mineral that was thought to ease childbirth. It was believed that a pregnant woman would deliver more easily if she drank water which had stood for three days and nights in a dish made of jet. Pieces of a small bowl made of jet which may have been used for this purpose have been found in London. Sympathetic magic (trying to cause events to happen by making symbolic gestures similar to the desired results) was practiced as well and appears to have been the most common form of magic used for deliveries. This magic involved various activities of opening in the attempt to help the mother's womb open. Doors, lids of chests, and any other closed items in the vicinity would be thrown open. More elaborately, the husband would wrap his belt around his wife and then remove it while reciting: "I bind you, let Christ unbind you!" He was to do this three times.

As the incantation above shows, the line between magic and Christian religion was quite blurry for many laypeople in the Middle Ages. Prayers were mixed with practices from folklore. Whether they involved prayers or not, the better educated clergy viewed all of these customs as superstition at best, demonic magic at worst. Still, such magic remained popular throughout medieval Europe though it came under increasing scrutiny and condemnation by the Church. And by the late Middle Ages, midwives or other practitioners who used magic too obviously or freely could well find themselves charged with witchcraft, especially if the child died during delivery.

As opposed to magic, praying for a safe delivery was fully endorsed by the Church. Before and during delivery expectant mothers, their husbands, friends, and families would routinely pray to God for the mother's and infant's health. Some might even promise to make a pilgrimage or a donation to the Church as evidence of their sincerity and piety. St. Mary, the mother of Christ, was a very popular saint in general and was especially popular with expectant mothers who hoped their deliveries would be as pain free and happy as hers. The girdle of St. Mary was thought to be especially beneficial to mothers during delivery. The girdle was a thin, ornamented belt which, apocryphal stories claimed, St. Mary dropped to St. Thomas during her ascension to heaven. Westminster Abbey possessed a girdle ascribed to St. Mary and loaned it to the English royal family for some births. Women of lesser standing had to content themselves with going to the shrine which held the girdle. However, this was not as difficult as it may sound since at least four other churches and abbeys around England claimed to have the true girdle. Further, England was not alone in claiming to have the girdle. France, Italy, and the crusader states in Palestine also had their holy girdles. In addition to St. Mary's girdle, both Aachen in Germany and Chartres in France claimed to possess the gown worn by St. Mary when she gave birth to Christ. However, many shrines to St. Mary, regardless of whether they possessed a girdle or a gown, became minor pilgrimage centers and were a focus for seeking divine help with births.

In addition to St. Mary, other saints popular with pregnant women were Saints Margaret and Anne. St. Margaret was a virgin martyred for her beliefs in the 4th century. According to apocryphal accounts, during the course of her martyrdom she was swallowed whole by a dragon. St. Margaret then made the sign of the Cross and the dragon's belly split open. She emerged unharmed. During the Middle Ages, St. Margaret's miraculous passage was transformed into a symbol for giving birth and expectant mothers prayed that their children would emerge from their bellies as safely as St. Margaret had escaped the dragon's. St. Anne's connection with pregnant women was less metaphorical and more direct: she was the mother of St. Mary.

While the Church offered some comfort to expectant women, the medieval Church's doctrine on procreation and birth was not entirely sympathetic. In the early Christian church, celibacy was the ideal. However, many clerics accepted that reproduction was a normal human function and that, while celibacy would be better, sexual intercourse within the confines of marriage for the purposes of procreation was to be tolerated. In fact, even clerics themselves were allowed to marry and have families for part of the Middle Ages. Yet despite this compromise, the pains and risks women endured in childbirth were seen by many clerics as divine punishment for the carnal pleasures of sexual intercourse. They appear to have been unconcerned that only half of the people who engaged in sexual activity were subject to this penalty. Clerics also noted that, in the biblical account of God casting Adam and Eve out of Paradise, God told Eve that the pains of childbirth would be part of her punishment. If the first mother was so cursed, the clerics reasoned, her descendants could expect no better. Still, pregnant women, their friends, and their families hoped that God would be merciful and prayed for His help.

Difficult Deliveries

All this help, physical, magical, and sacred, was used in varying combinations in routine births with varying degrees of success. But more extreme measures were needed when births were not routine. Breech births created insurmountable difficulties for mothers in the Middle Ages. A breech birth occurs when the baby is in the wrong position, i.e. anything other than head down towards the cervix (fig. 2). In a breech birth the baby's feet, buttocks, or other body parts, instead of the head, present themselves at the opening of the womb. It is impossible for the baby to exit the womb in this position. Then as today, the only two options are to turn the baby around so that his head is in the correct position to move through the birth canal or to perform a cesarean section.

Turning the baby involves substantial risks to both the mother and child. First, something must be inserted into the womb to hold on to the baby. To accomplish this in the Middle Ages, one of the attendants had to oil her hands well and insert one or, space permitting, both hands into the birth canal and try to turn the child around. This was a time when the midwife's long, slim fingers and short nails recommended by Soranus came in very handy. Late medieval instructions told attendants not to insert hooks or other objects into the birth canal to hasten delivery, but the fact that such instructions were needed suggests that this was not an uncommon practice. Forceps for assisting in turning the infant were not invented until the early 17th century.

The dangers for both the mother and her child were tremendous. The mother had a high risk of infection when the attendant's unsterile fingers or other instruments came in contact with the inside of the uterus. The baby, too, could suffer infection from this contact. Twisting

and with the tother honde put it vp ayein as we haue
schewid afore & so bryng hym forth yf you mayst.
The 19. is yf the child schewe first forth his fete &
tryng and his cord honde bytwene his fete & his
hede hangyng bakward. the mydwif abith hyr
honde putte in correctyng the chyld & leyng hys
cord honde by his other down by his sides & men-
dyng his hede on the best mad & the feete rightlich
dresses & than the mydwif bryngyng hym forth.
The 11. is yf the childes nekke come first foreward
than the mydwiff hyr honde putte yn & schoue hy
vp ayein by the shulders hyngyng lyst the chyld
& so to the orificium bryng hym down e so bryng hym
The 12. is yf the child schewe fyrst forthe ¶ forth
his knees bowed than the mydwiff schall put hy
vp ayein bakward the hondes of the mydwif sette
on oper in hir hyndes and pan hir cord honde
anoynded & put yn & per abith amendyng so the
knees And hym take by the schulders & so bakward
softely bryng hym forth. And so abland his fete be
amendid puttyng hym vpward vnto he be right
as he schuld be & than bryng hym forth by the
grace of god e the mydwifes comyng.

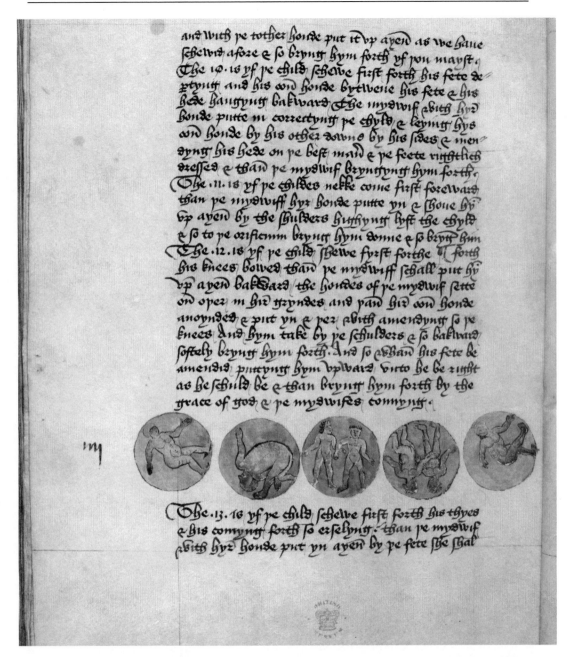

The 13. is yf the child schewe first forth his thyes
e his comyng forth so erchyng. than the mydwif
abith hyr honde put yn ayein by the fete she shal

Fig. 2. This illustration is part of a 15th century medical book. Despite being depicted as toddlers complete with full heads of hair, the children in the pictures are actually fetuses, and the five pictures depict different difficult positions for delivery. In all of the pictures, the circle represents the womb, and its opening is at the bottom of the circle. In an ideal delivery, the baby's head is pointed down and is ready to exit the womb. In the first, third, and fifth circles, the babies have their buttocks or feet pointed downward while the child in the second circle is doubled-over with one foot and one arm next to his head. Having the baby in any of these positions would result in a breech birth and require reaching up the birth canal and attempting to turn the baby to the correct position for delivery. The fourth circle depicts a pair of twins who are both pointed head downward. However, even with twins in the correct position, delivery of twins was still risky for both the babies and their mother.

and turning the baby could also damage its umbilical cord or cause other severe injuries which could easily result in death. The manipulations could also damage the placenta, which could trigger uncontrollable bleeding. Thus, the mortality rates for breech birth infants and their mothers in medieval Europe were likely quite high. While modern physicians occasionally try to move infants into better positions for delivery, sometimes with the use of sterile forceps, some of the same risks faced in the Middle Ages persist to the present day, and the mortality rate for breech birth infants remains significantly higher than for those delivered in normal births.

If trying to turn the baby failed and the baby was still alive, the only remaining option was a cesarean section. A cesarean section is an operation in which the mother's abdomen is cut open, allowing access to the womb and removal of the infant. In the United States today, cesarean section deliveries of babies are common, with approximately 1 in every 5 deliveries being performed by "c-section." The babies and their mothers typically experience few if any significant lasting ill effects. In the Middle Ages, while there were a few unsubstantiated reports of survivors, cesarean sections appear to have always been fatal for the mother. This terrible situation remained unchanged until the early 19th century, when advances in anesthesia and surgery improved the mother's chances of survival. The first successful cesarean section recorded in the English-speaking world occurred around 1815 and was performed in South Africa by an English woman who had disguised herself as a man so that she could serve in the British Army. (Another interesting side note is that, also in the 19th century, European explorers discovered native healers in several central African regions who successfully performed cesarean sections using methods that appear to have existed for generations.)

Returning to medieval Europe, in addition to being used in breech births, cesarean sections were also necessary any time the mother was dead or dying. Even for a healthy and well-fed mother, life-threatening dangers could arise during birth. There was always the possibility of excessive bleeding, especially if attendants attempted to help push or pull out the infant. Such internal bleeding could not be controlled by any of the medical practices employed in the Middle Ages and thus would likely have been fatal to the mother and her baby. Even without bleeding, a long and difficult delivery tired out both mother and child. Mothers who reached the point of exhaustion often died. In these circumstances, someone had to be prepared to perform an emergency cesarean section, cutting the mother's left side open and removing the baby in a last ditch effort to deliver it alive. If time allowed and one was available, a surgeon would be called in to perform the operation but the midwife or other attendants had to be prepared to act when a surgeon could not be found. Records of the survival of babies delivered by cesarean section are scarce. One documented case took place around the beginning of the 11th century. An infant was delivered two weeks early since his mother had died. After being taken from his mother's body, he was wrapped in the fat of a newborn pig "until his skin should grow." He survived and lived into adulthood, bearing the nickname "the Unborn."

The fatal consequences of a cesarean section for the mother were well understood. According to Church as well as medical guidance, a cesarean section was only to be performed when the mother was dead or dying and it was the only means for saving the life of the infant. Under no circumstances was the mother to be cut open solely to reach an infant so that he could be baptized before he died. However, the fact that such prohibitions had to be issued suggests that some midwives and others did believe baptism was more important than the mother's life. And baptism was certainly very important in Christian Europe in the Middle Ages. Birth attendants had to be prepared to perform emergency baptisms when a child appeared unlikely to live until a priest could arrive to perform the ceremony. Baptism and emergency baptism are discussed in more detail later in this chapter.

If the infant had died before delivery (stillbirth) or during it, the attendants were to take the necessary actions to remove it from the womb while avoiding inflicting harm to the mother. The dead infant had to be completely expelled from the womb or the mother would sicken and die. Hooks and other instruments were used to accomplish this gruesome task. Eagle-stones were also thought to help.

Other Difficult Births

While breech births were the most difficult, there were two other conditions which also created complications for deliveries. First, some mothers in the Middle Ages were extremely young even by contemporary standards. Very young brides were most common among the nobility. Some were child brides who were not expected to consummate their marriages until a suitable age, but a "suitable age" appears to have been as young as 12 in some instances. However, waiting until the girl was at least 14 to 16 years old was much more common. Still, there was considerable pressure on these noble brides to begin producing heirs, preferably male, as soon as possible to safeguard the future of the lineage. Thus, noble girls who were not even fully grown often became pregnant despite the high risks delivery posed by their smaller frames and relative frailty.

The other difficult condition was multiple births. Twins and triplets were rare but sufficiently common that they were included in medical literature and common lore. One common belief was that multiple births were the result of having intercourse with two or more different men. However, some people clearly did not believe this myth. For example, a French author of the late 12th century wrote a story in which a neighborhood gossip torments a mother who has given birth to twins. The gossip proclaims that the twins are proof that the mother has been unfaithful to her husband. But the gossip herself becomes pregnant within the year and gives birth to twins. The story ends with the townspeople concluding that the innocent mother has been divinely vindicated. Myths aside, twins and triplets were more likely to be underweight and so less prepared to survive. Multiple births were even more physically demanding on both the mother and the infants and had an increased risk of ending in breech births (fig. 2).

After the Birth

While tragic outcomes were all too common, many deliveries ended far more happily with a healthy newborn and a healthy though exhausted mother. After the baby had fully emerged from the womb, the umbilical cord was cut, leaving a few inches attached to the child. Thirteenth century Italian and English medical writers stated that a strong thread should be used as a ligature to tie the cord off on both sides of the cut to prevent bleeding. Following Soranus, they recommended using wool instead of linen thread since the wool was softer and less likely to cut into the cord than linen. Soranus had also advised that tying off both sides was necessary only when the placenta had not yet been expelled. Substances believed to promote coagulation, such as ash of snail, powdered dragon blood, or, more mundanely, cumin powder, were sometimes applied to the cut cord to help the cut seal faster. Bandaging with a soft cloth was also recommended. The infant was then gently cleaned with fine oils, rose-water or other pleasantly scented water. Obviously, many could not afford such luxuries and made do with plain water, preferably warm, and soft cloths (figs. 1 and 10). The baby was then wrapped to keep him warm. While swaddling, the wrapping of infants in tight bands of cloths, was common in the Middle Ages, it does not appear to have been routine practice to swaddle newborns. Illustrations indicate that the child was then given back to his mother for comfort and to begin nursing.

While the newborn was receiving his first care, the mother had to complete the birth process by expelling the placenta, which had nourished her infant during her pregnancy. The importance of the complete expelling of the placenta from the womb was well recognized. If it was not completely removed from the womb, the mother would sicken and die. This was among the gynecological problems addressed in the medical treatise ascribed to Trotula, a legendary 12th century female physician from Salerno. The section on giving birth states that the placenta must be completely expelled from the uterus soon after the baby has been deliv-ered. While this guidance is sound, the text then lists several different means for inducing the expulsion of the placenta, including burning the bones of salted fish, horses' hooves, or dung of a cat or lamb so that the smoke "fumigates the woman from below." Herbal methods were also used, including ingesting pennyroyal or drinking dittany juice. Pennyroyal is a member of the mint family still noted for its ability to promote menstruation. Dittany was used in wound treatment and was believed to help extract injurious materials from the body. As with removal of stillbirths, some texts cautioned against the use of drastic measures such as the use of hooks to hasten the removal of the placenta.

Mortality in Childbirth

As the information above illustrates, childbirth was extremely risky for both the mother and her child. The number of complications that could prove life threatening was stagger-ing. In times of famine or disease, the mother would be physically fragile even before the tri-als of delivery began. Her unborn infant would also be left weak and possibly underdeveloped by these same problems. Thus, both were left ill-prepared for any difficulties during delivery.

If the mother and her child survived their ordeal, they were still at risk. There was always a risk of infection for the mother, which could prove fatal in an age before antibiotics. The newborn baby was also at risk from infection and from complications stemming from any injuries he sustained during delivery. Further, once delivered, the baby was exposed to the same diseases as any other person and, unfortunately, the baby's developing immune system often proved no match for many viruses and bacteria.

Clearly, maternal and infant mortality was a serious problem in the Middle Ages. Since the surviving written records and physical remains of medieval Europeans do not provide enough information to precisely quantify the number of deaths of mothers and their chil-dren, we can only estimate. Combining the very limited medieval data available with data for other pre-industrial societies, some experts have estimated that approximately 1 in every 40 women died in childbirth during the Middle Ages while others think it was as high as 1 in 10. But keep in mind that these are very rough averages for the entire 1000 year period of the Middle Ages. Individual records reflect widely varying death rates above and below these aver-ages. As for infant mortality, it is just as speculative. The most common estimate is that nearly 1 in 3 children died before their first birthday but some experts estimate the average as having been lower, 1 in 5. Regardless of whatever the exact figures were, deaths of mothers and their babies were common in medieval Europe. Still, large numbers of mothers and their children beat the odds and survived, as the existence of many of us today proves.

Infant and maternal mortality remained high in Europe for centuries after the Middle Ages. Significant reductions in the rates of mortality have only been achieved in the last 100 to 150 years. Currently, in developed countries in Europe, North America, and elsewhere, maternal mortality has been reduced to an average of less than 1 in 10,000. Infant mortality (death from accident, disease, or any other cause before age 1) has been reduced to an average of less than 1 in 160. However, in many underdeveloped countries maternal mortality is estimated at approximately 1 in 100 and infant mortality averages about 1 in 5, rates which appear comparable to medieval Europe. The benefits of improved diet and access to advanced health care are obvious.

One last point about death during childbirth in the Middle Ages: burial. Under strict application of the Church's doctrines, if the mother and baby died during the birth before the baby could be baptized, the baby had to be removed from the mother's body before she could be buried in the parish cemetery. The cemetery was consecrated ground and only Christians could be buried there. Since the baby had not been baptized, he had not yet become a Christian and could not be buried in holy ground. However, a number of skeletons excavated from medieval cemeteries prove that this requirement was sometimes ignored and the mother and infant were simply buried together. There is also evidence that distraught families entered cemeteries at night and secretly buried their children who died during or immediately after birth and had not been baptized. These secret burials were common enough that Hereford Cathedral cited them as one of the reasons for enclosing its cemetery in 1398.

Baptism

As the prohibitions against burying unbaptized infants in church cemeteries suggest, baptism was of critical importance in Christian medieval European society. Under Christian beliefs, only those persons who had been baptized in the name of Christ had any chance of entering heaven. Thus, parents wanted their children baptized. And, conscious of high infant mortality, they wanted them baptized quickly. If the child was healthy, the baptism would take place within a few days after birth, allowing time to assemble the baptismal party and finalize arrangements for the accompanying celebration. But if the child was sickly, no time would be spared in performing the baptism.

The Need for Baptism

In the Christian belief system, all of mankind is tainted by the original sin of Adam and Eve. As part of this belief, every person bears their part of this sin from their first moments of life. Under Christianity, the stain of original sin can be removed by acceptance of the Christian faith through a ritual in which a person formally states his belief in Christ and other key elements of the faith. He then receives the sacrament of baptism and is accepted into the Christian community. Most importantly, freed of original sin, the person is now eligible to enter heaven upon his death. Of course, even after baptism, any sinful activity jeopardizes the heavenly reward.

In the early Christian church, only adults could be baptized. Typically, children were viewed as being too young to understand the significance and importance of accepting and entering the Christian faith, so they were barred from baptism until reaching an age when they could reasonably make such a commitment. However, in the first few centuries after Christ, Christianity evolved from a faith composed largely of adult converts from other religions to a faith into which an ever-increasing number of people were born. Christian parents were very concerned that their children who died too young to be baptized would not be able to enter heaven. Further, since only those baptized into the Christian faith could be admitted to heaven, the only alternative for the unbaptized was hell. In fact, St. Augustine (354–430 A.D.) and other important theologians of the early Christian church confirmed that unbaptized children, regardless of how innocent their lives, still suffered from original sin and would go to hell when they died. Despite the apparent contradiction of Christ's own views on the innocence and purity of children, implied in His teachings that Christians need to be "as little children" in their faith and humility, the consigning of unbaptized infants to hell remained a part of Church doctrine until the 13th century. Not surprisingly, Christian parents could not accept the bleak and terrifying prospect of their tiny loved ones being doomed to eternal torment. Beginning in Rome in the 3rd century A.D., the Church began baptizing children and, in the following three to five centuries, it became the standard practice throughout the Christianized parts of Europe. Initially, baptisms for both children and adults were performed only around Easter but, particularly with baptisms for newborns, the Church gradually shifted to permitting baptisms at any time throughout the year.

Even civil authorities felt a moral responsibility to encourage the rapid baptizing of infants. As early as the 7th century, fines and other punishments were to be imposed upon parents who failed to have their child baptized within a certain time, varying from seven to thirty days, after his birth. Fines and punishments were increased if the child died before baptism. However, such civil penalties appear to have been more common in areas in which rulers had recently converted to Christianity and were probably part of efforts to enforce full conversion of their subjects. Fear and guilt over the spiritual consequences of failing was usually a strong enough motivation for most parents to have their children promptly baptized.

The Ritual and Sacrament

Baptism of adult converts to Christianity continued and remained important. During the early Middle Ages, as Christianity spread to pagan areas, the conversion and baptism of adults, especially of kings, queens, and other nobility, was a key step in these areas' being integrated into the newly forming European community. Ideally, adults were to be baptized in groups around the holy days of Easter and Pentecost. Still, these baptisms were outstripped in sheer numbers by the ever-growing number of routine baptisms of children throughout the year.

As a sinful little creature, the unbaptized infant could not simply be admitted into the

Opposite: **Fig. 3. St. Eadburga's Church, Leigh, Worcestershire. The 14th century church has a wooden porch, which was typical of many churches in the Middle Ages. As with St. Peter's, this porch was the site of many events in the lives of its parishioners.**

church building. Some rituals and precautions were needed. The baptismal party met the priest in the shelter of a covered area immediately outside the church's door (figs. 3 and 4). The essential members of the baptismal party were the infant, of course, and its three godparents. The midwife or another attendant from the child's birth would also often attend. Her primary role was to confirm the child's gender. Surprisingly, the infant's parents were not members of the baptismal party. Fathers could attend but appear to have seldom done so. As for mothers, they were customarily barred from attending. The mother was deemed impure after the exertions of childbirth. She would not be readmitted to the church building until many weeks after the child's birth. This prohibition was drawn from the Old Testament and from the actions of the Virgin Mary, Christ's mother. The exact length of time was originally based upon whether the child was a boy or a girl. Delivery of a boy barred the mother for a period of 33 or 40 days while delivery of a girl imposed a 66 or 80 day ban. By the 13th century, the custom had settled at around forty days, regardless of the child's gender. After the prescribed number of days had passed, the mother could reenter the church after being met at the church door by the priest and receiving a blessing. This readmission ceremony was often called "churching." On a practical level, one hopes that some of time not spent attending church allowed the mother extra time to recuperate and to bond with her newborn.

Such sequestering of the new mother was not unique to the Judeo-Christian world. In dynastic China and other cultures, mothers have been similarly secluded after giving birth. While they had a respite from most religious obligations, many medieval European mothers had to return to their everyday work as quickly as possible because their labor was essential to maintaining their families' welfare. Only the nobility and the wealthy could typically afford to give a mother the prolonged rest she needed for rebuilding her health.

Godparents

As stated previously, the baptismal party included three godparents. For a boy, these were two men and a woman, and for a girl, two women and one man (fig. 5). The principal godparent would be one of the two who were the same gender as the child. However, in the early Middle Ages, this was not a strict rule and women are known to have been the sole godparents of some boys.

The exact selection of the godparents depended upon the parents' social contacts and the time available as well as upon the need to comply with customary and religious restrictions. The Church discouraged having close relatives, either by blood or by marriage, as godparents. As relatives, these persons already had some obligation to help foster the child's moral and religious upbringing, and the Church may have viewed it preferable to draw in people from outside the family to provide a broader network of people obligated to oversee the child's spiritual development. On a material level, this broadening of the child's connections to include a larger and more diverse group of adults may have also had the practical benefit of broadening the number of potential caregivers for the child should his parents die before he reached adulthood. This might not seem like an important consideration now in an age when we routinely expect parents to live to see their children grow to adulthood. However, in the Middle Ages, many parents died while their children were minors and so parents had serious concerns about who would care for their children after they were gone.

Returning to the spiritual aspects, the Church had another impact on selection of godparents. As will be discussed further in the chapter concerning marriage, the Church prohib-

Fig. 4. St. Peter's Church, Southrop, Gloucestershire, ca. 1100. By the end of the Middle Ages, many churches had stone porches. This stone porch was built in the late 14th century and may have replaced an earlier wooden one. As part of the baptismal rite, the godparents, the infant, and the priest met in the porch before entering the church. Weddings also often took place in church porches such as this one.

ited marriage between a broad range of individuals based upon whether they were related by blood, by marriage, or in spirit. This last group of spiritual relatives was godparents and their offspring. Marrying the son or daughter of one's godparents was prohibited as incest. Thus, parents did not want to select godparents who were also desirable future in-laws.

Subject to the Church's restrictions, the parents were free to select the godparents. While the evidence is very limited, it suggests that parents often tried to select at least one godparent who was above them socially and/or economically. For merchants or peasants, these desirable godparents could range from simply a more successful person within their own class and occupation to their immediate lord or one of his officials. For the nobility, godparents from one's own level or a higher one were suitable. Obviously, parents who could secure such desirable godparents hoped that these godparents would take a real interest in the child and possibly assist him with his career later in life. Surviving wills and other records reveal a mixed result. Some godparents made a token gift to the family at the time of the baptism and then appear to have had no further contacts. Some provided job opportunities to their godchildren, while others remembered godchildren in their wills with bequests ranging from small sums of money to significant land holdings and other valuables. But no pattern can be found. Clearly, some godparents took more of an interest in their godchildren than others, but the circumstances behind these relationships varied as much as the personalities and the financial resources of the people involved. In any event, having a prestigious godparent helped the social standing of the child and his family.

Despite the best preparations, all the parents' plans for selecting godparents could fall apart. Determining the date and time that a pregnant woman will deliver her child is still not an exact science and was even less so in the Middle Ages. Coupled with the urgency of having a child baptized, especially if it appeared likely to die, this meant that the most desirable godparents might not be available. Even when the child was healthy, the limited communications and transportation then available could result in long delays both in telling godparents that they were needed and in bringing them to the site of the baptism. Thus, in actual practice, relatives, who were otherwise barred from being the godparents, even including the child's father, and strangers found on the way to the church were sometimes pressed into service.

When the baptismal party had finally been assembled under the shelter of the porch (figs. 3 and 4), the priest asked one of the party, typically the midwife, to verify the child's gender. The priest asked the godparents what the child was to be named. He also quizzed each of the godparents to determine their basic understanding of Christian beliefs and their ability to recite a few standard prayers. Satisfied that the godparents met at least the minimum requirements for their future duties, the priest would proceed. But before entering the church, the child had to be exorcised just in case any demons were lurking in him. The exorcism entailed blessing the child, making the sign of the Cross and other gestures, and placing a small amount of salt in his mouth. Any hidden demons presumably exited the child's mouth along with gobs of drool as he tried to spit out the bitter salt. With a godparent carrying the infant, the baptismal party could now enter the church and begin the ceremony.

The Ceremony

Once inside, the party proceeded to the baptismal font. In early Christian baptism, the person being baptized was completely immersed in a large body of water such as a lake or river. This practice continued for adults but as baptism of children became the norm baptismal fonts were constructed inside churches. These stone or metal fonts provided a large, raised bowl of water which easily allowed total immersion baptism to be practiced on the small scale suitable for infants (figs. 5, 6, and 7). Water within the font had been solemnly and formally blessed and was thus "holy water." Often, the holy water had been in the font for some

This is 15th century illumination depicts a typical baptism of an infant. Here, the infant is male and so has two godfathers and one godmother to hold him and act on his behalf during the ceremony. The fourth figure (second from the left) is the priest. During the baptismal ceremony, the naked infant was usually immersed completely in the water-filled front.

time. It was considered valuable and held by some to have curative powers for the body as well as the soul. Thus, it could not be disposed of casually. In fact, there was such concern about the holy water being stolen and used for profane purposes that fonts were often fitted with large, lockable lids to guard the water within. The lids would also have protected the holy water from contamination, but that appears to have been a lesser concern. A guide for priests in the Middle Ages advised that the water in the font needed changing if a child defecated in the font during baptism but *not* if he only urinated.

At the font, the godparents removed the infant's clothes, usually consisting of a small gown, and presented the child to the priest. The priest asked the child his name, whether he

Fig. 6. Baptismal font and font cover at St. Mary's Church, Ewelme, Oxfordshire. The church, the font, and its cover date to the mid-15th century. Although the font cover was restored in the early 19th century, it retains its original form. The cover is 10½ feet in height. The cover is raised by means of a pulley in the ceiling and a counterweight. While quite ornate, this cover served the practical purpose of protecting the holy water within the font.

Fig. 7. Baptismal font, St. Peter's Church, Southrop, Gloucestershire, mid–12th century. Most font covers were more modest than that at Ewelme. Although the cover shown is a modern replacement, it likely resembles those used in many churches across medieval Europe. While the modern lid can simply be lifted off, there are remains of fittings for metal fasteners in several spots around the upper rim of the font. In the Middle Ages, these fasteners, along with a lock, firmly secured the lid and protected the holy water inside the font.

renounced Satan and all his works, and to confirm that he desired to be baptized. Obviously, the infant could not respond; part of the godparents' role was to make the responses on the child's behalf. The priest then proceeded to immerse the naked infant three times in the holy water while reciting that the child was being baptized in the name of the Father, Son, and Holy Spirit. Sprinkling water on the child's face three times was sometimes performed instead, but complete immersion was most common. The priest gave the child a final blessing while applying a smear of chrism, a blessed mixture of oil and balsam, in the shape of the Cross on the child's forehead. The child was returned to the godparents and redressed in its baptismal gown along with a hood or band over his forehead to secure the chrism.

The priest closed the ceremony by admonishing the godparents to fulfill their spiritual duties to the child, including teaching him the three basic Christian prayers (the Lord's Prayer, the Hail Mary, and the Apostles' Creed). The priest then routinely enjoined the godparents to help keep the child safe from fire and water, two leading but preventable killers of children then and now. Finally, he reminded them that the cloth covering the chrism had to be returned to the church for proper recycling. After all, it was then highly imbued with holy material and was suitable only for proper religious uses.

The ceremony was now over and the godparents could return the child to its parents. The child was now a true member of the Christian community, and the baptism was usually accompanied by such celebrations as the parents could afford. The parents would entertain and present gifts to the godparents while the godparents would give gifts for their new godchild. Like other occasions that were important within the community, the post-baptismal celebration and exchange of gifts served to build and reinforce valuable social ties. Participation in the event reaffirmed or even advanced the social standing of those involved. Thus, as with any such opportunities for public display of a family's standing, there was pressure on the parents to spend excessively on gifts and food, a point noted and criticized by contemporary moralists.

The priest might also be paid for his services. While performing baptisms was one of his fundamental duties and was thus supposed to be performed for free, many priests refused to perform baptisms unless they were paid. Extorting such payments was expressly prohibited by the Church but, despite repeated warnings, the practice continued.

Emergency Baptism

Administering the full ritual of baptism was not always practical. As discussed previously, birth was a risky process for both the mother and her baby. One of them, or even both, often did not survive. While the death of the mother was always a deep loss, the death of the baby had greater moral ramifications. As stated previously, if the baby was stillborn or died so soon after delivery that it could not be baptized, his soul was condemned to hell, forever. This belief was closely held by most medieval Christians. Fathers, midwives, and any others attending a birth were keenly aware of the stakes involved.

Recognizing that it was impossible for priests to rush to the scene of every difficult delivery, the Church permitted both laymen and laywomen to perform baptisms of babies at risk. In fact, performing baptism if required in an emergency became a duty of every Christian. For this, at least some portion of the baby had to have emerged from the mother's womb. Then, applying water to the exposed part, preferably the baby's head, the lay person simply baptized the child in the name of the Father, Son, and Holy Spirit.

But carrying out this simple ceremony was not always easy, especially when the mother had collapsed from exhaustion or had already died. In some of these instances, midwives and other attendants resorted to cesarean sections in their desperation to reach a dying baby to baptize it more than in any hope of delivering the child alive. However, despite the importance of baptizing the baby, such extreme measures were not to be done recklessly. As St. Thomas Aquinas (1224–1274 A.D.) and other medieval theologians cautioned, the mother's life was not to be sacrificed only in order to reach the baby in time for baptizing.

There was still one last ray of hope. As mentioned previously, the mother, her family, the midwife, and any others in attendance would be praying for divine assistance to help ease the birth for both the mother and her baby. It was always hoped that God could be moved to action in the case of a difficult delivery and the prospect of an otherwise innocent little soul in such danger. Thus, among the miracles attributed to divine intervention performed by saints during the Middle Ages are revivals of stillborn babies, but these were most often temporary reprieves, just long enough to allow the child to be baptized.

One last note on baptism: beginning in the late 12th century, prominent Christian theologians questioned the Church's position on where the souls of unbaptized children went after their deaths. In the early 13th century, the Church formally changed its doctrine and, instead of being consigned to hell, the souls of unbaptized infants were now believed to reside in limbo. This change meant that they would not be going to a place of hideous torments but that they were still not going to heaven, either. Instead of joining the blessed, presumably including their families, in heaven, these unfortunates were doomed to an eternity which held few of the joys of heaven, except, perhaps, knowing that they had escaped the tortures of hell. While this may have provided some slight measure of comfort to families who had lost infants before they were able to have them baptized, the creation of limbo clearly did not diminish the motivation for rapid baptism of children.

Naming

As Christianity came to be the dominant religion throughout Europe, baptism, besides inducting children into the Christian faith, became the ceremony at which children were given their names. In pre–Christian times, the peoples of Europe presumably had their own rituals for bestowing names on children, but few, if any, traces of these practices remain. A child was often given the name of his principal godparent, that is, the godparent who held the child and presented him to the priest during the baptism. This became such a common practice that books of instructions for priests mentioned that it was customary, but not required, to name the child after the principal godparent. Presumably, naming the child after his godparent was believed to strengthen the bond between them and increase the chance that the godparent would take an interest in the child and help him later in life. However, there is evidence that some parents may have selected the principal godparent on the basis of his name in order to give their child the name they wanted, occasionally selecting social inferiors. In these cases, getting the desired name was more important than a chance for future benefits from a higher status godparent. Still, parents did remain free to name their children as they chose and many did select names other than those of the principal godparent. But choosing a different name was not without risk of giving offense. In a few instances, some less than understanding godparents became indignant during baptism when they discovered that the parents had instructed the priest to give the child a name other than theirs.

Naming children after godparents sometimes resulted in a family with several children having the same name. In early 15th century England, one exceptionally large family had 7 sons and 7 daughters, who included 4 Johns, 2 Williams, and 2 Agneses. While we cannot be certain, this duplication of names was probably the result of naming after godparents. For some time, many historians had interpreted such naming as proof that people in the Middle Ages did not expect all their children to live and had given several children the same name to ensure that some favorite family name would be passed on to the next generation. Alternatively, some historians thought that names were being reused as children in a family died and new ones were born. In fact, there is evidence that this was sometimes the case and, admittedly, it cannot be determined whether all of the children in the example above were all alive at the same time. While premature deaths may have often lead to the reuse of names within a single generation of a family, baptismal records suggest that the naming of children after their principal godparents was the primary factor in multiple uses of the same name. To cope with having two or more children with same name, families used titles comparable to the use of "senior" and "junior." For example, the first son named "John" would be referred to as "John Major" while the second son "John" would be "John Minor." But it is less clear what happened when there was a third "John" born. Families likely relied on nicknames in such cases, like "Big John," "Little John," and "Young John." In fact, except when referring to their children in wills or on formal occasions, it is likely that mothers and fathers relied on nicknames any time that they had two or more children with the same name.

While naming a child after the principal godparent was customary, one group within Christian medieval society routinely ignored the custom and selected names as they liked. This was the nobility. At all levels, from minor lords to great kings, the nobility typically chose to perpetuate the names of the founders of their dynasties or nation or of other illustrious ancestors. Thus, for over 600 years, the names of French kings during the Middle Ages were primarily "Charles" (after Charlemagne), "Louis" (probably after Louis the Pious, son of Charlemagne), and "Philip" (possibly after Philip II, usually referred to as "Philip Augustus"). Altogether, these three names were given to a total of 23 out of the 34 French kings who reigned from 800 to 1462 A.D., much to the distress of any history student who has had to differentiate between what happened during the reigns of, say, Louis VII, VIII, and IX. A similar repeated use of names can be found in England, the kingdoms of Spain and many other royal houses during the Middle Ages. While names may have been given with a particular ancestor in mind, it seems likely that after a few generations it was difficult to say which particular "Louis" or "Philip" was being remembered and honored. Certain names had simply formed a pool of traditionally acceptable names.

Some noble families limited the pool of names even further and alternated between only two names so that the first-born son in each generation (who would usually be the principal or sole heir to the family estate) was named after his grandfather. A few families went further still and gave the first-born son the same name as his father, generation after generation. These naming practices were especially common among the urban nobility of Italy.

However, even among families with strong naming traditions, new names might be introduced. As part of alliance building, a weaker partner in alliance would sometimes name his son after the stronger partner. This showed his loyalty to that partner while also announcing to the world his bond to that partner, so that all would know that the two families were linked for mutual benefit and defense. Naming patterns could also be disrupted by the premature death of the first-born son. As mentioned above, for the nobility, the first-born son was commonly the primary heir in much of medieval Europe and he was usually the one given the special family name. However, if he died before inheriting or without producing an heir, the next heir in line under the law would inherit the estate and the leading position within that generation. Typically, this meant a brother or other close male relative would inherit and then their name could become part of the family's naming pattern.

Girls, too, were customarily given the name of their principal godparent: their godmother's name. However, families seem to have been more flexible in naming girls. Even among the nobility with its strong naming traditions for males, there appears to have been more variety and creativity in naming girls. For both nobility and commoners, the variety of names and weaker traditions for naming girls may have been based partly on the fact that most girls were expected to leave their birth families when they married. While marriages were sometimes seen as uniting the two families and brides would certainly still have some bonds with their birth families, marriage was typically seen as separating girls from their families and making them part of their husbands' families. This breaking of old ties and establishment of new ones usually meant that the wife and her offspring were seen more as part of her husband's family than of the wife's family. Thus, since it was her husband's line that she would be carrying on rather than her father's, there was less of an incentive for parents to try to perpetuate traditional family names for a girl.

The freedom in naming girls apparently led some parents to be a little too creative, at least in the eyes of a few English clergymen. At a church council in England held in 1281, one issue discussed was the problem of parents giving their children, primarily girls, sexually suggestive names as part of baptism. This practice was criticized but the only action proposed was to remind the parents that a bishop could choose to rename the child when he was confirmed. Since no list was made of the offensive names, we can only speculate as to whether the names were simply those of fictional or biblical characters noted for sexual improprieties or whether they were more explicit.

Sources of Names

The sources for children's names changed over the course of the Middle Ages. In the pre–Christian era and into the early Middle Ages, many peoples in Europe gave their children names that meant something in their language, a process similar to that used in many other cultures such as those of Native Americans. For example, in Anglo-Saxon, *Edward* meant "rich or happy guardian," *Heafoc* meant "hawk," and *Aethelflaed* meant "noble beauty." However, after a few generations, it is likely that children's names had less to do with their individual qualities and appearances, real or desired, than what had become the pool of common names. Still, some children continued to be given unique names well into the later Middle Ages. In some instances, the names were based on circumstances surrounding their birth. For example, in Italy, a child born in May was sometimes given the name *Maggio,* the name of the month in the local vernacular. Others were given names expressing their parents' joy and thankfulness for their births. Examples of these names include *Deodato,* meaning "given by God," and *Bonaventura,* which originally meant "good or happy event." A place associated with the birth was sometimes used in naming as well. For example, in one instance, a merchant was away on business in France when his son was born. The child was given the name "Giovanni" at his baptism. When the merchant finally returned home, he chose not call his new infant son "Giovanni." Instead, the father began calling the baby "Francis," a reminder of his own whereabouts on the day of the child's birth. This baby grew up to become a very famous Francis: St. Francis of Assisi.

As Europe was Christianized over the course of the early Middle Ages, naming practices were influenced by the Church. While traditional names did survive in many parts of Europe and continued to be common up through the 13th century, the practice of giving children the names of saints grew significantly in popularity during the 14th century. Naming children after saints could lead to new and even foreign names being introduced into the pool of names. One possible example is "Catherine." It was originally a Greek name and meant "pure" or "pure one." It was also the name of a popular saint who lived in the 4th century A.D., Catherine of Alexandria. This name gradually came to be used throughout Europe as Christianity gained converts. As missionaries and other clerics told stories about the saints, their devotion to Christianity, their miracles, and, in some instances, their martyrdom, names of saints like Catherine, James, and others became common in many regions where these names had not been part of the native language. From Ireland to Italy and from Spain to Hungary, these names spread. Though it is also possible that foreign names spread by contacts with other regions through trade, emigration, or other travel, it seems likely that conversion to Christianity was the primary force behind the introduction of these names into the pool of common names in so many diverse regions.

There is no evidence that children were named after celebrities as some are today, unless one considers saints or famous ancestors to be celebrities. While popes, kings, queens, and other nobility were the real celebrities of their day, they do not appear to have inspired parents to name their children after them. Perhaps it was considered presumptuous for people outside their own families to copy their names. As for the popularity of certain names, there were names that were used more often than others, but these varied so greatly between regions and over time that they cannot be listed easily or with a high degree of accuracy. The only names which appear to have regularly enjoyed popularity regardless of the language, location, or time were those of certain saints such as John (e.g., the French *Jean*, the German *Johan*, the Spanish *Juan*, the Russian *Ivan*, and the Italian *Giovanni*), and Mary (e.g., the French *Marie*, the Italian and Spanish *Maria*, and the Russian *Mariya*).

Family Names

Family names or surnames were common in Rome but disappeared from most of Europe after the fall of the empire in the West. Thus, family names did not exist at the beginning of the Middle Ages but gradually evolved over the course of the period. The nobility were the first to develop them. Members of the same noble lineage often came to be referred to by the name of the locale where the family had first risen to power. For example, Guy and his brother Amalric came from a family originally centered on Lusignan near Poitiers in France, and contemporaries continued to refer to them as "de Lusignan" even after they became, one after the other, kings of the crusader state of Jerusalem and of Cyprus. Sometimes families took their name from the place they currently ruled rather than their place of origin. For some, these were both the same place as for Enguerrand de Coucy, lord of Coucy, where his family originated and continued to rule for most of the Middle Ages. Of course, this practice of taking one's name after a place was not limited to France. While the French used "de" to mean "of" in many of their surnames, the Germans use "von" to the same effect. In England, "de" was used since England used French as its language of officialdom for most of Middle Ages. Thus, nobility and commoners alike appear in contemporary English documents with names like "Robert de Sothindon." However, the "de," "von," and similar expressions in other languages were increasingly dropped from names, leaving just the place name.

Physical characteristics of people were also a source of surnames. In French, the last name "Brun" was sometimes given to people with dark complexions or with brown hair. "Brown" was the English equivalent of "Brun." Humorous nicknames may have been used as well with men called "Little" or "Short" when they were really quite the opposite, such as "Little John" in the Robin Hood stories.

Some surnames like Plowman, Miller, and Carter obviously developed from the profession a family traditionally practiced. Others were patronymics, names derived from the father's name, such as Johnson and Jameson. Both "son" and "sen" were used and meant the same thing in Scandinavian countries, as in Anderson or Tobiassen. Also in Scandinavian countries, women sometimes received their fathers' names as well. Instead of "son," they would have the suffix "dotter," meaning "daughter of," creating names like "Hansdotter." To the east in Slavic countries, "ovich" was used, as in Ivan Ivanovich (Ivan son of Ivan). "Ovich" was eventually shortened to "ov." Some languages employed prefixes instead of suffixes, most notably in Scotland, Ireland, Wales, and Norman-held regions. The Irish "O'" and the Scottish "Mac" meant "son of." In Wales "ap" was used, as in Dafydd ap Llewelyn (David son of Llewelyn). The Normans used the prefix "fitz" to denote "son of," creating names such as William fitz Stephen. "Fitz" appears to have been a corruption of the Latin "filius" which means "son." The Normans introduced this naming practice to England after the conquest in 1066, and Anglo-Normans who settled in Scotland spread the custom there.

It is difficult to tell exactly when any of these names truly became surnames in the modern sense. Since the documentation is often spotty, one cannot be sure whether an apparent surname was actually just a descriptive name for an individual used only for the one transaction that a document records. For patronymics, it must have frequently taken several generations for a particular name to take hold since fathers' names sometimes changed with each generation. Only with repeated, consistent use did these names, regardless of their origins, become the family names we know today. The ever increasing recordkeeping for taxes, proof of land ownership, and other governmental purposes gradually encouraged families to retain the same surname.

Circumcision and Naming in the Jewish Community

Among the Jews scattered throughout Christian Europe, circumcision rather than baptism was the ritual which welcomed a male infant into the spiritual community. Circumcision, the removal of the foreskin of the penis, is an integral part of Jewish life which had been practiced for millennia before the Middle Ages and continues to be practiced today. In the biblical book of Genesis, God required Abraham and all his descendants to be circumcised as part of their covenant with God. The text further specifies that circumcision is to be performed when the male is eight days old. However, even in the Middle Ages, the eight day requirement was not rigidly followed if the infant was sick and needed more time to build his strength. The ceremony was often performed at home but the synagogue was the increasingly preferred venue (fig. 8). Regardless of where the circumcision was performed, it was preceded by a celebration the night before given by the happy parents in their home.

While boys were formally given their names at circumcision, girls followed a different custom, in part because they were not subject to circumcision. A girl was given her name by having it announced at the synagogue on the first Sabbath following her birth. As for the sources of names, Jews in Christian Europe traditionally did not give their children the same

name as any living relative but would often give them the name of a deceased relative instead. Jews in the Muslim-controlled parts of Spain, however, had different traditions and chose their children's names regardless of whether a living relative had the same name.

Birth Defects

We have been examining the activities that followed the successful birth of child. But what happened if the child had a birth defect? The range of birth defects recorded in the Middle Ages is the same as today: blindness, deafness, mental retardation, conjoined twins, and physical deformities, to name a few. While the defects were the same as those suffered now, the ideas about them and the understanding of their causes were radically different from today. Modern science and medicine have identified many of the causes of birth defects, from deficiencies in the mother's diet to inherited genetic flaws, and have provided measures to prevent or correct at least some conditions. In the Middle Ages, however, the real causes of birth defects were virtually unknown. As mentioned previously, a few medieval medical writers made some connection between diet and the birth of weak or otherwise defective children. But most medieval Europeans could not see any natural and rational causes themselves and so their imaginations ran wild, creating outlandish superstitions to explain why a woman had given birth to a "monster" (as the medieval chroniclers often called them) instead of a normal child. Some people saw them as omens of God's displeasure with sinful mankind while others believed that such a birth was a divine punishment of the parents for some sin they had committed. Such sins included having had intercourse and conceiving the child on a day when sexual relations were prohibited by the Church, such as on Sundays and during Lent, the forty days preceding Easter. Still others attributed such unfortunate children to diabolical forces and believed that the mother had actually been impregnated by a demon or that the Devil had somehow substituted one of his own flawed creations for her real baby. But others appear to have recognized that such children were simply the victims of cruel fate.

Some handicaps, such as some forms of conjoined twins, were so severe that the afflicted infants died within days after birth. Those with other less life-threatening handicaps survived longer. Yet, while most handicapped children do not appear to have survived childhood, some clearly did. Written records and skeletal remains show that people with physical deformities, such as congenitally misshapen or missing limbs or curvature of the spine, did survive into adulthood. Such survivals prove that at least some medieval families did care for their handicapped children and were able to provide the support needed despite the limited health care then available. Besides providing the best physical care they could, parents often made pilgrimages as part of seeking miraculous cures for their disabled children. According to the records of miracles kept by various churches that housed shrines, a few of these families did obtain divine cures but many must have gone away empty-handed, though this lack of suc-

Opposite: **Fig. 8. This illustration is from a book of hours. Books of hours were Christian religious texts for laymen. While their content varied, they usually contained prayers, excerpts from the bible, and other religious passages. This is a 15th century illustration of the circumcision of Christ from such a book. As was typical in the Middle Ages, the artist has painted the people in medieval clothing rather than garb from the 1st century A.D. Additionally, as the Christian artist who produced this work had almost certainly never witnessed an actual Jewish circumcision, he has used his imagination in depicting the costumes of the rabbi and mohel at right.**

cess did not dissuade them from undertaking additional pilgrimages to still other shrines in the hope that their faith and piety might win God's help for their children.

On the other hand, not all parents were willing or able to provide the special care their children needed. Some parents simply left their handicapped children at the doors of the nearest church, leaving it up to the local priest to find someone to care for them. In the first half of Middle Ages, some parents also took advantage of the growing number of monasteries and left their handicapped children, girls as well as boys, with the monks. Children were also occasionally abandoned with nuns at their abbeys. However, such communities of nuns were never as numerous as monasteries and appear to have focused far more on taking in the daughters of nobility for care than on accepting abandoned children.

Of course, handicapped children weren't the only ones who were placed in monasteries. Sometimes, parents formally made a gift of their child to the Church, a practice called oblation, which is discussed further in chapter 9. In other circumstances, such as during famines or when a family simply found itself lacking the resources to care for a child, healthy children were abandoned at monasteries. Parents abandoned their children to monasteries because, in many parts of medieval Europe, monasteries were the only institutions that appeared to offer stability and a refuge from the world as well as regular meals and some medical care. Monastic officials were hard pressed to cope with caring for these children and complained about the numbers of children being left in their care, especially those who had physical or mental defects. The children had to be fed, clothed, and supervised, all of which placed additional demands on monastic resources and disrupted the orderly observation of religious services that was central to monastic life. As a result of these problems as well as those caused by committing children to lifelong obligations without their consent, the Church largely ended oblation in the late 12th century and finally prohibited it entirely in the 15th century. As for abandoned children, monasteries appear to have taken a hard line and refused to accept any more foundlings as well. While monasteries closed their doors firmly against abandoned children, other institutions were created to fill the need for caring for foundlings. Beginning in the 12th century, larger numbers of hospitals were established and some of these took in abandoned children along with the sick and needy. Specialized foundling homes were also established. Foundling homes were frequently an outgrowth of hospitals and, in fact, were often referred to as "foundling hospitals." However, since they primarily functioned as orphanages rather than as medical hospitals, I have referred to them here as "homes." The creation and work of these homes are discussed below in the section on foundlings and abandonment.

Returning to the handicapped, regardless of where they were cared for, an unknown but significant number of children with physical handicaps survived to adulthood. Survival of people with physical handicaps was sufficiently common that the Church had a policy barring men with physical deformities from becoming priests unless the pope granted an individual exemption. This prohibition was not unique to the Church and reflected the prejudice of society in general. In the 15th century, household regulations for the household of King Edward IV of England specified that boys employed as servants were to be "clean limbed," that is, free of disfigurement and well-proportioned. Some guilds developed similar requirements for their candidates for apprenticeships. While these requirements had the legitimate function of screening out boys who lacked the physical abilities needed in service or trade, it also provided an excuse for turning away anyone whose physical appearance was in any way unattractive.

Depending upon the nature of the defect, the general public's reactions to persons with birth defects appear to have ranged from pity and concern to morbid curiosity and ridicule.

Amputations and crippling resulting from agricultural accidents, injuries in battle, and other misfortunes were probably sufficiently common that limbs missing or misshapen since birth were not particularly a stigma, except to the extent that they interfered with performing gainful employment. On the other hand, more extreme physical defects such as dwarfism drew the public's interest, and persons suffering these conditions often became living curiosities exhibited for amusement, like the sideshow "freaks" of the 19th and 20th centuries. Just as they employed musicians and acrobats, the nobility sometimes hired dwarves for their entertainment.

The mentally handicapped may also have found employment as entertainers in noble courts as well. But there is little evidence to establish how many jesters or "fools" were drawn from the ranks of the mentally handicapped and how many were mentally fit but feigned "simpleness" to allow themselves greater freedom in their performances. While it was generally acceptable to laugh at or ridicule the mentally handicapped, people did not usually hold them responsible for their words and actions. Thus, punishing "fools" was not typically condoned and so they could use their supposed mental incapacity as a shield against anyone offended by their jokes.

More concrete evidence of mentally handicapped children surviving to adulthood and making a living can be found in records of inheritances and guardianships. Some mentally handicapped but otherwise fit children appear to have been taken care of at home by their parents or other family members and contributed whatever labor they could to the family farm or trade. If they outlived their parents, the mentally handicapped could even inherit their parents' land. However, a lord could determine that a "simple" man could not cope with all the responsibilities of farming the land and keeping it productive and take the land, as happened in at least one case in England. But in other cases, lords made mentally handicapped persons their wards and appointed guardians to administer the land and provide financially for the handicapped owner out of the land's revenue. While such wardships were most common for heirs who were too young to be given their inheritances, they were also suitable for any situations in which an heir was found incompetent to manage his inheritance. While the handicapped person may have benefited from this arrangement, the lord would have been clearly acting in his own self-interest. His personal wealth depended upon having all the land under his jurisdiction worked to generate the highest possible revenues. But one might ask why the lord would go to this trouble and not simply have the handicapped person removed from the land and replaced by a new tenant. He might well do just that, but the lord was typically bound by customary inheritance laws and social pressures which curbed the unilateral dispossession of an otherwise legitimate tenant. Further, as explained in chapter 10, placing an estate under a guardian often allowed a lord to squeeze out some additional revenue. Unfortunately, few persons with severe disabilities, mental or physical, were fortunate enough to survive into adulthood. Fewer came into an inheritance that would support them for the rest of their lives. Those that did certainly had to be an extremely small minority of the total number of handicapped children born during the Middle Ages.

Infanticide

Before the Middle Ages, in the Roman Empire as well as among some of the barbarian peoples who overthrew the Empire and settled in Europe, infanticide of handicapped children was a socially acceptable practice. Healthy children, too, appear to have been victims of infanticide when a family determined that it was too poor to support another child. Infanticide continued to be practiced through the Middle Ages.

As previously mentioned, authorities in medieval cities were concerned about infanticide and some required midwives to report any cases in which they suspected it had occurred. The Church was concerned as well and considered infanticide to be a serious sin. Through the sermons of parish priests, the Church made clear how heinous a sin it was and the eternal torments awaiting parents, especially mothers, who killed their own infants. The Church also warned parents of the dangers of sleeping with their newborns. Newborns were sometimes suffocated when one of their sleeping parents rolled on top of them during the night. This was called "overlaying." While most cases of overlaying were likely accidents, the Church and secular authorities often suspected that overlain infants were actually victims of infanticide. In 13th century Germany, guidance issued by rabbis on this matter mirrored that of Christian authorities. Jewish mothers were advised to take care not that they did not fall asleep while nursing lest they smother their infants. And if an infant was found dead in his parents' bed, the mother was to be presumed guilty of maliciously causing the death.

Although some medieval Europeans did murder their own infants, there is insufficient evidence to determine how widespread the custom was and how frequently it was actually practiced. Skeletal remains of medieval infants have been recovered, but none that provide any proof that they died at the hands of their parents. Records of court proceedings of individual prosecutions and convictions for infanticide have survived but not from enough different regions and years in sufficient numbers to provide an adequate basis for determining the magnitude of the problem.

One point about infanticide in the Middle Ages of which we can be certain: it was not socially acceptable. As Christianity gained acceptance and became the dominant religion throughout Europe, attitudes toward infanticide changed. Just as the Church condemned abortion, it condemned infanticide. Both the Church and lay authorities prohibited infanticide and declared it, respectively, a grave sin and a crime. The punishments meted out by the Church included excommunication, for life or for a period of years, and performance of various penances to atone for the sin. The harshest penalties were imposed on persons who had killed an unbaptized infant since, in addition to killing an innocent person, they had condemned his soul to hell or, after the early 13th century, to limbo. As for secular justice, many lay authorities in the early Middle Ages appear to have left punishment for infanticide in the hands of the Church, but punishments gradually became a part of secular criminal law and became more severe over the course of the Middle Ages. In the 13th century England, infanticide began being classed as homicide and was thus a capital offense. In 14th century France, being burnt alive was the ultimate punishment for a woman who killed her baby. In parts of 15th century Italy, burning was also the prescribed form of punishment and one woman was forced to walk to her execution pyre with her dead infant tied to her neck. There is no question that infanticide was viewed as a serious crime which Church and secular authorities sought to deter.

The severity of the punishments and the concern that must have motivated them raises the question of whether the authorities were faced with an overwhelming problem and had to resort to increasingly extreme measures to fight rampant infanticide. Looking at the actual cases of infanticide brought before Church and lay courts, the answer is no. In England, very few cases of infanticide were brought before either court, which suggests that there was either a low rate of infanticide or that the crime was being extremely well concealed. In France, Germany, and Italy, there were a number of accusations of infanticide brought before the courts over the centuries. Some women were found guilty but many of the accused were found to have been insane at the time they killed their children. The descriptions of these cases are frighteningly similar to many of the cases of insane mothers killing their children in the recent past. These women were viewed as not being responsible for their actions and were sometimes released to the custody of their families rather than being judicially punished. Others were found guilty but obtained remission of their convictions. In France, the most common ground for remission was that the woman had been driven to the crime by the need to conceal a shameful pregnancy, such as the result of adultery or a pregnancy out of wedlock. Grants of remission were typically given only for first offences. Repeat offenders were usually denied remission and were subject to the full range of punishments, up to and including execution. When determining punishments, the courts did consider mitigating circumstances such as the desperate poverty of the mother. In hopes of lessening their punishment, mothers convicted of infanticide also frequently claimed that they had baptized their infants prior to killing them and had thus at least not damned their babies to an eternity in hell or limbo.

Abandonment, Foundlings, and Adoption

In the early Middle Ages in much of Europe, one alternative to infanticide was to sell the unwanted child into slavery. However, as Europe became Christianized, slavery of fellow Christians gradually disappeared. The other alternative used throughout the Middle Ages and up to the present day was to abandon the child. Medieval society appears to have judged parents who abandoned their children much less harshly than those who committed infanticide, provided that the parents were motivated by extreme poverty or by shame and the need to conceal a child that was the result of adultery or a pregnancy outside of wedlock. Even the Church grudgingly accepted that, while parents should take care of all the children that they brought into the world, it was better to abandon a child than to kill him. However, the child had to be abandoned in circumstances in which he was likely to be found and cared for, not left to die of hunger, thirst, or exposure.

Parents abandoning a child sometimes left a small packet containing salt with the infant as a sign to those who found him that he had not yet been baptized and so should be baptized as soon as possible. Still, children found without salt were routinely baptized as well, just to be sure. At the baptismal ceremony, priests often named abandoned children after the saint on whose day they were baptized.

As mentioned previously, handicapped children as well as healthy ones were sometimes abandoned at the gates of monasteries and abbeys and doors of churches. As with infanticide, illegitimate children appear to have been victims of abandonment more often than legitimate ones. In Italy, even the rich were known to abandon children that resulted from their extramarital affairs. Regardless of their health and legitimacy, children were abandoned by parents of all classes in great numbers during times of upheaval such as wars and famines. The Church, particularly its monasteries, was an attractive place to abandon children because it was the only institution in medieval Europe that offered care for the sick and vulnerable. Further, some bishops actually encouraged bringing unwanted children to churches so that homes could be found for them. However, as with handicapped children, the Church was seldom prepared to provide long term care for abandoned children. As noted previously, beginning in the 12th century, there was an increase in the founding of hospitals to help the sick and the needy, and these institutions provided an alternative to monasteries as a place to seek help.

However, many hospitals did not accept foundlings and so the increase in hospitals provided only limited relief for abandoned children. Faced with little institutional support, individual bishops and other clerics sometimes took the initiative to help foundlings.

In the late 8th century, the bishop of Milan established the first recorded foundling home in Western Europe. Children at this home were cared for and taught basic skills until they reached the age of seven. At seven, they were free to leave. This typically meant that they were then found positions as apprentices or as domestic servants. (Apprenticeships are discussed further in chapter 8.) Foundlings were also cared for up to age seven in London at the hospitals of St. Bartholomew and St. Mary Spital near Bishopgate, but this care was only available to infants whose mothers died while giving birth at the hospital. Elsewhere in England, foundling homes were established at York in the 12th century and Lincoln in the 13th century. As with many foundling homes throughout Europe, these were small operations that could provide care for only a dozen or two children at a time, although a few cities, primarily in Italy, established homes that accommodated far larger numbers.

In other parts of Europe, additional sources of help for foundlings gradually developed. In southern France around 1160, a new religious order was founded which included caring for foundlings and orphans among its missions. This group, the Order of the Holy Spirit, spread throughout France and into other parts of Europe as well. Its confraternities (groups of laymen and women who volunteered to help the clerics in the order) frequently took in and cared for foundlings on behalf of the order. This order was so successful that the Pope summoned the order's head to Rome and had him establish foundling homes there. Following the order's guidance and, perhaps, the earlier example of Milan, foundling homes were established in Siena, Pisa, Florence, and other Italian cities. In Florence by the end of the Middle Ages, there were three foundling homes: the Santa Maria da San Gallo (founded in the 13th century) and the Santa Maria della Scala (founded in 1316), which were both general hospitals that also accepted foundlings, and the Santa Maria degl'innocenti (founded in 1445), which was purely a foundling home. In 1435, da San Gallo cared for over 200 foundlings.

Unfortunately, placement in a foundling home was no guarantee of survival. Although the homes provided the best care that they could afford, many of the infants who were received by foundling homes did not live long enough to be placed with a family. Rates of infant mortality were high in medieval Europe, but foundlings had significantly higher mortality rates than children who remained with their families. Forty percent of the infants admitted to foundling homes commonly died during their first year and mortality rates sometimes reached over 90 percent during epidemics and famines.

Adoption

Besides providing homes for foundlings, some clerics took steps to encourage the adoption of foundlings. In the 6th and again in the late 9th century, bishops in areas that are now part of France encouraged mothers wishing to abandon their children to bring them to the churches so that they could be placed with other families. Even without the sanction of the Church, it is likely that abandoned children were adopted throughout medieval Europe as families with adequate resources took in children from poorer relatives or even from destitute neighbors. While adoption today involves very formalized and often complex legal proceedings, most adoptions in medieval Europe were performed with little or, indeed, no ceremony at all. Children appear to have been simply taken in and so became part of the family.

One final observation: currently, families wishing to adopt children usually try to adopt infants. The older a child is, the more difficulty he typically has in finding a family willing to adopt him. In the Middle Ages, the situation was the opposite. Foundling homes made no attempts to immediately find families for the infants left in their care. In fact, the homes waited until the children reached at least the age of seven and then placed them with craftsmen for apprenticeships or with families for domestic service. Medieval Europeans appear to have rarely adopted foundling infants. Rather, they adopted children who had already survived the perils of early childhood and were sufficiently developed, both physically and mentally, to do chores and other work and so could be productive members of their new families right from the start. There were instances when infants were adopted, but these appear to have been largely limited to cases in which families took in the children, both legitimate and illegitimate, of relatives. Examples of the latter are found in Italian records, where children born to female servants and slavewomen who had been impregnated by their masters were sometimes taken into the household and became part of the family rather than being cast out. However, when adopting the child of a complete stranger, most medieval Europeans seem to have been quite pragmatic and limited their selection to older children who appeared able to immediately make a contribution to their family's resources in exchange for their upkeep. In fairness to the people of the Middle Ages, it should be noted that such a businesslike approach to adoption was not uniquely "medieval," as the writings of Charles Dickens and the real-life circumstances upon which they were based prove. Still, this is not to say that such adopted children were viewed as mere slave labor. Records of inheritances show that these children were often remembered with affection by their adoptive parents.

2

Caring for Infants and Children

After surviving birth, infants in medieval Europe advanced to the next step in their perilous progress toward adulthood: early childhood. As shown in coroners' records, accounts of miracles attributed to saints, and other documents, young children in the Middle Ages were often in danger of grievous injuries or even death. Drowning, attacks by supposedly domesticated animals, fire, and many other accidents claimed young victims. In addition to these calamities, birth defects, disease, and hunger took their toll as well. Some historians have even theorized that the mortality rate for young children was so high that parents in the Middle Ages did not form strong bonds with their children because of the likelihood that they would die. However, documentary and physical evidence shows that most parents were not indifferent to their children. As discussed in chapter 5, many parents clearly loved their children and strove to give them the best care possible, especially during early childhood when their lives were so fragile. And when that care was not enough, parents mourned the loss of their children.

In this chapter, we will examine how children were cared for from birth up to about the age of seven. At or around age seven, children traditionally began receiving training for their adult careers although, through imitative play and watching their parents and other adults, many children began this process earlier. Before the age of seven, little appears to have been expected of children, other than that they would eat and sleep, play and grow. As for their care, surviving written guides, illustrations, and other evidence of childrearing practices show that some things are obvious regardless of the time or the place: all children have to be fed, clothed, and protected. Keeping them clean and loving them are good ideas too.

Nursing

After a child was born, one of the first things he needed was food. Mother's milk is recognized today as the best food for infants and was widely recognized as such in the Middle Ages. It is hygienic, conveniently located, and usually readily available at any time of the day or night. Further, assuming that the mother is getting an adequate diet, her milk provides all the nutrition her infant needs for growth and development as well as providing antibodies vital to protecting his health. As reflected in the writings of one English author in the 13th century, nursing was also recognized as helping a mother to bond with her new child and begin nurturing him. As though these reasons weren't enough, the Church endorsed the practice as well. In church sculpture and other religious art, Mary, the model of motherhood, was frequently depicted nursing the infant Jesus. In the eyes of the Church, to nurse one's own child was part of being a good Christian mother like Mary. Thus, it comes as little surprise that most mothers in the Middle Ages appear to have nursed their own children.

What could be simpler and more straightforward than a mother nursing her own child? But it wasn't always that easy. Some babies refused to nurse and wasted away if the parents could not find a way to get them to take the nipple. Some mothers had difficulties as well. A few appear to have suffered postpartum depression and refused to nurse their babies. Others had physical problems and could not produce the milk necessary. This problem was sufficiently common that a few medical books and other writings addressed this along with other health problems that afflicted women's breasts. Some texts recommended consuming fennel and other herbs that were believed to promote lactation. These texts also warned against eating onions and other strong tasting foods since it was believed that the flavors would pass into the milk and spoil it or at least make it unpalatable to the baby. If these cures failed, some other source of milk had to be found. Infants whose mothers had died or been left too weak or ill by childbirth to nurse also needed a source of milk. Baby formula would likely be used as a replacement for mother's milk in most of these situations today, but baby formula was not developed until the 19th century. Animal milk was available but it was not an adequate replacement and was often unsafe to drink. Thus, the best solution available in medieval Europe was to hire a woman who was lactating to feed the infant. Such women were called wet nurses.

Wet Nursing—An Overview

Before discussing the details of wet nursing during the Middle Ages, some information about the general history of the practice is necessary. Hiring someone to breastfeed one's child may seem alien and even somewhat repugnant today. However, it was practiced by many cultures around the world before and since the Middle Ages. In fact, wet nursing was much more widely practiced in Europe after the Middle Ages. In 18th century Hamburg, for example, four to five thousand women are estimated to have been employed as wet nurses out of a total of approximately 90,000 residents. In the early 19th century when Paris had a population of 800,000 to 900,000, one researcher has estimated that only about half of the approximately 20,000 babies born each year in the city of Paris were nursed by their own mothers. The rest were fed by wet nurses, many of them residing in towns some distance from Paris. Wet nursing was such a well established and widespread practice in Paris and other large French cities that government agencies were set up to help find wet nurses for newborns and regulate the business of wet nursing.

Commercial wet nursing wasn't restricted to Europe. It was practiced in China and Japan as well as in many Islamic countries, while European colonization helped to spread it to other regions around the world. In colonial America, advertisements by women offering their services as wet nurses and by families seeking such services regularly appeared in newspapers. In the Spanish and Portuguese colonies in Central and South America, Catholic religious orders opened homes for foundlings which employed wet nurses just as their European counterparts did. Female colonists served as wet nurses as did women from the indigenous population. Women from enslaved peoples served as wet nurses as well.

Despite the growing number of infants who were wet nursed from the Middle Ages through the 19th century, the inadequacies of wet nursing became increasingly apparent. First, there were often not enough wet nurses to meet the demand. While families accounted for a large portion of the market for wet nurses, infants abandoned at foundling homes accounted for an ever-growing demand. These babies were always in desperate need of mothers' milk, but the institutions sheltering them could seldom compete with private families in the pay they could offer wet nurses. Thus, they often could not find enough wet nurses for all the infants in their care. The lack of nurses meant that these infants frequently starved or died from complications caused by a diet of pap or animal milk. Second, to make matters worse, popular opinion held that a woman had only enough milk for one child at a time so women desiring to become wet nurses were routinely expected not feed their own infants. This was not a problem when the wet nurse's infant had died. In the Middle Ages many wet nurses may have been women who had miscarried or had a stillbirth or whose child had died within a short time after birth. A woman whose own children had died was often preferred as a wet nurse, since her employers could be certain that her milk was going solely to their child. Alternatively, if the wet nurse's own child was old enough to be safely weaned, this too could free her to nurse the infant of another although, since she would have given birth at a least a year if not two before becoming a wet nurse, some fastidious parents may have considered her milk to have been too "old" to feed to their child. Thus, there was pressure for a prospective wet nurse to prematurely wean her child. Her other options were to place him with another wet nurse or she could simply abandon him. Wet nurses before and after the Middle Ages frequently hired other women to nurse their children. Of course, this practice could only be done when the first wet nurse was earning enough to cover paying her own wet nurse and still make a profit. However, it meant that they typically had to employ wet nurses who would accept low pay. When a wet nurse could find a lactating relative or neighbor, such as one who had recently weaned her own child, who was willing to take such pay, the wet nurse's child probably fared well. Such an arrangement allowed the wet nurse to frequently visit her child or even keep him at home for much of the time. It also likely permitted her to continue to feed him at least part of the time, a practice which many employers of wet nurses often suspected occurred. However, wet nurses sometimes had no choice but to place their children out with other wet nurses. This practice became increasingly common after the Middle Ages. A wet nurse willing to serve for low pay was likely unfit in some way for employment in the higher paying wet nurse position which the nurse employing her had been able to obtain. The care that wet nurses' children received from these cheaper wet nurses appears to have often been deficient. As for premature weaning, it likely resulted in malnutrition and other problems which could prove fatal. And abandonment all too frequently led to death from inadequate food and care in foundling homes. Thus, the children of the wet nurses often suffered from their mothers' employment.

Substitutes for breast milk were tried repeatedly, primarily in experiments on the infants in foundling homes when wet nurses could not be found, but no real breakthroughs took place until the late 19th century. At that time, inventors and scientists created several new items and processes which provided alternatives that contributed to the demise of wet-nursing. Sanitary glass bottles and artificial rubber nipples capable of being sterilized were developed in the early 19th century, and Henri Nestle is credited with inventing baby formula in 1867. Louis Pasteur's famous method for sterilizing animal milk provided yet another substitute for human milk. While they do not provide the complete nutritional value for infants that human milk provides, formula and pasteurized animal milk are reliable and hygienic foods suitable for infants. Together, sanitary bottles and artificial nipples, formula, and pasteurized milk created safe and cheap alternatives to hiring wet nurses. Besides these technological advances, there was a growing awareness of the problems of commercial wet nursing and increasing acceptance of maternal breastfeeding among influential segments of society in Europe and the United States. These changes in attitude, combined with the advances in artificial feeding, helped largely end commercial wet nursing by the beginning of the 20th century. Hospitals and homes for abandoned infants, however, continued to employ wet nurses for premature infants, newborn foundlings, and other babies with a special need for the complete nutrition and antibodies provided by mothers' milk until at least the 1930s. Today, "milk banks" operated by hospitals and filled with donations from nursing mothers fill this need. Apart from occasional reports of "cross nursing," which is a new term for wet nursing coined in the 1980s, wet nursing is virtually extinct.

Now, with this information about wet nursing in hand, we can return to the Middle Ages.

Why Would a Woman Become a Wet Nurse?

Just as it is difficult today to understand why one would employ a wet nurse, it is difficult to comprehend why so many women would agree to provide such an intimate service, often to the detriment of their own children and their own health. Some, such as slaves, had no choice, but free women and noble ladies also filled this role at one time or another.

Slaves

Slavery was practiced throughout Europe at the beginning of the Middle Ages. It was a legacy of both the Roman Empire and the barbarians who toppled the empire in Western Europe. However, slavery was gradually curtailed throughout most of medieval Europe, partly as a result of the spread of Christianity. While the medieval Church never issued an outright prohibition against owning slaves, the Church and lay society increasingly found the practice of Christians owning fellow Christians as slaves unacceptable. Thus, as more of Europe converted to Christianity, the supply of potential slaves shrank until at some point during the 11th century A.D. the only acceptable sources of slaves were now from outside Europe, though Greek Orthodox Christians and followers of other branches of Christianity that did not adhere to the rites of Rome were viewed by some as fair game at times. So, by about halfway through the Middle Ages, slavery remained common only in areas that had ready access to non–Christian slaves such as captured Muslims in Spain and Central Asians, Slavs, and others brought to markets in Italy as part of Italy's extensive commerce with the eastern Mediterranean. Not surprisingly, therefore, most records of the use of female slaves as wet nurses come from Italy and Spain. In these countries, female slaves who had recently given birth were used as wet nurses for their masters' children. In fact, female slaves who were still nursing their children were considered quite valuable and are known to have commanded high prices in the slave market in medieval Castile. The slaves' own children, if they had survived birth, were often given to other slaves to nurse, although in Italy they would sometimes be placed in a foundling home instead. If a family did not have a child that needed nursing, they would often loan or rent out their slave wet nurse to others who needed her services.

Besides private owners, homes for foundlings operated by religious orders in Italy also utilized slaves as wet nurses. Some of these women were gifts given by donors as a donation to support the order's good work, but these religious orders also directly bought non–Christian wet nurses to feed their Christian foundlings.

Free Women

Slave women constituted only a small part of the total number who performed wet nursing during the Middle Ages. The vast majority of wet nurses were free women who served for pay. None of the surviving contracts or regulations indicates that any of these women were serfs. Though they were free, they were not rich. Contracts for wet nurses usually record the occupation of both the wet nurse and her husband. While some were wives of millers or prosperous farmers, most were wives of ordinary farmers or laborers. The income they could bring in by wet nursing was frequently vital to the survival of their families. And wet nursing was the highest paid work that a semi-skilled or unskilled woman could hope to get during the Middle Ages and for long afterwards. Regulations on pay from part of 13th century Spain show that a wet nurse could earn nearly twice as much as an ordinary female day laborer, almost as much as a male day laborer's wages. One hundred years later in France, a wet nurse still earned almost double the wages of a typical female domestic servant. Further, families typically offered additional benefits such as good food and comfortable housing to live-in wet nurses, while wet nurses who remained in their own homes could continue to help around the farm or perform craft work in between feeding and caring for their guest nurslings. Thus, wet nursing could provide a family with vital primary or significant supplementary income and gave women a strong financial motive.

It should be noted that there was no shame attached to being a wet nurse. It was accepted as a respectable trade for women and likely spared many destitute women from resorting to prostitution to survive. During the Middle Ages, husbands appear to have usually offered no opposition to their wives becoming wet nurses. This is somewhat surprising since a husband was expected to give up sexual intercourse with his wife during the term of her service as wet nurse. (The reason for this is discussed more fully below.) In situations where the wife was going to live with the family she served, he also suffered the loss of her service in their own household. However, the husband must have considered the money she earned to be well worth the sacrifices. In fact, many husbands appear to have been quite ready to hire out their wives and acknowledged their consent in written contracts for their wives' services. In medieval and renaissance Italy, husbands did more than merely consent. They routinely sought out employment for their wives as wet nurses and served as their agents in contract negotiations.

As for single women, except for the recently widowed, they were generally not considered suitable wet nurses in medieval Europe. Single women were largely excluded from wet nursing until the 19th century when changing social values and the increasing availability of work in factories reduced the numbers of married women willing to serve as wet nurses and forced Europeans to increasingly employ "fallen women" (unwed mothers) as wet nurses.

Noble Ladies

Noble women were far more likely to be customers for wet nurses than to become wet nurses themselves. And, as discussed further below, the nobility were certainly able to retain the best of the commercial wet nurses. So why would a noble woman nurse another's child? For prestige and social advancement. From the Middle Ages through the 18th century, there are repeated instances in which woman of lesser nobility served as wet nurses for the infants of their social superiors. Most often, this appears to have been done only for short periods such as while hosting the child's parents as guests, although some women of the minor nobility seem to have left their own homes and joined the households of royalty or other great nobility for years of service. The social standing of the wet nurse and her family was enhanced by rendering such intimate service to her superiors and their future heirs. Further, while some payments were likely received in those cases when the woman joined the court, the primary reward was the strengthening of social and political ties between the family of the wet nurse and the family of the nursling. These ties could result in "favors," such as grants of land or lucrative and important offices that were often worth more than mere monetary sums since they conferred prestige along with tangible gain. Thus, some noble women were willing to become wet nurses when the potential rewards were worth it. As for the greater nobles these women served, they gained prestige as well by displaying that they could command the services of a nobly born wet nurse and not just that of a hired commoner. Still, it should be noted that commoners constituted the clear majority of wet nurses for the nobility.

One last point: what happened to the child of a noble woman who served as a wet nurse? Assuming that he hadn't died in childbirth or shortly thereafter, such an infant would have been suckled by a wet nurse hired by his family. As mentioned previously, employing a wet nurse to feed the child of a woman serving as wet nurse was a common practice outside the nobility as well, and even the lesser nobility could typically well afford a good wet nurse.

Wet Nurses for the Nobility

While some noble ladies served as wet nurses, noblewomen were primarily employers of wet nurses. In fact, while commoners increasingly employed wet nurses over the course of the Middle Ages, the percentage of infants fed by wet nurses was always highest among the nobility and wet nurses appear to have been an essential part of noble households from the very beginning of the Middle Ages. For example, in the 7th century, the king of Wessex in England issued a law recognizing that a reeve (an official in charge of supervising a noble's estates), a smith, and a wet nurse for his children were the three servants that a nobleman was expected to bring along when traveling. This formal recognition suggests that employing a wet nurse was a symbol of noble status. Since commoners did not employ reeves or retain smiths as personal servants, the inclusion of the wet nurse likely indicates that her services too were above the reach of the common people. The nobility appear to have retained their monopoly on wet nurses through the early Middle Ages but the practice was eventually adopted by prosperous commoners, especially those living in cities.

Why did most noble mothers not nurse their own children? Many contemporary clerics denounced them for behaving unnaturally, and some thought that noble ladies were simply vain and did not nurse in order to more quickly regain their pre-pregnancy figures and avoid the discomforts of nursing. Based on these assumptions, clerics praised the virtues of those noblewomen who did nurse their own children while citing those who failed to do so as being guilty of the sins of pride and vanity. Although vanity may have been a factor in some instances, most noble mothers may have been bowing to the obligations that their class imposed upon them. Wives of the nobility were expected to give birth to many children, creating heirs that would ensure the survival and continued prosperity of the family line. To meet this expectation, noblewomen needed to be as fertile as possible during their childbearing years. Fertility is lowered when a woman is lactating. If a woman stops nursing, she gradually stops lactating and fertility returns to normal levels. Thus, a noblewoman could more quickly restore her fertility after a pregnancy if she did not nurse her newborn. (Curtailing lactation was not without problems. Relieving the engorgement of the breasts without nursing or otherwise stimulating lactation was often painful and sometimes injured the mother's health. Binding the breasts until woman's body reabsorbed her milk was one method of accomplishing this task.) So in not nursing her own child, a noble mother may have just been carrying out another of her duties to her husband and family rather than acting out of pride and vanity. Further, as the Middle Ages progressed and the employment of wet nurses became such a longstanding and routine practice among the nobility, many noblewomen likely just accepted the practice as part of their traditional customs and never even considered making a personal decision on the matter.

As for finding and hiring wet nurses, noble mothers and fathers appear to have seldom if ever had problems in retaining the services of high quality wet nurses. While royalty and the higher nobility might have had women of lesser nobility serve as wet nurses, even these lofty families appear to have more often employed commoners, although they certainly never had to settle for boarding their children with the wet nurses as many non-noble families did. The nobility could usually offer better compensation to their wet nurses than could most common people. In addition to money and the enhanced social standing of being a noble's servant, noble employers offered the perks of access to the better food and accommodations that typically went along with being part of a noble household. With her intimate connection and constant presence with the nobleman's wife and children, a wet nurse sometimes came to be so fully accepted into the family that she would be given a given a pension or other substantial gifts in recognition of her service. She might even be remembered with a bequest in their wills. Wet nurses were sometimes even retained as favored permanent household servants long after their charges had grown up. Juliet's nurse in *Romeo and Juliet* is one fictional example of such a servant.

The wealth of the nobility also allowed many of them to employ several wet nurses simultaneously. This was most common when a noble family had more than one child still at an age to nurse but was also done to have a back-up nurse on hand should the primary nurse fall ill or otherwise lose her ability to provide milk, such as by becoming pregnant. Employment of multiple back-up nurses was especially common among royalty beginning in the later Middle Ages. Using their great wealth, royalty could also offer wet nurses contracts for much longer employment than commoners or even most nobility could. Contracts for between two to four years' service appear to have been typical, but in medieval Castile the royal family sometimes contracted with wet nurses to serve for ten to twenty years. However, they were not expected to nurse the royal infants for the entire time. Rather, after weaning, the wet nurses served as the children's nannies until they reached adulthood.

Wet Nurses for Commoners

As mentioned previously, noble ladies were not the only women who relied on wet nurses instead of nursing their own children. By the later Middle Ages, wives of wealthy urban merchants and craftsmen imitated this and other customs of their noble superiors. Documentary evidence indicates that the employment of wet nurses outside of noble households was widespread by the 14th century. However, most of the surviving records are from a limited number of large Italian cities. Italy was the most urbanized region of Europe at this time and so its practices may have been significantly different from many other parts of Europe where population density and concentration of wealth were lower. Customers for paid wet nurses appear to have been much scarcer in towns and rural areas. Thus, in Italy and elsewhere in Europe, the vast majority of commoners nursed their own children and employment of wet nurses was limited to prosperous urban residents who could afford it and enjoyed it as one the tokens of their superior social status.

Some families engaged in trades or crafts appear to have hired wet nurses so that the mothers could return to work in the family business more quickly, but most of the women whose children were wet nursed were employed primarily or solely in managing their own households and not directly in the production of income. It would be easy to assume that this latter group of women were simply trying to enhance their social status by imitating noblewomen. However, they too were sometimes pressured to produce large numbers of children. Commoners might not appear to have had the same need to produce heirs as the nobility but most families, regardless of their class, wish to perpetuate themselves. No less than the nobility, common people also preferred that their immediate descendants inherit their accumulated wealth rather than having it pass to distant relatives or even outside the family entirely. Admittedly, this would have been a concern for only the more prosperous, but this is exactly the group who took steps to produce more children by employing wet nurses. Besides creating heirs, having a large number of children had other advantages. It provided a bigger pool of people to help take care of parents in their old age, an important consideration in a time before retirement plans, pensions, and health insurance. Further, in many trades or crafts, children provided a built-in workforce for the family's business. Thus, though vanity or a desire to increase their social status may have been factors, many commoners appear to have had valid economic motives for employing wet nurses so that their wives' fertility would return more quickly and so enable them to bear larger numbers of children.

While middle- and upper-class merchants and craftsmen were able to bear the costs of employing wet nurses and supporting large families, those less well off could not. For peasant farmers who owned only small amounts of land or worked the land of others and for urban workers with no prospects for building their own businesses, having any children, let alone a large family, was often too big a financial burden. Regardless of how much they might want or need large families, some simply could not afford them. The inadequate diet of the poor probably limited their fertility and, when they did conceive, it also likely contributed to a higher rate of stillbirths as well as birth defects and other problems that left their infants weak and unlikely to survive. Thus, their families were often small and, when their infants did survive, the mothers would nurse their own children. The mothers might even hire out their services as wet nurse if their child died or had been weaned. In those instances when one of their children had to be wet nursed such as when the mother had died, the poor had to rely on the charity of a lactating friend or neighbor, but such charity was extremely rare, so most must have had to resort to animal milk and other liquids.

While the focus has been on wet-nursing as a means of increasing fertility, some historians have observed that freeing mothers, noble or common, from nursing would have allowed them an important respite from some of the physical demands of childrearing. Providing a period of rest and recuperation immediately after childbirth would have given a mother the chance to rebuild her health and strength and thus increase her odds of survival. In fact, in his work on women's health, Soranus of Ephesus noted that a mother would both recover from the exertions of childbirth and maintain her long-term health better if she passed the task of nursing her newborn to a wet nurse. However, he also observed that she would consequently get back in shape for further childbearing more quickly too. Thus, employing wet nurses relieved mothers of the physical strains of nursing but it appears that it was often done with an eye toward speeding their return to childbearing.

Selecting a Wet Nurse

Throughout the long history of wet nursing, medical guides and general advice show that selecting a wet nurse was to be done carefully and to be based on a thorough examination of both the physical and moral qualities of the candidates. In many ways, both the selection process and the parents' expectations of the care to be provided by the wet nurse foreshadow similar concerns with modern daycare. While providing milk for the child was the primary concern, wet nurses typically served as nannies as well: keeping the child clean, safe, and entertained along with keeping him fed. Wet nurses were also expected to teach the child the basics of speech, walking, and other fundamental skills. An accurate assessment of how well she would perform these collateral duties was especially critical when the child was leaving his own family and going to live with the wet nurse and her family.

Medical experts of the time differed slightly over the physical attributes of the perfect wet nurse. All were in complete agreement that she needed to be healthy and well fed with a robust constitution and good complexion. Having her bear some resemblance to the child's mother was a bonus since children were believed to absorb some of the physical features of their nurses along their milk. Some writers added that it was quite acceptable for the nurse to be slightly fat and all assumed that she would not be skinny or have a small frame. As for her breasts, medium-sized were considered the best (fig. 9). Small ones were thought to contain too little milk. If her breasts were overly large, there was believed to be a risk that the infant would not drain the breast completely at each feeding and that the leftover milk that would somehow go bad before the next feeding. Regarding the wet nurse's age, most said that she should be young, but Soranus specified that she should be between the ages of 20 and 40. Regardless of her age, she had to have given birth recently. One writer added that it would be best if she had given birth to a boy one and a half to two months before becoming a wet nurse though some other writers preferred that her child was the same gender as the one she was going to nurse. Soranus wrote that she should already have given birth two to three times so that her breasts were fully developed and she herself was well practiced in caring for small children.

Apart from the 12th century text attributed to the female medical practitioner Trotula, medical experts and popular opinion were unanimous that an expectant mother was completely unacceptable as a wet nurse. And pregnancy among wet nurses was a common problem since lactation only diminished fertility rather than preventing conception entirely. Today, provided that the mother is receiving adequate nutrition and rest, nursing while pregnant is recognized as not being harmful to the nursing infant, the mother, or her fetus. However, until the 17th century, most Europeans believed that the mother's blood was transformed directly into milk in her breasts. They also believed that a pregnant woman nurtured her fetus with the best part of her blood. Thus, there was perceived to be a significant problem when

Opposite: **Fig. 9. This picture from a book on health shows a woman, likely a noblewoman, examining the breast of a potential wet nurse. The firmness and size of her breasts were among the factors considered when selecting a wet nurse. The figure above the two women is a man making a grotesque face. He has been traditionally interpreted as a monk expressing his disgust with the scene beneath him.**

ous
olt
n deue
et bras.

quil dit
turel
s sor
bient
il dit
q dauo
ete a
il doit.

fes soit
en ha
deliurer
grant.
v fiez
es. e se
e v pl
sauuue
ce en

pres
oh e
li fe
sera
luu
si be
cou
sau
cou
v d

ues lenfant garder. Sachie
ke si tost com ilest nes le co
ent en voleper en roses brou
mellees enseu delie e deues
re crenchier le bouteril au
lone de iiij poces e metre p
desus poure desandragon e
sarqua col e de comin e de n
re e vn drapiet delin moill

a wet nurse became pregnant since there were now conflicting demands within her body. Since her developing fetus was getting the best part of her blood, what was left to be turned into milk? Applying the theory of bodily humors which was widely believed in by medieval Europeans, the blood left to be transformed into milk in her breasts would have been mostly phlegm and bile, creating an inferior if not outright noxious liquid. It was not uncommon for a child's illness to be attributed to his nurse's milk, especially when she was found to be concealing a pregnancy. Contracts for wet nurses often specified that the contract would be terminated if the wet nurse became pregnant. Some contracts included penalty clauses requiring the wet nurse to forfeit most or all of her pay if she became pregnant and failed to disclose it to the child's parents within a reasonable time. In parts of medieval Spain, a pregnant wet nurse and her husband were even subject to prosecution for homicide if the nursling died after being fed her tainted milk. Thus, women who had recently given birth, not those who were currently expecting, were the most desirable candidates for employment as wet nurses.

While the woman should have recently given birth, her child was often an impediment to her becoming a wet nurse. As mentioned previously, women were believed to only have enough milk for one child. Letters and personal documents from early 15th century Italy show that families seeking wet nurses could be ruthless regarding children of wet nurses. Wet nurses whose own children had died or been placed in foundling homes were openly preferred. The insensitivity to the wet nurse's own loss is sometimes shocking. In one instance, a woman helping another family to find a wet nurse wrote that she had found a mother whose two-month-old baby was deathly ill and that she had gotten her to promise that she would come be their wet nurse as soon as her baby died. One can only hope that such ghoulish behavior was exceptional.

Along with examining the wet nurse's physical condition, parents would also look for desirable personal characteristics. Experience and good judgment were two of the most desirable attributes sought by parents in a wet nurse. In fact, Soranus made it clear that his reason for setting a minimum age of twenty for prospective wet nurses was to ensure that they had some experience and maturity in judgment as well as being mature physically. Other personal characteristics that parents looked for included honesty, compassion, sobriety, an even temper, and general good morals. Among the bad traits parents sought to avoid were low intelligence, heavy drinking or drunkenness, bad temper, promiscuity, and other forms of lax morals. While the theory was that these characteristics, good or bad, passed into the child along with the nurse's milk, examining the behavior of potential wet nurses had a twofold practical value.

First, an honest, compassionate and experienced nurse who exercised good judgment and kept her temper well under control was far more likely to take good care of an infant than a drunken, ill-tempered, promiscuous one. The potentially harmful consequences of a wet nurse's poor judgment or lack of self-control while caring for an infant were all too obvious. Many small children died from accidents or inadequate care while living with their wet nurses. Drunkenness was particularly recognized as creating dangers for the child. Soranus observed that a drunken wet nurse was likely to be inattentive to the infant in her care and, by her neglect, allow him to come to harm. Further, Soranus and others noted that the inebriating qualities of wine were absorbed into the nurse's milk and then passed on to the infant. Consuming wine-tainted milk was known to cause a baby to become sluggish or even comatose. It was also known to trigger tremors or convulsions in infants. So, while they may have been examining the wet nurse's behavior to determine the quality of her milk, medieval parents appear to have known that they were also protecting the safety and well-being of their baby by assessing the quality of care that he would receive from the wet nurse.

Second, from a very early age, children learn by example. If a nurse was slovenly or sullen, cursed, or openly displayed other undesirable traits, a child could be expected to pick up these habits. At the other end of the spectrum, a child raised with warmth and kindness in an orderly and pious household was expected to develop these positive attributes. Admittedly, when a child developed habits or traits similar to those of his wet nurse, medieval writers and parents routinely attributed such transference to the nurse's milk but many were aware of the impact that surrounding people and their activities had upon a child. For example, the great artist Michelangelo once joked that he had sucked hammers and chisels along with the milk of his wet nurse, who was a stonecutter's wife. Thus, to avoid having their children returned to them as unpleasant little strangers with bad manners and worse habits, medieval parents likely compared the wet nurse's household to their own to determine whether their child would be brought up with appropriate values and behaviors.

Not surprisingly, parents often had difficulty in finding a wet nurse with all the desirable physical and moral attributes, especially in northern Italy, which appears to have had the highest demand for their services. In 14th century Italy, parents were advised to start looking for a wet nurse early, presumably before the child was born. Even with an early start, they often had to make compromises to find an affordable wet nurse. Many parents had to settle for placing their child out with the wet nurse's family rather than bringing the nurse to live with them. In Italy, it was usually substantially cheaper to have the child go live with the wet nurse than to have her come live the child's family. It may appear odd that having the child board full-time was cheaper than having the nurse live in, but a live-in nurse was a family servant who was expected to perform her duties all day long and not be engaged in any outside employment, while a wet nurse who stayed in her own home could continue to take care of her own family and engage in other occupations while simultaneously caring for the infant. Further, in areas with high demand for wet nurses, many parents had to settle for wet nurses who lived some distance away out in the countryside. Then as now, the costs of living typically became lower the further away one lived from an urban center. Thus, Italian wet nurses commanded lower fees the further they lived from the city. In contrast, 14th century French authorities apparently believed that the food and accommodations provided by the family employing the wet nurse were quite valuable. In French regulations, a live-in wet nurse's wages were set at half those of a wet nurse who took the nursling away to live with her family.

Wet Nurses of Different Faiths

As medieval Europe was predominantly Christian, most wet nurses were Christians, but there were Jewish communities scattered throughout the region, and Muslims lived in Spain and Sicily for part of the Middle Ages. Where these different faiths lived together, they interacted socially and commercially and part of that interaction included wet nursing: Christian, Jewish, and Muslim women are all known to have nursed infants of other religions. They hired themselves out based on who needed their services and could afford them. However, people did not always agree with this practice and, during the 12th century, Church and secular authorities began prohibiting Christian women from nursing children other than those of their own faith. This prohibition was based in part on the concern that wet nurses living with Jewish families would be pressured to convert to Judaism. But Christians were not alone in their distrust of other faiths. Jews had similar fears that Jewish wet nurses living with Christian families would be encouraged to convert or that they would at least be compelled to eat foods that were contrary to their dietary laws. Some Jews were also concerned that Christian wet nurses serving in Jewish homes would inculcate their nurslings with Christian beliefs through such subtle means as singing Christian hymns as lullabies. Perhaps for the same reason, Muslims did not always find Christian women to be acceptable as wet nurses for their children either. On top of all these suspicions, rumors often circulated that wet nurses of the other faiths were only providing that milk which they thought wasn't good enough for their own children. Not surprisingly, by the end of the Middle Ages, the only surviving interfaith wet nursing appears to have been that provided by the slaves in the foundling homes of Italy.

The Impact of Wet Nursing on the Infants

So how did infants fare while they were in the care of wet nurses? Those infants who were nursed in their own homes appear to have done the best. For the nobility, their live-in wet nurses seem to have met their expectations and were seldom blamed for the sickness or death of the infants in their care. For commoners, the care provided by their live-in wet nurses appears to have been usually satisfactory as well. Problems were most common when the infant went to live with the wet nurse and her family.

Away from the day to day supervision of the parents, things seemed more likely to go wrong. As mentioned previously, the wet nurse and her family could be in the same town or city as her employer, but they were often in outlying villages or farms that were so far away that the child's family seldom visited and had no oversight of the child's care. Studies of wet nursing in the 14th century have revealed that the survival of infants generally decreased as the distance between their families and the wet nurse increased. And this did not go unnoticed in the Middle Ages. It appears that Italian families were aware of the risk and placed their children accordingly. Males, especially first sons, were typically placed with the closest nurses available, while daughters were often placed with more distant nurses. This is one of the most obvious examples of discrimination between genders in the Middle Ages and provides support to those who argue that medieval parents were far more indifferent or even callous toward their children, especially daughters, than modern parents.

The causes for the higher mortality rates for infants placed out with their wet nurses are not easily explained, although negligence was certainly one cause. There were cases when a child fell ill or was injured and the wet nurse failed to call for medical help or notify the family in timely manner. When she finally did, it was too late, although it was often doubtful whether the child's death would have been avoided even if she had acted sooner.

Death records also indicate that nurslings tended to die in higher numbers in the late summer. Late summer was harvest time. Many wet nurses were farmers' wives and had to go out to help bring in the harvest along with every other able-bodied adult in the community. During the long, hard days of harvesting, wet nurses likely nursed the infants in their care less both because the strenuous activity of harvesting left them with less milk and because they were out in the fields for most of the day. The infants were left behind at home, usually in the care of children too young to help with the harvest. Less feeding and inadequate supervision took their toll.

As mentioned in chapter 1, the common practice of having the infant sleep in the same bed as an adult, such as the wet nurse, could also have tragic results. While the dangers of this practice are well recognized today, parents as well as wet nurses and their husbands in the

Middle Ages often slept with the infants in their care. Some families could not afford cradles, and keeping the infant in bed also made late night feedings easier. But it was very dangerous for the infants since, simply by rolling over during the night, a sleeping adult could overlay a baby, smothering him or crushing him against the hard bed frame or floor beneath the thin mattresses then commonly in use. Such tragedies spurred the invention in 15th century Florence of a device called an *aruccio*. This was a protective cage that was placed over the infant to protect him from overlaying while still allowing feeding. After the Middle Ages, wet nurses were sometimes required to show that they had either a cradle or an *aruccio* before they were allowed to take an infant away to be nursed.

While negligence certainly claimed the lives of some infants who were put out to nurse, negligence occurred even when infants were kept at home and nursed by their own mothers, as shown in cases in which infants were overlain by their own mothers or fathers or in which they died in accidents in the home when the mother and father had left them alone or in the care of another child. Although some wet nurses may well have been grossly negligent, it is difficult to establish whether the quality of the care given by wet nurses was significantly inferior to that given by parents. Further, wet nurses had a strong financial incentive to provide the best care that they could. After all, when an infant died, the parents stopped paying immediately, and it seems possible that a wet nurse who lost too many infants would gain a bad reputation that would put off prospective employers.

The health of children placed out with wet nurses may also have been a factor in their higher mortality. As mentioned in chapter 1, infant mortality in the Middle Ages was very high by modern standards. The infants sent to live with wet nurses may have been among those least likely to survive, such as ones whose mothers had died or who had otherwise undergone a difficult delivery that had left the mother too weak to nurse. It is even possible that some parents factored in the child's health and likelihood of survival when making the decision on placing the child out to nurse. Besides infants from families, a large number of the children who were sent out to wet nurse were foundlings, often newborns, who had received very poor care and were quite ill and malnourished by the time they reached the wet nurse. These children had little chance of survival regardless of their nurses' efforts.

Obviously, wet nursing had many shortcomings and was not an ideal way to feed infants. Bringing the wet nurse into her employer's home yielded the best results for the nursing child. But apart from the nobility, many, if not most, parents settled for placing their child out with the wet nurse. Many of the infants placed out by their own families may have better survived if they had been kept in their own homes, but for foundlings and infants who mothers had died wet nursing was the only viable option at the time. As for the children of the wet nurses, while many must have survived, their deaths were likely all too common.

Animal Milk and Pap

While human milk was (and still is) the best food for infants, it was not always available. As mentioned before, when a mother died or was left too weak or ill from the delivery an alternative had to be found to feed her infant. Similarly, an alternative was needed if she had started to nurse but her milk supply failed for some reason. But sometimes there were not enough affordable wet nurses available. During plagues and other disasters, even the wealthy might find it nearly impossible to find a suitable wet nurse. And even on a day-to-day basis, a substitute for mother's milk was needed as growing infants were weaned and had to be given other foods to sustain them. In these circumstances, people in medieval Europe turned to two liquid foods: milk from animals and pap. Pap was made of grain, flour, or bread that was soaked into milk, broth, or water until very soft or mostly dissolved. Sweeteners such as honey or diluted wine may have been added to make it more appealing. When given as a supplement to breast milk for infants or as a primary food for children old enough to be safely weaned, animal milk and pap provided some nutritional value. But for younger infants who still needed human milk, these foods were harder to digest and did not provide the complete nutrition they needed. Further, as discussed below, the methods for serving these foods were often very unhygienic. As a result, although animal milk and pap were the only foods available, they were often a poor or even dangerous substitute for human milk.

Cows, sheep, and goats provided milk for human consumption in medieval Europe. However, these milks are not ideal foods for infants. While they do provide calories, calcium, and some usable vitamins, some of the other nutrients in animal milk can't be digested and absorbed by the infant in the same way that nutrients in human milk can. Thus, animal milk had less nutritional value than human milk to the infant. Further, animal milks do not provide the antibodies that human milk provides, and so the baby's immune system does not receive vital strengthening on this diet. Worse yet, in an age before inoculations for dairy animals and pasteurization of their milk, animal milk was not always a safe beverage and could contain many diseases, such as tuberculosis and cow pox, which a baby, or indeed anyone, could contract from consuming the milk. Even in the Middle Ages, a few medical writers made a connection between milk consumption and contracting some diseases. However, these learned writers were more concerned about another thing that animal milk could transmit: bestial behavior. These authors shared a belief common among medieval Europeans: that consuming animal milk would convey bestial traits to the growing infant in the same way that the infant was believed to absorb character traits transmitted from the mother or wet nurse along with her milk's nutrients. And so they warned against feeding infants animal milk for this reason too. Aside from the dangers of having a child develop the personality of a cow or sheep, a final (and very real) problem with milk itself is that liquid milk spoils rapidly without refrigeration and so fresh, potable milk was usually not easily available in cities and other locations which were any significant distance from dairy animals. Still, despite these problems and biases, animal milks appear to have been widely and routinely used as a substitute for human milk for feeding infants. For example, after successfully blessing a previously barren woman with the birth of a child, one early medieval saint is said to have sent the woman a gift of a cow to help her with feeding the child. And some 16th century foundling homes maintained herds of goats to provide milk for the infants in their care. While post-medieval, this likely reflects a use of animal milk by these institutions that began in the late Middle Ages to cope with a growing number of abandoned infants. As for more fortunate infants who were not abandoned, archaeological finds, manuscript illuminations, and some contemporary inventories provide evidence of feeding implements that indicate that these children too were fed animal milk or other liquids while they were still too young to feed themselves.

How did medieval Europeans solve the problem of how to get animal milk and other liquids into a baby before there were bottles and rubber nipples? One of the tools used for feeding animal milk to a baby was a small animal horn which had a little hole drilled in its pointed end (fig. 10). While the infant could suck the end of the bare horn, a nipple made of parchment (not the fine paper we usually think of today, but the skin of a calf or lamb carefully prepared into thin, supple material) appears to have sometimes been attached to making sucking easier. Another form of feeding vessel was a small clay pot in the shape of a woman's breast. One of these rare objects was found buried with an infant in an Anglo-Saxon cemetery in England dating to the

Top: Fig. 10. When their mothers were unable to feed them and no wet nurses were available, infants were sometimes fed using a cow's horn. The tip of the cow's horn was cut off and a nipple of parchment or cloth was then attached over the hole in the end of the horn. In this picture, a woman is pouring a liquid, possibly cow's milk, into the horn while another woman holds the horn to the baby's mouth. *Bottom:* Fig 11. There were devices other than a cow's horn for feeding babies. This pottery vessel was found buried with an infant in a 7th century Anglo-Saxon cemetery at Castledyke

in Humberside, UK. It is approximately 4 inches long. Its upper end is open and is about 2½ inches in diameter. Its lower end is molded in the form of a nipple. As with cow's horn, a parchment or cloth nipple was attached to provide a soft surface for the infant to suck. Dr. Kevin Leahy of the North Lincolnshire Museum has noted that there is a shallow groove around the base of the nipple, which allowed the parchment or cloth nipple to be secured with a cord or string.

7th century (fig. 11). Grooves on the outer surface of the pot indicate that, as with the feeding horn, some type of artificial nipple was attached to the pot and held in place with a cord. Babies also appear to have been fed by soaking a small piece of cloth in milk and having the baby suck the milk out of it. These sucking cloths could also have served as pacifiers. All these methods could also have been used for feeding very thin pap as well as milk but none of the surviving feeding vessels have yielded any residue to analyze. However, all of these feeding methods further increased the risk that the infant would contract an infection since none of the items were sterile. Horn and pottery could not be adequately cleaned and the parchment nipples and sucking cloth were presumably reused for repeated feedings, with perhaps only rinsing in between uses. While they kept these items as clean as their other eating utensils, medieval Europeans were quite unaware of the need to sterilize their infants' feeding horns, cloths, and nipples, had it even been possible. Thus, during the Middle Ages and for centuries afterward, babies fed animal milk and pap were at risk from contamination of their feeding implements as well as from the lack of antibodies and possible diseases (and undesirable personality traits) in the milk itself. Despite these problems, animal milk and pap were still fed to many babies since there were no alternatives.

Solids and Liquids

Just as today, as babies grew and cut their first teeth, solid food was gradually introduced into their diet. Without the bottles of prepared strained vegetables or pureed fruits which are so convenient and indispensable now, medieval Europeans used other means to feed their growing infants. Babies old enough for solid foods were first fed very soft foods such as thicker forms of pap, likely the consistency of modern cereals for infants. One Anglo-Saxon source mentions that bread made of fine white flour, rather than the more common and cheaper whole grains, was the best bread for small children. As the child grew, other foods were added. Simply mashing foods such as cooked fruits and vegetables into a paste was likely a common method for making food soft enough for an infant to eat. Another acceptable method suitable for meats was for the parents or wet nurse to pre-chew some food and then feed it to baby with their fingers. One text describes the individual servings of pre-chewed food as being morsels the size of an acorn. Thus, the child's diet was gradually broadened while he grew enough teeth to chew for himself.

Along with solid foods, the infant was gradually introduced to beverages other than milk or thin pap to help him grow and to prepare him for weaning. Currently, water and fruit juice are the two most common drinks other than milk for infants. Thirsty medieval infants were certainly given water to drink, either plain or with honey or wine added. However, most people in the Middle Ages were aware that water quality was important. They recognized that water from some sources, such as rivers in urban areas, was sometimes unhealthy to drink, especially for weak people such as infants and the sick. Thus, they would use water from the best source available or would use alternative beverages if any were available. While we today might turn to fruit juices if water is unavailable, fruit juices were very uncommon in the Middle Ages. Without refrigeration and pasteurization or other means for stabilizing the juice and halting fermentation, fruit juices either rapidly spoiled or, more typically, matured into alcoholic beverages such as wine, cider, or perry. While this meant that fruit juices were very seldom available, this was not perceived as a problem in the Middle Ages since the properly fermented juices could be stored and kept for later use. Further, surviving medieval recipes and dietary guides suggest that unfermented fruit juices were most commonly used as an ingredient in sauces rather than consumed as a drink. In any event, the result was that fruit juice was seldom, if ever, given to infants, except in its fermented form.

Given the lack of other reliably hygienic beverages, parents turned to the same beverages they themselves consumed, wine and beer, for their children. While these were more common drinks for older children, wine and beer, both usually diluted with water, were given to thirsty infants. Wine was more common and affordable in France, Italy and southern Germany, the major wine producing regions, and so children in these areas were more likely to be given diluted wine. To the north, most wine had to be imported and was thus more expensive. While the wealthier residents of the Low Countries, England and other northern areas could afford to give their children wine, beer was more common and usually much cheaper than wine. In these countries, brewers produced *small beer* which was naturally low in alcohol and intended as a hygienic thirst quencher for everyone, even children. For very small children, small beer was likely diluted with water to further lower its alcohol content. While a few medical writers were concerned about giving wine to small children, especially infants, medieval parents were still limited to those beverages that were available and which they perceived as safest, so diluted wine and very low-alcohol beer were likely very common drinks for thirsty children, including infants.

Weaning and Teething

As mentioned previously, the age at which a child was weaned varied widely and depended on factors such as whether his mother needed to wean him early so that she could hire herself out as a wet nurse. Some medical experts cautioned against such premature weaning and warned that introducing solid foods too early could harm the child. In ordinary circumstances, the age for weaning appears to have varied from anywhere from six months to three years, but it appears to have been most commonly achieved around the age of two. Some experts made a connection between weaning and the fact that a child's first set of teeth should be complete by around age two. They reasoned that since the child could then chew more solid foods he could therefore be safely weaned. In the Jewish community, weaning at the age of two was the practice approved in the Talmud, and the writings of a Jewish author in 12th century Spain indicate that this was still the preferred practice.

To encourage a child to stop nursing, some medical experts advised applying mustard or bitter aloes to the wet nurse's or mother's nipples. Such materials seem likely to have irritated the poor nurse's or mother's flesh as much as they repelled the child. Several contemporary experts acknowledged that nursing should be stopped gradually and not halted abruptly. Further, an infant who vomited or exhibited other severe problems while making the transition from the breast to other foods was to receive special care. He was to be allowed to return to breastfeeding. After his health returned, he was then to be offered other foods again.

The discomfort of teething infants did not pass unnoticed in the Middle Ages. Medical experts advised rubbing the child's gums with honey mixed with a little salt or giving him a licorice root to suck. The sucking cloths like those used to feed young infants may have also served as teething material for older ones. Other items may have been used to soothe teething infants as well. Branches of coral, one with a silver ring, are recorded in two inventories of items sent along with infants who were being wet nursed away from home. These inventories are from early 15th century Italy. From post-medieval examples, we know that these pieces of coral were valuable red coral from the Mediterranean and that they were polished until they were quite smooth. Additionally, they were probably about the size and shape of a finger and were likely mounted in silver settings that included a ring through which a ribbon was tied so that it could be hung around the child's neck. The Romans of the classical age thought that hanging red coral around the neck of an infant would protect him from danger. Apparently, this practice survived in Italy, but it does not appear in other parts of Europe until after the Middle Ages. Italy was the primary source for coral in medieval Europe. Thus, the use of coral for teething may have survived in Italy since coral was available locally. In any event, while the coral was thought to have some supernatural power to ward off harm, the small stick of coral provided an infant something relatively cool and smooth to work his gums against just as a teething ring is used today. Of course, only children of wealthy parents enjoyed such luxurious teething aids.

Bathing and Cleaning

Hygiene for infants was definitely a concern. Medieval Europeans did not bathe as frequently as we do today. But that does not mean that they preferred being dirty or were oblivious to the benefits of good hygiene. Obtaining large quantities of clean, warm water in which to bathe was a major obstacle to personal hygiene up until recent times and remains so in many parts of the world. Still, even in the Middle Ages, frequent bathing in warm water was recommended for infants. One expert advised washing infants at least once and even two to three times a day, if needed, and the number of drownings and near-drownings of infants when they were left unattended in washtubs indicate that many infants were, in fact, bathed on a regular basis. Bathing of infants was such a commonplace activity that female saints and other devoutly religious women who reported seeing mystical visions of Christ in the form of an infant sometimes said that they saw Him playing happily as St. Mary washed Him. This vision of the infant Christ enjoying His tub mirrored most babies' enjoyment of water-play, then and now. Another medieval medical writer commented that bath-time was a good opportunity for swaddled infants to stretch and exercise a little. Thus, bath-time was both hygienic and fun, even in the Middle Ages. As children grew bigger, things sometimes changed. One 13th century English writer noted that, starting around the age of 7, little boys frequently liked getting dirty when they played and strongly resisted taking baths.

After bathing, the infant or child was then gently and thoroughly dried off. After drying off, rubbing with oil was recommended for infants to help protect their delicate skin. In addition to bathing, mothers and nurses also groomed their infants and children by examining their hair and gently picking out lice since lice were a common problem for both adults and children in medieval Europe.

Swaddling

For the first several months of his life, the infant would be wrapped up in cloth with only his face left exposed. The cloth was held in places by fabric bands or strips that crisscrossed the infant, leaving him immobile. This was swaddling. Along with one of the pieces of coral previously mentioned, six swaddling bands and six pieces of woolen cloth as well as bibs, caps, little shirts, lined cloaks, robes with and without sleeves, and a cradle with a pillow and blanket were also listed in one inventory of items sent along with a child to his wet nurse. Note that diapers were not included in the inventory. Diapers, or rather the lack of diapers in the Middle Ages, will be discussed later in this chapter. Returning to the six swaddling bands and cloths, this may have been a two day supply of these items, allowing three pairs of bands and cloths to be cleaned and dried while the others were in use. Changing the swaddling three times a day is mentioned in songs traditionally sung by wet nurses from the Casentino region in Italy during carnival time. Casentino was a region noted for its wet nurses, and the song advertised the women's nursing prowess as well as the quality of care they provided. Here are a few verses:

> With lots of good fine milk
> our breasts are full.
> To avoid all suspicion,
> let the doctor see it,
> because in it is found
> the life and being of the creature,
> for good milk nourishes
> with no trouble and makes the flesh firm...
> We're young married women,
> well experienced in our art,
> we can swaddle the baby in a flash
> and no one has to show us
> how to use the cloth and bands;
> while caring for him we arrange them carefully
> because if he catches cold,
> the baby is harmed and the *balia* blamed.
> [*Balia* was an Italian word for "wet nurse."]
> We change three times a day
> the wool and linen cloths and white bands,
> and we never get tired or cross
> being with him so he won't cry...

[From *Canti Carnascialeschi del Rinascimento*, C.S. Singelton, ed. (Bari: Laterza, 1936), as cited by James Bruce Ross in "The Middle-Class Child in Urban Italy, Fourteenth to Early Sixteenth Century" in *The History of Childhood*, L. De Mause, ed. (New York, 1974).]

Thus, an infant that was well cared for would likely have had his swaddling completely changed three times each day. Given how often a modern infant has his diaper changed during a day, this number of changes appears inadequate, yet it must have been found quite acceptable at the time since the wet nurses expressly mentioned it as part of the good quality services they provided. However, another verse of the song mentions changing the infant frequently when he is sick as part of the additional care a wet nurse would give to help him recover more quickly. While it is unclear whether this passage refers to changing the swaddling or other clothing the child may have worn, the language suggests that more frequent changes may have been done but only when there was extraordinary need such as when the baby had diarrhea. Still, this is only speculation and there is no clear evidence of how often children had their swaddling changed in actual practice during the Middle Ages.

Swaddling was removed at bath time, but it may have been taken off at other times too. One 13th century English guide on childrearing states that infants should be given some time to stretch and crawl around. Though not expressly stated, such movement would not be possible if the infants were swaddled. Further, a few of the documented injuries and deaths of infants suggest that these infants had to have been left at least partially unswaddled since they were mobile enough to get themselves into trouble by such actions as crawling and falling into ditches as well as finding things, picking them up, and putting them in their mouths. Thus, while many infants were swaddled for many hours during the day, they may have been routinely given some time to stretch and play.

Before examining the problems posed by the frequency and quality of swaddling, let's examine why infants were swaddled in the first place.

Peoples around the Mediterranean Sea swaddled their infants long before the Middle Ages.

There are references to swaddling in ancient Egypt, and Greeks and Romans of the classical age continued the practice. After the Middle Ages, the use of swaddling persisted in Europe for several centuries. In Russia, it was still practiced in the late 20th century, and in regions outside Europe, such as in parts of the Middle East, swaddling continues to be practiced today.

After an infant was born and had been washed, he was typically swaddled immediately. This kept the infant warm and snug and so provided him some comfort and reassurance after the travails of birth. People in the Middle Ages understood the need for keeping a baby warm, and this was probably one of their principal motives for swaddling. Besides keeping the baby warm, one medieval author also thought that swaddling an infant prevented an infant from injuring himself such as by keeping him from accidentally scratching his eyes. This same concern was mentioned by Soranus in the portion of his text which addressed caring for newborn infants. And a few texts note that swaddling helps ensure that an infant laid down in his cradle will remain face up and thus reduce the risk of him accidentally smothering by turning over on his face.

Restricting the infant's movement may also have prevented other accidents in homes that were far from child-safe. Open central hearths (often with cooking pots full of boiling liquids suspended above them), roaming animals, and other hazards were common in many medieval homes and children, even infants, were not always as well supervised as they should have been. Further, playpens and cribs were unknown and cradles typically had very low sides which an active, unrestrained infant could easily surmount, so swaddling could also have been a means for keeping an infant from rolling or crawling around unsupervised. However, no medieval texts include this among the explanations of the need for swaddling. Thus, ensuring that the baby would stay put and hopefully out of harm's way appears to have been an unintended benefit of swaddling.

In medieval Europe, the primary reason for swaddling was that it was believed to help shape the child's body, particularly the arms and legs. Infants were believed to emerge from the womb still soft and somewhat unformed. Their bodies were thought to be pliable like wax. To ensure that a baby would grow into the proper shape, medieval people believed that they had to correct the natural tendency of the newborn baby to curl up tight into a ball, the position to which he was so accustomed from his time in his mother's womb. By placing the infant's arms straight down along the sides of his body and by straightening his legs so that they were fully extended and then wrapping him up in swaddling bands, parents believed that they would help their baby develop long, straight, well-shaped limbs. Similarly, it was believed that parents and wet nurses could help a child develop pleasing features (or correct unpleasant ones) by gently and repeatedly pushing or pulling the affected part into the desired shape. Warm baths and applications of warm cloths sometimes recommended as well to help the process. Through these processes, some believed that children's legs could be stretched to make them long and attractive and that the nose, ears, lips, and other facial features could be pushed and pressed to make children more beautiful or handsome. However, not all people believed in these practices. One 12th century writer who had traveled in Ireland observed that the Irish did not swaddle their children or attempt to artificially shape their children's features and left the molding up to nature. He noted that the results were strong and upright bodies and handsome faces with good complexions.

As for the disadvantages of swaddling, these are more readily apparent than any supposed benefits in shaping the child's body. Encasing a baby in tight layers of cloth creates significant health risks. From spit-up on his clothing to excrement and urine in his diaper, a baby requires frequent cleaning and changes of clothing. Today, disposable diapers and diaper wipes, easy to wash fabrics, and washing machines have made these tasks much simpler and easier to accomplish than it was for earlier generations, although, as any parent will tell you, it is still a constant and tiring struggle. Mundane a task as it is, keeping a baby clean and dry is important since failure to do so can result in conditions ranging from merely annoying to truly life-threatening. Confinement in a soiled and wet diaper can result in diaper rash and chafing. Prolonged confinement leads to open sores. These sores are susceptible to infection and, given their constant exposure to excrement, infection would be quite likely to occur. In the Middle Ages, as at any time before the invention of antibiotics, infections could easily lead to disability or death. Since swaddling required extensive wrapping of the baby and then re-wrapping each time the baby was changed, the labor and inconvenience involved presumably deterred changing and cleaning infants as frequently as they needed to be. Further, aligning the child's limbs carelessly or tying the swaddling too tight could cause chafing as well as circulatory and other problems, even if the bands and cloths were clean. These problems were recognized in the Middle Ages, and contemporary experts warned of the dangers. While many mothers and wet nurses did take the time and effort to regularly and carefully re-swaddle the infants in their care, some clearly did not. Among the conditions for which parents sought miraculous cures from saints for their children were skin conditions, bleeding sores, abscesses, and other severe problems caused by dirty or overly tight swaddling. Unfortunately, divine intervention was not always forthcoming and deformity or death were not uncommon results in such cases. However, large numbers of children survived swaddling without incident, and it is impossible to determine just how pervasive and severe the problems caused by swaddling were. Further, there is also no evidence which can tell us whether infants were swaddled 24 hours a day, seven days a week, except when being changed, or whether they may have been swaddled only part of the time, such as while resting or sleeping, and were allowed at least a few moments free of swaddling to stretch and play.

As to at what age infants were finally freed from swaddling, there is some evidence but it is quite limited. Medieval medical writers are silent on this issue, although the venerable Soranus wrote that people commonly stopped swaddling when the child was either forty days or sixty days old. He advised ending swaddling when the child was firm enough that there was no longer a risk that its body would become distorted without the support of the swaddling bands. To allow the child to become accustomed to his new physical freedom, Soranus also recommended that swaddling should be stopped gradually: the child's right hand should be freed first, then, after a few days, his left. Finally, the feet should be freed. Soranus stated that the right hand should be freed first to encourage the child to use his right hand instead of his left. This practice may have continued into the Middle Ages since medieval Europeans believed as much as their Roman predecessors had that right-handedness was very desirable. In fact, being left-handed in medieval Europe was viewed as unlucky and may have been thought of as an outward sign of evil character as well. Turning from Soranus' writings to evidence of actual practice, there are very few clues to the age at which swaddling was stopped. In one story of a miraculous cure from the 13th century, a child is recorded as still being swaddled when he was well over a year old. However, since this boy was born with a physical handicap (the story doesn't describe the handicap), he may have been kept swaddled longer than usual either to hide his handicap or to try to correct it. Looking later than the Middle Ages, one 17th century English text recommended freeing the infant's arms after four months but keeping the rest of the body swaddled until the baby was a year old. However, a few records of actual practice from 17th century England show that at least some ended their swaddling between one to three months after their births. It is interesting how closely these ages correspond to the 40 to 60 days mentioned by Soranus. Looking at more recent history, Germans in the 19th century typically kept their children swaddled for the first six months of their lives while Russians in the 19th and 20th centuries kept theirs swaddled for the first six to twelve months. As for medieval illustrations of swaddled infants, these depict small, easily carried little bundles but their size gives no firm evidence of how old these "babes in arms" were. Thus, the age at which infants in the Middle Ages were considered old enough to no longer need swaddling cannot be established with certainty, but it seems likely that this typically took place at some point during the first year of their lives. In fact, it may have often occurred as early as third month after their births. In any event, it appears that the period of swaddling was a matter of months and was not prolonged to the point that it interfered with normal physical development.

Diapers

Even in the detailed inventories made by Italian parents in the 15th century of the clothes and other items sent along with their children when they went to their wet nurses, there are no mentions, descriptions, illustrations or other evidence of the use of diapers in medieval Europe. Beginning in the second half of the 16th century, English sources begin mentioning items called *clouts*, *double clouts*, or *tail clouts*. These were all names for the same thing: pieces of cloth which were folded and used to cover a baby's bottom. By the 19th century in England, these terms had been superceded by a more euphemistic word: *napkin*. Today, the British just call them *nappies*. In other parts of Europe, terms formerly used for swaddling began being applied to diapers as they came into use, such as in Germany where the current word for diaper, *Windel*, was previously applied to swaddling clothes. *Windel* was derived from the German word for winding, capturing the idea that swaddling bands were wound around the infant. Regardless of what they were called, diapers were a post-medieval invention, and the first recorded use of the word *diaper* to mean a covering for an infant's bottom did not occur until the 19th century. Before that time, *diaper* referred to a type of cloth woven with a repeating pattern of small shapes, usually diamonds. How and why this change in meaning of occurred is unclear.

Toilet Training

At some point after he was no longer being swaddled, the medieval infant had to have been toilet trained. Surprisingly little was recorded about toilet training in Europe before the 19th century. In the Middle Ages, medical writers were as silent on this point as they were about what age to end swaddling. However, one of the few surviving clues about toilet training can be found in a work by Francesco da Barberino, an Italian who wrote about child care in the late 13th and early 14th centuries. He advised that children around the age of two should have a little chair with a hole in its seat for relieving themselves.

Apart from the one text by Barberino, there is little, if any, other evidence of when and how children were toilet trained. In the absence of conclusive evidence, there are a few hypotheses about methods of toilet training other than the use of "potty chairs." One possibility is that after a child stopped being swaddled, he or she was dressed in other clothing but was not given any clothing to cover his or her bottom. Without such covering, the child's urine or feces simply ran down his or her legs. The child then gradually associated the discomforts of this experience with the sensation of a full bladder or full bowels and then realized that he or she should have relieved him- or herself in a latrine or chamber pot instead. This hypothesis is supported by the fact that diapers do not appear to have been developed until the 16th century so that young children in earlier times likely ran around without any clothing that covered their bottoms. This method of toilet training would seem to have been particularly suitable to the peasantry. Peasants, including their children, spent much of their lives out of doors. Additionally, their homes often had floors only of pounded earth or clay and they are not recorded as possessing potty chairs. In contrast, the nobility and the wealthy, who were the intended audience of Barberino's writings, could afford both potty chairs and homes with furnishings worth protecting from being soiled by their children.

Another factor in toilet training may have been the comparative lack of privacy which historians believed most medieval Europeans experienced. With fewer provisions for privacy and fewer qualms about displaying bodily functions, at least in front of one's family and associates, it is likely that children witnessed their older siblings, parents, and other adults relieving themselves. As a consequence, medieval children may have learned proper toilet habits by example, just as children learn so many other aspects of behavior. As for when they were toilet trained, we can only estimate. Based on Barberino's writing and on modern experience and on studies of non–European cultures, sometime around two years of age appears likely.

Cradles and Other Sleeping Arrangements

Once they had been fed, cleaned up, and swaddled, many infants must have been ready for a nap. As mentioned previously, small children, especially infants, were at risk of being accidentally killed by overlaying when sharing a bed with an adult such as his parents or wet nurse. This was not a problem during the daytime since children napped alone, but it was a significant problem when the whole family went to bed at night. Having the child sleep apart from adults in his own cradle avoided this danger and, for this reason, the Church advocated the use of cradles to provide infants with their own safe, little beds.

Then as now, parents were concerned about the safety of their children while they were sleeping in their cradles. Parents were aware that their babies could suffocate if they were placed face down in the cradle. Swaddled infants were particularly at risk since the swaddling would likely prevent them from turning themselves over. Some medical writers debated whether it was best to place the swaddled infant in the cradle on his or her back or side. Although it was believed to make the back of the head become somewhat flattened, most parents in the Middle Ages appear to have laid their infants on their backs in their cradles to prevent them from accidentally smothering, just as parents do today.

Although infants were immobilized by swaddling, some cradles were fitted with straps to further restrain the child and ensure that he did not fall out if the cradle tipped over. As this feature indicates, cradles in the Middle Ages did rock (see cover illustration). Most cradles rocked side to side but descriptions of cradles in Italy indicate that at least some rocked the baby head to toe instead. As early as the 13th century, royal and other noble households employed assistants for their children's nurses, and rocking the cradle was one of their duties. In lists of servants, these women were referred to as "rockers" or "rocksters."

Along with paid rockers, some royal infants are known to have had elaborate cradles considered as befitting their rank as heirs to the throne. At the end of the Middle Ages, royal infants in the household of Henry VII, king of England, had two cradles, an everyday one and one for special occasions such as when the baby was attending the royal court and so was on display to the public. The everyday one was about four feet long and two feet wide and made of painted wood decorated with silver and gilt. The buckles for its straps were silver and its blankets were trimmed with fur and cloth of gold. The cradle for public display was much larger: seven and a half feet long and two and a half feet wide. It, too, was made of wood, but it was upholstered in leather. The royal coat of arms was engraved on the headboard.

Unfortunately, placing a child in a cradle rather than leaving him loose on the floor or elsewhere did not guarantee his safety. Cradles were all too frequently placed too near the fire. While this kept the infant warm and allowed a mother to keep an eye on him while cooking, it also increased the chance that he would be burned. One study of infant mortality in the medieval England found that nearly one-third of the deaths of one-year-old children were caused by being burned while in a cradle. Sparks from the fire, animals such as pigs wandering into the house and tipping the cradle over, and just plain carelessness all contributed to these preventable deaths. Some infants were injured or strangled when they tried to crawl out of their cradles and became entangled in the straps that were supposed to keep them safely confined. And older children sometimes managed to slip out of their cradles entirely despite restraints. For example, around the end of the 13th century, a two-year-old boy escaped his cradle one evening while his parents were attending an all night funeral service. His sisters were at home but were asleep. After shedding his clothes, he left the house and proceeded to the nearby castle where his father worked as a cook. Unfortunately for the boy, the castle's drawbridge was raised for the night and he managed to fall into the dry moat below. His naked and frost-covered body was discovered early the next morning, but he was rescued and, with aid attributed to the intervention of a saint, was revived. Thus, as these incidents show, placing an infant in a cradle was no guarantee that he was out of harm's way. Still, cradles did at least protect them from the dangers of being overlain by their parents or wet nurse at night by providing them with their own little beds.

For infants of those too poor to afford cradles and for many other children as they outgrew their cradles, sharing their parents' bed appears to have been a common practice. Medieval homes were frequently small by today's standards. The smallest houses had only one or two rooms and mattresses, in the form of large, flat cloth bags stuffed with wool or straw, were laid out in any available open space at night and then rolled up for storage during the day. Even in larger homes, there was often only one bedroom.

When children were young and small, having them join their parents in their bed was the simplest sleeping arrangement. As they grew bigger, children appear to have been frequently given their own bedding. Fortunate children had trundle beds which were stored under their parents' bed when not in use. More commonly, they appear to have had mattresses which were placed on the floor and rolled up to store during the day.

Other rooms in the house with suitable floor space as well as lofts could be pressed into use as bedrooms at night if a family outgrew its bedroom.

But additional bedding did not necessarily mean an end to sharing beds. Siblings were expected to share a bed. The problems that could be caused by such sharing did not go unnoticed. Children were generally recognized as being innocent but parents were advised by some medical authorities to begin separating their sons from their daughters at bed time as early as the age of three and no later than age seven. This was to prevent them from engaging in inappropriate behavior at an age when their curiosity about the bodies of the opposite sex was developing. Interestingly, given that most adults in medieval Europe appear to have slept in the nude, concerns about children sleeping with their naked parents do not appear to have been raised. Perhaps children were expected to have moved on to their own beds before they reached an age when this practice would cause problems.

As all this discussion of sharing beds suggests, regardless of their exact sleeping arrangements, medieval children and adults rarely enjoyed the private space most modern people take for granted in their own homes. Only the very privileged children of royalty and the nobility would typically have had their own private rooms, and even then they were seldom alone. Noble siblings often had to share bedchambers. Further, their nurses or other personal servants frequently slept in the same room with them, just as their parents' closest servants slept on bedding on the floor of their bedroom. Thus, beds and bedrooms were primarily places for sleeping and not so much the private refuges that they are today.

Learning to Walk

Once children were out of swaddling, they were crawling and soon were trying to stand and walk. Freed from the cradle, they were ready to explore. Further, since there were no playpens or cribs to help corral them, infants and small children were frequently able to range quite far. And, when they weren't well supervised, they sometimes got into trouble, especially since medieval homes were far from childproof. Medieval toddlers were just as likely as small children today to pick up coins, pins, and any other small object they found and put them in their mouths. Putting seeds, fruit pits, and other items up their own noses or in their ears was also a problem. In addition, open fires, uncovered wells, ditches, and streams, as well as roaming farm animals were also hazards frequently encountered around many medieval houses. Thus, the admonition to godparents to help protect their godchildren from fire and water was based on concerns over very real dangers. Still, despite the risks posed by increased mobility, medieval parents appear to have been as anxious as modern ones to have their children walk as early as possible. This was such a common desire, in fact, that some medieval medical writers cautioned parents against rushing children to sit up and walk before they were ready.

There were some attempts to help protect children learning to walk. In Spain and Italy, as well as other parts of Europe, padded bonnets were made to cushion any impacts for children learning to stand up and walk. Another common accessory was a walker (fig. 12). This was usually in the form of an open, four-sided frame with small wheels at the bottom of each leg, somewhat similar to the modern walking frames used by the elderly.

Supervision

Padded bonnets and walking frames may have helped but, as the dangers outlined above show, medieval children needed the same constant supervision that children need today to keep them from getting into trouble. A little is known about the day to day care and supervision of medieval infants and young children from a few late medieval manuals and some illuminations, but most of what was recorded by contemporaries addressed the times when care-giving went wrong and the unfortunate child ended up either as the subject of a coroner's report or, more happily, among those miraculously helped by divine intervention. Obviously, these reports skew our view of child-rearing in the Middle Ages in the same way that basing a study of modern child care primarily upon child protective service case files would. Keeping this in mind, we can still discern some common aspects of medieval child care.

Fig. 12. In this picture, the Holy Family is depicted as a prosperous urban family of the mid–15th century. On the right, St. Joseph is in his workshop while St. Mary, on the left, weaves cloth on a loom. Between them, the toddler Jesus is using a walking frame to scoot around the house. Wheeled frames such as this one appear to have been common by the late Middle Ages.

Parents, primarily the mother, were expected to care for and supervise their children. There were a few exceptions. In late medieval Italy, some children lived with their wet nurse and her family for the first two to three years of their lives. In a few exceptional cases, some children even stayed with their wet nurses up to the age of ten or so. For these children, the wet nurse and her family were obviously the most important caregivers for the earliest part of their childhoods. In noble and other wealthy households, mothers supervised the care of their children, but the menial tasks such as the cleaning and feeding of infants were frequently entrusted to servants. As previously discussed, these servants appear to have often included the wet nurses, who stayed on with their charges after nursing was completed.

Wet nurses aside, most parents in medieval Europe cared for their children themselves day in and day out. However, just as parents today sometimes must rely on relatives or babysitters to watch their children on occasion and on daycare providers for longer term care, medieval parents frequently had to call on others to watch their children when obligations, such as working in fields, called them away from their homes. Older siblings, aged relatives, and neighbors frequently helped medieval parents care for and supervise their children. From coroners' reports, we know that some of these caregivers were not up to the task, and this is not surprising when we discover that some of the siblings set to watch their little brothers or sisters were only five or six years old and that some of the aged relatives were blind or otherwise infirm. Having such people watch over small children was clearly negligent and, today, would bring legal intervention and possibly punishment as well. Yet, it is unfair to hold parents of the Middle Ages to modern standards in all these cases. These parents likely had a very limited selection of people willing to help watch their children and had to make do with who they could find. In fact, at times, some parents could find no one and left their children alone, with tragic consequences. (Although it should be noted that fatal accidents sometimes occurred when a young child was simply sent outside to play.) However, we only know of the cases in which a child wandered off and drowned in a river or tipped over a pot full of boiling soup on himself. Just as today, all the myriad times when someone took care of a child and nothing bad happened went unrecorded. Deaths of children resulting from inadequate supervision were (and are) mostly preventable tragedies, but they are not always proof of the parents' indifference to welfare of their children. As discussed further in chapter 5, many parents in the Middle Ages were clearly willing to make great sacrifices for their children. For example, a mother escaped her burning home but then rushed back in to save her son, only to be overcome by smoke and heat and die in the attempt. In another case, a father was killed while trying to protect his daughter from a rapist. Thus, most medieval parents likely did the best they could when supervising their children and when entrusting their care to others. Unfortunately, that wasn't always enough.

One last point on the supervision of children: parents and caregivers were not the only ones who watched out for children in medieval Europe. Adults were aware that children are all too frequently oblivious to dangers around them. There were good Samaritans even in the Middle Ages who helped prevent accidents or rescued children, regardless of whether they knew the child or not. For example, residents of one London neighborhood in the 14th century intervened to protect a boy being beaten by two men. Even though they did not know the boy, the neighbors challenged the men and fought them when they refused to desist. Similarly, when a child went missing, many people, if not the entire community, routinely turned out to help search. Admittedly, there were also cases in which passers-by did not want to get involved, failed to provide any help, and left the child in peril. Such a case occurred in 13th century England. A group of young men and women saw a girl's body in a pond but made no attempt to help and even stopped someone else from going for help. They thought that girl was already dead and, since she was no one that they recognized, they apparently wanted to avoid the inconvenience of having to appear as witnesses in the investigation of some stranger's death. Luckily, the girl was later rescued and revived. Thus, some adults were callous or indifferent, but most appear to have been moved to action when they saw a child in danger.

Caring for Sick Children

Returning to children's primary caregivers, their parents: one of the most convincing pieces of evidence that many medieval parents loved their children as much as their modern counterparts is the care given to sick children. When a child became ill or was injured, most parents did not simply shrug and wait for the disease to run its course or leave the injury untreated. They took action to help cure their child.

While little was recorded of such treatments, many parents presumably provided the initial care themselves: making the child comfortable, ensuring he rested, preparing nutritious and easily digested foods, such as broth and chicken, and cleaning any wounds or sores. Many of the diseases suffered by children in the Middle Ages are still with us: chicken pox, diarrhea, upset stomachs, colds, and fevers. Parents appear to have been able to cope with these as effectively then as now. Other conditions such as intestinal worms and the fungus called "ringworm" that plagued medieval children are less common today among children in most industrialized countries, but medieval parents were able to cure or at least mitigate even these problems as well.

As with parents before and since, many medieval parents appear to have been selfless and tireless in their care of their sick children. One father made sure that he checked his children's temperatures at the same time each day for eight months when they all came down with a persistent fever, probably malaria. Through constant care, one mother kept her daughter alive after she contracted a disease that caused her to vomit almost everything she ate. After four years, the exhausted mother prayed that her daughter be cured or die to end her misery. The daughter soon died and her death was considered a miracle.

If home remedies failed, some parents sought out physicians and surgeons to treat their children. Such treatment was quite expensive and often of questionable worth. In at least one case, the parents are known to have gone to several different physicians seeking cures for their sick child. As with treatments for adults, medieval physicians often prescribed medicines and changes in diet as part of their treatment. For nursing infants, it was recognized that they could not change their diet and that they would have difficulty ingesting medicines. Thus, the mother or wet nurse had to take the medicine or make the change in diet so that her milk would be imbued with the palliative qualities that the infant needed.

In addition to diet and medication, medieval physicians commonly employed bleeding, but this treatment was rarely recommended for children. As mentioned previously, bleeding, also called venesection, involved making a small incision into a vein and releasing a prescribed amount of blood in order to restore the patient's balance of bodily humors. Physicians and surgeons recognized that children, along with elderly and pregnant women, might be too weak to withstand bleeding. One prominent 14th century surgeon and medical writer specified that children under the age of 14 should not be bled nor should they undergo any major surgery unless there was no other option.

Along with medical treatment or when the treatments failed, parents routinely turned to God for help in saving their children. The simplest means was to pray for a cure. Many went beyond this and solemnly vowed to undertake a pilgrimage, usually to the shrine of a saint noted for helping in such cases. Sometimes the vow of pilgrimage was conditional on the child being cured first. This was common when the illness or injury was immediately life-threatening and there was not enough time to undertake a pilgrimage before the child was expected to die. In other situations, such as when a child was suffering a chronic illness, one or both of the parents and even the child, if he was well enough to travel, went on pilgrimage to seek a cure. As with physicians, saintly shrines also did not always deliver a cure, and some families made many pilgrimages to several different shrines, always hoping for a miracle.

Less benign than the belief in the value of pilgrimages was the belief in fairies and changelings. In parts of Europe before the spread of Christianity, some people believed that fairies would sneak into homes and harm any babies they found or that they would take the human infants and leave their own infants in their place. These substitute children were called changelings. Among the characteristics attributed to changelings were incessant crying, weakness, sickliness, and constant hunger despite showing no signs of growing. Today, through the help of modern medicine, such infants might be diagnosed with colic or other conditions which we can understand and usually treat. However, in the Middle Ages, even after Europe became Christianized, some people could find no reasonable explanation for such problems themselves and so turned to superstition. As late as the 14th century, an English monk wrote that some people were still leaving food out near their infants' cradles to protect them from fairies. This practice dated back into the pre–Christian era and was done either as an offering to appease the fairies or as a lure to distract them from their evildoing. If preventive measures failed and a changeling was swapped for a human baby, the only "remedy" was to somehow compel the fairies to come take their child and return the human one. Unfortunately for the innocent child, it was thought the fairies would come to retrieve him if he was being tormented. Thus, suspected changelings were sometimes physically abused. There were alternatives to physical torture. Abandoning the child at a crossroads or riverside and rituals carried out in groves of trees followed by repeated dipping in a river were also employed to force the fairies to undo their harm. Even in these rites, the child was still in danger of being injured or killed. While the belief in changelings was found in many regions across Europe, most accounts of the harrowing practices used to force the fairies to return the normal child are drawn primarily from isolated locales in France. With such limited evidence, it cannot be established how commonly parents of suspected changelings resorted to such extreme and life-threatening measures to "save" their children. One can hope that it was a rare procedure.

Mourning and Burial

Although there is insufficient evidence to quantify the rate of child mortality, it was clearly high during the Middle Ages. Parents often outlived some of their children. Some even suffered having all their children predecease them. Still, it was considered a tragedy when a child died, and parents mourned the loss of their little ones. Even when the Black Death killed staggering numbers of people, young and old, parents still grieved most over the loss of their children. During the recurrences of the Black Death in the 15th century, fathers in some Italian cities wrote of their lost children with great tenderness, recalling all their good characteristics and the joy they had brought. Some recorded feelings of guilt and regret as well, berating themselves for not having been better fathers for their now departed children. Mothers seldom left written records of their mourning themselves, but others wrote of mothers who were driven mad with grief over the death of their children. While weeping and other expressions of loss were expected, bereaved mothers sometimes fled and refused to come home. Others lost all interest in life and fell into deep depression. Some, unable to fully face the sad truth, even refused to part with their dead little ones and had to be forced to allow them to be buried. Further proof of the universality and intensity of parental mourning over the loss of their children can be found in surviving sermons. Clergymen frequently preached against excessive grieving and reminded parents that their children, assuming they had been baptized, were assuredly in heaven since they died so young that they were still innocent of any serious sins. One hopes that this thought provided parents some comfort.

Medieval burial practices for children indicate that they were typically accorded the same respect and dignity as adults. Royal and noble children received funerals befitting their rank, which could include ceremonies conducted in one of the great cathedrals and interment in a desirable burial chamber, such as one located in the cathedral's floor. Like most adults, humbler children were sewn up in shrouds and laid to rest in child-sized graves in the parish cemetery.

In the early Middle Ages, Europeans who had not yet converted to Christianity often buried items along with the bodies of both adults and children. Whether these objects were expected to be of use in the afterlife or were simply placed there as signs of respect and affection, we may never know. In any case, little clay birds, balls, tops, dolls and other toys have sometimes been found in the graves of pagan children buried during the early Middle Ages.

Christian burial practices forbade interment of goods along with the body. However, children sometimes continued to receive special treatment. In some medieval Christian cemeteries in England and France, graves of children, especially young children, have been found grouped along the sides of the churches that adjoined the cemeteries. Many medieval Christians wanted to be buried as close as possible to the church's altar, so the placement of these graves close to the church's walls, and thus close to altar inside, may reflect special affection for those buried. Further, the graves were placed so that the rainwater running off the eaves of the church roof flowed over the graves. Historians and archaeologists have speculated that the siting of the graves may have also been motivated by the belief that the church, as a holy structure, in some way "blessed" the water that came in contact with it. So, these children's graves and the bodies in them were washed and blessed with "holy" water with every rain. However, this blessing was not a substitute for baptism. As discussed in chapter 1, unbaptized infants were excluded from burial in the consecrated ground of Christian cemeteries in the Middle Ages.

Role of Fathers

One final note on childcare: raising children is traditionally women's work and medieval mothers appear to have been the primary caregivers for their children. The role of the father was to provide for and protect his family. However, these traditional roles were often shared. The income produced by working mothers was often vital to their families' survival and fathers were often involved in their children's upbringing. For example, in Italian cities, fathers were typically responsible for hiring the wet nurse. Further, the diaries kept by some of these men show that they could be every bit as attentive to their children as their mothers. Such fathers clearly took great pride and pleasure in their children and seeing them develop. Fathers are also known to have shared the childcare burden on a day-to-day basis. Some took their young sons and daughters to work with them so that they could keep an eye on them while working. (This might explain how the wayward little son of the castle cook mentioned above became so used to making his way from home to his father's workplace.) In some instances, fathers were the primary caregivers for their children. When a mother died or became mentally or physically disabled, this was one of the few options available. Thus, while mothers routinely took care of their children, fathers sometimes assumed or shared this duty too.

While some fathers were directly involved in raising their children, some were clearly less engaged. For example, among the nobility, fathers were frequently away from home conducting business such as wars, attending court, and administering their often far-flung land-holdings. Even when they were home, some noble fathers may have had little contact with their children on a daily basis. The children were typically raised by the women of the house-hold. Their mother, their nurse, and other female servants appear to have been the adults with whom they had the most contact in early childhood. Still, it should be noted that noble houses ranged from small estates which barely supported a single family up to royal palaces which housed small armies of servants and supporters as well as the royal family itself, so the degree to which children were insulated from their parents varied tremendously. Further, hav-ing to spend significant amounts of time away from your children and having to entrust their care to others does not mean that one does not love and care about one's children, a point that working parents, especially working mothers, still have to assert today. Therefore, it would be unfair to assume that all noble fathers were indifferent to their own children except for their need for them as heirs, based on the limited evidence available. In fact, fathers from all classes in medieval Europe appear to have run the gamut from caring and loving to negligent or abusive.

3

Play

As we will see in chapter 8, children were expected to begin performing helpful chores around the home, farm, and workshop by around the age of five or six. However, they were not expected to work full time by any means and were left with free time for play. The need for children to play was recognized even in the Middle Ages. One writer in the 13th century put it simply: Children should be allowed to play because nature demands it. Playing games and sports as well as with toys kept medieval children amused and it helped them develop their strength, their coordination, and their mental abilities, just as play still does today.

Despite the grim picture we have of growing up in medieval Europe, children back then did play and have fun. In fact, many of the things they enjoyed are still enjoyed by children today. However, as we will see, it may be difficult for modern people to understand why some of these pastimes were considered to be fun. Technological progress over the past century has drastically changed the forms of entertainment enjoyed by children as well as adults today. At the present, many, if not most, children and adults in industrialized countries routinely entertain themselves with CDs, DVDs, and, of course, a wide variety of computer-based games. While they were only created in the past few decades, all these items are now considered essential means for keeping oneself entertained. In contrast, as we will see in this chapter, European children in the Middle Ages played a wide variety of games and sports, from the simple to the complex, which required only the most basic of materials. Although people today may not see the appeal of some of these amusements, they were clearly enjoyed back then.

As with so many other aspects of life in the Middle Ages, the class to which a person belonged influenced the availability and choice of recreational activities. Even for children, the pastimes they enjoyed depended, in part, on their social class. For example, horseback riding was restricted to those whose families who could afford to keep a horse. Even more select was the group who read for pleasure. As will be further explained in chapter 6, literacy was a relatively scarce skill among medieval Europeans. Further, all books had to be painstakingly copied by hand, so they were very expensive. As a consequence, only the children of wealthy families grew up to enjoy the accounts of the adventures of King Arthur and romances about knights and their ladies. Even the selection of board games played was also influenced by a person's wealth and social standing. Games such Nine-Man Morris, draughts (checkers), and tic-tac-toe were enjoyed at all levels of society but chess and *tric-trac* (backgammon) were primarily played by the nobility and the wealthy (fig. 13).

Fig. 13. The couple on the left is playing chess while the one on the right is playing Nine-Man Morris. While chess was primarily played by the aristocracy, Nine-Man Morris was enjoyed by all classes of medieval society.

Infants

Like children before and since the Middle Ages, children in medieval Europe enjoyed games and playing appropriate for their ages. Babies in the Middle Ages were entertained with such activities as piggyback rides, bouncing on an adult's knee, and playing "peek-a-boo." Their parents or nurses also told them stories, recited rhymes, and sang to them. As they grew older, they played the venerable game of guessing in which hand a small item was hidden. This game was called *Handy Dandy* in England. As for infant toys, rattles can be traced back in time to at least classical Greece and babies in the medieval Europe were likely given them as well. By the late Middle Ages, rattles were sometimes made out of metal and were in the form of a small stick with little round bells (the sort we associate with "Jingle Bells") attached to them. While none have survived, there were also small, wooden blocks for little children. The existence of these toys is revealed by their mention in lists of toys which were often part of moralists' complaints that parents spoiled their children by giving them too many toys.

Older Children

As children advanced from infanthood and became more mobile and more coordinated, their playing became more complex and varied. Older children played hide-and-seek, leapfrog, tag, and hopscotch. They ran races and jumped, tumbled, and leapt for the sheer pleasure of it. They threw rocks at targets and competed to see who could throw them highest or furthest. Some even walked on stilts, while others carried their fellow children piggyback. They sometimes had contests in which those being carried attempted to knock each other off. Many of these activities can be found in a painting by Bruegel of children at play (fig. 14). While this painting was created in 1560, written descriptions from the Middle Ages indicate that most, if not all, of the games and toys depicted were common well before this date.

They also got into mischief, particularly boys. Stealing fruit appears to have been a fairly common pastime for boys who lived anywhere near orchards (fig. 15). They stole fruit because it was the primary form of sweet treat available in medieval Europe, since sugar was a rare and expensive luxury good and even honey was relatively costly. Children, boys as well as girls, went exploring in the lands around their homes, climbing trees and poking around piles of wood and anything else interesting as they went. Evidence of these last activities is found in accounts of miracles where saints intervened to revive a child who fell while climbing a tree or who was crushed when the pile of wood on which he was playing collapsed.

Fig. 14. This fanciful painting by Pieter Bruegel is teeming with children at play. Over 200 children are shown participating in at least 70 different games and activities. For example, in the upper left corner, a boy climbs a tree. In the lower left corner, two girls are playing the jacks-like game of knucklebones. In the middle ground, six boys are playing leap-frog. To the right, another group of boys are playing a game in which each tries to throw his cap the furthest. Other games are more obscure and difficult to identify. Several different groups of children appear to be imitating religious processions. Other groups are playing very rough games, such as the five boys on the right side of the painting who are gathered around another boy and pulling his hair. Regardless of the exact nature of games, these pastimes reveal both the ingenuity of children in making their own fun and the time-lessness of some of those activities.

Banding together in groups was also a common practice among older children. For example, one Anglo-Saxon document mentions such a group of children playing at the seashore. Besides forming groups for embarking on adventures around the neighborhood, children appear to have often simply gathered to play with one another. As early as the 14th century, writers observed that children preferred the company of other children rather than that of adults. Some things never change.

Imitative Play

Children of the Middle Ages seem to have enjoyed imitating the activities of adults as much as children do today. Chronicles of the lives of saints occasionally mention that, as children, future saints shunned childish games and instead acted out the roles of priests and bishop, imi-

Fig. 15. Candies were rare and expensive in medieval Europe. Instead, the most commonly available sweets were fruit, and stealing fruit appears to have been a common pastime for many children, especially boys.

tating religious ceremonies they had seen. Even less saintly children engaged in such play and reenacted religious activities such as processions, weddings, and other Church activities (fig. 14).

On a more mundane level, children were also given toy pots, pans, dishes, and other miniature models of implements and tools with which to play. Most of these were made of fired clay but, by the last centuries of the Middle Ages, more were being made of metal. One particularly luxurious example of such metal toys was a set of little silver bowls and dishes made for a two-year-old princess in the 14th century. Like tea sets and play dishes today, these items were made for girls so that they could imitate their mothers at work around the house.

Boys among the nobility were also given smaller versions of adult items. Toy wooden swords were likely quite common, and royal princes were sometimes given their own metal swords by the time they were eight or nine. By the end of the Middle Ages, kings and other members of the higher nobility had small suits of plate armor made for their sons as well (fig. 16).

Toys

Toys are among the rarest artifacts of medieval living. This scarcity certainly does not mean that they were rare in the Middle Ages, but it does reflect the perishable nature of the clay, wood, and fabric used to make most toys and, probably, the hard use they saw at the hands of the children who played with them. There is also the problem of determining whether items belonged to children or adults. Both children and adults played games involving dice and game pieces (such as chess, checkers, and backgammon) so that the age of the former owners of these items cannot be absolutely established.

Wooden Toys

Wooden toys were likely the most common since wood was a readily available material and easily worked. These included wheeled wooden toys to push or pull along. Examples of such toys have been found in Novgorod, Russia, where wheeled wooden horses have been recovered in excavations of deposits ranging from the 11th through the 14th centuries. The Novgorod horses vary in length from about eight to twelve inches. These toys are simplified representations of horses but were quite suitable for children's use. Tops were another common, simple toy. Some were in the form of large wooden cones, several inches in height, that were kept spinning by lashing them with small whips (fig. 14). Others were smaller and were spun with the fingers.

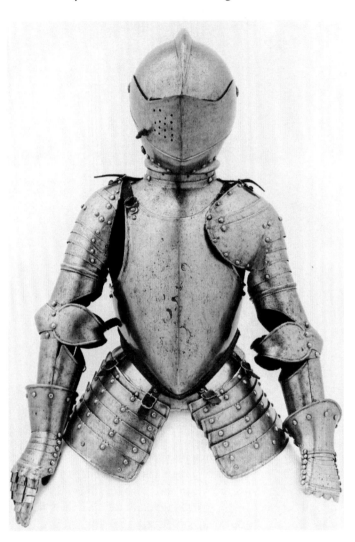

Fig. 16. While this particular armor was made after the end of the Middle Ages, it is part of a tradition of making scaled-down armor for sons of the high nobility. Such armor was every bit as well-made and sophisticated as that made for adults. By wearing harnesses of armor, boys became accustomed to the weight and feel of armor. Additionally, they could engage in mock combat while wearing such armor. For example, this armor was designed for the sport of fighting against an opponent while separated by a waist-high barrier. Since the armor was designed for this specialized type of sport combat, it covered the boy only from the waist up.

Hobby-horses were frequently mentioned in medieval lists of toys and were frequently included in depictions of children at play. Children often simply made their own from long sticks. By the end of the Middle Ages hobby-horses were being made commercially, at least in the Low Countries, with carved and painted heads and little leather reins similar to modern ones (fig. 14). There were also rocking horses. Again, while none survive, the tracts of Italian moralists prove that they existed at least as early as the 14th century.

Children also played with large wooden hoops which they rolled, usually with the aid of a stick (fig. 14). These hoops were the same ones used in manufacturing barrels. Children continued to play this game into the 19th century, wherever barrels were available. Cup-and-ball was another wooden toy which enjoyed popularity during the Middle Ages and for centuries afterward. As the name suggests, this toy was a cup on a handle with a wooden ball attached by a string. The goal was to flip the ball up and catch it in the cup.

There were early forms of pinwheels, often called "windmills," as well. Unlike modern pinwheels in which the bladed wheel is held by a pin on the side of a stick, medieval pinwheel blades were pinned onto the top of the stick so that they were at a right-angle to the stick's tip. To make the pinwheel spin, a child held it straight out in front of him and ran. Children playing with windmills are often shown in mock jousts, charging at each other with their pinwheels extended like lances (fig. 14). This pinwheel jousting may have been the origin of the phrase "tilting at windmills" to describe attacking imaginary enemies, although Cervantes is generally credited with coining the phrase in *Don Quixote* in the early 17th century.

By the late 14th century, another windmill-like toy appeared. It was made in two pieces. The first piece was a round stick several inches long with blades fixed to one of its ends. The other end of the stick fit into the second piece of the toy, a small, wooden ball or a large nut with a small hole drilled in it. The stick fit into the hole with a few inches exposed between the blades and the ball. A string was wound around the exposed part of stick. A child held the ball in one hand and quickly pulled the string with the other, making the blades spin rapidly. (A toy like this is being held by the boy in green shown in the upper left-hand branch of the Tree of Consanguinity on the cover.) Unfortunately, the illustrations do not show whether or not the stick lifted off like a little helicopter. Most likely, it simply spun around.

Kites

Kites were another late medieval toy. The earliest medieval depiction of a kite-like object was in 1326, but it was in the form of a windsock rather than the sort of kites common today. More windsocks, this time made to look like dragon heads, appear in illustration from the first half of the 15th century. Flat kites with trailing tails were developed during the late 15th century, but the diamond-shaped kite most familiar today did not appear in any European illustrations until 1618. It is most likely that European merchants such as Marco Polo, who had observed Chinese kites and kite competitions in 1282, brought kites or, at least, the knowledge for making them back from the Orient.

Balls and Marbles

Children also played with balls of various sizes. Instead of wood, specimens found in locations across Europe reveal that balls were typically made of pieces of leather stitched together and then stuffed with moss, chaff from grains, or other wadding. These were used in a variety of games as discussed later in this chapter. Marbles made of clay or stone were yet another simple but popular toy and appear to have been used in games similar to those played for centuries after the Middle Ages.

Metal Toys and Toy Castles

In addition to leather and wood, some toys were made out of metal. While metal is more durable than either of the other materials, only a few metal toys have survived. This low survival rate can probably be attributed to the relative expense of metal during the Middle Ages. Far fewer people were able to afford metal toys for their children than toys of leather and

Fig. 17. This little bronze knight likely delighted some little boy six centuries ago. While it is only a little over an inch high and an inch long, this metal figure would have been relatively expensive and so was likely made for a noble boy.

wood so comparatively fewer metal toys were produced. Further, the high value of metal meant that broken metal toys were melted down and recycled.

As with wooden toys, metal toys came in a variety of shapes, such as the little metal jugs and dishes mentioned previously. There were also more complex toys made out of metal. One such toy was a small bird found in London. While incomplete today, the bird originally perched on a rod and its tongue moved in and out of its beak when its tail was pushed. Models of birds appear to have been a popular toy. In 14th century Italy, birds made out of painted wood and ceramic were also included in lists of children's toys.

Metal was also cast to make figures of knights. These forerunners of the tin soldiers of later centuries ranged from very simple, almost abstract, ones such as the one illustrated (fig. 17) to more detailed and realistic specimens. Some of these metal knights were quite complex. For example, one such toy which has survived from 15th or early 16th century Germany is pair of mounted lance-wielding knights who charged at each other on wheeled steeds. The horses were fitted with small sets of pulleys so that they could be drawn towards each other by having a child behind each knight pull a cord. When the knights collided, pivots built into each one allowed them to topple backwards in their saddles. A toy which appears to be identical to this one is also depicted in a German woodcut, dated 1516. However, while children are present, adults are shown playing with the knights on a tabletop, showing that even back then adults couldn't resist playing with really neat kids' toys.

There were other military toys as well. In the late 13th century, Edward I, an English king noted for the number of castles built during his reign, had toy castles made for his sons. One of these castles was likely furnished inside and was such a showpiece that it was displayed in one of Edward's palaces. Some royal children were given toys weapons suitable for attacking castles as well. One of Edward's sons received a little siege engine along with his castle while, in the 14th century, Richard II, then only ten years old, was given a pair of little cannons.

Dolls

Toy knights were not the only figures of people made for children. Dolls appear to have been common toys for girls. There are several references to girls playing with dolls, including descriptions of child brides among the nobility who were so young that they continued to play with dolls for some time after their weddings. Girls of all classes appear to have often used dolls in imitating their mothers and "playing house."

As with some of the toy birds, by the late Middle Ages, many dolls were made of fired clay or brightly painted wood. Some German towns and cities, such as Nuremberg, appear to have become well established producers of ceramic dolls before the end of the Middle Ages. In 15th century woodcuts depicting various trades in Germany, dollmakers are shown molding and firing clay dolls while others are assembling dolls with moveable limbs. Despite being mass produced from a relatively cheap material, these dolls were still expensive and were likely bought for children of the nobility and wealthier merchants.

While manufactured dolls were available by the end of the Middle Ages, homemade dolls made of cloth and wood were likely the most common form of dolls throughout the period. Cloth and wood are highly perishable and no dolls of this sort have survived. However, as the descriptions of the behavior of child brides illustrate, there are written accounts which prove the existence of such dolls. Other references appear in medieval England where, by the late Middle Ages, dolls were often called *poppets*. In one English text, cowardly or weak people were likened to dolls with legs made of cloth. This suggests that some poppets may have been rag dolls made entirely of cloth. Still other dolls and figures were made from flowers and other pieces of plants, not unlike the cornhusk dolls of American pioneers.

Imaginative Play and Improvised Toys

Many children improvised their own toys. In a 15th century Scottish poem, the writer included a lengthy list of children's activities. Among these were taking a stick, pretending it was a horse, and riding around on it. The poet further describes children taking pieces of bread and imaging that they were little sailing ships, while girls could make dolls just from scraps of cloth, a few flowers, and some other odds and ends. For boys, on the other hand, long plant stems and leaves became make-believe spears and swords. A story from the early 12th century illustrates some imaginative play with such items. King Stephen I of England was recorded as playing a game with a young boy, a hostage son of one his rebel nobles. While the details are unclear, the two took long plant stems and either tried to hit and break the tip of their opponent's stem or swung the stems to knock down "soldiers" made from other plants. Improvised toys such as these were likely the most common form of playthings. Many families, particularly the peasantry which made up the vast majority of the population in medieval Europe, could not afford purpose-built toys. The children of these families had to make do with things they could find or make themselves, much as many children around the world still do.

Medieval children also sought to imitate the buildings they saw around them. With a little creativity, they made models of various structures. For example, sandcastles are nothing new. They date back to at least the 12th century, when a monk from Wales wrote that, when he was a child, his brothers built castles, palaces, and even towns out of sand on the beach while he, as befitted a future cleric, built churches and monasteries. There are also references to building little mills complete with dams for channeling the water. In the 15th century Scottish poem mentioned previously, the poet described children building miniature manor houses out sticks. So, even in a world without Legos, many children had an irresistible urge to build models of the structures they saw around them.

Children also played with a variety of items which were not meant to be toys. Then as now, children played with everyday items such as coins, beads, and even pieces of broken jewelry. Children appear to have kept such objects as "treasures" just as boys and girls today still prize the little odds and ends they've found. Some of these items have been found in early medieval graves of children and were likely placed there because they had been favorite trinkets of the deceased child.

Musical Instruments

Children today are encouraged to enjoy and make music at an early age, and some children in the Middle Ages were similarly encouraged by their parents. The same Italian 14th century list of toys which included toy birds also recorded little drums, cymbals, and tambourines as common toys among the middle and upper classes of the Italian city-states. Whistles were also popular. Some whistles appear to have been in the form of small flutes and were possibly similar to the "penny-whistles" of more recent times.

Staged Entertainments

While most traveling performers catered to adults, a few provided entertainment especially for children. The first illustrations of puppet shows as well as written records of payments for such shows appeared in the 14th century. As with later puppet shows, these early ones used glove puppets and were played out on little stages like those used in later Punch and Judy shows. In fact, the performance shown in the illustration is likely an early Punch and Judy show, with Punch being the male figure on the left holding a club and the female figure on the right being Judy (fig. 18).

Sports

As discussed previously, older children in the Middle Ages engaged in numerous physical activities from running and jumping to leapfrog and throwing rocks. They also played on improvised seesaws and swings (fig. 19). Besides such unstructured exercise, older children in the Middle Ages also engaged in activities that we would consider sports today. Most of these sports were popular with adults as well as children but some were primarily for older children and teenagers.

Swimming

Eighth century chronicles record that, among other physical exercises, Charlemagne enjoyed swimming in the Roman-style baths constructed at his palaces. However, while there are scattered references throughout the Middle Ages, swimming appears to have largely fallen out favor with the nobility by the 11th century. However, swimming wasn't a pastime reserved for the nobility. Illustrations of pastoral scenes set in the summer occasionally include depictions of farm laborers "skinny-dipping" in a pond or stream to cool off after a long, hot day of hard work. Similarly, in calendar illustrations for the summer months, there are pictures

Top: Fig. 18. This crowd of children is eagerly watching a puppet show staged just for their entertainment. The puppet on the left appears to be male and holds a small club and is likely an ancestor of "Punch," while the female puppet on the right is probably an early "Judy." As the puppets in later Punch and Judy shows often fought and struck each other, medieval puppet shows also likely involved physical humor, including some comic violence. Such entertainment has obviously appealed to some children in every generation. *Bottom:* Fig. 19. Specialized outdoor play equipment, such a monkey bars and jungle gyms, did not exist in the Middle Ages. Still, medieval children created their own equipment. In this picture, some boys have made a swing out of some rope and a pulley. Similarly, in figure 14, barrels, fences, and a rail for hitching horses have similarly been temporarily transformed into play equipment.

of groups of naked boys swimming in streams, complete with some of them shivering from the coldness of the water and others attempting to dunk their playmates (fig. 20). The strong association of swimming with the warm months highlights the limited opportunities for swimming in most of Europe. For much of the year, the water, whether in streams, lakes, or the seas, was too cold for swimming. This, rather than fear or dislike of getting wet, may explain the relative unpopularity of swimming among medieval Europeans.

Fig. 20. Swimming was limited to only the warmest months in most of Europe. Still, despite the short season for swimming, some children enjoyed this pastime while they could. This is the illustration for the month of June from the calendar portion of a book of hours. While one boy is shivering, the other three are enjoying a cooling dip in the water.

Most swimmers appear to have been boys and men. As for girls and women swimming, apart from two accounts from 13th century England of women drowning, there are virtually no examples of female swimmers in medieval Europe. The prevalence of male swimmers may be explained by the fact that swimming was only performed in the nude. It may have been considered an inappropriately immodest activity for girls and women. Even among males, modesty may have been of some concern since no onlookers are portrayed in the pictures of naked men or boys swimming.

Water Jousting

Water jousting was one sport which proved that many young men were not afraid of the water. It took place on rivers instead of in castle tilt-yards, with a team of oarsmen in a long, narrow rowboat in place of a warhorse (fig. 21). The water jouster, standing up near the bow of the boat, wielded a long pole and attempted to knock his opponent, who was similarly armed and positioned in the prow of an oncoming boat, over and into the water while avoiding being knocked over himself. As shown in medieval illustrations, water jousting also included passes at the quintain, a practice dummy that swung around when struck and was designed to knock over any jouster who didn't get out of the way in time. Unlike real jousting, water jousts were usually held as part of civic festivals in the summer (when the water

Fig. 21. Water jousting appears to have been enjoyed in many parts of Europe. This Flemish picture from the mid–14th century shows the basic elements of this sport. A young man stands in the back of a small boat and holds a long pole while four or five other young men paddle the boat towards a target on the left of the scene. The jouster's goal is to strike the target with the pole without being knocked into the water.

was warmer) rather than as aristocratic entertainments; the participants in water jousting were young men from the sponsoring towns rather than nobles practicing for war; and the most serious damage inflicted was usually a thorough soaking of the loser rather than any grievous wounds.

While water jousting seems like a rather odd sport, it enjoyed popularity in many parts of medieval Europe. It appears in sources ranging from a written description of activities in London from around 1180 to French manuscript illuminations in the 14th and 15th centuries.

Ice Skating and Other Winter Activities

While some sports were best suited to summer, there were others unique to winter. In northern countries, notably England, Scandinavia, and the Low Countries, ice skating was a popular winter sport for children as well as adults. The blades of medieval ice skates were typically made of sections of animal leg-bones. Metal skates did not appear until some time in the 15th century. Along one side, the bone was slightly sharpened for its entire length to form an edge that served the same propulsion and steering functions as the edges of modern steel blades. The opposite side was flattened and possibly attached to a small length of board so that the skater's foot rested firmly on the blade. The blades were then strapped to the boots or shoes of the skater. Skaters also often used long poles to push themselves along the ice.

From a brief description of skating in London written by Thomas Becket's secretary in 1180 to Dutch and German woodcuts of the 15th century, skating was depicted as an exhilarating, but often painful, pastime. These depictions of skating are filled with images of experienced skaters gracefully gliding across the glistening ice while novices clatter about and fall or, just as bad, manage to get moving but are unable to stop themselves.

Another way of enjoying the ice was to find a large chunk of ice and sit on it while others pull it along the ice like a sled. Ordinary sledding across the snow was more common. There were also snowball fights. These appear in a variety of illuminations, including a late 15th or early 16th century Dutch illumination that shows rosy-cheeked children gleefully pelting each other with snowballs and a 15th century French illumination that shows both children and adults throwing snowballs while others roll up a big ball of snow, presumably to make a snowman.

Ball Games

Medieval children played many different ball games, some of which are still popular today. Younger children likely played simple games like catch. As they grew older, they played more organized sports. These sports evolved gradually over the course of the Middle Ages and included the forerunners of the modern games of soccer, rugby, tennis, badminton, handball, racquetball, and probably baseball and cricket as well. Golf also developed in the late Middle Ages from games akin to croquet and, perhaps, field hockey. While some of the early forms of golf appear to have been played exclusively by adults, some, such as the croquet-like *closh*, were played by children and adolescents.

Football

Football was a common game. Although there are few contemporary records of medieval football, the illustrations and written descriptions that have survived show that that it was played without any specialized protective clothing and that points were scored by carrying the ball into a goal area defended the opposing team. Fall typically marked the beginning of football season because the balls were often made from the bladders of animals, particularly pigs. Since fall was the primary time for slaughtering pigs and other animals, balls were more plentiful then. Carefully removed bladders could be made virtually air-tight by sealing their openings. The bladders were often filled with dried peas before they were inflated. The peas made the balls rattle and also gave them some additional weight, which may have made them easier to handle. Based on specimens recovered from excavations of medieval sites, some footballs appear to have been made of pieces of leather stitched together rather than from a bladder. These balls were stuffed with moss or some other materials instead of being inflated.

While the exact rules of play cannot be determined and the nature of the games likely varied between different regions and over time, many football games appear to have been akin to rugby. One account mentions that both hands and feet could be used in moving the ball. The games were generally very rough and injuries were not uncommon. Football was already a spectator sport in the Middle Ages. In 12th century London, for example, older men rode out to watch football games played by apprentices and other young men in fields just outside the city.

Tennis

Tennis developed in the late Middle Ages and was usually associated with the nobility, particularly young noblemen, although girls may have played as well. For example, in his youth, Henry V of England appears to have been a tennis-player since Charles VI of France allegedly chose to insult him by sending him a chest of tennis balls during diplomatic negotiations in 1415. This gesture implied that Henry V was an immature boy who should stay home and play tennis instead of daring to embark on a war with France.

Nobles weren't the only ones to play tennis. Commoners in cities such as Paris played in whatever spaces they could find. Whether noble or common, tennis was played with small leather or cloth balls which were sometimes feathered like badminton shuttlecocks. Some players used wooden racquets with some type of netting, likely just strings of ordinary fibers such as wool or linen. In other versions of game, players wore gloves and hit the ball back and forth to each other. Many of these games appear to have involved each player hitting the ball against a wall in turn, like modern handball. Finding suitable walls for playing often caused problems. The only large, hard vertical surfaces available, even in cities, were often the walls of churches. Not surprisingly, church officials were not pleased with such use of their walls. For example, in 1448, the dean of Exeter Cathedral complained that tennis players were breaking the cathedral's windows and damaging its walls.

Baseball and Cricket

In a few medieval illustrations, there are depictions of boys playing games which may be the forerunners of baseball or cricket. In a typical one of these pictures, a boy is shown throwing a ball at another boy who holds a paddle or stick ready to hit the ball (fig. 22). Unfortunately, these illustrations do not show any other players so the full nature of the game cannot be determined.

Wrestling and Stone-Throwing

Among the nobility, wrestling appears to often have been part of the martial training of noble boys. Besides the physical exercise it provided, wrestling trained boys in grappling with their opponents and forcing them to the ground. Such skills were useful on the battlefield since close, hand-to-hand fighting was a common form of combat.

Commoners also wrestled, but for sport rather than to train for war. Boys wrestled with each other while playing, and wrestling continued as a pastime into early adulthood. While most wrestling matches were casual contests of strength and skill, some were public competitions with prizes such as a ram for the winner.

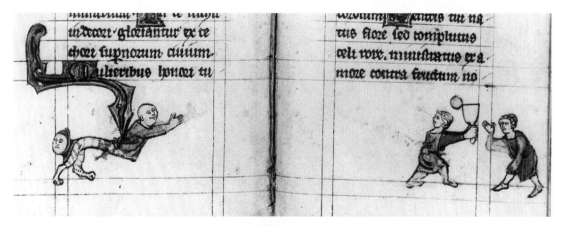

Fig. 22. In this little scene from the margin of a manuscript, the boy on the right has thrown a ball to another boy who is wielding a bat or paddle. However, the grotesque figure on the left seems to have distracted the batter and caused him to miss the ball. While the exact nature of the game depicted cannot be determined, ball games such as these were likely the forerunners of baseball, cricket, and other similar games.

Stone-throwing was another activity shared by nobility and commoners. As in wrestling, older boys and men among the nobility threw stones primarily to build up and maintain the strength needed for combat, while commoners did so to display and test their strength against one another. Still, even among the nobility, throwing large, heavy rocks greater distances than one's peers was certainly as much a display of personal pride and prowess as it was a part of a regimen of body-building.

Archery

For much of the Middle Ages, the English were famous for their archery, and many boys across rural England and Wales trained to become archers from a very early age. Even some boys in cities took up archery, as will be discussed later in this chapter. Boys were sometimes as young as four when they were given little toy bows. As early as the age of seven, boys were given their first real bows. These bows were small and light and drawing the string back required relatively little strength. However, for a young boy, some exertion was required to pull the string back far enough to properly launch an arrow. From this beginning, a boy learning the skills needed to shoot with a bow. He also began developing the physical strength needed to become a good archer. As he grew up, he was given progressively larger and more powerful bows. With repeated practice, the muscles in his upper body developed so that he could generate the force needed to draw back the bowstring. He also developed his skills in aiming and releasing his arrows to hit targets at greater and greater distances. Finally, as an adult, he could wield a bow which was about as tall as he was. He could draw the bowstring, despite the 130 or more pounds of force it required, and hit targets a hundred yards away or even further. This skill had applications in hunting (or poaching) as well as in war.

Horseback Riding and Horse Racing

Besides being the primary means of transportation in peace and war, horseback riding was also enjoyed as pastime by the nobility and those others who could afford the expense of buying and maintaining riding horses. Riding was an essential skill among the nobility, and noble boys learned to ride at an early age. Most noble girls appear to have learned to ride as well, but there is no evidence of when they typically began their training (see chapter 9). Children sometimes participated in horse racing as well. In London, local boys were used as jockeys because of their light weight.

Games

In addition to sports that developed and tested strength and agility, people in the Middle Ages played and enjoyed a wide range of other, less physically demanding games of chance and skill. Some of these, such as cards and backgammon, are still familiar to players today while others have disappeared. Let's see what games children and teenagers played in an age long before the advent of video and computer games.

Cherry Pit or Cherry Stones

As the name suggests, this game was often played with the pits or stones of cherries. Small rocks or nuts were also used, perhaps when cherries were out of season. To play cherry pit, players tossed or flicked cherry pits at a target such as a hole in the ground. Not unlike various marble games popular until recent times, a good eye and manual dexterity were needed to win.

Knucklebones

Played by children as well as adults, knucklebones was a common game throughout medieval Europe. Like cherry pit, it was named after its playing pieces, which were made from the toe or "knuckle" bones of sheep and other livestock. These were about two inches long and an inch wide. Children commonly played knucklebones like the modern game of jacks, with a player having to flip up one bone, scoop up the other bones, and catch the first bone before it hit the ground. However, descriptions of other methods of play also survive. These methods included precision flipping of the bones to hit targets such as other bones or to pass through a sort of goal post formed by the fingers of another player, not unlike, respectively, modern marbles and tabletop football.

More Physical Games

Some children's games required more physical activity than knucklebones and cherry pit. Hide-and-seek, tag, and others have already been mentioned. There were others which were more popular with older children and even with adults. One of these games was *Hoodman Blind*, more commonly called *Blindman's Buff* ("buff" was short for "buffet") in later times. This game involved blindfolding one player by taking his hood, a common piece of clothing for men and boys, and placing it backwards on his head so that his face was covered. The other players then had to strike him without getting caught (fig. 23).

Another physical game was *Prison Base*. Prison Base was played by two teams and was a sort of serial tag game in which the first team sent out a player, then the second team then sent out a player to tag the first team's player, followed by the first team sending out a player to tag the second team's player, and so on. The goal was to tag out the other teams' players before they reached their designated "home." As with Hoodman Blind, this game was pop-

Fig. 23. There were several different games which involved blindfolding one of the players. One such game was Hoodman Blind. As shown in this illustration, this game involved having one of the players wear his hood backwards so that his face is covered and he cannot see. The other boys have taken off their hoods and are using them to hit the blinded player. The goal of the game for the blinded player appears to have been to snatch the hoods away from the other players as they hit him. The other players' goal is to strike the blinded player as many times as possible without getting caught.

ular with adults as well as children. In fact, it was so popular with some citizens of 14th century London that Edward III banned it from being played on the grounds of his palace of Westminster because the games were so noisy and rambunctious that they distracted his government ministers at work in the palace.

Board Games

Children also learned how to play board games. To some degree, the games which they learned depended upon their class, but many board games were popular among all classes. These included games such as draughts (checkers), *tables* (a chase game played on a rectangular board marked out in small squares), and Nine-Man Morris (which was sometimes called *merills*) (fig. 13). Nine-Man Morris was akin to tic-tac-toe but involved more strategy since the number of possible arrangements of pieces was significantly greater than in tic-tac-toe. Another game was Fox and Geese, which was based on an earlier Roman game. In this game, two players sought to outmaneuver each other, with the Fox attempting to seize individual Geese without becoming trapped by the rest of the flock. Backgammon (often called *tric-trac* in the Middle Ages) was very popular but appears to have been particularly favored by the nobility and the wealthy, while chess seems to have primarily been reserved for these privileged classes.

Though the games were the same, the quality and expense of the playing boards and pieces varied considerably. Simple wooden disks sufficed for most players, but the nobility and the rich used intricately carved disks of ivory or bone for their game pieces in checkers or backgammon (fig. 24). Chess pieces were commonly made from these same materials. Similarly, most people played on painted boards, while the privileged used beautifully inlaid tables of exotic woods made by expert craftsmen. Even precious metals were used in some extravagant game sets. For example, Edward IV, king of England in the mid–15th century, owned not one but two complete sets of pieces made of silver and silver-gilt for playing Fox and Geese.

Fig. 24. This game piece, which is about two inches in diameter, may have been used to play backgammon or checkers. Made from part of the tusk of a narwhal, it is decorated with a carving of a castle which has two figures within its walls. Most game pieces have carved decorations and the motifs vary widely, from depictions of animals to scenes from clasical mythology. As with all medieval game pieces, it cannot be determined whether this one was used by an adult or by a child.

Chess

Chess, although a board game, was in a class by itself, even as it still is today. Invented in India in the 6th century, chess reached the Islamic countries of the Middle East by the 7th century. From there, after the passing of some four centuries, it began to infiltrate Europe but did not gain wide acceptance until after the First Crusade ended in 1099 when returning Frankish crusaders brought the game back to their courts. Then, it finally broke through and became one of the most sophisticated and popular pastimes of the European nobility. The warlike nature of the game and the hierarchy of pieces on the board undoubtedly suited the nobility and their outlook on the world well. Among the nobility, men and women frequently began learning to play chess when they were children (fig. 13).

Reading

It sounds rather dull compared to the other amusements we picture children and adults enjoying, but reading was actually one of the most elite forms of entertainment, a point that wasn't lost on the status conscious aristocrats of the time. To acquire the skill of reading, whether in Latin or in a "vulgar" language such as French or English, one had to obtain an education. As discussed in chapter 6, schooling was scarce and difficult to obtain. Further, it was often expensive.

The subject matter of medieval books ranged from poetry and romantic fiction, such as stories about King Arthur's court, to serious studies of law, science, and religion. Romances and poetry were obviously preferred when reading for enjoyment. Regardless of their subjects, books were expensive and relatively rare before the advent of printing presses in the 15th century. This was another factor which contributed to reading being a pastime primarily for the wealthy.

Riddles and Word Games

Medieval children enjoyed rhymes, riddles, and tongue-twisters much like modern children. Many of the riddles were in the form of "what am I?" and are rather bizarre by modern standards. For example:

> Who comes neither driving, walking, nor riding; neither clothed nor naked; neither shod nor unshod; neither in the road nor out of it? (Driving, in this case, refers to driving animals, such as horses pulling a wagon.)

The answer is a man who is driving, walking, and riding all at the same time. He is described as astride a goat but his legs are so long that they reach the ground. As a consequence, he is walking as much as he is riding. Additionally, he is "driving" the goat by clasping one of its horns to control it. He is neither clothed nor naked because he wears a hood but not any other clothing. He is both shod and unshod since he is wearing a shoe on only one foot. Finally, he is traveling along the edge of the road so that half of his body (and the goat's) is in the road and the other half is in the ditch adjoining the road.

Another, simpler riddle was:

Who died but was never born? Adam.

Tongue-twisters involved alliterative sounds just as they still do today. Here's an example from late medieval England:

Three grey greedy geese
Flew over three green greasy furrows.
The geese were grey and greedy;
The furrows were green and greasy [Adapted from *Medieval Children*,
    by Nicholas Orme (New Haven, 2001)].

Enjoyment of such riddles and wordplay often carried over into adulthood.

Pranks

Children in medieval Europe were not above playing practical jokes. The 15th century writer Christine de Pisan recorded a particularly dangerous one: To get rid of their governess, some noble girls spread dried peas on the stairs in the hope that she would slip on the hard little balls and break her neck falling down the stairs. Young apprentices at an Italian bank carried out a far less malevolent prank at their workplace: they smuggled in a box filled with mice and then released them to the surprise and discomfort of older co-workers and customers alike.

Less Wholesome Entertainments

The Middle Ages certainly had vulgar and cruel entertainments. Many involved animals. Cockfights were not uncommon and, as discussed further in chapter six, were a traditional activity for schoolboys. Cocks and hens were also abused and killed by children in a "sport" in which the unfortunate birds were buried in small pits so that only their heads remained above ground. In other instances, rather than being placed in a pit, the bird was immobilized by trapping its head with a forked stick. In either case, children then threw sticks called *cock-steles* at its head until the wretched bird was dead.

Children also attended other cruel spectacles along with their parents and other adults. Among these were bear-baiting, in which bears were placed in a pit or other enclosure and then attacked by a pack of dogs. The crowd watched and bet on how many of the dogs the bear would kill before being overcome. Other animals, including badgers, bulls, asses, and even horses, were sometimes subjected to similar suffering. These cruel forms of entertainment were not uniquely medieval. They continued to be staged well into the 17th century. Further, cockfights have survived to the present in many places around the world and are still legal in two states in the United States.

In addition to watching animals suffer, children watched people being publicly subjected to physical punishments. These punishments ranged from public beatings and confinement in the stocks to executions, either relatively swiftly by beheading or strangulation by hanging or prolonged and painful deaths by mutilation. In at least a few illustrations of notable executions in medieval chronicles, children were depicted among the onlookers.

Pets

While the mistreatment of animals was not uncommon in medieval Europe, animals were sometimes kept as pets. Song-birds and squirrels are known to have been kept as pets by children, most often by girls. Families, both noble and common, also often kept other animals around the house. Dogs were the most common animals in medieval households, but they were typically a working animal as much as they were a family pet. From guarding livestock to chasing game, dogs performed a variety of duties. A few lucky dogs, such as the prioress' spoiled lap dog in Chaucer's *Canterbury Tales*, were kept purely as pets, but this appears to have been a custom only of the wealthy and the nobility. Families also kept cats but, again, they served more as working animals than as coddled pets and earned their keep by catching rats and mice.

Adolescent Pastimes

Then as now, adolescence was a time of transition. As medieval children grew up, their interests changed. While they would continue to play games such as Nine-Man Morris and others even as adults, they stopped playing with toys. In the place of childish pastimes, they took up other pursuits. Like teenagers before and since the Middle Ages, some of their activities were wholesome, or at least benign, while others were antisocial. In this section, we will examine these pastimes.

Youth Groups

Too young to be a member of adult society and too old to be a child, teenagers in the Middle Ages sought out others of their own ages for social activities. Youths in some cities formed themselves into clubs or gangs. Some of these were relatively organized while most appear to have been very loosely structured. In Italian cities, these groups were composed primarily of sons of the middle and upper classes. Outside of Italy, apprentices and young servants appear to have formed the bulk of gang members. Urban gangs went largely unrecorded. Only when there was civil unrest did these groups come to the fore. In medieval cities, young males, including those in their early twenties as well as teenagers, were a volatile group. Whether apprentices or servants, they appear to have always been ready to join in any riots. For example, in London, there were occasional outbursts against foreign businessmen, such as some Italians, who enjoyed special trading privileges in exchange for cash payments and loans to the English king, and the Flemings, who came to work in cloth manufacturing. When popular resentment about foreigners taking commerce or work away from native Londoners boiled over, apprentices, often egged on by their masters, took the streets and beat any non–Englishman they could find.

Vandalism

Even in an age when glass windows were rare and relatively expensive, boys were already breaking windows in churches and other buildings. In many cases, the damage was accidental: the boys were throwing rocks or shooting arrows at birds perched on the buildings and missed. Physical evidence of the boys' errant shots has been found at Westminster Abbey, where a medieval arrow was uncovered in one of the abbey's rain gutters. Damage to buildings and wounding of citizens by stray shots became so common in London that the city government banned all shooting at birds in 1327. The city's ban must not have solved the problem since, in 1385, the bishop of London moved to excommunicate boys who damaged the stained glass windows and statuary of St. Paul's Cathedral with arrows and rocks aimed at birds nesting on the building. The bishop also sought to stop boys from playing ball in the cathedral's gateway and churchyard since mis-thrown balls were causing similar damage. Not all damage to churches and other buildings can be ascribed to simply careless aiming of balls, arrows, or rocks. In some instances, the admonitions of Church officials and others indicate that boys were quite intentionally vandalizing churches and other buildings.

Vandalism also occurred in the countryside. As discussed further in chapter 7, university students sometimes damaged the crops in fields and orchards near their schools. However, while they were known to damage their neighbors' houses on occasion, the sons of peasants who lived in the country appear to have never destroyed crops. Unlike the students, they likely appreciated the value and importance of the crops as well as the hard work that went into their production. As a consequence, they seem to have been more likely to steal fruit from their neighbors' trees rather than to inflict wanton harm.

Drinking and Gambling

There were no minimum age limits for drinking alcoholic beverages in medieval Europe. As discussed in chapter 2, low-alcohol beer was even a common beverage for many young children. As they grew to adulthood, the amount and the alcoholic content of the drinks consumed by children increased. By the time they were adolescents, many boys in the towns and cities were already frequenting taverns. Many apprentices and young servants, some as young as twelve or fourteen, spent much of what little money they earned on beer and wine. Excessive drinking sometimes made these boys easy prey for con men and thieves.

Along with drinking, boys in the countryside as well as in the towns and cities often took up gambling. The Church condemned gambling and even civil authorities occasionally tried to curb it. For example, in the 15th century, King Henry VII of England forbade servants and apprentices across the country to gamble except during Christmas holidays. Despite these efforts, gambling was a very popular pastime throughout medieval society. Betting on games of dice and knucklebones was quite common. Smaller children bet beads and buttons on such games while adolescents and adults wagered money on how the dice or bones would land. Playing cards were unknown in Europe for most of the Middle Ages, but they rapidly gained popularity after they were introduced in the late 14th century. They quickly joined dice as the most popular tools for gambling. Gambling often led adolescents as well as adults into trouble. Accusations of cheating and other disagreements led to fights, sometimes fatal ones. (Finds of medieval dice which have been "loaded," that is, made so that certain numbers always come up, confirm that claims of cheating were sometimes quite justified.) Gambling also led to other crimes. Apprentices and servants were known to steal from their masters in order to pay their gambling debts.

Dancing

Despite the examples above, not all adolescents in medieval Europe were juvenile delinquents. Nor were all their activities violent or debauched. Dancing was a common part of most celebrations in the Middle Ages and teenaged boys and girls of all classes enjoyed dancing. Most adults appear to have enjoyed dancing as well. While medieval dances were more stylized than the largely free-form dancing common today, dancing still gave members of the opposite sex a chance to meet, mingle, and flirt. Dancing was often part of the courtship process (see chapter 10).

Fig. 25. In this scene, two groups of men and women dance to music played by three musicians. On the left, one plays a fiddle with a bow while another musician in the middle plays drums attached to the back of a boy in front of him. To the right, a third musician plays a portative organ. He holds the organ and works its bellows with his left hand while playing its keyboard with his right. The group on the right is dancing in a ring as the group on the left dances in a long, winding line. The dancers sometimes sang as well to provide music they needed for their steps.

Describing the various dances common in the Middle Ages is outside the scope of this work. However, here is a brief synopsis of the principal forms of dances:

- Ring dances (fig. 25). The dancers held hands, formed a ring, and danced in a circle or in a line winding around the room or field where the dance was held. This form of dancing appears to have been common in many parts of Europe throughout the Middle Ages.
- Estampie. Music for this dance from the 14th century indicates that it was performed in three-eight or three-quarter time. The dance itself involved slow, gliding steps.
- Salterello. This was a faster dance with music in four-four or twelve-eight time. It appears to have been a lively dance with romping steps.

Music

In an age before recorded music, people had to make their own music. Singing was the most common form of music since it did not require any instruments, and all classes of society enjoyed singing. Some singing was performed as an entertainment in itself but it was often an accompaniment for dancing. For example, ring dances were typically performed to the tune of carols sung by their companions. These songs were not Christmas carols but were choral dance music on a variety of themes such as romance and the adventures of heroes.

Apart from training boys to sing in choirs, there is little evidence of formal instruction in singing in the Middle Ages. Children appear to have learned by listening to older children and adults and then joining in. Daughters of the nobility are known to have learned at least some songs while doing embroidery and other cloth work. Women often performed such work in groups and sang to keep themselves entertained, and so the girls learned songs from the women. Moralists thought that it was better for the women to occupy themselves with singing rather than gossiping. However, the few surviving bits of lyrics suggest that many songs were about love and lovers.

For instrumental music, small drums and pipes were the most common. Bagpipes also appear in many depictions of dances, particularly in rural settings. While bagpipes are most associated with Scotland today, they were common in many countries in medieval Europe. Stringed instruments were rarer and were most likely to be found in the homes in the homes of the wealthy and the nobility. How people learned to play these instruments is not recorded.

Presumably, as with singing, they started out by watching adults and then practicing themselves. Additionally, as mentioned previously, some children were given toy musical instruments and learned at least some musical skills by playing with them. Professionals may have given some instruction to those who could afford their services but there are no records of such tutoring. Most musicians were amateurs and likely provided training to their children and any others who were interested.

4

Clothing and Dress

Once they were toilet trained, children in medieval Europe were dressed in clothes which were largely identical to those worn by adults. The children's clothing was made out of the same fabrics and in the same colors as adults' clothing. The only significant difference was the smaller size. Some historians have cited the fact that medieval children were dressed as miniature adults as support for the theory that children in the Middle Ages were treated like adults rather than as children. However, this reasoning is faulty as shown by the following example:

T-shirts worn with blue jeans became a popular outfit for teenagers some forty years ago and, with minor variations, have remained popular with that group to the present. Meanwhile, wearing blue jeans and T-shirts has since become common among adults of all ages. Additionally, parents often dress their young children in this fashion.

Now, applying the logic that children in the Middle Ages were treated like adults because they were dressed like adults, the evidence in this example would lead historians in the future to conclude that children and adults today were all treated like teenagers. Clearly, this is not the case. While popular fashions for people of all ages are frequently patterned on those created for the youth market, adults and children today do not behave like teenagers nor do they expect to be treated like them. Similarly, just because a child in medieval Europe was dressed like an adult did not mean that he or she was expected to act like one.

It is only within the last one or two centuries that clothing has been specifically designed for children. Examples of such clothing range from the little sailor suits for boys and very frilly dresses for girls made at the beginning of the 20th century to the very colorful outfits marketed to boys and girls today. In contrast, during the Middle Ages, people saw no need to create clothing especially styled for children. Children's bodies are shaped like adults, only smaller, so the simplest thing to do was just to make them smaller versions of the same items of clothing worn by adults made out of the same materials used for adult clothing.

Fashions changed over the course of the Middle Ages and detailing the evolution of clothing styles in medieval Europe would take us rather far off the topic of growing up. Instead, a very brief summary must suffice. Readers who would like to know more about clothing in the Middle Ages may refer to the bibliography at the end of this book. Additionally, please consult the illustrations throughout this book for examples of the clothing described in this chapter.

Boys' Clothing

During the early Middle Ages, boys wore tunics. These were loosely cut, long-sleeved, T-shaped garments. While men's hemlines were usually down to about the knee or little lower, boys' tunics were often higher. Under the tunic, they wore another tunic, usually referred to by fashion historians as an undertunic. They also wore undershorts, which were typically referred to as breeches or braies and covered the same part of a boy's anatomy as most modern undershorts. To cover their legs, they wore long stockings or hose that reached to the middle or top of the thigh. These hose were sometimes held up by garters or by bands of cloth wrapped around the outside the hose. Long hose that reached the top of the thigh were held up by a lace, commonly called a *point*, tied from the top edge of the hose to the waistband of their breeches. Their ensemble was completed with shoes and a hat or hood, although children often wore no head coverings.

Over time, clothing for men and boys became more fitted. The tunic, especially its sleeves, became more tightly fitted. Its hemline gradually rose until, in the 14th century, it just covered the buttocks and tops of the thighs. Along with changing its fit and coverage, the tunic's name changed to *gypon*, *gipon*, or, more familiarly, doublet. The doublet remained a common item of men's and boys' clothing through the end of the Middle Ages and on into the Renaissance. During this same time, hose evolved too. The two separate hose came to be joined together and a piece of cloth was added to fill the space between the legs at the back. In front, a triangular flap, the codpiece, served as the fly. These additions helped maintain the modesty of the wearers as hemlines rose and exposed more of the lower body.

Other pieces of clothing were sometimes worn over the tunic or doublet. One such item in the early Middle Ages was the surcoat, a large, loose fitting, sleeveless garment which was worn over the tunic. Another was the supertunic, which was cut like the tunic, only slightly larger so that it could fit over the tunic. Both surcoats and supertunics often had slits from the waist down, either at the front and back or down the left and rights sides, so that the skirt did not interfere with riding horseback or other physical activities. In the 14th century, supertunics were made to fit more snugly through the chest and typically had tighter fitting sleeves just as doublets did. Their hemlines also rose. As with the tunic, the name of the garment changed along with its cut, and this style of supertunic became the cote-hardie. Another variation on the supertunic which also evolved during the 14th century was the houppelande. While the cote-hardie was fairly form fitting and had a high hemline, the houppelande retained more of the qualities of earlier supertunics and was more like a gown, loose fitting with a long skirt reaching the mid-calf or the ankle. The sleeves of houppelandes were loose fitting and often had flared cuffs. High, standing collars were another feature of houppelandes. Before the end of the 15th century, the houppelande evolved into or was simply replaced by the gown. The gown had long sleeves and a long skirt. It was fitted but was generously cut so that it could be worn comfortably over several other layers of clothing, much like modern overcoats.

One final point about boys' fashions: hairstyles. The length of men's and boys' hair varied over the course of the Middle Ages. The shortest hairstyle for men and boys in the Middle Ages was that worn by 11th century Normans. The Norman style was a bowl-shaped haircut that was so short that the hair in front covered only the very top of the forehead and the hair on the back of the head was shaved off up to a line parallel to the tops of the ears or even an inch or so above that point. This style disappeared by the beginning of the 12th century, but a less severe version of the bowl cut became popular again in England and France in the early 15th century. At other times, men and boys wore their hair in a variety of more moderate lengths, including bobs that covered down to the bottom of the ear. There were also longer styles that would be down to or slightly over the back of the collar. These styles appear to have been worn either with a center part or with no part at all. Longer styles with hair flowing down to the shoulders or even lower were sometimes popular. Viking men were most noted for this style, but other men wore it as well. For example, in England during the early 12th century, some noblemen grew their hair so long that it was described as rivaling the length of the tresses of the ladies at court. Fashions shifted back and forth with long hair for males falling out of favor during the 13th century and then reappearing in the 14th century followed by a return to short hair in the 15th century.

Girls' Clothing

For girls, the standard item of clothing was a long-sleeved dress or that hung down to about their ankles. The dress, often referred to as a gown, was cut much like the tunic worn by boys. Under their dresses, girls wore chemises, which were garments cut much like the dress but usually of a lighter-weight material. They too wore hose to cover their legs. Their hose covered up to around the knee and were supported with a band or garter at the top edge. Unlike boys, they did not wear breeches or any other form of underpants. Nor would they wear any when they grew up and became women. References to "drawers" for women began to appear only in the late 16th and early 17th centuries. Returning to their outer garments, along with the dress, girls wore shoes and belts.

As with clothing for men and boys, girls' and women's clothing gradually became more fitted. However, unlike male fashions, hemlines on clothing for girls and women always remained long. Women's hemlines reached to at least a few inches below the knees and were more often lower, reaching down to the ankle or even to the ground. Further, even when they wore the shorter, knee- or calf-length dresses, medieval women and girls still wore chemises that covered their legs down to the ankle.

By the late 11th century, fashionable dresses fit the arms and upper body snugly. To achieve the tight fit, dresses were made with long slits which typically started at the neckline and ran down either the front or back of the dress down to the waist. Sometimes the slits were placed on the sides of the dress on the seams that ran down under each armpit. Laces were fitted through holes along the edge of the slits and drawn tight to make the dress snugly fit its wearer. Similar arrangement of slits, holes, and laces at the cuff or up the forearm of each sleeve allowed the sleeves to fit snugly as well. Over the years, buttons gradually replaced laces in dresses. With other variations, such as the use of wide, flaring sleeves instead of tight fitting ones, dresses of this basic type continued in use through the Middle Ages.

During the 13th century, women and girls began wearing sleeveless surcoats similar to those worn by men. However, these surcoats went beyond merely being sleeveless and were often referred to as sideless surcoats since the openings in the sides of these garments were rather wide and extended down to the waist or even to the hips. In the 14th century, the cote-hardie became a popular piece of women's outerwear. Though it was given the same name as the man's jacket-like outer garment that was also then in fashion, the woman's cote-hardie bore few resemblances to the man's and was actually a long gown which fitted the wearer's upper body closely and emphasized its curves. The cote-hardie also had long, tightly fitting sleeves and a flowing skirt that reached the ground. Like the sideless surcoat, the cote-hardie remained in fashion until the end of the 14th century. Near the end of the 14th century, fashionable girls and women began wearing houppelandes. Unlike cote-hardies, girl's and women's houppelandes were largely identical to men's garments of the same name: generously cut gown-like garments with high necks and very wide sleeves.

As for hairstyles, girls grew their hair long. Long hair was seen as a natural attribute of femininity in the Middle Ages. Wearing their hair loose was also quite acceptable for girls though it was not considered proper to allow it to hang over their faces. A girl who cut her hair short like a boy's or wore boy's clothing, such as Joan of Arc did, risked being punished severely for her unnatural behavior. Some women and girls in medieval illustrations appear to have short hair but closer examination usually reveals that they actually have their long hair pinned up in buns, braids, or coils or otherwise styled it to look short. After marrying, a woman usually wore her hair up and covered it and the rest of her head with a veil. A veil was a piece of fabric, usually worn with a headband, which covered most of a woman's head but left her face exposed. The veil was often supplemented with a rectangular cloth called a wimple. The wimple was pinned to the wearer's hair or veil just above each of her ears and then draped down, leaving her face exposed but covering her throat and the sides of her head. In the later Middle Ages, the veil and wimple were supplemented and largely replaced by a wide variety of hats.

Fabrics and Colors for Children's Clothing

Children's clothing was usually made out of the same types of fabrics as their parents' garments. Like their parents, sons and daughters of royalty and other nobility had clothes made of silk as well as fine velvets made from the best wool. Even cloth of gold, a fabric in which very fine golden wires were interwoven with silk or other luxurious fibers, appears in the inventories of the clothes of some royal boys and girls. The trousseau of Princess Philippa of Lancaster, who was married at the age of 12 to the king of Denmark in 1406, had three dresses made of cloth of gold, two of which were trimmed with fur. Her wedding dress was white satin edged with two types of very expensive fur, including one that was a luxurious white fur. Some of her other dresses were embroidered with pearls and the coloring of many of her dresses required rare and costly dyes. Such clothing was meant to impress her future husband and in-laws as well as anyone else who might see the princess. But this was more than an exercise in vanity and pride. Among medieval nobility, conspicuous consumption such as this was part of maintaining and improving a family's social and political standing. It displayed the wealth and good taste of the bride's family and, implicitly, the power they had that allowed them to enjoy these things.

Of course, most boys and girls weren't princes and princesses. Children of peasants wore the same coarse but sturdy linen and woolen fabrics as their parents. Merchants and craftsmen clothed their children in better grades of wool and linen that were finer and softer. The wealthiest merchants could afford silks and velvets comparable to those bought by the nobility. However, for everyday wear, even the nobility appear to have frequently worn more practical woolen and linen clothing rather than elaborate and delicate silk brocades and satins.

As for colors of clothing, the shades of cloth available in the Middle Ages were far more limited than those available today because dyers had to rely exclusively on dyes derived from various plants, animals, and minerals. Further, as mentioned above, some dyes were very expensive. Shades from peach through tan and brick red to brown were relatively cheap to produce while rich, dark reds were quite expensive. Yellow dye was also fairly cheap but, except for golden yellow, yellow was not a very popular color in the Middle Ages. However, yellow dye was combined with other dyestuffs to color cloth orange or green. Blue dye was commonly available and used to produce shades ranging from light sky blues to dark, purplish blue when mixed with red dye. So, with these dyes at hand, medieval dyers created a broad spectrum of colors for clothing. While the expense of some of the dyes meant that not everyone could afford every color, many different shades were available even to common people in the Middle Ages. Thus, medieval Europeans, both adults and children, dressed in colors more varied and interesting than just the drab browns and grays which they are so often imagined to have worn.

5

Care and Discipline

Both mothers and fathers were active in caring for their children and supervising their behavior. As discussed in later chapters of this book, other adults, such as master craftsmen training apprentices and teachers, also exercised control over children in their charge. Medieval records reveal that the care which children received from their parents and others ranged from loving and tender to harsh and abusive. Unfortunately, the records are too sparse to determine how many children were cherished or mistreated. Still, while corporal punishment was certainly more accepted in the Middle Ages (and remained so until the very recent past in most industrialized countries), there is little reason to assume that the percentage of children who were genuinely loved and well cared-for and those who were neglected or beaten was significantly different than today. Admittedly, public consciousness about the evils of child abuse and the social mechanisms to protect children are clearly far more developed now than in medieval Europe. However, it is questionable whether the underlying nature of human beings has improved that much since the Middle Ages. Large numbers of bad parents, whether physically or mentally abusive, neglectful, or dangerously careless, are still with us today. Fortunately, there are large numbers of good parents as well, but it is impossible to determine how many of each type there are now, just as it has been for any time in the past.

There is one final point to consider about the level of care which children received in their homes. Living conditions in the Middle Ages were certainly much harsher and less comfortable for children than today. For example, their homes lacked running water, central heating, labor-saving appliances, and so many other things we now consider essential. Even among the nobility, accommodations were crude by modern standards. Additionally, food was not as easily obtained as it is now and its preparation was more labor intensive than modern, pre-processed foods. Further, famines disrupted food supplies and sometimes caused death by starvation. However, children were not alone in suffering through all these difficulties. Their parents and other adults had to survive the same trials. Thus, when we read of peasant children who slept on mattresses stuffed only with straw and ate a diet composed largely of gruel made of boiled grains, we should not assume that these children were being abused. These conditions were not the result of their parents' malice or neglect. Parents, in most cases, provided their children with the best housing, food, and clothing that they could afford.

Caring for Children

Several decades ago, some historians claimed that parents in medieval Europe did not form strong emotional bonds with their children. They asserted that high mortality rates, the difficulties of everyday life, and other factors made parents largely indifferent to their children. Fortunately, other historians did not accept this theory and have compiled much convincing evidence that, throughout the Middle Ages, parents commonly had great affection for their children. For example, in the 9th century, Alfred, king of the Anglo-Saxons in England, wrote of the worst imaginable pain as that experienced by a father who witnesses the death of one his children. There is no evidence that his audience had any difficulty in understanding his comment.

Later in the Middle Ages, evidence that parents loved their children so much that they spoiled them can be found in sermons and manuals written by clerics and others. As early as the 14th century, moralists in England complained that parents were too soft and lenient with their children. Similar sentiments can be found in tracts from the cities of northern Italy that were directed at the merchant families of the middle and upper classes. In one such manual, Giovanni Dominici, a Dominican friar of the 14th century, advised parents that they should not hug, kiss, or otherwise have physical contact with their sons once they had turned three years old. They should also make their sons walk barefoot, perform hard labor, and sleep in drafts and other harsh conditions. Further, sons should be fed coarse, tough foods such as peasants ate and wear cheap, rough clothing. Finally, Dominici went so far as to advise giving boys small doses of purgatives to prepare them for being ill in the future. The writers of advice such as this stated that the goal of these exercises was to toughen the boys and prepare them in case they fell on hard times, but the real goal seems to have been to encourage parents to provide less luxurious clothing and accommodations for their beloved sons.

As for daughters of the Italian middle classes, St. Bernandino of Siena, a Franciscan friar, bluntly advised to make them drudges. They were to be taught to perform the labor needed to run a household, from preparing food and cleaning the house to making cloth and then sewing it into clothing. They were also to take care of their younger siblings to train them for their future roles as mothers. Further, they were to accomplish all these tasks while being fed little. One writer said it should be just enough to keep a girl alive! Again, the real point of moralists' guidance on childrearing was to convince parents to change their ways and not let their daughters lead the idle and privileged lives which their families' wealth provided.

Few parents appear to have followed the harsh advice of the friars and other moralists. Girls from middle and upper classes were certainly taught to keep house, but this was so that they could supervise servants, not slave away themselves. Boys, the heirs to their families' businesses and fortunes, enjoyed all the luxury their families could provide. As for their food, there is no evidence that any girl from a successful bourgeois family was ever placed on a starvation diet or that any boy had to eat coarse and bitter food, let alone suffer intentional distress from unneeded purgatives. In fact, some diaries kept by parents, personal correspondence, and other contemporary accounts describe the care of children in upper and middle class Italian families and often express the delight parents took in watching their children play and in giving them treats such as toys and sweets. Diary entries also record the pride which parents, especially fathers, took in their children and the love they felt for them. Unfortunately, beginning in the mid–14th century, many of these diaries also contain the laments of the parents over the loss of their cherished children. As much as the joy they expressed in happier times, the grief these parents recorded in their diaries reveals the depth of their love for their children.

Throughout the Middle Ages, there is also recurring evidence of parents' love for their children in numerous accounts attributed to the divine intervention of saints. From across Europe, parents were recorded as displaying concern, grief, and despair when their children fell seriously ill or were injured or thought to be dead after an accident. In some instances, mothers wailed so loudly when their lifeless children were found that all their neighbors turned out to discover the source and many then provided whatever help they could. Like parents today, some even expressed feelings of guilt or remorse for not having protected their children from danger.

For both boys and girls, parents typically made every effort possible to revive and heal their children. As discussed in chapter 2, when earthly means failed, they implored saints for aid and offered donations to religious institutions or vowed to go on pilgrimages if their children were saved. For poor parents, the offerings were sometimes only a silver penny but that might represent most of their ready cash. Similarly, their pilgrimages were sometimes only to a local shrine, but this was still a genuine expression of both their faith and their desire to help their children. Among the wealthy and the nobility, offerings were sometimes quite substantial. Some pledged to donate candles, money, or other treasure to a church, often a cathedral which possessed relics of a saint whose aid they sought. The candles might seem like a rather cheap donation but this was not the case. These candles were made from fine beeswax which was often imported from eastern Europe and was relatively expensive. Further, the candles were quite large since the common practice was to measure the child's height and then have the candle made the same height. The resulting candles often weighed many pounds. As for pilgrimages, the wealthy were also able to afford journeying to much more distant destinations which presumably housed more potent relics than local shrines. For English parents, for example, these could range from one of the principal shrines in their own country, such as St. Thomas Becket's at Canterbury, to a major shrine in another country, such as St. James of Compostela in northern Spain. Again, regardless of the distance involved, parents who vowed to go a pilgrimage were expressing their love for their children and their willingness to sacrifice money and time to save them.

Other evidence of parents' love for their children appears in coroners' inquests. For example, in one case in 1298, a shop caught fire one night. The owners, a husband and wife, lived in part of the shop. The fire spread quickly but the couple escaped. However, when the wife discovered that they had left their young son behind, she ran back in to rescue him. Tragically, both she and her son died in the blaze. In another case, a teenage girl was gathering kindling in the woods when she was attacked by a rapist armed with a bow and arrows. Her father responded to her calls for help but was shot by the rapist. Clearly, these parents loved their children and were willing to sacrifice even their own lives to protect them.

Parental Instruction of Children

As part of caring for their children, parents taught them the basic skills needed to function in society. Obviously, this was not unique to the Middle Ages and has always been a vital role of parents. Such training was seldom, if ever, formal, and children simply learned by watching how their parents behaved. Through this means, they learned such fundamentals as how to eat, dress, speak, and keep themselves clean. Not unlike children today, medieval children also learned more complex things from their parents, such as moral values and religious beliefs.

Another complex matter which parents taught their children through their words and actions was their place within society. With the class structure of medieval Europe, this was an important matter: Peasant children learned that it was their lot to work the land and serve their lords while the nobility learned to expect the obedience of their inferiors and to rule by force and diplomacy. While this is a simplification of the classes and their roles, it is important to understand that most people in the Middle Ages were prepared from a very early age for their future careers. Admittedly, people today still learn much that affects their future employment from their parents but, in many parts of the world today, education and personal initiative provide a much greater range of choices and economic and social mobility than was possible in medieval Europe.

Discipline and Punishment

When children failed to follow their parents' guidance, parents often enforced their will with physical punishment. Parents were commonly recorded as administering whippings or beatings to their children when they misbehaved. Some parents exercised restraint in doling out such punishment, while others seem to have used any excuse to strike their children. Similar disparity can be seen in the severity of the punishments, with some parents beating their children terribly for the most minor of transgressions and others maintaining some degree of proportionality between the misbehavior and its "correction" through force. However, its merits and efficacy aside, physical punishment of children was certainly not unique to medieval Europe. It is only in very recent times that there has been any general movement away from it as the primary means of disciplining children.

While corporal punishment was certainly common, there were those that questioned the effectiveness of beating children as a means of correcting their behavior and recognized that there were better methods. One such person was the English saint Anselm. Near the end of the 11th century, an abbot complained to Anselm that the boys in training to become monks at his monastery were incorrigible and that even with beating them day and night that he was unable to make decent monks out of them. Anselm, himself an abbot, found this abbot's approach to discipline completely unacceptable and explained that good habits could not be achieved by threats and force of blows. Such treatment only bred fear and hatred. Encouragement, love, and kindness were better tools. Correction, when needed, should be gentle and appropriate to the fault. Anselm was not alone in these views. Among others, a 13th century German poet summed up this approach:

> Children won't do what they ought
> If you beat them with a rod.
> Children thrive and grow
> When taught by words, and not a blow....
> Evil words, words unkind
> Will do harm to a child's mind [From *An Anthology of Medieval Lyrics,*
>   Angel Flores, ed. (New York: 1962), as cited in "Survivors and Surrogates:
>   Children and Parents from the Ninth to the Thirteenth Centuries"
>   by Mary Martin McLaughlin, published in *The History of Childhood,*
>   L. De Mause, ed. (New York, 1974)].

Still, despite the opinions of St. Anselm and others, strict discipline backed by corporal punishment was the most commonly recommended approach to childrearing. But even some of texts containing such recommendations clearly indicate that moderation should be used. Many parents likely used spanking or whipping with a light switch on a regular basis to correct bad behavior. Unfortunately, even as today, some parents took their "disciplining" too far and beat their children so severely that they died. There were also instances in which adults other than parents struck children in response to their misbehavior. For example, a boy attempted to steal a small amount of wool from a shop by placing it under his hat. The wife of the shopkeeper caught the boy and hit him in the head with her hand. The boy died from the blow. While cases in which children died from excessive force were occasionally reviewed by the local authorities, there appear to have never been any criminal prosecutions and punishments of abusive parents. Further, other adults who severely injured or killed children in the course of correcting their behavior were rarely found guilty of a crime. The wife of the shopkeeper mentioned above was found to have acted reasonably and the boy's death was deemed an accident. On the other hand, teachers who beat their pupils excessively were sometimes successfully prosecuted by the students' parents. The fact that cases of severe "disciplinary" beatings, whether by parents or by other adults, were brought to the attention of authorities suggests that communities had some idea of reasonable limits on physical punishment. Admittedly, these limits were far less restrictive than today's, but they still indicate that unbridled corporal punishment was likely not accepted by many ordinary people.

On the other extreme, some parents had standards of discipline much lower than the accepted norms. These extremely permissive parents spoiled their children. Among these were parents who were amused when young children swore or engaged in other offensive behavior in imitation of adults. Contemporary moralists were shocked and dismayed by parents who laughed rather than were angered when their children called them "whores" or "cuckolds."

As these examples suggest, while strict discipline and physical punishment were the standards, actual childrearing practices varied considerably. Not all children were beaten but far too many likely were. Some parents used discipline as a cover for abuse while others genuinely loved their children and chastised them with little or no force. Other parents let their children run amok, becoming hazards to themselves and others.

There appears to have been little difference between Christians and Jews in the disciplining and punishment of children. Some Jewish children were beaten and abused by their parents while many others were cherished and treated tenderly by their parents. However, even in loving Jewish homes, correcting children's behavior by corporal punishment was as acceptable as in Christian households. Unfortunately, such punishments could become excessive. For example, Maimonides, a noted rabbi in 12th century Spain, confirmed the opinion that a father who accidentally killed his son by striking him when disciplining him should not be punished for the death. Further, Jewish teachers, like their Christian counterparts, were expected to routinely use physical punishment such as whipping to enforce discipline in the classroom and spur their pupils to do better. In contrast, guidance written in the 9th century advised Jewish parents not to place their sons with teachers who punished students excessively. The acceptability of beating and other physical punishing of children appears to have been viewed as ambiguously among Jews as it was among Christians.

6

Formal Education

Along with playing and growing, children in the Middle Ages were expected to learn so that they would be ready to make their own way in the world. Learning the basic knowledge and skills necessary for surviving as an adult has always been part of growing up. In the United States and other industrialized countries today, a significant part of preparing children for adulthood is accomplished through formal education. Children in the U.S. and other developed countries are expected, indeed required, to receive ten to twelve years of formal schooling. However, the provision of free public education for all children is a fairly recent development. Universal education began in the 19th century in Europe and the U.S. and has spread to many parts of the world, although there are still major areas of the world where free education is limited at best.

One of the reasons that societies provide free education to their children is the economic value of having an educated workforce. Educated citizens can typically contribute more to society in terms of productivity and innovation and so make their societies more prosperous. As we will see in this chapter, some of the wealthiest cities in medieval Europe were those that encouraged education. On a more personal level, education generally qualifies an individual for a wider range of job opportunities. Further, this range of employment usually includes more lucrative jobs than are available to those with little or no education. This fact has been recognized for thousands of years. In an Egyptian text from 1300 B.C., for example, a father advised his son to get an education so that he could get a well paying and comfortable job and avoid being stuck with low paying work that required hard, physical labor. In medieval Europe, many people appreciated the value of education but it was seldom easy or cheap to obtain. As a consequence, relatively few children received formal education. Most children learned their future occupations through apprenticeships and other forms of "on the job" training. This type of education will be examined in chapter 8. In this chapter, we will examine the education of the fortunate few who were taught to read, write, and use mathematics.

Education in Europe Before the Middle Ages

In the era immediately preceding the Middle Ages, Europe can be divided roughly into two regions: the Roman Empire and the lands of the so-called "barbarians" outside the empire.

There is no evidence of formal schooling among the barbarian peoples. None of these groups appear to have developed written language and used it to record or transmit knowledge. Laws, customs, and other information were transmitted orally rather than in writing and so there were no texts that children could study. There may have been adults who instructed children in the religious customs and other specialized areas of their tribe's traditions, but the little evidence that survives, such as Roman descriptions of barbarian practices, suggests that children simply learned from watching and listening to their parents and other adults. Through these means, they learned the skills that they needed to survive and to function in their society.

In the Roman Empire, education was valued and recognized as a means for advancement. Therefore, many Romans began their children's education at an early age to give them as much of an advantage as possible. Those parents who were literate typically taught their young children the basics of reading and writing at home. When a boy reached the age of seven, he was deemed ready to begin more rigorous study. In wealthy households, parents hired tutors or bought them to educate their sons. Educated Greeks were highly valued as tutors and were often bought as slaves to instruct the children of privileged families. Such children enjoyed the luxury of one-on-one teaching in the comfort of their own homes. Those families that could not afford tutors sent their children to freelance teachers. These teachers for hire were found around the temples, forums, and other busy locations in cities and larger towns throughout the empire. They would teach in any available space. In warmer climates, this meant that they often taught outside. The more established and successful teachers rented space on the ground floor of shops and established more permanent classrooms. Additionally, in some of the provincial cities, civic authorities employed teachers to provide education to children of residents. In other instances, city officials recognized exceptional teachers by paying them a salary and giving them exemptions from taxes as well as from burdensome civic obligations such as jury duty. In fact, even the imperial government was aware of the value of education and the benefits of making it more accessible. In an effort to increase the number of teachers, Julius Caesar issued a decree conferring Roman citizenship, with all its benefits, on all teachers of the liberal arts. Despite such recognition, teaching appears to have been a low paying occupation except for a few teachers who found patrons among the patrician class.

Whether the instructor was a private tutor or a public teacher working in exchange for fees paid by the parents or by municipal officials, the first subjects taught were grammar and rhetoric. Literature was usually taught as well, both for its own value and to illustrate examples of grammar and rhetoric. Drawn from the Greek liberal arts, grammar and rhetoric were the foundations of Roman education since the former was essential for reading and writing and the latter was the basis for persuasive speaking. While the value of being able to read and compose documents is readily apparent, the reasons for teaching boys the fundamentals of public speaking are less obvious. Rhetoric developed a boy's ability to think on his feet and speak effectively in public. These attributes were highly valued in classical Greece and Rome. Rhetoricians could use these skills in everyday life, and those who excelled in public debating and delivered moving speeches could build careers as powerful politicians. Thus, both grammar and rhetoric were considered essential aspects of a boy's education.

After being introduced to grammar and rhetoric, the pupil was taught logic. Often referred to as *dialectics*, logic was the art of reasoning and was recognized as a necessary adjunct to the other two arts. Together, grammar, rhetoric, and logic formed the *trivium*, the first three of the seven liberal arts. Students were expected to take four to five years to master the trivium. Once the trivium was completed, a student could go on to higher education. Again following the classical liberal arts education of the Greeks, the next subjects studied were geometry, music, mathematics, and astronomy. These four subjects were referred to as the *quadrivium* and required four to six years of study. The mix of subjects in the quadrivium reflects that, under the Greek ideal adopted by the Romans, the purpose of the liberal arts education was to help the student develop his mind and spirit, not train him for job. Understandably, most pupils, especially those from poor and middle-class families, did not complete their education or even the trivium. In fact, many of the grammar schools, especially those catering to the poorer classes of society, appear to have concentrated on providing a practical, basic education in reading and writing supplemented by some fundamental mathematics. Even this limited education gave students the necessary skills to pursue careers which were far more profitable than those open to the illiterate.

As for the tools used to teach children, letters cut out of wood or carved from ivory have survived from Roman classrooms. These were used to familiarize children with the shapes of the letters of the alphabet just as blocks and other toys and learning aids do today. Additionally, some Greek and Roman teachers used pastries or fruit cut into the shape of the letters and awarded these treats to students who learned their lessons. Once the basic alphabet was mastered, pupils learned to read papyrus scrolls, since bound books were unknown in the Roman world.

All students learned to read but many stopped their educations before learning how to write. This seems odd given that reading and writing are inextricably paired in teaching today. However, from both antiquity and the Middle Ages, there are many examples of people, such as Charlemagne, who could read but not write. For some of these people, it may have been that they had only enough time or money for a very limited but useful education. After all, even this much education meant that a person could read and interpret documents for himself and not be forced to trust others to read them to him accurately. As for writing, a person could always hire a scribe and dictate any documents he needed written and then proofread it himself. Many of these semi-literate people may have intended to pick up writing later on, and some did. However, the longer they delayed, the more difficult the task became. Charlemagne illustrates this point as well since he learned reading and some arithmetic relatively early in life but never mastered writing despite his later efforts.

Writing in the Roman world was taught using small framed boards coated with a thick layer of wax. A student would write on the wax using a stick or stylus made of bone, ivory, or wood. When the lesson was over, the student simply rubbed the wax smooth again to create a fresh blank surface. Wax tablets continued to be used in the Middle Ages, and specimens have been found in York, Novgorod, and many other locations. The medieval wax tablets were used as notebooks by merchants and others as well as by students for school work.

After sufficient practice on wax, the student would move up to writing with pen and ink on scraps of used papyrus or on thin boards coated with whitewash. Both these surfaces could be reused either by scraping away the top layer of the papyrus or by applying a fresh coat of whitewash on the board.

For math, the student learned to use an abacus. Roman abacuses took several forms. One of the most common forms was a board with several parallel grooves carved in its surface. Each groove represented a different magnitude of value (ones, tens, etc.). Counters made of materials such as stone or metal were placed in the grooves and slid back and forth to represent different values. Another alternative was to draw or paint lines on a board and move counters along the lines. There were also smaller, more portable versions made entirely of metal. These were in the form of cards about five inches high and eight inches long, made with several parallel slots. Bead-like counters were permanently fitted into the slots and were slid up and down to perform calculations. While they may sound clumsy, these early calculators were used for millennia by many different cultures in Asia and Europe, and well trained users could perform their operations with great speed and accuracy. Written equations were seldom used, it appears, to solve math problems. This may have been due in part to the difficulty of performing written calculations with Roman numerals. However, students appear to have used their wax tablets and styluses to write out at least some of their math work as well as to draw figures for geometry.

For most subjects, learning involved a large amount of rote memorization. Chanting and mnemonic devices were common teaching methods to help students memorize. Today, making children simply memorize information is often criticized and is an unpopular learning method, but it was clearly necessary in an age when information could not be easily stored and retrieved. Today, we can simply jot down a note on a pad with a pen or pencil or enter the information in a PDA or other portable electronic device. If we need to find a piece of information, we can look it up in a book at home or in a library or go on-line and find it quickly and easily. Obviously, these weren't options back then. Writing materials were bulky and relatively expensive so that making a quick note or reminder was not an option. Further, reference materials and other reading matter were available in cities and larger towns, but they were expensive and seldom easily accessible to the general public. Thus, the best way for a person to have information at his command was to have memorized it. Besides allowing people to carry the basic references they needed around in their heads, their memorization skills also likely trained them to more easily remember new information without having to write it down. However, memorization did not always come easily to children even back then. Roman teachers complained about students who fidgeted too much or fell asleep during their classes much as teachers do today.

Classes were typically small, with only a handful or perhaps a dozen or so pupils, and discipline in Roman classrooms was traditionally strict. Students typically sat down on the ground or floor while their teacher was seated on a chair. All teachers carried rods. Teachers used their rods to maintain order in their classes and correct their students by beating them when they misbehaved, whether by being disruptive or by simply not learning their lessons satisfactorily. However, even back then, some people questioned the effectiveness of corporal punishment, especially when it when was used to "correct" slow learners.

One final point, throughout this section, I have used the word "boy" interchangeably with "child" or "student." This was not an oversight. Education in the Roman Empire was largely reserved for males. Some girls were taught to read and write, but this education was primarily done within the home. Only a few girls appear to have been sent out to public teachers. And these girls were typically sent at a later age than was common for boys. Further, they did not pursue the higher learning of the quadrivium. As we will see, this aspect of Roman education as well as many others was continued in the Middle Ages.

Education After the Fall of Rome

As with other Roman institutions, education was dealt a serious blow by the final collapse of the Roman Empire in western Europe at the end of the 5th century A.D. Classical education survived in the eastern Roman Empire (later known as the Byzantine Empire), centered on its capital, Constantinople. However, in the cities and towns of the former Roman provinces in western Europe, teachers and schools gradually disappeared. Parents who were literate likely educated their own children but, with the decline of urban centers and general upheaval of society, this was an increasingly difficult task. Reading materials must have become harder to find as old texts wore out or were destroyed. The contraction of trade left many areas isolated so that traditional writing materials such as papyrus were difficult or impossible to obtain. And so, with the disruption of commerce and the political and social fragmentation of the empire, the skills of reading and writing faded from collective memory in many of the outlying regions of the fallen empire within a few generations.

But literacy and education were far from extinguished in western Europe. Schools in the outer reaches of the empire, such as in Germany and northern France, perished, but closer to the heart of the empire in southern France and in Italy itself, some teaching survived in the remaining urban centers. From Marseilles to Ravenna, teachers of grammar and even rhetoric continued to ply their trade in the centuries immediately after the fall of Rome. Thus, rather than being annihilated, education retreated back toward the Mediterranean coast where it had its strongest roots, and so the tradition of secular education persisted even in these "dark ages."

Barbarians and Education

Surprisingly, another factor that helped the survival of education within the core of the former empire was the needs of the barbarians who now ruled in place of the Roman emperors. Not all of the Visigoths, Ostrogoths, Franks, and other peoples who had invaded the empire sought to wantonly destroy what they now held. Many of these people had served the empire as military auxiliaries or had at least been living on the fringes of the empire for generations. They were aware of the empire's wealth and coveted it. Rather than simple looting, some wanted to stay and rule and so enjoy the riches that the lands and people of the empire could produce. Because of their previous contacts with the empire, many of their leaders recognized the need to maintain some parts of the imperial government to control and tax their new subjects. As illiterate outsiders, they needed civil servants who could already read, write, and keep accounts to do the work for them. Admittedly, the fragmentation of the empire between the various barbarian peoples meant that governments were not as large or as sophisticated as they had been in the heyday of the empire, but trained administrators and tax collectors were still needed. Further, inspired by the Roman law codes, many of the new rulers determined that they needed to write down the laws of their own peoples for the first time. Thus, jurists were needed to codify the laws and to interpret them. And so, within Italy at least, some boys continued to be educated so that they could serve their new masters just as their forefathers had served the emperors.

The Church and Education

Along with the political, legal, and fiscal structures of Rome, the barbarians inherited the religion of Rome: Christianity. Having survived various efforts to exterminate it, Christianity had become the official religion of the Roman Empire in 380 A.D. As part of their assimilation of Roman culture, many of the barbarian leaders and their peoples converted to Christianity after settling down in their new lands. This wholesale conversion may appear surprising. However, as with other aspects of Roman culture, many of the barbarians had long been exposed to the Christian religion through their contacts with the empire, and some were already practicing Christians. It should be noted, though, that Christianity as practiced in Rome and overseen by the pope was not the only form of Christian belief. Along with others in Europe and around the Mediterranean, some of the barbarians practiced Nestorianism and other forms of Christianity. A discussion of these beliefs and the eventual predominance of Roman Christianity within medieval Europe is outside the scope of this book. However, all forms of Christianity shared a common need for an educated clergy. Literacy was fundamental to Christianity. The life and teachings of Jesus Christ had been written down by His followers and these writings became the core of the New Testament of the Bible. The practice of Christianity was based upon these texts and a literate clergy was needed to pass on Christ's teachings in a world in which most people were illiterate.

The early Church drew its clergy from followers who had already learned reading and writing. These men had been taught by tutors or in schools, as previously discussed. Up to the fall of Rome, the only education provided by the Church appears to have been religious instruction for its followers and theological training for the clergy. All other education was left in secular hands. With the severe reduction of secular education following the collapse of the Western Empire, the Church was faced with a dwindling supply of literate clergymen. By the 6th century A.D., leaders within the Church recognized the crisis and determined that they had to act to preserve the Latin language so that the practice and dissemination of Christianity could continue. Why Latin? Latin was the language of the empire and had become the language of the Church as well. All the principal texts of the Church had been translated into Latin. Most new theological works and other religious guidance were written in Latin and religious services were performed in Latin. Thus, the Church needed men who were literate in Latin to serve the Church.

To save the Latin language, the Church began gathering together and storing many of the remaining documents of classical Rome which secular society had largely abandoned. This task fell primarily to monasteries and their monks since they could provide relatively secure storage spaces as well as disciplined staff to oversee the collections. Fortunately, documents were not saved because of their content, and so these early libraries had very eclectic collections. Many works, such as those of Ovid and other great classical writers, included pagan themes and imagery of which the Church did not approve. However, rather than destroy these masterpieces, the Church kept them because they were fine examples of Latin composition and grammar which could be used to teach the language to future generations of churchmen.

Monastic Schools

Along with developing libraries, monasteries also created schools to meet their needs for educated personnel. Monastic education focused on the skills which the monks needed to perform their duties. Thus, those training to become monks, the oblates (young children who

Opposite: **Fig. 26. This page of music is from a breviary. A breviary was a book for priests which contained the basic information for celebrating masses, weddings, baptisms, funerals, holy days, and other religious observances. In the Middle Ages, priests sang or chanted the liturgy rather than simply reciting it, as shown in the these illuminations, and had to learn this skill as part of their training.**

had been committed to the monasteries by their parents) and the novices, were taught to sing and read so that they could participate in the mass and other religious services (fig. 26). Many were also taught how to write so that they could perform tasks such as copying manuscripts or, more mundanely, drafting correspondence and keeping records such as charters documenting donations to their monasteries. Some were instructed in math as well so that they could perform the accounting necessary to manage the monastery's assets.

While the monasteries maintained their own schools throughout the Middle Ages, education within monastic schools was almost exclusively limited to monks and those training to become monks. In the late 8th century, Charlemagne, king of the Franks and later the first Holy Roman Emperor, had tried to change this. In addition to all of his military and political pursuits, Charlemagne was also interested in promoting education. As a devout Christian, Charlemagne wanted an educated clergy, and as a ruler he recognized the need for literate and educated administrators to staff his government. In fact, he drew some of his administrators from the ranks of the Church. To better meet these needs, he wanted schools established at every monastery and at every bishop's court (fig. 27). At these schools, the sons of both serfs and free men would be taught reading and writing and given religious instruction as well. While Charlemagne did establish a school for the sons of the nobility at his own court, his larger plan for education was resisted by the monasteries and was never implemented. In fact, by the 12th century, many of the monastic orders came to prohibit accepting children who were under the age of fourteen even as novices in their monasteries. The basis for these restrictions was that the presence of children was disruptive and detracted from the monasteries' primary purpose as places of religious contemplation. However, records of official inspections of monasteries indicate that these prohibitions were not always observed and that royal and other noble families did place their sons in monasteries for some education and then later retrieved them. Still, as a rule, laymen were seldom permitted to disrupt the disciplined and enclosed life of the monks by studying with them or even by consulting their libraries. As for the bishops, they did continue and eventually expanded their educational roles, as discussed later in this chapter.

Secular students were not the only ones excluded from monastic schools. Even other clergymen such as parish priests were generally unwelcome in the monasteries. These priests were members of the *secular* clergy, which meant that they lived in the outside world amongst the lay people to whom they ministered. Monks were *regular* clergy. They belonged to religious orders which imposed strict rules on their conduct and required them to live communally under the direction of a superior, usually an abbot. Celibacy was also a requirement for monks. Secular priests had been discouraged from marrying from at least the early 4th century A.D. but were not absolutely forbidden from having wives until the early 12th century. Given their discipline, their celibacy and their rejection of all other worldly temptations as well as their daily round of religious services, monks were often viewed as being the ideal clerics. Thus, to the medieval mind it was quite understandable that these paragons should not be contaminated by allowing anyone, even lesser clerics, to share their schools.

Before moving on to the schools for the secular clergy, there is one other group to be addressed: nuns. The formal roles for women within the medieval Church were very limited.

Opposite: Fig. 27. This picture shows a cleric instructing other clerices. This could be a depiction of teaching at a cathedral school or a monastery. As was typical for the Middle Ages, the teacher is seated on a chair while his students must sit on the ground. Additionally, he holds a bundle of long sticks, which he uses to enforce discipline and to punish students who fail to meet his academic standards.

et dont ilz procedent parcialement et de leur na
ture. Puis parlerons du monde et comment
il est compose a la Reonde. Mes auant toute
euure nous voulons parler des sept ars libe
raulx qui ne sont pas a oublier Et premie
rement nous toucherons del art de gram
maire qui est la premiere des sept ars et sans
la quelle les aultres six ne poeuent auoir
entiere perfection

Cy parle de gramaire

La premiere
des sept ars
si est gramaire dot
pour le temps de
maintenant il ne
est pas seu le quart
temps sans la quel
le art touteffoie
toutes aultres sci
ences de clergie en
espetial sont de petite recommandation po

Women were prohibited from becoming priests or, indeed, entering any of the other minor or major orders of clergy (see chapter 9). As a consequence, apart from a few exceptions such as women who were permitted to become holy hermits known as anchoresses, the only choice for women who wanted to serve God through the Church was to enter an order of nuns. Like monks, nuns typically received a basic education in singing and reading, the skills needed to participate in religious services. However, their educations usually ended at this point. Accounting and recordkeeping for communities of nuns were typically performed by clergymen or other males assigned to oversee the management of the convent, so nuns were seldom taught math or writing. This was the sort of limited education which even such a noted nun as St. Hildegard of Bingen received. Born in 1098 A.D., St. Hildegard became the leader of her convent and was famed for both her spirituality and intelligence. She corresponded with popes, kings, and many other people throughout Europe, and she composed works on a number of topics, both sacred and secular. However, while she could read, her command of writing was very limited. As a consequence, she dictated all her letters and other writings to a monk who acted as her secretary. Further proof of the limited literacy of nuns can be seen in the administrative practices of bishops. When issuing guidance or writing other correspondence to monasteries in their dioceses, bishops wrote in Latin but, when they were addressing communities of nuns, some bishops wrote in the vernacular instead. These bishops knew that the nuns would be able to read the vernacular but not Latin. Still, it should be noted that there were a few nunneries whose members were quite literate and, unquestionably, intelligent and accomplished as well. Such nunneries existed primarily in northern Germany and reached their intellectual peak in the early Middle Ages. Unfortunately, even they were unable to sustain this level for very long. Thus, while some monasteries became great producers and repositories for books and occasionally developed reputations as centers for learning, the great majority of medieval nunneries were not noted for their intellectual achievements.

Bishops and Cathedral Schools

With monastic schools closed to the secular clergy, bishops undertook the task of training young men to serve as priests within their dioceses. Bishops were often members of noble families and maintained large households just as their lay relatives did. These households, whether lay or religious, attracted ambitious men who sought to advance themselves by serving their social superiors. In addition, families seeking to curry favor with their superiors or strengthen relations with their equals often sent their sons to households such as those of bishops to serve and be trained. Thus, bishops frequently had an entourage of young men and boys who were eagerly seeking training and advancement. Unfortunately, there is little evidence of how these future clerics were trained. However, since bishops typically had priests and other clerics in their retinues as well, it is likely that these clerics instructed the boys and young men in reading and writing Latin. Along with these basic skills, those who were destined for careers in the Church learned the rites and rituals which a priest needed to fulfill his duties. This part of the training was accomplished by having them serve as acolytes and assist in the performance of religious services. From these informal beginnings, schools were gradually established at the administrative centers of the bishops: their cathedrals. Further, the Lateran councils (special convocations of the higher clergy) in 1179 and again in 1215 issued decrees requiring bishops to maintain free schools to teach young clerics in training as well as the sons of the poor. And so, throughout Europe, from Cologne and Vienna to Angers and

Reims, cathedral schools undertook the task of educating boys. However, only a small group of boys were fortunate enough to attend these schools. While a few cathedrals established large schools, some with total enrollments of 60 and even up to 180 students, most cathedral schools were small and many accepted only 12 students at a time. The number twelve and its multiples were likely chosen in honor of the original 12 Christian students, the disciples of Christ.

At the cathedral schools, students usually started at the age of seven. Most of them continued to live at home while attending school. Boarding appears to have been limited to small numbers of the older students. As part of their training for a career in the clergy the students were taught to sing, since many parts of religious services had to be chanted or sung rather than merely spoken. Some cathedral schools were referred to as choir schools or song schools and the students often served in the cathedrals' choirs. However, their studies covered far more than just choral work. They learned to read and write in Latin and received religious instruction. In some schools, they also learned grammar and a little classical logic as well as some additional training in Christian theology. They were expected to stay in school until around the age of 10 to 12. Some would then leave to enter minor orders and begin their career in the Church, while others slipped back into secular life. The promising ones stayed on at school until they were 16. In their additional years at school they completed their study of the trivium and were taught some, if not all, of the quadrivium as well. Interestingly, the math and astronomy portions of the quadrivium were useful for clerics since they were needed for calculating the dates to observe certain religious celebrations such as Easter and the start of Advent. The dates for these events, known as movable feasts, shifted each year unlike other holy days such as Christmas. As the Middle Ages progressed, separate schools for advanced education, including the entire quadrivium, developed in a number of the cathedral cities. Some of these schools progressed even further and taught theology and law. As discussed in the next chapter, a number of these schools evolved into the first universities.

Returning to the students, pupils who completed their entire course of studies often went on to successful careers in the Church. However, there were secular opportunities as well for such educated men. While many of those who trained in the households of bishops and, later, in cathedral schools went on to religious vocations and advancement within the Church, others who had not taken vows or had only taken minor vows left and pursued secular careers. Education was valuable and scarce so men who had mastered the skills of literacy were often sought after as administrators and jurists by many rulers, from petty lords to kings. Further, some educated men who had taken religious vows still became the advisors and confidantes of great nobles while nominally remaining part of the clergy. Some even officially served two masters and held high clerical posts while occupying important positions in secular government as well, such as Simon of Sudbury, who was archbishop of Canterbury and the chancellor of King Richard II of England. While Archbishop Simon and a few other government officials were killed by mobs in the Peasants' Revolt of 1381, most clerics had few difficulties holding down two jobs and, unlike today, mixing of religion and politics was the norm in medieval Europe. In fact, even if they did not hold any formal political positions, many of the higher clergy still wielded considerable power in the secular world.

Priests as Teachers

Below the level of the bishops and their cathedral schools, education was carried out by other members of the secular clergy as well. In addition to providing instruction in their own households and later at the schools attached to their cathedrals, some bishops issued guidance to parish priests that they should provide free education to their congregations. For example, in 1403, a council of French bishops decreed that priests must educate the sons and daughters of their parishioners in the basic prayers starting at the age of six or seven. However, apart from such efforts, there was no specialized religious education for the laity. Catholic CCD (Confraternity of Christian Doctrine) education and protestant Sunday schools were not developed until after the Middle Ages. As a consequence, the vast majority of children in the Middle Ages learned their religious beliefs from their parents and other adults and by attending church and listening to sermons.

When priests did provide religious instruction to their parishioners' children, they often taught them some fundamentals of reading Latin as part of this education since a rudimentary knowledge of Latin was needed to read prayers and other common religious verses. Teaching Latin was also done to help cultivate potential clergymen. However, many of the priests had very meager educations themselves and, judging by the bishops' repetition of this guidance, some appeared to have simply resisted assuming yet another unpaid duty. Yet the specification that they, the priests, must provide the education free of charge suggests that some priests were, in fact, doing some teaching but were charging for it.

While the success of these grassroots programs was limited, many priests scattered across Europe did provide some basic education to their parishioners. Some took their responsibilities very seriously. For example, one priest in 13th century France had the three basic prayers (the Lord's Prayer, the Hail Mary, and the Apostles' Creed) painted in large letters on signs and then displayed them in the churchyard so that all his flock could see them. Presumably, he hoped that they would learn to read a little by matching the written words to the words they so often recited in church and at home.

Girls were not excluded from receiving such education, but most of the children taught by priests were boys. For some boys, especially sons of peasants, this education provided an invaluable opportunity to embark on a career in the Church rather than remaining a laborer. In the early Middle Ages, even the sons of serfs, the peasants who were bound to the land, could escape their servile status if they could find a way into the Church. However, this avenue of advancement was eventually restricted so that only free men could become priests, although some other lesser positions appear to have remained open to those who were born serfs. For others, both free and unfree, learning to read provided a skill they could use to advance themselves and their families while remaining in their own communities. Reading enabled them to decipher contracts and deeds as well as the charters that spelled out their obligations to their local lord. Further, if they learned to write, they could also keep their own accounts and other records of the services and payments they had provided and which were owed to them. This increased ability to understand and argue for one's legal rights might have been a reason that receiving an education was sometimes among the actions for which a serf had to obtain his lord's prior approval and pay a fee before the lord would grant his permission. However, the recorded instances of such licensing of education in 14th century England indicate that most, if not all, serfs who sought an education did so as the first step towards a career in the Church. Thus, while some lords likely found the idea of a serf trying to rise above his station in life through education repellent and contrary to the good order of society, the rationale for controlling the education of serfs was probably the very real risk that a lord would permanently lose a serf's services once he completed enough of his education to enter the clergy. Licenses for education issued by some lords addressed this issue directly and specifically barred the serf from proceeding on to holy orders, while others allowed the serf to enter the clergy but decreed that he must return to his unfree status if he ever left the clergy. When a serf was allowed to be educated *and* continue on to enter the clergy, the fee he paid his lord was intended to compensate the lord for the loss of his services. The amounts of these fees varied greatly. Some religious institutions, such as monasteries, which had the rights of lordship in the lands they owned, charged only token amounts. Other lords, religious as well as lay, charged stiff fees that reflected either their assessment of their real financial losses caused by the loss of the serf or their estimate of the highest amount of money they could extort from the serf at that moment.

While many commoners had to rely on whatever education they could extract from their local priest, some families, especially the nobility, could typically afford a better education for their children. The nobility often employed priests as chaplains and had them tutor their children in addition to performing religious duties. Moreover, some noble families as well as wealthy merchant families hired clerics especially for the task of tutoring. This education enabled the nobility and rich urban class to read prayer books, but it also provided them with the skills needed to understand the financial accounts of their estates and businesses, legal documents, and even works of fiction. As these examples reveal, despite the intimate connection of education with the Church and the use of clerics as teachers, the students were not always clerics and their educations were not always applied to religious purposes. Thus, as with bishops who were also government officials, there was often not a clear distinction between secular and religious education and the applications of that education. With this in mind, let us examine teaching outside the Church.

Secular Education

The Church was the primary, although not sole, source of education in western Europe for the first several centuries of the Middle Ages and remained dominant throughout the period. It was only in the late Middle Ages and early Renaissance that secular scholars assumed a major role as preservers and promoters of education. However, as mentioned previously, some teaching independent of the Church appears to have survived in cities in Italy and southeastern France. And, by the 12th century, secular schools are recorded in a handful of cities across Europe (fig. 28).

The Growth of Secular Schools

Within Italy, secular schools flourished in the cities, particularly in the north. By the 14th century, many of these cities had numerous schools providing a range of practical education for their residents. For example, among the many boasts about his home city which one Florentine wrote in 1339 was that somewhere between eight and ten thousand boys and girls, about half the city's children, were being taught to read and write in the vernacular in grammar schools throughout the city. This same proud Florentine goes on to state that there were ten more advanced schools for boys: six that taught arithmetic and use of the abacus and four that taught Latin grammar and rhetoric as well as logic to prepare students to attend universities. Approximately 1,000 students attended the so-called abacus schools while around 600 attended the secondary or university preparatory schools. The numbers of schools are credible, but the number of students attending them needs further explanation. Attending

Fig. 28. The Ewelme School, Oxfordshire, was founded in 1437 and still serves as the village grammar school. It is a unique survival of a medieval school building. While the interior has been modernized, its exterior is original.

school in a medieval city was quite different than today. Unlike modern students who are expected to attend primary and secondary schools full time for 10 or more consecutive years, students in medieval Europe attended secular schools for only a short time. While some stayed in school longer, many, if not most, probably attended school for no more than a total of six months. Many urban schools were oriented towards providing a brief, practical education in skills that the student would be able to immediately apply in business. Thus, they were first taught reading. In the earlier Middle Ages, they were taught to read Latin since this was the primary language of record. At some point, vernacular languages were added, but there is little evidence of when such instruction began. These languages were clearly being taught by the late Middle Ages when Latin was being replaced by local languages in many official records as well as in works of literature. Those who could stay at school longer learned to write as well as read. At the abacus schools, students learned basic math and accounting using abacuses. These abacuses functioned in the same way as their Roman forerunners although they typically had lines or grids drawn on their surfaces instead of grooves or slots to channel the markers. They often resembled checker boards. The abacus schools also frequently offered instruction in drafting business documents and correspondence along with arithmetic and bookkeeping. As these subjects suggest, most of the students at schools in medieval cities were the children of merchants and other businesspeople. These parents wanted their children to learn the skills needed to earn a living and to help with the family business.

Florence was not unique in having business schools. Milan had "schools for notaries" which offered instruction in drafting business documents and other mercantile matters. Milan also had grammar schools which employed at least seventy teachers by the late 13th century. There were also eight secondary school teachers at work in Milan as well. Secular schools grew in many cities outside of Italy as well. By the 12th century, Orleans in France had a school noted for its teaching of grammar, rhetoric, and classical literature. In cities across Germany and Switzerland, from Lubeck to Zurich, private as well as some municipal schools sprang up from the 13th to 15th centuries. One of the reasons for the creation of the city-run schools was that the municipal officials and residents were not content with the limited educational opportunities provided through the Church-run schools, such as those at the cathedrals. For its part, the Church, or at least the local bishops, often did not welcome this expansion of schools outside their control. However, the cities usually overcame this resistance and took action to establish the schools needed to educate their children. Some of the best documented instances of such civic action come from the Low Countries, particularly in towns and cities now in Belgium. Ghent in Flanders created a municipal school in 1179. The neighboring city of Ypres set up a school in 1195. In 1253, Ypres also issued a civic ordinance which allowed anyone to open a grammar school, although secondary education was limited to three existing schools. In 1320, the duke of Lorraine approved the opening of five new schools in Brussels. These schools appear to have been open to both boys and girls and increased the number of schools in the city to at least seven. In a further advance, beginning in the late 13th and early 14th centuries, at least some of the municipally-operated schools were free to children of all residents. In such instances, citizens indirectly paid the salary of the teacher through taxes or other charges assessed by the town or city council.

By the 14th century, there were significant numbers of schools in towns and cities across Europe. For example, even after the first visitation of the bubonic plague, Paris had 41 schoolmasters and 21 schoolmistresses scattered throughout the city in 1357. However, it should be noted that most schools were one-person operations, so the master or mistress, despite their grand title, was often the school's only teacher and not the head of an entire faculty. Schools proliferated at such a high rate in the late Middle Ages that there was competition, sometimes fierce, for students. For example, in 1321 the master of the city grammar school in Canterbury sued a local priest who was also running a school for enrolling more students than he was permitted under municipal regulations. In Paris, city officials forbade the opening of a new school unless it was located at least twenty houses away from any existing school. Ferrara in Italy took similar action in 1443 and required prior approval of the city council before anyone could open a new grammar school. Limiting the number of schools may seem contrary to the public good but these cities likely acted for the same reasons that medieval cities regulated other trades and services: trying to meet the needs of their citizens but also protecting the tradesmen and service providers from potentially damaging competition. Typical of the anti-competitive protectionism that covered most trades in Middle Ages, city officials were likely attempting to ensure that there were enough school teachers to meet the demand for education while simultaneously ensuring that each teacher had enough pupils to earn a living. Despite these measures, teachers still competed with each other for students. Some even resorted to displaying signs in front of their schools advertising how well and how gently they taught and how quickly their students learned to read and write.

The Value of an Education

The rapid growth in urban secular schools in the 14th and 15th century strongly suggests that medieval Europeans realized the economic value of education. Hard-nosed, pragmatic parents would not have invested their money in education for their children unless they expected to see some real return on that investment. While enabling a child to read his prayerbook was obviously considered a virtuous act, these parents were more interested in having their children learn how to keep accounts, write bills of sale, and understand how to apply all these skills shrewdly so that they could succeed in business. And parents weren't the only ones who made this connection. By the 15th century, many guilds had made being able to read and write a prerequisite for their new apprentices. Civic officials must have understood the connection between education and wealth too or they would not have been so willing to encourage and even finance schools for their citizens' children. While having schools and an educated populace enhanced a city's prestige, having an increasingly educated class of merchants and craftsmen yielded real monetary benefits as well. One has only to look at the cities which were the most commercially successful: the northern Italian cities, many of the cities of the Low Countries, and some of the cities that were part of the Germanic mercantile league known as the Hanseatic League. It is not a coincidence that most of these cities were among those that promoted education. Before the end of the Middle Ages, secular schools and the education they provided were so well recognized as benefiting the public good that wealthy citizens increasingly included bequests in their wills for the support of some of these schools along with other donations for civic improvements.

The Faculty

Initially, most of the teachers at secular schools were likely drawn from the ranks of clergy, particularly those in minor orders (see chapter 9), who had received some basic education at a cathedral or from a priest. These men would likely have been able to teach the basics of reading and some grammar. However, secondary school teachers and increasing numbers of grammar school masters appear to have been drawn from the ranks of those men who had attended universities but not completed their degrees (fig. 29). Over the years, the standards for teachers increased further still. For example, by the late 14th century, Bologna was already requiring teachers hired to teach in public secondary schools either to have a university degree or to complete one within a year of being hired or else be terminated.

Fig. 29. Teaching techniques in secular schools were the same as those in Church schools. In this depiction of a typical secular classroom, the teacher is seated in a chair while his students must sit on the ground. In his right hand, he holds a paddle with a long handle that permits him to hit offending students without having to rise from his seat. The student kneeling in front of the teacher is holding an open book from which the teacher is lecturing.

As mentioned above, there were schoolmistresses as well as schoolmasters. The first reference to schoolmistresses in Paris appears in a tax list for 1292 with a single entry. This number increased to 21 schoolmistresses by 1357. Reims had at least one schoolmistress in the 14th century. Another reference appears in Brussels in 1320, when the city government decreed that both male and female teachers were to receive equal pay. There are also a few leases and other property documents in Paris and elsewhere which mention women using houses as schools. As in other areas of education, England appears to have lagged behind the Continent since, by the early 15th century, there were only 2 schoolmistresses recorded in the metropolis of London.

While there is evidence, albeit limited, for their existence, there are no surviving records which provide information on the training and education of the women who became teachers. Girls as well as boys were eligible for free education by priests, but this training was likely too rudimentary to have given many students sufficient knowledge to become teachers. As for the cathedral schools and universities, they were closed to women. Thus, schoolmistresses most likely received their educations outside the Church. Some, especially the earliest female teachers, may have been the daughters or even the wives or mistresses of educated men, such as members of the clergy or schoolmasters. These women could have been taught at home by their fathers or husbands just as women learned other trades and skills (see chapter 8). Others may have come from families wealthy enough to hire a tutor to educate their daughters. However, such tutoring was rare and there is no evidence which indicates that such privileged daughters went on to teaching careers. Over time, some of the schoolmistresses may have been women who attended a secular school when they were children. Unfortunately, given the lack of evidence, one can only speculate on how these pioneers in education obtained their training.

Schooling for Girls

As the previous section suggests, there is only very limited information available about the education of girls. In general, women were not thought to need any formal education to carry out their roles in life. However, in the families of merchants and craftsmen, wives frequently played an active role in the family business. And, as mentioned before, these were the sorts of families which understood the value of formal education and had the resources to employ tutors or send their children to school. Thus, some of these families had their daughters educated so that they would be better prepared to make a living. With this education and training in family trade, they could help out with the family business or find other employment. For example, in some of the breweries in northern Germany, women were often employed as clerks and kept the accounts and other business records. Further, a young woman who knew a trade and was educated could be a valuable business partner for any man she married. Such husband and wife teams were common, and widows frequently carried on their husbands' trades. Similarly, in noble households, some women received sufficient education and training so that they could assist in overseeing the family estates.

Daughters of noble or other wealthy households were sometimes fortunate enough to be educated. For example, in 1397, King Henry IV of England was recorded as buying "A B C" books for his two little daughters, who were then three and five years old. Some may have been taught by the same tutors who instructed their male siblings. Others were likely instructed by the household chaplain but, due to concerns about propriety, some families appear to have hired governesses or other women to teach their daughters. After all, the legendary and tragic romance in the 12th century between Heloise and her male tutor, the cleric Peter Abelard, provided an all too notorious example of the perils of private tutoring of girls by men. In the cities of northern Italy, moralists went further and cautioned parents not to risk exposing their daughters to immodest and unchaste behavior by allowing them to attend school, but to have them taught at home by a nun instead. Some parents took this a step further and placed their daughters in nunneries to be educated by the nuns. However, as with monasteries, convents did not routinely accept the daughters of the laity merely to teach them. The majority of girls placed in nunneries were expected to remain there and enter religious orders.

The use of nuns as teachers raises an interesting issue: given the limited education which most nuns received, what did they teach? By the latter half of the Middle Ages, many nuns were probably sufficiently literate that they were able to teach their pupils to read the basic prayers, a few psalms, and some other brief religious texts. A few were even skilled enough to produce illuminated manuscripts like their male counterparts in the monasteries. However, research has revealed that nuns who copied manuscripts likely had obtained their educations and begun developing their artistic talents before they entered the religious life. They were not taught them as part of their training within the nunnery. Thus, very few nuns appear to have been educated well enough to teach writing. Instead, the nuns likely provided some religious instruction along with what limited instruction in reading they could, but probably little more than that. The real point of having a daughter educated by a nun was so that she could learn and imitate the virtues of chastity, modesty, humility, piety, and obedience which the nun modeled. This conclusion is also supported by the fact that some parents even sought out anchoresses to act as teachers for their daughters. This was a sufficiently common practice that a 13th century set of rules for these holy female hermits specifies that an anchoress should not act as a schoolmistress, although her serving maid was permitted to teach little girls if there was no other education available to them. Since the anchoresses were rarely, if ever, noted for their learning but were famed for their devotion to God and their virtue, it seems that their teaching, like a nun's, would be limited to teaching religious virtues through the examples of their own lives.

Returning to less spiritual matters, those families who wanted to have their daughters educated in more pragmatic subjects like writing and math but who could not afford to engage tutors sometimes sent their daughters to secular schools. There were secular schools open to girls in many of the northern Italian cities, in Paris and a few of the larger French cities, in the larger cities of the Low Countries, and in at least a few German cities as well. There were likely schools for girls elsewhere in Europe but evidence of them has not survived. There is conflicting information about whether the schools girls attended were single-sex or coeducational. It appears that girls and boys usually attended separate schools and, generally, schoolmasters taught boys while schoolmistresses taught girls, although some schoolmistresses are known to have taught boys as well. In Paris and elsewhere, coed schools seem to have been permitted only with a special dispensation from the local authorities. Perhaps coed schools were allowed in those cities, towns, or urban neighborhoods which lacked either sufficient teachers or a sufficient number of pupils to support two separate schools. However, at least in some of Italian cities, there were coed schools even when these exigencies likely did not exist, hence the moralists' warnings mentioned above about the dangers such schools posed to the modesty and chastity of girls. Yet, it should be noted that parents were sometimes advised that these public schools were not suitable for their sons either. Thus, this guidance may just reflect a bias against any education being conducted outside the auspices of the Church. In any event, there were some coed schools in medieval Europe but they do not appear to have been common.

Facilities

As with the Roman schools, the secular schools of the Middle Ages did not have specially built facilities. Teachers taught wherever they could find space. Typically, they taught in their homes, but some rented space. Even when cities began operating schools, they did not construct buildings especially to be schools. Instead, they utilized existing facilities of adequate size although some were aware that schools needed to be in suitable locations as well. Not unlike modern school officials, some medieval civic governments had to cope with the issue of getting students safely to the schools. Just like those who attended Church schools, children attending secular schools were sometimes as young as seven and were typically sent off to school with no adult to escort them. Walking to school through the streets of medieval cities was sometimes risky, even fatal, for these little students. Some cities justified opening additional schools so that students walking to school would no longer be forced to cross busy, dangerous streets or walk across bridges that were crowded with heavy commercial traffic.

Inside the school, medieval children routinely sat on the floor because, as with Roman schools, there were never any desks and very rarely even benches or other seats for the students in the classrooms. Further, the classrooms were usually on the ground floor and, as with many medieval buildings, the floors were often just flattened and hardened earth covered with a layer of rushes. This made for uncomfortable seating, especially in the winter when the floors were very cold. The teacher, on the other hand, had a chair or at least a stool to sit on. The only specialized furnishings found in medieval classrooms were numerous lamps so that the students could see to read and write.

These early schools were usually just a single room. Given that most schools had only a single teacher and pupils of differing ages and abilities, medieval schools likely functioned in the same manner as the "one-room schools" of the American frontier. This meant that teachers probably broke the students up into groups according to their abilities and may have had older or more advanced students help the younger or newer students with their studies. However, there is virtually no evidence on this aspect of medieval education.

Village Schools and Itinerant Teachers

Up to this point, the focus has been on secular education in the cities and larger towns. What about the rural areas and their populations? While the urban centers were wealthy and influential, most medieval Europeans were engaged in agriculture and lived in small towns, villages, and farmsteads. Opportunities for even basic education in the sparsely populated agricultural regions remained extremely limited for most of the Middle Ages. Those who lived relatively close to cities often sent their children into the city for school. In Reims during the 13th century, half the children attending school are estimated to have come from the surrounding farms and villages. In small towns and villages that were too distant from cities with schools, the town or village councils sometimes collected money to pay for teachers and established schools that were free to all the children of the residents. Such public schools are known to have existed in small towns in Germany as early as the 13th century. Paralleling the growth in urban schools, the number of town and village schools is believed to have increased significantly over the course of the 15th century. There is evidence, especially in Germany, that town and village schoolmasters were primarily drawn from the ranks of men who had attended university but failed to complete their degrees. By the late Middle Ages, the number of such men, while still a small percentage of the total population, was enough to provide a large pool of potential teachers.

In the absence of town or village schools, parents who wanted more education for their children than their parish priest was willing or able to provide had to employ itinerant instructors to teach their children. But these parents had no way to verify the qualifications of the itinerant teachers. Some of these traveling teachers appear to have been men, lay or cleric, who attended universities for some time, or at least claimed they had. Others were possibly monks or other clerics who had abandoned their positions within the Church and were roaming the country. A few were simply laymen who had managed to pick up some learning at some point in their lives. Some actually lived up to their promises and taught their students, but all too many appear to have been incompetent, lazy, or simply outright frauds. Even village schools were not always able to weed out such undesirable teachers. Parents in one village in medieval France petitioned the local authorities to remove a schoolmaster who was so lax in maintaining discipline that the children gambled at dice while at a school instead of being taught. Such teachers would stay on and collect whatever fees they could until they were found out and then move on.

Teaching and Disciplinary Techniques

Regardless of whether a school was operated by the Church, by secular authorities, or by an individual teacher-entrepreneur, all teachers appear to have used the same basic methods of teaching and enforcing discipline.

Teaching Reading and Writing

Just as in the days of the Romans, young children were sometimes taught their ABCs using fruits and little cakes cut into the shapes of the letters and given out as rewards. Through the 19th century, gingerbread was sometimes made in molds in the shape of tablets with all the letters of alphabet on them. In England, these edible alphabets were commonly sold at fairs. To persuade customers to buy them for their children, gingerbread vendors claimed that eating the delicious treats would help a child learn his letters if he was required to recite each letter before he was allowed to eat it. Given the existence of other medieval gingerbread molds, such as those in the shape of saints, these gingerbread alphabets may have developed in the late Middle Ages, although all alphabet molds found so far date from after the period.

Inedible but still food-related, bowls have survived in England from the 14th and 15th centuries which have the alphabet engraved on them. Bowls with the "Hail Mary" prayer on them have been found in France, Spain, and the Low Countries. All these bowls were made from luxurious materials such as silver and silver-gilt. While there is no documentation to prove the use for which these dishes were made, helping children learn their ABCs and first prayers seems like a reasonable explanation. And, given their expense, these items and others, such as a set of golden letters which the duke of Orleans had made for his five-year-old daughter in 1415, show that wealthy medieval families sometimes tried to give their children a head start in learning the alphabet and reading while they were still quite young.

Less extravagant but just as effective, alphabets were often painted on boards displayed in the classroom. An inventory of Angers Castle in 1471 listed one room that had a large board with the alphabets of several different languages drawn on it. This may have been used by a chaplain for teaching the noble children of the castle. Students frequently had their own copies of the alphabet as well. One such learning device, a plaster disk with the alphabet on it, was found in a medieval site near Paris. More durable and more common were small wooden boards or tablets with the alphabet written or painted on them. The tablets often had a single, small handle at the bottom which gave them a paddle-shape. Written references to such tablets occur as early the 13th century but, given their utility and ease of manufacture, it seems likely they were in use much earlier. During the early 15th century, the increasing availability of paper and the continuing development of carved wooden blocks for printing led to changes in the alphabet tablets. Increasingly, the alphabet was printed on sheets of paper which were then nailed or otherwise attached to the large, flat surface of the tablets. Biblical verses or common prayers were sometimes printed along with the alphabet on these sheets. Beginning in the second half of the 15th century, the alphabet sheets were often protected by a thin, transparent layer of horn permanently attached to the wooden tablet. (The thin sheet of horn was made by boiling, cutting, and flattening a cow's horn.) With the addition of the sheet of horn, the alphabet tablets came to be commonly called *hornbooks*. As with the painted tablet, students could repeatedly use the hornbook, tracing the letters with their fingers if needed, without damaging the printing on the paper. The hornbook was such a successful teaching aid that it was used until at least the late 18th century. In addition to alphabet tablets, children learned their letters and other aspects of reading by chants or repeated recitations and other memorization techniques like their Roman predecessors. As for their initial learning of writing, many students appear to have first used styluses of bone or wood and scratched their first letters onto wax tablets just as Roman students had. As they became more proficient, they moved up to quill, ink, and parchment.

Once students had learned their ABCs, they were taught to read the basic prayers as well as some psalms. The students sometimes learned to read these prayers and other works from little booklets. However, even small books such as these were often scarce and somewhat expensive before the advent of printing in the 15th century. To cope with the shortage of textbooks and to help them learn to write, the teacher would read the passages aloud and students would copy them down. To help take all this dictation, students learned systems of abbreviations and shorthand during their time in grammar school. By abbreviating common terms and other means, the students were able to take notes quickly and in less space as well as compose documents with equal speed and brevity. It also allowed them conserve writing materials, especially parchment, which was relatively expensive and which remained the primary writing surface for most of the Middle Ages. After mastering the basics, students advanced to passages from classical Roman writers such as Cato, Ovid, and Virgil. In both Church and secular schools, they were taught these texts not for their content but for their examples of grammar and composition in Latin.

Teaching Math

As mentioned previously, students were taught to perform mathematical operations using an abacus since the Roman numeral system inherited by the medieval Europeans was ill-suited to written computations and since the abacus could be used easily and quickly to carry out even difficult computations. Students could also learn how to count up to a million using their fingers and a combination of other body parts. For example, 70,000 was represented by placing one's left hand on the left thigh with the palm facing outwards with thumb pointing down while the gesture for one million was to clasp both hands together over one's head. Additionally, math and logic were taught using riddles, although we might call them "word problems" today. Here are some examples that are at least 1,000 years old:

> Six workers were hired to build a house. Five were master builders and one was an apprentice. At the end of the day, the five masters were paid a total of 25 deniers. The masters divide their pay equally. From their pay, the master builders must pay the apprentice and each master must pay the same amount. The apprentice is paid half as much as a master. How much did each man receive?
> A boy chased a boar and killed it but then stepped on a poisonous snake and received a fatal bite. While dying, his mother tells him, "If you had lived for as long as you have and yet that long again and then half as much plus a year, you would have lived to been a hundred years old, my son." How old was the boy? (Answers in appendix 3.)

Students were expected to figure out the answers to these sorts of problems in their heads.

While various forms of abacuses continued to be used throughout the Middle Ages, Roman numerals were gradually replaced with the numerals we use today and which are often called "Arabic numerals." However, this new system of numerals actually originated in India. The Arabic world had obtained this number system and much other mathematical knowledge from their contact with and later conquest of India. Scholars in the Islamic world assimilated this information and disseminated it. Through texts written by Arab scholars, the Indian numerals reached Europe through Spain by the 10th century. Along with such other Indian developments as place value and the concept of zero, the new system of numerals eventually helped to revolutionize mathematics in Europe by making it possible to write out increasingly complex computations and results in forms which were far more understandable than had been possible with Roman numerals. However, the new numerals did not become widely used until the 13th century, and even then many businesses appear to have retained the use of Roman numerals and mathematical shorthand for their business accounts and other records. Still, by the late Middle Ages, arithmetic was increasingly taught using the new Indian numerals.

Discipline and Corporal Punishment

Just as it had been a part of education in Rome, corporal punishment continued to be a part of teaching, both clerical and lay, in the Middle Ages. The teacher's birch or switch cut from the thin, whip-like branches of birches, willow, and other trees was an indispensable academic accessory. The branches were sometimes tied into a bundle to create a larger, broom-like switch (fig. 27). In some illustrations, teachers are shown holding a long-handled paddle instead of a switch. The length of the handle may have allowed teachers to hit a student without having to rise from his seat (fig. 29). Students who were disruptive or who failed to learn as well or as quickly as their instructors wished were subject to whipping with the switch or a paddling, although some teachers appear to have terrorized all their pupils, regardless of their academic performance. Physical punishments ranged from taps and slaps up to bruising, even killing, blows and scarring whippings. Such correction was a regular part of education, whether in school or in private instruction with a tutor. Not surprisingly, some of the earliest independent writing we have from schoolboys are records of how much they hated their brutal teachers. As early as the 15th century, boys scribbled their thoughts in the margins of books and slips of paper. Many dreamt of turning the tables and beating their persecutors. One imaginative young writer went even further and fantasized about having his teacher transmogrify into a hare and all his books into hunting dogs. He would then hunt his teacher down. On very rare occasions, some school boys appear to have gone beyond merely thinking about retribution. The noted monastery of St. Gall suffered a major fire in 937 which started at the monastery's school. The fire was believed to have been set by one of the oblates in retaliation for being whipped, along with other monks-in-training, for misbehavior during a festival. The alleged arsonist's target may have been the whips stored in the school.

However, not all corporal punishment went unchecked. As noted in the previous chapter, St. Anselm and others recognized that harsh physical punishment was not conducive to either learning or the development of good character. One late medieval example of such enlightened thinking can be found in the writings of Guarino of Verona, a 15th century Italian educator. He advocated that students should be treated in a gentle manner, quite similar to that favored by St. Anselm, and that whipping students was counterproductive. Instead of encouraging the boys to learn, it made them hate education. Teachers should use kindness first and resort to punishment only when all else has failed to change their students' behavior. Further, while evidence is scarce, some parents took action against abusive teachers and tutors. Some even sued for damages for injuries inflicted on their sons. At the very least, teachers, many of whom relied on tuition payments for their livelihood, risked losing paying customers if they treated their students too roughly.

It should be noted that not all teachers in Middle Ages were unfeeling, dictatorial brutes. Certainly, most appear to have been very strict, especially when judged by modern standards, and many routinely used force. However, we cannot establish how many did so excessively and there is evidence, such as the use of fruit cut into the shape of letters mentioned previously, that some teachers did use gentler teaching methods. Further, there were those in the

Church and elsewhere, in addition to St. Anselm and Guarino of Verona, who recommended positive ways to help children to learn. For example, in the 11th century, St. Peter Damian suggested several different games to break up the long hours of instruction and make learning reading and proper speech more interesting to the students. Later in the Middle Ages, one moralist recommended awarding small prizes such as sweets or school-related items such as inkwells to those who did well in class. While we cannot determine the impact of this advice, it is likely that it encouraged some teachers to use gentler, more positive teaching methods. Finally, a good sense of humor has always been a valuable asset for any teacher, and at least a few teachers in the Middle Ages were fondly remembered for using humor to make their points and keep their students' interest.

Student Amusements

School wasn't all work and no play. Schoolboys enjoyed the same games and celebrations as other children. And there were even a few activities which appear to have been especially reserved for boys attending schools. One of these pastimes was the pre–Lenten cock fight. As part of the revelry or carnival preceding Lent (the forty day period of fasting before Easter), schoolboys were allowed to bring roosters to school on Shrove Tuesday. The boys then conducted cock fights between the unfortunate birds. Alternatively, but equally cruelly, the poor birds might be buried in pits up to their necks or otherwise immobilized and then pelted with rocks or sticks until dead. When the brutal entertainment was over, the teachers appear to have commonly claimed all the chickens and taken them home to be eaten.

The holidays in December were more gentle. On 6 December, the feast of St. Nicholas, the patron saint of children, schoolboys in some parts of Europe were allowed to gamble at dice during the school day by permissive teachers. Such activity was ordinarily prohibited but Christmas season was a special time of the year for children, especially those at school. On 28 December, just after Christmas but still during the holiday season, is the feast of the Holy Innocents. This holy day honors the innocent children who, according to accounts in the New Testament, were massacred by order of King Herod in his attempt to slay the young Christ. As far back as the early 13th century, boys attending many of the cathedral schools in England celebrated this holiday by electing "boy-bishops." Some went even further and created entire courts for their bishops with mock archdeacons, chaplains, and others, all dressing up in clerical garb. Following his installation, the boy-bishop would deliver a sermon in the cathedral to his congregation. These sermons appear to have been satirical, with their teachers likely bearing the brunt of the jokes. The boy-bishop and his followers then toured their "diocese" and collected money from the cathedral's clergy as well as from local monasteries and even indulgent local nobles. These fund-raising forays could cover a considerable area since the staff of some cathedrals provided their students with horses for the occasion. In exchange for the donations, the boy-bishops bestowed blessings and sometimes gave out small presents as well. At some cathedrals, the boy-bishop retained the day's takings, but at others the funds were used to pay for a feast for him and his court.

Jewish Education

Education had strong connections with religion for medieval Jews as well as medieval Christians. In fact, the importance of studying the Torah, Talmud, and other sacred texts made learning to read a religious duty within the Jewish community. Jewish fathers were to teach their children to read or else find a tutor for them. Some families, primarily wealthy families and families of rabbis, taught their daughters as well as their sons to read and even write but, as with Christian education, Jewish education was generally limited to males. Only boys and men were admitted to the yeshivas (schools for studying the Torah and other texts) and given other advanced education.

Education began at home. Just like any other parents, Jewish parents in the Middle Ages first taught their young children how to speak. Those parents who knew Hebrew likely instructed them in speaking Hebrew as well as the vernacular used in the surrounding Christian community. Some parents also taught their children the alphabet and possibly some of the other fundamentals of reading. After basic instruction at home, Jewish boys went on to formal schooling at around the age of five or six. In cities and larger towns, such education typically took place outside the home in schools supported by the entire local Jewish community. Schools were sometimes attached to the synagogue, but instruction frequently took place in the teacher's home. However, many communities were too small to support a school and so parents employed tutors to teach their children in their own homes. Some families were too poor to afford tutors. These families had to rely on the charity of wealthier families to pay for tutors for their children.

Tutors were often itinerant. Some were students traveling between centers of higher learning while others were scholars simply trying to eke out a living. These men presumably taught their students as well as they were able. However, just as with traveling teachers for Christian children, there were some who were lazy or were complete frauds who taught their students little or nothing and fled with any money they had collected when they were discovered.

In the Ashkenazi Jewish communities in medieval Germany and France, formal education began with the teacher displaying a tablet or board with the letters of the Hebrew alphabet written on it. This act highlights one significant difference from Christian education. Instead of Latin, Jewish texts were written primarily in Hebrew, and this was the universal language of Jewish education. The teacher then read the alphabet forwards, backwards, and finally with various letters combined. The new student was encouraged to repeat the letters after his teacher. When this process was complete, the teacher smeared honey over the alphabet and the student licked it off. The student was then presented with little sweet cakes and shelled hard-boiled eggs which had verses from the Bible written on them. The teacher read the verses aloud with the student again repeating after him. When all the verses were read, the student ate the cakes and eggs. The teacher then instructed the student in some of the basic study practices, including various memorization techniques such as chanting. For the same reasons discussed in Christian education, development of good memorization skills was important. Finally, the student finished the first day of school with additional treats of fruits and nuts. While all the various foods and acts had symbolic value, the boys must have simply enjoyed all the attention and, especially, all the delicious foods. These treats likely encouraged the little boys to have positive associations with going to school and learning. In this respect, these special foods were similar to the cakes and fruits cut into the shapes of letters used by teachers in the Roman Empire to encourage and reward their students. By the late Middle Ages, these rituals appear to have largely died out as the Bar Mitzvah became the focal point of a boy's progression into adulthood.

Also like the students in both Roman schools and the schools of Christians in the Middle Ages, students in Jewish schools were sometimes pushed to achieve academically by more coercive means. Jewish teachers routinely employed the same corporal punishments as their Christian counterparts did to force students to be attentive to their studies and to correct disruptive or otherwise unacceptable behavior. Jewish parents appear to have expressed as much concern as Christian ones that their children should not be beaten or spanked excessively by their teachers. Jewish teachers, like Christian ones, were generally exempt from punishment if they accidentally beat students too severely and caused injury or even death. However, as with Christian parents, Jewish parents sometimes sought redress from teachers who were too quick or too hard with their blows. At the very least, Jewish parents, like Christian ones, could punish an abusive teacher by withdrawing their child from his school and so deprive him of the teaching fees he would have otherwise received.

Teaching methods aside, the primary goal of education was to enable Jewish men to understand and participate fully in their religion and its ceremonies. Students who excelled in their studies were encouraged to pursue higher education at a yeshiva, an academy for studying the Talmud, and become rabbis. Many of the Talmudic academies were temporary. They formed around a noted and respected rabbi and then disappeared upon his death or departure. However, some cities with larger Jewish communities did develop more permanent centers of learning. In Germany, Cologne, Mainz, Worms, and Speyer in the Rheinland formed the heart of Ashkenazi Jewish community. In some of these cities, Jewish communities had existed since the last centuries of the Roman Empire. They weathered the passage of the First Crusade and other persecutions and survived as centers of Jewish culture through the Middle Ages. In the Languedoc, which is now part of southern France, Narbonne was noted for its vibrant Jewish community and its yeshiva. Yeshivas which were likely founded by scholars from Narbonne also existed in other Jewish communities around the region, including at Beziers, Lunel, and Montpellier. As with the Rheinland, these towns and cities as well as others such as Marseilles had Jewish communities which dated back to the Roman Empire. The conquest of the region by the kings of France in the Albigensian Crusade led to increased pressure on Jews throughout the Languedoc in the 13th century but some of their schools survived until the expulsion of the Jews from France in the early 14th century. In addition to the Rheinland and the Languedoc, there were centers for Jewish learning in Toledo and other Spanish cities. Under the Muslims, the Jews and their culture were tolerated as long as they paid their taxes and obeyed their Muslim rulers. During the 11th through 15th centuries, Christian forces reconquered the Iberian peninsula from the Muslims. Jewish communities survived for some time under Christian rule but, as in most of the rest of Europe, they were eventually expelled.

7

University Education

While the number of people who received any formal schooling was a small fraction of the total population of medieval Europe, the number who went on to higher studies was smaller still. However, since attending a university or other institution of higher learning is a common part of growing up for many young men and women in many parts of the world today, we will examine the medieval universities and their students in order to better understand their similarities to and differences with their contemporary counterparts.

In the 12th century, there were perhaps a few thousand scholars studying at the first four universities: Bologna, Paris, Montpellier, and Oxford. By the end of the Middle Ages, thousands of new students enrolled each year in more than 60 universities spread across Europe. For example, by the end of the 15th century, it is estimated that new enrollments in the universities of Germany alone totaled around 2,500 to 3,000 each year. As these figures suggest, the number of Europeans who attended the universities grew substantially over the course of the Middle Ages. Yet despite this increase, the number of university scholars, as a percentage of the total population, remained quite small. Those few thousand scholars of the 12th century were drawn from a population that likely exceeded 40,000,000, which meant that they constituted less than a fraction of one percent of the total populace. In the 15th century, when Europe was beginning to recover from the losses inflicted by the bubonic plague, the population is estimated to have been slightly more than 50,000,000, including some 10,000,000 in the regions that provided most of the students for the German universities. Applying these estimates and those for enrollments, university scholars may have accounted for approximately one percent of the total population by the end of the Middle Ages. Clearly, despite the increase in the numbers of students and universities, such higher education was not an ordinary part of growing up in the Middle Ages. Further, unlike today when most university students start their educations while still in their late teens, many medieval university students were already adults and had begun careers as members of the clergy by the time they entered the universities.

The Rise of the Universities

While much of the content and some of the pedagogical techniques of medieval education were drawn from Greco-Roman culture, the universities as institutions were not based on classical precedents. In the ancient world, scholars seeking advanced education sought out noted masters in their particular fields of interest. Often traveling great distances, students congregated around these experts wherever they might be found. When these masters moved, their temporary academies moved as well. When a master died, his school disappeared and his followers dispersed. Further, unlike the faculties found in medieval and modern universities, masters of different subjects were seldom to be found in the same locale. A noted medical expert might be found practicing in a town on a Greek island while a famed jurist might live and work in a city in Italy. There was simply no motivation for these men to gather together in a single spot, especially since teaching was often only a sideline to their primary careers. But there appears to have been one exception to this general lack of permanent centers of higher learning: Alexandria in Egypt. In late antiquity, Alexandria was noted for its massive library. Scholars from around the Mediterranean came there to do research. Consequently, experts in a variety of topics as well as students routinely came in contact with each other and exchanged ideas. In fact, recent excavations suggest that the library complex may have included facilities used as lecture halls. However, no evidence has yet been found on what may have been taught in these rooms or to whom. Further, the library was destroyed centuries before the Middle Ages began and it could not have served as a model for the universities that arose in medieval Europe. Thus, universities, as permanent centers of higher education with faculties that provided regular instruction on a variety of subjects, were a new creation by the medieval Europeans.

The universities developed slowly. For the first several centuries of the Middle Ages, scholars seeking advanced training appear to have had no choice but to study under individual masters, just as their classical predecessors had. Over time, some cities did become centers for certain specialties. For example, Bologna became a center for teaching the civil law inherited from the Romans while Montpellier in the south of France developed a medical school and Paris became a center for theological studies. By some point in the 12th century, these three schools, along with Oxford in England, attracted growing numbers of students and masters, some of whom had traveled from other countries to reach these new centers of learning. Among these scholars were masters from a number of disciplines. These schools were then able to offer instruction taught by qualified experts in the basic masters of arts curriculum as well as in at least two of the four courses of higher study: theology, civil law, canon law, and medicine.

The combination of attracting students and masters in a variety of areas of study, having qualified masters as instructors, and offering degrees in several of the then-recognized fields of advanced studies elevated these schools to being *studia generalia,* the medieval Latin term for places of general studies: universities. This status differentiated these schools from the ordinary *studia* which offered instruction and conferred degrees in only the classical liberal arts and perhaps one of the higher subjects. For example, Reims had a noted school of theology and Lyons, Orleans, and Angers were all centers for studying law, but none attained the rank of *studium generale* during the Middle Ages. Similarly, Parma, Verona, and several other cities in Italy had *studia* that offered degrees in arts as well as law, but these too were not considered universities since they did not offer a more complete range of degrees. Further, these and many other *studia* were schools of only regional importance and did not attract any significant number of scholars from outside the immediate vicinity, in part, because of their limited curricula and lower prestige. Still, many other centers did grow from *studia* to *studia generalia,* while some universities were successfully created by royal patronage in cities where no significant higher education had previously existed. By the end of Middle Ages, there were over 60 universities across Europe in France, Italy, England, Portugal, and Spain as well as in Sweden, Denmark, and Scotland and the areas now comprising Germany, Hungary, Poland, and the Czech Republic.

While all these schools met the requirements for being a *studium generale*, their sizes varied greatly. Further, even at major universities, attendance fluctuated widely over the course of the Middle Ages. In peak years, the enrollment of students at a major university, such as Bologna or Paris, is estimated to have often exceeded a thousand. Most universities had far fewer students with perhaps three to four hundred attending each institution. And some were smaller still with enrollments of only a hundred or so students. However, in times of political crisis or other disasters, attendance at even some of the great universities plummeted to levels so low that their continued existence was sometimes in doubt, yet most of the medieval universities, both large and small, weathered these storms and became permanent centers of learning.

The Students

Who attended the universities of medieval Europe? For a number of reasons, the students at medieval universities were almost exclusively Christian men.

Universities were licensed by the pope and were typically under the jurisdiction of the local bishop or archbishop. As Christian institutions, admittance to the universities was restricted to Christians. However, there were a few exceptions. At Padua and likely at Montpellier as well, a few Jewish men studied and taught medicine. Further, in the 12th and 13th centuries, Arabic scholars may have attended and taught at Montpellier and a few other universities located near the Mediterranean. But such intercultural exchanges were limited to universities located in cities which had significant trade contacts with the Arabic world and, even in those instances, were extremely rare.

Besides simply being Christians, most of the men studying at the universities were, in fact, clerics. Particularly in the first centuries of their existence, universities drew most of their instructors and students from among the clergy because, except for some of the educated laity of the urban centers of northern Italy, these were the only people who were sufficiently educated to pursue advanced studies. But it must be remembered that the clergy encompassed a much broader spectrum of men than it does today (see chapter 9). Many of these clerics were only in minor orders, which meant that they had not yet taken the final vows that committed them to a lifetime of service to the Church. This was no small matter since such vows were taken very seriously in the Middle Ages, and the Church rarely allowed men to return to the secular world after taking these vows. Further, many clerics in minor orders were still quite young, as discussed later in this section. On the other hand, there were also cleric-scholars who had already taken their final vows, held positions of responsibility with the Church, and were men of mature years. Thus, while many students were part of the clergy, they were not a homogenous and strictly disciplined group.

Besides being the supplier of university scholars, the Church was also the primary employer of university-educated men for most of the Middle Ages. The Church needed the skills and services of the theologians, canon lawyers, and even the arts scholars which the universities produced. This gave clerics a strong motive for attending a university, since such higher education could significantly improve their career opportunities within the Church. In the secular world, the value of a university education was only gradually recognized and even then was limited primarily to civil law and medicine, two careers that were potentially very lucrative. However, for reasons discussed later in this chapter, the balance shifted over the course of the Middle Ages and laymen eventually came to be the majority of university scholars.

As for women, no female scholar ever attended a university in medieval Europe. Still, there were women who pursued learning on their own. The most notable example is Christine de Pisan (1365–ca. 1430 A.D.). Her father was a university-educated physician and astrologer who moved from Italy to Paris to serve the king of France in 1368. Growing up in Paris, she learned French as well as Latin, arithmetic, geometry, and the rest of the subjects that were part of a classical education. She married a nobleman who served as one of the king's secretaries, but he died when she was only 25. Left with little money to support herself and her three children, she applied her education and went on to become one of the first successful female writers. Her writing displays her familiarity with many texts, including those that formed the core of the university arts curriculum. Near the end of the Middle Ages, a few women who, like Christine, were daughters of professors at the southern universities are known to have received advanced educations as well. These women did not attend classes at the universities and so were likely tutored privately by their fathers and other scholars of the universities. However, such education was exceptional and the number of learned women remained very small.

Student Qualifications

Along with their knowledge, the Church-educated scholars who taught and studied at the universities brought with them the language used both in their earlier studies and in the performance of their official duties: Latin. Principal texts for the universities were written in Latin or translated into Latin from Greek or other languages, and lectures and other instruction were conducted solely in that language as well. As a result, Latin became the language of education as well as of the Church.

Initially, relatively few men outside the Church possessed sufficient knowledge of Latin but, over the course of the Middle Ages, more were able to obtain it, and lay enrollment in the universities steadily increased over the centuries. Additionally, in some university cities, there were grammar schools that provided specialized remedial education for students, both lay and cleric, who found, after arriving at the university, that they had overestimated their proficiency in Latin. Thus, the language barrier was not insurmountable for a motivated scholar.

Besides the language requirement, it cost money to attend a university. To encourage them to undertake higher education, clerics were allowed to be absent from their posts for up to five years and still collect the compensation from those posts if they were attending schools recognized by the pope as *studia generalia*. In the 14th century, this sabbatical was lengthened to seven years. This incentive wasn't needed for monks and friars since their religious orders paid for selected members to attend universities. Not surprisingly, those monks and friars selected were usually sent to study theology. But there were many clerics who were not in monastic orders and who either did not hold paid positions or held only poorly paid ones. Some of these poor clerics sought to improve themselves by attending the universities but could only afford it if they could find a relative or other patron to subsidize their studies. Failing to find such support, some poor clerics supported their education through begging.

As for laymen, they received no subsidies and so their attendance at the universities was generally limited to those who could afford the university fees as well as rent, food, and other costs. A few of the lay university students were sons of the nobility, but most were the sons of urban businessmen. Some were from wealthy families but most appear to have been from middle class families who were investing in their sons' education as part their overall efforts to enhance their families' wealth and position. The numbers of lay students grew over the centuries. Combined with the decline in clerical enrollment, this increase resulted in lay students constituting a majority of the scholars at universities by the end of the Middle Ages.

The Age of Students

Today, we think of most students entering college at the age of eighteen or nineteen, immediately following their graduation from secondary school. However, as described in the last chapter, there were no organized school systems in the Middle Ages and students did not make an orderly progression up through the grades as they do now. Instead, medieval scholars began their university education whenever they were ready. In practice, this meant that most started when they had mastered sufficient Latin to understand the lectures and texts and had sufficient resources to finance their education. As a result, the age for starting university studies was very flexible. Some students are known to have been as young as ten or twelve when they first enrolled, but fourteen appears to have been the usual minimum age for a student entering university in the Middle Ages. Still, not all students were so young. Some arts students began their university studies later in life since they simply did not have the resources to start when they were younger. And, not surprisingly, most scholars pursuing advanced studies, such as law or medicine, were significantly older than many of the arts students. Some of these more mature students had completed their arts studies at a local *studium* and then went on to the universities to pursue higher education which was only available there. The age of these older students ranged from the mid-twenties to the early forties. So, in summary, younger students ranged in age from around fourteen to their early twenties and constituted the majority of arts students, while most scholars studying one of the advanced subjects were older. This meant that, since most universities had far more arts students than law, medical, and theology students combined, the majority of university students were relatively young.

Student Organizations and Foundations

From the earliest years of the universities, students came together for a variety of purposes in addition to learning. Many of them were strangers in an alien city and often their language set them apart from the local inhabitants. For protection as well as for friendship, they sought out fellow students. They also needed to find housing. Many needed some financial aid. To meet all these needs, different forms of student organizations developed.

Nations

While scholars were united by the common tongue of Latin, they were still divided by their native languages and cultures. At most of the universities, students from the same country or region joined together for mutual support and protection as well as for recreational purposes. These groups were commonly referred to as *nations*. At Paris, for example, there were originally four nations: Normandy, Picardy, England, and France. Students who were not from one of the principal countries usually joined their nearest linguistic or geographic neighbors. As a result, students from the Low Countries joined the Picardy nation while Germans and others from northeastern Europe joined the English one. At Oxford, there were two nations: North and South. North included Scotland and the northern half of England. South included Ireland, Wales, the southern half of England, and all students from overseas. However, the Oxford nations were abolished around 1274 in an attempt to end the prolonged, and sometimes violent, conflict between the two groups.

The nations periodically collected dues from their members as well as from new students when they joined. These funds were used to help out sick students as well as to pay for a banquet on the feast day of the nation's patron saint and for other purposes. The nations also acted as administrative bodies of the universities by collecting the lecture fees its members owed the masters and by providing some oversight of its members' conduct. Over the course of the later Middle Ages, the nations gradually disappeared at most universities. This was due, at least in part, to the rising number of universities. As the number of universities multiplied, students more frequently attended universities in their native countries rather than going abroad and so there was much less need for organizations for foreign students.

Housing and Halls

On a smaller scale, students organized themselves through their housing. Rich students could afford to rent entire houses and frequently staffed their new households with servants from home who had journeyed to the university with their young masters. Most students could not afford such luxury. Some rented spare rooms wherever they could find them. In the early years of the universities, such boarding was common and students sometimes even lodged in the homes of their instructors. Some masters took this a step further and created boarding houses or hospices solely for students. Students also joined together into small groups to lease whole houses. House servants, especially cooks and laundresses, were hired by these groups as well. These hospices and group houses, sometimes called halls, *bursae*, *aulae*, or hostels, developed at most of the universities. While they had started simply as shared housing, they became increasingly formalized and were fixtures at the universities until the end of the Middle Ages. Some even received donations from former members. They established rules for their members and all were eventually governed by a master who had authority to maintain discipline. The size of these halls ranged from as few as three students up to 30 or more.

Colleges

The establishment of colleges created another way in which students were organized (fig. 30). Despite being permitted to collect money from their regular duties while attending a university, even clerics could not always afford all the fees and other expenses. Poor scholars frequently turned to begging, and some universities issued begging licenses to their poor students so that they could beg without fear of being prosecuted as vagrants. As with aid for other impoverished groups, it came to be a recognized form of Christian charity to give alms to poor students. Gradually, some charitable individuals established permanent foundations

Fig. 30. Walter de Merton, bishop of Rochester and lord chancellor of England, founded Merton College in Oxford in 1264. The original admission policy of this college gave perference to relatives of Bishop Merton.

to help poor students studying. These endowed group homes were the original residential colleges. In return for praying for the founders' souls and assisting at masses, students admitted to the colleges were provided with room, board, and money to defray their educational expenses. Some founders may have also hoped that they were helping to produce a more educated clergy that would better serve the Christians of Europe.

The first colleges were quite small, often accommodating only a dozen or so scholars. As with cathedral schools, twelve and multiples of twelve may have been chosen in honor of the original Christian students, the Apostles. Even by the middle of the 15th century, many English colleges seldom hosted more than two dozen students at a time although some had as many as seventy. In contrast, some of the colleges founded at German universities in 15th century were quite large and housed 200 to 300 students. For some early colleges, their small size was well suited to their purpose since they were created by their founders primarily for the benefit of poor relatives who wished to advance themselves by obtaining an education. But even these colleges soon admitted other deserving students when there were no suitable relatives to be found. Preference was generally given to students who needed some financial aid to enable them to attend school, but many colleges appear to have developed policies of accepting students who were of middling means rather than actually destitute. In fact, most students attending universities were likely from what we would consider to be middle class families (sons of prosperous merchants and landowners, younger sons of knights, and the like) rather than truly poor ones. Many needed additional money to afford all the costs associated with attending a university, but they were far from starving. Increasingly, the most that truly impoverished students could hope for from a college was to be allowed to work serving the college's members. In exchange, these poor students were given meager room and board like other servants, but they were also allowed to attend lectures at the college, a sort of early work-study arrangement. At the other end of the scale, colleges founded by kings and queens typically catered to the sons of families who had won royal favor. Often, these were families of the lesser nobility or even commoners who had provided some valued service to the royalty, and a place at college for their sons was part of their reward. Accommodations at these colleges were suitably comfortable. A few students found life in the colleges so pleasant that they did not want to leave even after successfully completed their studies and were ejected only with some difficulty by the college's other members.

In the colleges, the students shared rooms. At an English college, a typical arrangement was for three to four junior students and one senior to share a chamber. At the more massive colleges in Germany, such as at Erfurt, twelve or so students lived in each room. Meals were prepared by a cook employed by the college and were eaten communally in the college's hall. Laundry, a nagging problem even for early university students, was taken care of by the college's laundress. The college also employed an official, sometimes called a *manciple*, to manage the college's employees and oversee the day to day operations. Over time, colleges added other benefits to their basic room and board. Some employed tutors to assist their students. Before the end of the Middle Ages, many colleges, such as those at Oxford and Cambridge, employed their own masters to lecture for their fellows. Alumni and other benefactors also donated books to their colleges and so created libraries. The advantages provided by the colleges became so desirable that students began paying to be admitted to colleges. However, these paying members did not enjoy all of the college's privileges, such as periodic cash and clothing allowances, and they were viewed as inferiors by those who been selected to attend the college.

The colleges also provided a means for imposing some controls over student behavior. Some required their scholars to attend mass daily. Misconduct such as coming in after curfew could result in the offending student being given only bread and water for one day, while repeatedly keeping late hours could result in expulsion. Sneaking out of the college after curfew and having a woman, other than one's mother or sister, in one's room were also grounds for expulsion. In addition to encouraging the students to behave morally, college rules also sought to compel their members to excel academically. Colleges made attending lectures compulsory, held their own mandatory study and review sessions, and instituted examinations for their members to ensure that they were learning at a satisfactory pace. Those who failed these exams faced expulsion from their colleges. By the end of the Middle Ages, many, if not most, universities required students to be enrolled in a college or a regulated hall. This requirement was part of the increasingly tighter discipline which the colleges and universities imposed upon all their students in the 15th century.

The Faculty

Like the students, many instructors at medieval universities were members of the clergy. But, as with the students, their clerical duties appear to have typically been a distant second to their academic ones. And there were some lay teachers even in the earliest years of the universities, although they were initially limited primarily to medical instruction and were most common in universities in southern Europe such as Montpellier and Bologna. However, as the number of lay students grew, so too did the number of lay instructors since some of the lay students stayed on at the universities after graduation and became teachers. Whether lay or clerical, teachers at universities were usually referred to as *magisters* or masters, but other titles like doctor and professor were sometimes used instead. As discussed later in this chapter, *master* and *doctor* were designations for specific degrees of education as well, but even those who held doctorates appear to have been satisfied with the honorific of *master*.

Initially, masters were likely men who had become recognized experts in their area of study. Some may have been graduates of the earlier learning centers that gave rise to the universities. Eventually, a master had to have undertaken a complete course of study at a university, been examined by others who were already masters, and found competent. These masters then awarded him a degree. He still needed a license to teach. The teaching license was conferred under the authority of the local bishop or archbishop and gave the master the right to teach at any university in Christendom. In practice, foreign masters seeking to teach at a university which they had not attended frequently had to undergo some examination by the local masters before they were admitted to the faculty.

The original university faculty members were independent lecturers. Their income came from the fees students paid to hear their lectures, and so their livelihood depended on the number of students they were able to attract. Students arriving in a city that hosted one of the early universities were often greeted by these lecturers or their agents, each one proclaiming the superiority of their qualifications. Students were advised not to contract with a master until after they had attended three of his lectures to determine his suitability. In fact, some universities, such as Bologna, prohibited the collection of lecturers' fees until several days or even a couple of weeks after the start of the term to allow students time to make up their minds. Once a student had contracted with a master, other instructors were not to try to lure him (and his money) away. But not all masters must have observed this point of professional etiquette since university administrations in Paris and elsewhere had to formally prohibit masters from poaching each others' students. Such rivalry between masters also reflects the fact that early faculties were simply coalitions of independent instructors. It took many centuries for faculties to develop into organized staffs of professors who were directly employed and controlled by university administrations as they are today.

Not surprisingly, the dependency of the faculty on lecture fees gave the students some leverage over how classes were conducted. However, in Paris and most other universities, the faculties were able to neutralize much of the students' advantage by organizing themselves into a corporate body. Comparable to other medieval guilds, the organization of masters was able to set conditions for their employment and generally gave the masters the upper hand in dealings with the students. However, at Bologna, the students organized first and were long able to set many of the terms for the operation of the university and working conditions of the faculty. Among these were the following:

- Classes had to start on time. Any instructor who failed to start lecturing at the appointed time was subject to a fine.
- Classes had to end on time. Any instructor who failed to stop lecturing on time was also fined. Further, any student who stayed past the bell to listen was also subject to a fine.
- Instructors could not be absent on a day they were to teach without the permission of their students. Students who failed to report their instructors for being absent were also subject to punishment.

- Instructors had to cover all the material required for the class. This requirement was primarily for courses in law and was to deter rushing or skipping chapters, especially at the end of the term as a result of spending too much time on early chapters at the start of the term. At the beginning of each term, an instructor had to post a substantial bond with a bank. Official representatives of the students withdrew set amounts any time the master fell behind in his teaching schedule.

Professors at Bologna complied with these strict conditions since their pay came exclusively from the lecture fees paid by the students. Further, even the amount of these fees were not completely under the control of the instructors. Representatives of the students wishing to attend a class would meet with the prospective instructor and negotiate the fee. Student representatives then collected a share of the fee from each student enrolled in the class to pay the instructor. Both students and professors were hard bargainers, and the latter frequently complained that everyone wanted to learn but nobody wanted to pay for it. Some masters had to threaten to stop teaching to persuade the students to pay a reasonable sum for their services. Eventually, instructors at the Italian universities gained increasing independence when city authorities and other benefactors began providing subsidies and finally outright salaries to professors. At other universities, such as Oxford and Cambridge, lecture fees were also meager, but masters collected a significant portion of their pay from the fees paid by students to the faculty when they were awarded their degrees. Over time, the fees paid at the time of enrollment became the primary source of revenue collected from the students at most universities. Ultimately, by the end of the Middle Ages, faculty compensation throughout Europe became more stable as lecturers were paid by endowments established by the colleges as well as by the universities themselves.

The value of a noted master in enhancing a university's reputation and attracting students (and their money) was well recognized by civic governments in Italy. Thus, in the early years of the universities, some cities which were trying to establish universities attempted to lure masters away from their existing posts with bribes and offers of better privileges and conditions at their new universities. To counter this threat, cities bribed professors to stay and required them to swear an oath not to teach anywhere else for at least a year after leaving their current posts. Some cities backed the oaths up with substantial fines on masters who violated their agreements and left to teach at a rival city. The amounts of the fines were sometimes based on the professor's age with fines substantially higher for masters fifty years old or older than for younger ones. This appears to have been in recognition of the older professors' presumably greater expertise and reputation.

The masters also came to form part of the administration of the universities. While the bishops and their chancellors controlled the issuance of licenses to teach and had disciplinary oversight of the conduct of the students, the masters controlled the curriculum, requirements for degrees, examinations, and the awarding of degrees. Initially, all masters participated in administration but, eventually, these matters were controlled by a subset of the faculty called the regent masters or *regents*. Regents were initially required to be celibate, but this requirement was abolished before the end of the Middle Ages.

Masters were sometimes also students. Some scholars who had completed their studies in the arts and obtained the degree of master of arts stayed on at the universities to pursue still higher degrees. As masters of arts, they were part of the faculty and taught while they worked on their advanced studies. In part, they took up teaching to support themselves, but some universities required those who earned master of arts degrees to stay on and teach for up to two years after graduation. This requirement was probably motivated by a shortage of qualified instructors for the growing number of students. By the end of the Middle Ages, however, this period of compulsory teaching was gradually reduced and eventually disappeared. Ever increasing numbers of university graduates and the desire of faculty members to maintain their status and income by avoiding having too many instructors likely contributed to ending this burden on new degree-holders.

In addition to the masters, students who were nearing completion of their degrees also taught at some universities. After completing most of the work towards a degree, students were sometimes required to give a course of free lectures on their subjects. In part, this was training for those who planned to become teaching masters themselves. Additionally, regardless of how they planned to use their degrees, it also required the scholars to have mastered their subjects well enough to explain them to others. As with requiring new masters of arts to teach, some historians have suggested that the primary purpose of this requirement was not for the benefit of the scholars giving the lectures. Rather, there were times when there weren't enough qualified masters to meet the demand for lectures, especially at the prices students were willing to pay. Forcing senior students to give lectures for free may have been meant to solve this problem, although some contemporary accounts of university life mention students having to be bribed to attend some of these free lectures, presumably so that the scholars giving them would get the credit they needed for graduation. However, it may have been that bribery was necessary only for truly bad lecturers. In any event, the use of students as instructors shows that the position of "teaching assistant" is almost as old as the universities themselves. As with requiring new masters of arts to teach, by the end of the Middle Ages, students were no longer required to give lectures either.

Subjects Taught at the Universities

Today, universities offer degrees in the arts and sciences in subjects ranging from literature and foreign languages to chemistry and engineering. The choices in majors at medieval universities were far more limited. What we would think of as undergraduate studies were limited to a single major, *arts*.

In theory, the arts curriculum covered the entire trivium and quadrivium: grammar, rhetoric, and logic plus arithmetic, music, astronomy, and geometry. In practice, however, some of these subjects, such as rhetoric and music, typically received little attention while others, primarily logic, were studied at length. The study of logic was also expanded to cover topics that were not part of the classical arts curriculum. This expansion was due largely, if not entirely, to the works of Aristotle, which were used to teach logic. While masters did use them to illustrate logic and reasoning, these writings covered a broad range of subjects which captured the interests of many scholars. For example, in his works on natural philosophy, Aristotle wrote about the natural sciences: astronomical phenomena, human behavior, different forms of animal and plant life, reproduction, and many other aspects of the natural world. Applying modern terms, Aristotle's natural philosophy touched on topics from astronomy, zoology, biology, botany, and psychology among others. Additionally, Aristotle wrote about ethics and related topics in his works on moral philosophy, and he addressed sophisticated abstract concepts, such as the nature of the human soul and of existence, in his metaphysics. Many of Aristotle's works became part of the arts curriculum at the universities and came to be taught for their own content and not just as exemplars of logic and reasoning. As a result, many scholars at the universities became great admirers of Aristotle's teachings. But, while the logic and other educational merits of Aristotle's works were generally appreciated and respected, there was concern that some scholars were becoming too influenced by the philosophical and metaphysical content of his writing, some of which conflicted with Christian beliefs. This conflict prompted university authorities, in accordance with guidance from the Church, to restrict the teaching of certain parts of Aristotle's works. It should be noted that Aristotle was seen as a challenge to religious orthodoxy in the Islamic world as well. In the 12th century, the Muslim scholar Ibn Rushd, known in Europe as Averroes, wrote brilliant commentaries on Aristotle's works, but contemporary Islamic theologians criticized and opposed his work since it helped spread knowledge of beliefs which were contrary to their religion.

In addition to instruction in the arts, universities also taught four advanced courses of study. As mentioned previously, these were canon law, civil law, medicine, and theology.

The significance of canon law, the law of the Church, may not be readily apparent today. However, the Church occupied a central place in medieval society, and the guidance issued by successive popes and Church councils affected Christians throughout Europe. The interpretation and harmonization of all this guidance was the job of the canon lawyers. Further, the ecclesiastical courts had jurisdiction over many aspects of life, such as marriage. Canon lawyers were needed for obtaining legal separations or even dissolution of marriages as well as for defending marriages against claims of invalidity for reasons such as incest (see chapter 10).

Civil law was taught using the legal code compiled by the order of the Emperor Justinian. This work codified the laws of the Roman Empire as they existed in 534 A.D. As a result, civil law was also known as Roman law. Although the Roman Empire ceased to exist as a political entity in western Europe, its laws still provided precedents in medieval legal proceedings. Further, the renewed study of Roman law at the universities contributed to its revival in much of Europe and to its introduction into some parts of Europe which had never been conquered by the Romans. However, many countries had developed their own customary and common laws and statutes after the collapse of the empire. As a result, some universities supplemented their civil law instruction with teaching on the laws governing the regions in which they were located.

While most medieval European legal systems were based, to some degree, on Roman civil law, there was one exception: England. The English developed a legal system which was based entirely on their own common laws and statutes. Roman civil law played no significant role in the English legal system, and so Roman law received little attention at English universities. After attending a university for a few years, those men who wished to become civil lawyers in England went to the inns of court of London to study the practice of common law.

The teaching of medicine in medieval universities was grounded in the humoral theory of the classical world (see appendix 1). As discussed later in this chapter, the study of medicine benefited from newly translated classical works as well as from newly written texts by both Arabic and European medical practitioners which became available during the course of the Middle Ages.

Theology was the epitome of education, at least in the view of the Church. The development of great theologians who had studied the Christian religion at great length and who could ably defend and advance the cause of Christianity was a noble goal. But theology held no attraction for laymen and, even among those university students who were clerics, theology was frequently not as popular as law since law often led to successful careers both inside and outside the Church. Further, the Church actually restricted the study of theology by permitting only the universities of Paris, Oxford, and Cambridge to confer degrees in theology for much of the period. The Church's restrictions were likely an attempt to prevent the development of competing, and possibly conflicting, centers of Christian religious thought. Keeping theology almost entirely centered in Paris facilitated the Church's monitoring and, if necessary, intervention in debates and discussions about issues of Christian orthodoxy. Such efforts would have been even more difficult had each of the growing number of universities had its own fully accredited theology program. As part of keeping Paris the acknowledged center of Christian theology, the Church prohibited teaching civil law at the University of Paris in 1219 to prevent theology students from being distracted and drawn into alternative careers.

Subjects outside those required for degrees were occasionally offered as well. In the 14th century, as part of efforts to prepare for reconquering the Holy Land, universities were encouraged to offer foreign language courses in Hebrew, Greek, and Arabic. A few universities actually did add these languages to their curricula, but they soon disappeared along with the dream of a new crusade. In the sciences, astrology was occasionally offered, usually as part of the medical curriculum since the heavenly bodies were thought to exercise influence on the human body. However, astrology had a rather checkered career as a university subject. It was frequently condemned as a form of magic by the Church and its practitioners were subject to persecution, including burning at the stake.

At some of the Italian universities, courses in drafting legal documents and business correspondence as well as in accounting and notarial skills were offered in addition to the courses required for degrees. At the English universities, such instruction was offered by business schools that were not part of the university although, at Oxford, such schools were overseen by two of the university's regents. These courses, whether taught at the university or at independent schools, provided practical business training for the students, regardless of whether they completed their degrees. This business education could be readily applied in a number of profitable careers, from serving as a legal clerk to managing the estates of a noble household or working as a municipal official.

Methods of Instruction and Learning

The Middle Ages is general viewed as a time of intellectual stagnation. Rather than thinking independently and critically, scholars in medieval Europe are often pictured as only absorbing and repeating whatever scraps of information they could find, whether from classical Rome or from Arab sources. As we will see in this section, while there is some truth in these stereotypes, teaching, learning, and, indeed, thinking did evolve during the Middle Ages and received knowledge did not always go unchallenged. Although intellectual progress was uneven and stalled at times, medieval Europeans, including many of the scholars at the universities, were not all superstitious and backward. Without this progress, the advances made during Renaissance might never have occurred.

Lecturing

The primary form of instruction at medieval universities was lecturing. There were three basic types of lectures. Since books were scarce and expensive before the printing press made their mass production possible, special lectures were sometimes given for students who lacked the fundamental texts needed for their studies. At these lectures, texts written by recognized authorities were read aloud, usually by a senior student rather than a master, while the students worked furiously to write it all down. Tedious as this process was, it allowed students to create their own copies of the books they needed but could not obtain. Other means for coping with the scarcity of books will be discussed later.

The second and most common form of lecture was the *ordinary* lecture. In the ordinary lecture, a master presented material from the texts required by the syllabus for the course. He read selections from the text and provided his own interpretation of its meaning, his *gloss*. Glossing was the primary means of providing more up to date information, since the master would cite the views of other experts, both past and current, on the material in addition to his own. Further, especially as new information became available through newly translated or newly written texts, the master could use his gloss to reconcile the content of the primary texts with any other conflicting information that arose. This practice reflects an approach common in medieval society: established authorities were respected and seldom directly and openly challenged. Rather, when authorities were found to disagree or were proven false, the correct, updated information was put forward but the change was typically styled as a mere clarification or elaboration of the original, not as an outright rejection. For example, a medieval doctor who had discovered some aspect of human anatomy about which Galen, the famed Roman physician who lived in the 2nd century A.D., was in error or had never commented upon would likely have described his new information as being a clarification of Galen's observations rather than flatly declare the great Galen to have been wrong or to have missed something. Thus, at first glance, the masters at the universities appear to have slavishly taught the classical texts, right or wrong, but in reality these scholars applied reason when confronted with problems, assimilated new information, and passed it on to students through the glosses.

In addition to the *ordinary* lectures, masters and senior students also gave *extraordinary* lectures. As the name suggests, these were extra lectures which supplemented the basic required lectures. The extraordinary lectures given by students were part of the course of free lectures they were required to deliver as part of their degree requirement. These student lectures were given in the afternoon, in part because the ordinary lectures were given in the morning and students were forbidden from giving lectures at the same time as the masters. At an extraordinary student lecture, a senior student read selections from one of the required texts and gave his own explanations and interpretations of their meaning. The content of the lecture appears to have frequently mirrored the ordinary lecture given by the master in the morning. Having a second hearing of the material, and possibly some open discussion of it, presumably helped students to learn it more thoroughly or at least gave them another chance to copy it all down. It may have also given late-risers a chance to make up the material they missed that morning. The extraordinary lectures given by masters were less common than those given by students. Like the student lectures, they were also held in the afternoon after the ordinary lectures were out of the way. However, rather than rehash the morning's lesson, some masters appear to have used these sessions to present materials pertinent to the course but not part of the prescribed syllabus. These could include newly translated or newly written works on the course subject as well as discussions of any recent developments or controversies on relevant topics. In some instances, the lists of texts required for courses changed over the years, with some of the standard texts replaced by works which first appeared as part of extraordinary lectures. And so, while some texts remained standard for centuries, the material taught at the universities gradually changed to include the latest information.

Disputations

In addition to attending lectures, students also had to participate in disputations after their first two years of study. Disputations were public debates that were refereed and judged by the masters. The topics for these debates were often predetermined but were sometimes left open for the participants to put forward. The arguments and results of disputations were sometimes recorded and used as supplementary course materials.

While today we might think that such debating was only necessary for training lawyers, these exercises were thought suitable for all areas of study since they tested the students' mastery of their subjects as well as their ability to reason. In fact, apart from oral examinations given by the masters to students applying for their degrees, these were the only tests most students ever underwent. There were no written tests or term papers in the medieval universities.

Dissections

Apart from lectures and disputations, there were no other specialized teaching sessions except for medical students. As part of their education, medical students needed to be familiarized with human body, inside and out. To meet this need, human dissection was conducted as part of their instruction in anatomy. By the early 14th century, medical students at Bologna and Montpellier were expected to witness at least one human dissection as part of their instruction in anatomy. (Such dissections had likely been taking place at these universities for some time before this, but written regulations on their conduct only appear beginning in the 14th century.) During the dissection, the instructor read aloud from a book on anatomy to explain to the students what they were seeing. Surgeons appear to have done the actual dissecting. The bodies were frequently those of executed criminals. For example, in the 14th century, the king of Aragon dictated that the university in Lerida was to receive the body of one executed criminal each year for dissection at the medical school. The king further specified that the luckless criminals were to be specially executed by drowning, presumably to leave their bodies in the best condition for study. At Bologna, attendance at a human dissection was limited to medical students who were at least in their third year of studies. Further, the audience was limited to no more than twenty students at the dissection of a man and thirty at the dissection of a woman. Dissections of female bodies were likely conducted less frequently and so more students were allowed to attend. Finally, no student was permitted to attend more than one female and two male dissections. All these limits suggest that these anatomy lessons were very infrequent and that the university wanted to ensure that each student had the opportunity to observe one at least once during their education. When corpses were not available and at universities that did not conduct human dissections, pigs, apes, and other animals appear to have been dissected to familiarize students with basic anatomy. Instructors sometimes used large illustrations that were somewhat similar to modern anatomical charts as well.

Taking Notes

As indicated above, taking notes has been a part of university studies from the beginning. The necessity of taking lengthy notes at lectures and disputations coupled with the relatively high cost of parchment were some of the reasons that students employed systems of abbreviations and shorthand, likely learned during their earlier education at grammar schools. By abbreviating common terms and other means, the students were able to take notes quickly and in less space as well as to compose documents with equal speed and brevity. The memory training which students had previously undergone in grammar and secondary school education also helped them to remember and fill in gaps in their notes.

Reading

As mentioned previously, books, while essential to education, were difficult and expensive to obtain in an age before movable type made printing books comparatively cheap and easy. In the Middle Ages, each book was laboriously handwritten by a scribe onto sheets of parchment made from the skins of goats, sheep, and calves. Parchment was a critical material for the universities. Even after the introduction of paper to Europe in the later Middle Ages, parchment remained essential for the production of books and as note paper for most of the period. In Paris, all parchment entering the city had to be offered for sale at the university first before any other consumers had the chance to buy it. Along with ensuring the university's supply, this right also gave the university some control over the price at which the paper was sold to the faculty and students. Each book made for university use had to be copied by hand from an approved original and then checked for errors and corrected. The sheets of parchment were then stitched together and bound between thin wooden boards, usually covered in leather. Because of the time and materials that went into their production, even without the illustrations and decorations often associated with medieval manuscripts, these books were more expensive than many students could easily afford.

To obtain the necessary texts, many students attended the special lectures described previously where books were read aloud while the students copied them down. For students with more money to spend, stationers approved by the universities sold plainly made copies of the required texts. For those with less money, some stationers were also permitted to rent out sections of the texts as well. Called *peciae*, these sections were rented to students on a short-term basis so that they could copy them. Another alternative was to find someone who had the book one needed, borrow it from him, and copy it. This likely required much begging and frequently involved giving the book's owner a deposit or pledge of some kind to ensure the book's return. The value of books and concern over their loss was so great that universities frequently had rules prohibiting owners of especially valuable and rare books from selling them to anyone outside the university community without first giving masters of the university an opportunity to buy them. Additionally, even within the university community, sales of valuable books were required to be publicly witnessed, presumably to head off any accusations that a book had been stolen rather than bought. Students were sometimes prohibited from pawning or selling their books as well since, if they no longer had their texts, they could not study.

The value of books also led to their chaining within libraries. At the colleges, as they began to form their own libraries, parts of the collections were often kept chained to prevent their theft or other loss or damage. Iron loops were attached to the book's spine and a chain threaded through the loops and attached to the bookcase. The chain was just long enough to allow the book to be taken from the shelf and placed on a desk nearby for reading. Not all library books were subjected to such high security; only especially valuable ones or, perhaps, ones for which there was a high demand.

The Texts

What were the contents of these books that were so essential for higher studies? As mentioned before, the arts curriculum focused on the works of the famous Greek philosopher Aristotle for logic as well as for many topics that were outside the scope of the traditional definition of the arts. Grammar was taught using the works of Donatus, a Roman of the 4th century A.D., and Priscian, who lived in Constantinople in the 6th century A.D. The works of Cicero (106–43 B.C.) provided the examples for teaching rhetoric. For arithmetic and music, the standard works were by the Roman scholar and philosopher Boethius (c. 480–c. 524 A.D.). He also translated some of the works of Aristotle into Latin. The works of Euclid, a Greek of the 3rd century B.C., were used for geometry and those of Ptolemy, a Greek born in Egypt in the 1st century A.D., for astronomy.

Some new texts were gradually introduced into the arts curriculum over the course of the Middle Ages. For example, while some of Aristotle's works on logic had remained in circulation in Europe despite the fall of the Roman Empire, many of his other works, including those on metaphysics and natural philosophy, were lost for many centuries and only rediscovered beginning in the 12th century. The recovery of most Aristotle's surviving works and their introduction into the universities took until the early 13th century. Other areas of the arts gained new texts from other sources. Through Arabic channels, European scholars gained significant new information on mathematics, including a new system of numerals to replace the old Roman numerals. The Arabic world had obtained much of this mathematical knowledge from its contact with India. The so-called Arabic numerals we still use today were first developed in India and were introduced to Europe through Arabic texts in 10th century Spain. While the new numerals did not become widely used until the 13th century, these and other Indian innovations, such as place value, eventually help revolutionize mathematics in Europe by making computations far easier to understand and perform.

For civil law, as mentioned previously, the fundamental work was the *Code* of the Emperor Justinian, which codified the laws of the Roman Empire as they existed in 534 A.D. Another essential work was the *Digest*, which recorded important legal decisions by Italian jurists. There was also the *Novellae*, a supplementary text of laws enacted by Justinian after the Code had been written, and a textbook on all these laws and decisions called the *Institutes*. Finally, there were many works by medieval jurists commenting on and providing further explanations of the original laws and legal decisions.

For canon law, the two primary texts were the *Decretum* by Gratian and the *Decretals* of Pope Gregory IX (fig. 31). Gratian was a monk who lived in Italy in the 12th century. He compiled the writings of the early fathers of the Christian church, decrees issued by Church councils, letters and other documents containing guidance issued by the popes (such documents are called *decretals*), and any other records containing the laws of the Church. Gratian added his interpretations of these texts and when these records gave conflicting guidance, he attempted to reconcile the differences in his comments. The *Decretum* was effectively accepted as a codification of the laws of the Church. Since the *Decretum* was not periodically revised, it quickly became outdated as popes and Church councils issued new rulings or amended old ones. Further, there were some gaps in the *Decretum*. Thus, in 1234, Pope Gregory IX had a new compilation containing all the laws and guidance issued since the *Decretum* had been written, plus additional earlier material which been omitted. Subsequent popes issued similar updates in 1298 and 1317. As with civil law, there were also numerous commentaries and glosses written by medieval canon lawyers, which students were required to read as well.

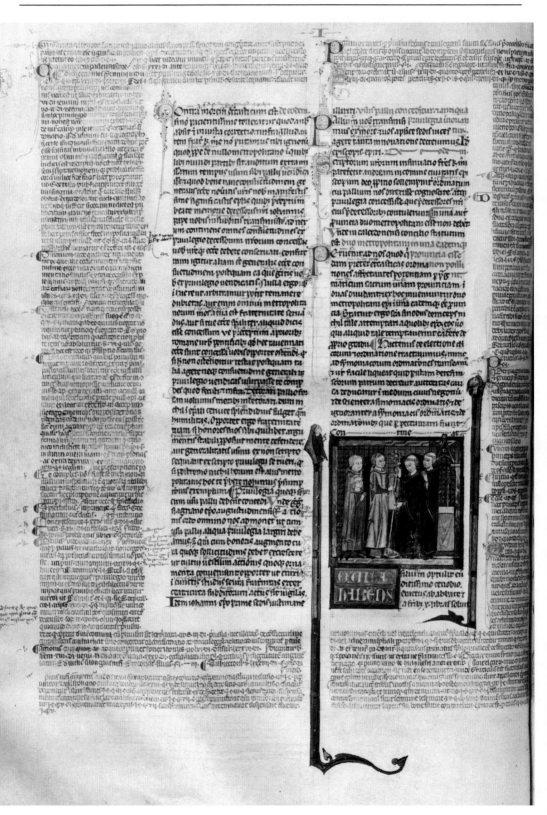

For theology, the primary text was the Bible. Along with the Bible, theology students studied the *Sentences* of Peter Lombard. Peter Lombard was a 12th century cleric and theologian. His *Sentences* used a question and answer format to present and explain Christian theological doctrine. Texts containing the works of the early Church fathers were also part of the required reading. Books on preaching and collections of sermons were typically included as well, to help train the theologians in communicating the basic as well as the finer points of Christian belief to their congregations.

For medicine, the essential texts were the various works of Galen, the noted Roman physician of the 2nd century A.D. Some texts by the legendary Greek physician Hippocrates (c. 460–c. 377 B.C.) and by other medical experts of the classical world were also used. Along with these classical works, books by Arabic medical writers such as Abu al–Qasim, known in the Europe as Albucasis (c. 936–c. 1013 A.D.), and al–Husain bin Abdallah Ibn Sina (980–1037 A.D.), who was called Avicenna in Europe, were also part of the standard list of medical texts. These were the core readings, but medicine received many new texts over the course of the Middle Ages. Some were translations of classical Greek and Roman works which had disappeared in Western Europe but which had survived in the Byzantine Empire and elsewhere around the eastern and southern shores of the Mediterranean in the former lands of the Roman Empire. These works had been translated from Greek and Latin into local languages by a variety of scholars, primarily Muslims, but by Jews and native Christians as well. From the languages of the Middle East, these texts were eventually translated into Latin. New writings by medical experts in the Arabic countries were similarly translated. These works, both recovered ancient texts and new books, entered Europe one by one, mainly through centers of learning in Spain and southern Italy where Christian, Jewish, and Arabic societies interacted. They then became a valued part of European medical knowledge. However, the supply of new translations and texts from the Arabic world gradually tapered off until, by the end of the 14th century, few if any new medical works came from this source. Meanwhile, new medical books were being written by Europeans. Many of these books repeated the contents of classical and Arabic works, but they increasingly contained new discoveries or, at least, new, first-hand descriptions of medical conditions and information drawn from the writers' own experiences in treating patients rather than mere restatements of traditional theories on treatment.

The Facilities

Today, when we think of universities, we usually imagine large campuses with big and expensive buildings ranging from dormitories and stadiums to lecture halls and laboratories. When universities first developed and for several centuries thereafter, they had no permanent buildings. For lectures, instructors initially taught in their own homes. As the number of students grew, masters rented buildings to use for lecture halls. To help the masters secure adequate spaces for lectures, secular authorities sometimes took action. For example, at Cambridge

Opposite: **Fig. 31. This is a page from Gratian's *Decretum*, one of the fundamental texts of canon law. The primary text is in the central two columns in large, dark script. The surrounding writing is the *gloss*. The gloss provided comments on the primary text along with explanations of difficult terms and other information useful in interpreting the text. In this particular excerpt, one can see annotations made by one of the book's previous owners.**

and Oxford, landlords who had rented out buildings to be used as lecture halls were restricted from renting those buildings out for any other purposes. Churches and monasteries in university cities also occasionally permitted masters to use their large rooms as classrooms as well. Monasteries also frequently stored the universities' records.

Within the lecture halls, furnishings were typically as sparse as in the grammar and secondary schools. Just as they had during their earlier education, university students were expected to sit on the floor at their masters' feet. To make the floors a little more comfortable, especially in winter, the floors were covered with a layer of straw. As a consequence of this practice, the street where most of the lectures were given at the university in Paris came to be called the Rue du Fouarre, the Street of Straw, from the constant supply of straw brought in to refresh the floor coverings in the lecture rooms. Seating gradually improved and, by the 14th century at the latest, students usually sat on benches.

At some universities, such as Orleans, seating arrangements in these early lecture halls was determined by a student's social standing and wealth. Front row seats were reserved for noble students and for those who could afford to pay a relatively high fee. The price of the seats decreased with each subsequent row. Those seats at the back of the room, furthest away from the master, were the cheapest.

As for student accommodations, as mentioned previously, students lived in rented rooms or houses. Some even boarded in the homes of their instructors. In England and elsewhere, to ensure the availability of reasonably priced housing for scholars, kings ordered the establishment of official rent surveyors in university cities to determine rental rates for properties rather than allowing landlords to dictate rates. This prevented landlords from colluding and setting higher rents for students than they charged other residents. However, landlords were still allowed to require the students to whom they rented to post sureties for their rent and for damages. Even in the Middle Ages, damage deposits and payment of the first and last months' rents in advance were standard lease terms.

Students, of course, tended to live as close to their instructors and their lectures as they could. Businesses that supplied students with school supplies, food, drink, and other essential services and products gravitated to these areas as well. As a result, the neighborhoods where the masters first gave their lectures became the university quarters within the cities, many of which have survived to the present day.

Universities seldom owned any buildings until near the end of the Middle Ages. In the early 15th century, individual colleges, such as those in Oxford and Cambridge, were the first to construct buildings especially designed for the needs of higher education. Drawing on the plans of contemporary monasteries and the large townhouse complexes of the wealthy known as *inns*, these buildings took the form of a large hollow square or rectangle whose sides contained housing for the students, lecture halls, a kitchen, a chapel, and other facilities (fig. 32). In the center of this quadrangle, there was an open space which was landscaped and kept as a garden. This design became the model for university buildings for centuries afterwards.

The earlier lack of permanent facilities was actually something of an advantage for students at the universities. Students could easily pack up, leave, and study elsewhere if a plague or war threatened the city or if the ordinary citizens of the city did something that displeased the university students. For example, when a student was killed by a city resident and the city failed, in the eyes of the students, to adequately punish the wrong-doer or otherwise make redress for the slaying, the students would call a halt to studies and threaten to leave unless the city made reparations. The students sometimes took similar action on occasions when city officials punished a scholar, rightly or wrongly, for some offense. If the city did not capitulate, the students left and

Fig. 32. A college quadrangle in Oxford. Although these buildings are post-medieval, the ground plan is typical of English colleges in the late Middle Ages. Buildings containing classrooms, a library, residence halls, kitchen, and dining hall form a square enclosing a central open space.

were followed by the instructors, money lenders, prostitutes, manuscript copyists, stationers, and other tradespeople that relied on the students' business. Usually, they didn't have to follow them very far. Neighboring towns were often quite willing to offer students generous accommodations and liberal terms in exchange for all the revenue the university would generate as well as the prestige that hosting a university conferred. Students sometimes dispersed to various cities which already possessed either a university or at least a *studia* that offered instruction in their specialty. Regardless of the destination, these migrations were usually temporary. The students returned to their original host city after its citizens made amends, although intervention by kings or other high secular authorities was often necessary to bring about this rapprochement. Royal intervention frequently took the form of coercion or outright punishment of the city's residents and the conferral of additional rights on the students at the citizens' expense. Without such strong intervention, migrations were sometimes prolonged and resulted in new universities being founded. However, every migration did eventually come to an end. And, while some of the new schools survived, many of them lasted no more than a few generations since most students were eventually drawn back to the original university.

Life in the Universities

It is difficult to describe the "average" medieval university student and his experience while pursuing his studies. As previously discussed, many of the students were clerics, but this did not mean that all of them were sober, mature churchmen. There was also an ever-increasing number of lay students. These were mostly sons of the urban middle and upper classes but there were a few sons of the nobility as well. In addition, the ages of the students varied greatly, with mobs of arts students in their teens sharing campuses alongside serious law and medical students in their late twenties and thirties. With all these variations in mind, let us look at some aspects of medieval university life. In some of these matters, some of the activities of medieval students appear comparable to those of modern college students, but other were uniquely medieval activities.

New Students

The youth and relative inexperience of many new students meant that they needed to be protected. As was common for travel in the Middle Ages, students often joined together with other students or with merchants, pilgrims, and other travelers for mutual protection on their journey. In England, parents sometimes employed professional "fetchers" who escorted their sons from home to the university. Students from wealthy and noble families journeyed to the universities with their own retinues of guards and servants, just as they did on any other trip. The prospective students frequently carried large sums of money to pay for their fees and other expenses of their first term, and so were appealing targets for highwaymen. Traveling as part of a group protected these young men from such predators, but they were still subject to arbitrary tolls, often simply extortion, exacted by the various local lords of the lands through which they happened to pass. Some kings and other nobles addressed this problem by declaring scholars to be immune from all tolls within their realms.

Besides professional fetchers, some families sent a relative or a trusted family friend or servant along with the young student or to meet him upon his arrival at the university. Parents of younger students also relied on these relatives or friends to help place their sons in suitable lodgings and find a good master if the parents had not made such arrangements in advance. As the number of colleges grew, it became easier for parents to pre-select both housing and schooling for their sons, assuming that the sons met the admission standards or that the families had the right connections to get them into the college of their choosing. Some of the youngest students appear to have been placed directly with tutors. In these circumstances, the student lived with his tutor and was subject to that tutor's discipline much as though he was the student's surrogate parent. Such tutors were often older scholars who were working on their own course of studies.

While entrance examinations became increasingly common for the colleges, there were no formal entrance requirements for the universities themselves, although a working knowledge of Latin was necessary. If a man could find a master willing to enroll him, he could become a university student. Thus, at least in the early years of the universities, many freshmen enjoyed considerable freedom in choosing their educational arrangements.

Once the new student was safely delivered, enrolled, and housed, he was then faced with being initiated into the brotherhood of university scholars. Hazing of new students occurred despite repeated efforts at some universities in the later Middle Ages to prevent it. Some of these initiation rituals were quite complex. At some universities, new students were often referred to as *bejauni*. This was a contraction of the French phrase *bec-jaune*, literally a "yellow-bill" or "yellow-beak." This term was comparable in meaning to the modern English "greenhorn" or "rookie." The *bejauni* were treated mockingly as wild animals that had to be "civilized" before they were fit to mingle with the other scholars. They had to undergo various operations to remove their horns, tusks, and noxious body odor. The "operations" involved much rough handling by senior students and applications of irritating substances to the luckless freshman. In other universities, primarily in France, new students were sometimes treated as criminals who had to atone for their crimes or as sinners who had to be purged of their taint. Their atonement or purgation was achieved through their submission to numerous blows, often inflicted using books or other objects. Regardless of the locale and the pretenses for humiliating the new arrivals, the results were the same in the end: the newcomers were battered and then had to treat their tormentors to a party with food and wine. The expenses for these parties could drain the new student of much of the cash intended to sustain him through his first term. Money was also extorted from new students by stealing their books and forcing them to pay a ransom for their return. Universities attempted to protect newcomers, many of whom were only in their early teens, from these abuses, but the fact that measures against exploiting new students had to be repeatedly reissued suggests that these customs persisted.

Besides monetary penalties, new students were some times subjected to other indignities such as having to stand aside to allow upperclassmen to pass by. In some colleges, new students had to serve meals to their seniors before they could sit and eat. Breaches of etiquette were punishable by blows. Universities sometimes acted to halt this sort of bullying as well. For example, in 1466, the University of Heidelberg forbade upperclassmen from throwing dirt on new students and forcing them to sing. However, these and other prohibitions were presumably unsuccessful since the tradition of picking on freshman certainly continued for centuries after the Middle Ages.

Benefit of Clergy and the Special Status of Scholars

University students and masters generally enjoyed special legal status in medieval society. Most of the early university scholars were members of the clergy and were accorded the same special treatment regardless of whether they were studying or were actively performing their religious duties. An important part of these special clerical privileges was protection from secular authorities. This protection was commonly referred to as *benefit of clergy*. When a cleric was accused of criminal activity and arrested, secular authorities did not have the right to try and punish him. Only the Church had that right, and so the accused cleric had to be handed over to the Church for trial and punishment. In practice, this meant that felonious monks and priests received much lighter penalties that ordinary people for their criminal conduct because ecclesiastic courts had a different range of penalties than secular courts. Lay courts, such as those administered by a noble lord, could impose fines, permanent banishment, mutilation, or even death on convicted criminals, but the goal of the ecclesiastic courts was to reform the offender and help him to save his soul. As a result, ecclesiastic punishment was usually intended to correct the guilty on a more spiritual level. Thus, a person who violated a law of the Church would be ordered by an ecclesiastic court to perform penance to purge his sins. For laymen, ecclesiastic courts imposed penances such as making a donation to the Church, going on a pilgrimage, or undergoing a humiliating public ceremony, which sometimes involved being stripped and whipped. As for clerics found guilty by ecclesiastic courts, they were punished by penances as well. These included pilgrimages, imprisonment, being stripped of their offices, and being reassigned to onerous tasks. As these examples show, *benefit of clergy* allowed guilty clerics to escape the severe physical punishments, such as mutilation, branding, or death, which a lay court might have imposed for the same offenses.

Under *benefit of clergy*, clerics attending universities who were accused of criminal acts were tried in the court of the bishop or archbishop who had jurisdiction over the university instead of being tried by a municipal court. However, this privilege was extended to lay university students as well as clerics from the earliest days of the universities. Thus, all university scholars were a protected group. Some later university charters further expanded the jurisdiction of the courts of the bishops or archbishops to cover all the employees of the universities, stationers and other tradesmen closely tied to the universities, and all their families as well. At many universities, the bishops and archbishops delegated their authority to try scholars and others to the chancellors whom they had appointed to govern the universities in their stead. Minor offenses were sometimes punished by a short stint in the chancellor's prison while severe offenses, such as murder, were often punished only by expulsion from the university.

In addition to the privileges which were derived from the clerical status of the first university students, scholars often benefited from other preferences bestowed on them by secular authorities as well. Kings conferred such financial benefits as entitling scholars to buy their foodstuffs and wine free of taxes. Kings also frequently assumed the role of protector of the scholars and universities within their realms. As discussed in the next section, scholars sorely needed such powerful protection at times.

Violence

Scholars were frequently armed and sometimes dangerous. Court records show that, from 1297 to 1322, members of the faculty and student body of Oxford University killed 13 people, including fellow scholars as well as ordinary citizens of Oxford. However, based on the limited evidence available, it appears that scholars were no more prone to committing homicide than any other people in the Middle Ages. These fatalities simply show that scholars typically behaved no better than anyone else did. Still, there were violent outbursts in some cities which are clearly attributable to the presence of the universities and the conflicts which arose between scholars and ordinary citizens. Students provided a source of revenue for many townspeople, from rent for lodging to sales of food and drink. But even money was not always enough to make up for the arrogant, disruptive, and sometimes riotous behavior of the students. Further, the special status and privileges enjoyed by the scholars was a constant source of irritation to many local residents. Officials in late 13th century Paris complained that university scholars went unpunished for committing robberies and burglaries, attacking and killing innocent citizens, abducting women, and ravishing virgins because of the protections provided by benefit of clergy. While these accusations likely exaggerated the extent of the problem, the youth of many of the students, combined with their freedom from most ordinary responsibilities and their protected status, probably did encourage students to treat the citizens with contempt as well as to actually commit some crimes. As might be expected, tensions between town and gown boiled over at times.

For example, in Oxford in 1355, an argument between some students and a tavern keeper over the quality of wine being served led to a brawl which escalated into an all out battle the following day, with both factions armed with bows, arrows, and other weapons. The scholars were badly beaten by the townspeople, with several scholars being killed and many others severely wounded. The enmity between the two sides was so intense that some of the fallen students were allegedly scalped by Oxford residents. Many of the students' halls were sacked and a few were put to the torch. The surviving scholars fled and all university activities in Oxford stopped. Upon hearing of the disturbance, King Edward III quickly ordered a special commission to investigate the incident and punish those responsible. As a result, Oxford's mayor and bailiffs were sent to prison for a time and the local sheriff removed from office. The king unilaterally pardoned all the scholars for any offenses they may have committed and formally requested the university to resume lectures. Further, the king took away some of the city's legal authorities, ranging from the regulation of food brought into the city to the punishment of people for carrying unauthorized weapons, and gave them to the university. The city was also ordered to restore all the property taken from the scholars. Finally, the mayor, bailiffs, and sixty leading citizens of Oxford had to make a donation to a local church, part of which was then given to the scholars, and attend a mass on the anniversary of the attack in perpetuity. Despite the Reformation and intervening centuries, the residents of Oxford were not freed of this obligation until 1825.

Comparable riots and battles occurred at Cambridge, Paris, Orleans, Toulouse, and other universities during the Middle Ages. The outcomes were usually the same: the citizens were forced to admit they were in the wrong, pay a fine (some of which went to the university and its students), make valuable concessions to the university, and undergo public humiliation. But it should be remembered that neither side was completely innocent. In Paris, for example, citizens sometimes broke into buildings used as classrooms at night and vandalized them. This and other hostile actions towards the scholars were enough of a problem that authorities in Paris took action to stop them.

While much of the students' hostility was directed at the townspeople, students also fought amongst themselves. Friction between rival halls and colleges as well as between students of different nationalities also lead to assaults and even murder at times. However, none of these conflicts approached the level of the pitched battles in which all students united against city residents.

Men who pretended to be students as well as students who had dropped out of school but stayed on in university cities also engaged in violence and criminal activities. Many of these idlers sought the protection afforded by the genuine students' clerical status while eking out a living by gambling or other less savory means. A few became bandits and haunted the roads leading into the university cities. To police the student body and weed out the false scholars, enrollment with one of the university's masters or with one of the colleges became a requirement for proving one's status as a legitimate scholar. Some universities went further and required all students to enroll within thirty days of their arrival. Students who could not produce proof of enrollment were periodically driven out of the cities.

Student Pastimes

The only pastime which university officials formally encouraged for scholars was taking quiet walks in the nearby countryside. This wholesome exercise, along with the fresh air, was recommended for maintaining the students' health. As clerics, university students were expected by the Church to shun all other idle pursuits and devote themselves to their studies with same fervor that they should show in performing all their religious duties. The Church expected this of all its servants. After all, priests and other clergy were prohibited from hunting, gambling, and many other common forms of recreation. However, many members of the clergy, from humble parish priests to noble archbishops, routinely violated these restrictions, so it comes as little surprise that university students did as well.

Some students enjoyed hunting and fishing, even when it involved poaching. In the early 15th century, a statute issued by King Henry V on discipline at the universities specifically cited students at Oxford for poaching and reminded them of the prohibition of such activity. But this and other laws appear to have had little impact. Colleges still found it necessary to continually remind their members that they were prohibited from keeping dogs, hawks, and ferrets, which were all animals used for hunting, in their rooms. Sometimes the list of animals was even more extensive, as at Peterhouse College in Cambridge, which extended its ban on pets in the early 15th century to apes, wolves, bears, and harts. One can only imagine the pranksters who made these additional prohibitions necessary.

Even more than poaching, scholars enjoyed drinking wine. Any event, from religious feasts to celebrations for earning a degree, provided an excuse for drinking. However, it may be unfair to single out the scholars as especially heavy drinkers, since most members of society also consumed alcoholic beverages whenever the opportunity was presented. Still, at least in the eyes of many of their contemporaries, university scholars were notorious for their thirst for wine. And, wine and taverns often played a part in students' misconduct. Besides being a factor in major public disorders, such as the riots at Oxford discussed previously, wine and taverns contributed to more mundane problems such as the violation of the civic curfew. Curfew was a crime prevention measure, and anyone abroad at night in the dark streets was presumed to be up to no good and so was subject to arrest. City watchmen enforcing the curfew sometimes encountered groups of students who had been drinking all evening and were out on the streets only because they had been thrown out of the taverns when they closed at curfew. Late night brawls often resulted from these confrontations. The students appear to have won many of these fights, likely because they often outnumbered the watchmen. Even when the students were arrested, all that the city officials could do was turn them over to bishop or his chancellor. Any ordinary citizen who broke the curfew was fined, while those who repeatedly or violently broke law, as some students did, were punished more severely.

In addition to fishing and hunting (or poaching) and drinking, university students amused themselves with other pastimes which were also enjoyed by the rest of medieval society. These included gambling with dice and later cards, when they were introduced in the late 14th century, and attending public spectacles such as wrestling matches, bull- or bear-baiting, and performances by traveling musicians, actors, and other entertainers. Scholars also played chess as well as ball games, including early forms of tennis or handball, and participated in martial sports including archery, practicing with swords, and tilting. While such activities were popular, bishops and others responsible for administering the universities banned students from participating in many of these pastimes, even chess, on the grounds that they should be spending their time studying and not engaging in idle pursuits. Further, university administrators knew that some of these activities led to worse ones, such as the deadly quarrels that all too often followed shady games of chance at taverns. At Bologna, officials tried hardest to keep students from gambling during the three months before they took their degrees. This may have been to keep prospective graduates focused on their studies, but the strict ban also extended to the month *after* receiving a degree. Thus, their goal was more likely to keep students from running up big debts and then fleeing. Despite these bans and restrictions, all these forms of recreation, along with drinking wine, remained popular among students.

Students enjoyed some seasonal activities as well. Like schoolboys, university students celebrated the feasts of St. Nicholas and of the Holy Innocents. In England, students in the colleges elected their own *lord of misrule* or *king of the beans* who acted much like the boy bishops of the cathedral schools. Dressed up in the most outlandish outfits they could create, these "lords" and "kings" led their followers in Christmas revels. Students at Perpignan also dressed up in costumes on St. Nicholas' Day and on St. Catherine's Day (25 November) and St. Eulalia's Day (12 February) as well. For the latter two saints' days, the students dressed themselves in outfits that caricatured women, Jews, and Muslims. Such mummery may have originated in plays or processions honoring the two female saints. But, by 1381, only forty-two years after the university was founded, officials banned students from wearing costumes for these festivals. This ban, like others, may have been motivated by increasingly outrageous or disrespectful behavior by students who were emboldened by the anonymity that the costumes provided.

Not all wintertime celebrations involved costumes. On the day of the first snowfall in Bologna, students made snow balls and gave them to residents of the city in exchange for money, wine, or food. The students used their takings to throw themselves a party later that day. Given the mischievous and occasionally destructive nature of students, one might suspect that there was originally an element of extortion in this practice and that citizens "bought" the snow balls to prevent the students from throwing them at passers-by.

Like the rest of Christian medieval society, university students also celebrated in the period just before Lent and its forty days of fasting began. In many cities, the students joined in the general pre–Lenten carnivals. At some universities, the students conducted their own special amusements. Like younger pupils, students were permitted to conduct pre–Lenten cock-fighting at some universities. Students at Cambridge in the 14th century also observed the days before Lent with burlesques similar to the mock "lords" and "kings" of the Christmas season, except the targets of the jokes at this time of year were the university officials. Dressed as chancellors and the like, the students paraded through the city while ringing bells and blowing trumpets. The university administration was not amused and acted to ban this humorous display of contempt for authority.

Unfortunately, students engaged in some even less socially acceptable forms of recreation. In addition to the late night carousing and clashes with city watchmen previously discussed, vandalism was already a part of university life in the Middle Ages. On occasion, students at some universities wantonly destroyed crops in nearby fields and orchards in the fall. In Leipzig, university officials had to warn students to stop interfering with the city's hangman when he was performing his duties. And at all universities, there were students who patronized prostitutes despite attempts by authorities to curb such activity. At Heidelberg, for example, students discovered going to brothels were fined and their names publicly listed to shame them.

Clothing

Students who were clerics were encouraged to wear the plain, dark tunics and robes appropriate for their religious vocation. As clerics, they also wore their hair tonsured. The tonsure was a style of haircut in which the crown of the head was shaved completely, leaving a fringe of hair encircling the head. As discussed in the chapter 9, this distinctive haircut was an outward sign of a man's religious vows. In addition, clerics in western Europe were also customarily clean shaven. As for lay students, there were no requirements that they be tonsured or that they shave their beards or moustaches, although they were expected to dress themselves seriously and soberly. But wearing clothes and hairstyles that shock one's elders seems to have been a part of university life from at least the late 13th century. Those students, both lay and cleric, who could afford them wore clothes cut in the latest styles and made from brightly colored fabrics and had expensive, fashionable shoes as well. Further, some also wore the latest hairstyles, regardless of any religious obligations to be tonsured and clean shaven. Thus, in the 14th century, students who kept up with latest fashions in personal grooming wore their hair long and flowing and had full beards and moustaches. Some colleges required their members to dress conservatively, but university authorities often found that there was little they could do to compel all students to dress properly. However, a group of bishops in England responded to the problem by agreeing that they would not allow any degrees or offices to be conferred on any clerical scholar until he shaved and dressed appropriately. As a result, clerics attending the English universities may have been able to dress as they liked while in school, but they had to conform if they wanted to graduate and get a job. By the end of the Middle Ages, universities began to be more successful in requiring students to wear plain, uniform clothing. This and other restrictive measures were all part of the higher degree of discipline which university officials imposed on students in the 15th century.

As for the clothing of the masters, chancellors, and other university officials, by the 14th century, they had started to wear distinctive robes which signified their academic standing or their office. They typically wore long robes called *cappa clausa*. They also wore hats. Two of the most popular styles were the *pileus*, which was a form of beret that was worn pulled down tightly on the wearer's head so that it resembled a beanie with a small stem projecting at the top, and the *biretta*, which was another form of beret which more resembled the modern beret with a snug, wide headband but with a very floppy and loose top. The *cappa*, *pileus*, and *biretta* were derived from the garments worn by contemporary clerics, which is not surprising given that so many of the masters and others at the universities were clerics. Incidentally, the mortarboard hat commonly used at graduations today did not appear until the 16th century. It was originally a variation on the *biretta*, which had the top portion of the hat made in the shape of a square instead of a circle. Known as the *pileus quadratus* or *bonnet carre*, the square top was large and floppy at first, but some unknown scholar soon came up with the idea of placing a small square board inside his to stiffen the top and keep it from falling over his face. As for the color of these academic costumes, scarlet was a popular shade, likely in part because it was more expensive to produce than many other dyes and so conveyed prestige. However, the colors and trims of these robes and hats varied greatly between the universities. For example, theologians at some universities wore black robes, while those elsewhere wore white. From these beginnings, universities later developed complex schemes of color and styles of robes to signify a scholar's area of study, academic status, and any offices he held within the university. Complete academic dress appears to have been worn primarily on formal occasions since records at some university include complaints about masters failing to wear their proper attire to official faculty convocations. This also suggests that medieval masters likely wore plainer and more functional versions of the *cappa* and other garments for everyday teaching.

Discipline

While some aspects of medieval student life, such as dressing as one pleases, still have parallels at universities today, some fortunately do not. One such unpleasant practice developed from the general requirement that all students had to know and speak Latin to attend the universities. In Heidelberg and other universities in German-speaking areas this requirement led to the creation of the *wolf*. The wolf was an official, presumably drawn from the ranks of the students, who spied on the students to ensure that they spoke only Latin and not their native languages with other students, whether in their residences or in lecture halls. Students who slipped up and were found out by the wolf were fined. Other universities demanded that their students speak only Latin as well, but only the German universities carried enforcement to such an extreme. In England, students were sometimes allowed to speak French as well as Latin but, regardless of the language, it was usually a matter for the individual colleges to enforce this requirement. At some colleges in England and France, not speaking in Latin, leaving a door open, and other minor offenses of house rules were typically punished by *sconcing*. A student who was *sconced* had to buy wine for the benefit of his fellows. The amount to be purchased varied with the severity of the offense. One of the most severe offenses appears to have been accusing the senior fellows of imposing a *sconce* simply because they had run out of money to buy their own wine. Such a rude assertion provoked calls for the accuser's expulsion.

As for other forms of discipline, physical punishment, apart from punishments such as confinement in the chancellor's jail for criminal acts, was not a feature of the medieval higher education until the late 15th century, when some universities began instituting corporal punishment. As discussed previously, before this time, a scholar who engaged in disruptive activity was punished by the bishop's or chancellor's court, with expulsion being the most severe penalty that the court could impose. Even when some universities began employing this as part of their stricter discipline for students, only the youngest and poorest students appear to have been subjected to such humiliating punishments. Records at some of these universities suggest that wealthier or other higher status students were let off with fines or even lesser punishments for offenses for which poorer students were publicly whipped.

The School Day and School Year

Schedules varied between universities but a typical day at a medieval university started with a two hour lecture beginning at 9:00 AM. The first lectures of the day were those delivered by the masters. At 1:30 or 2:00 PM, there was another two hour lecture followed by a one-and-a-half hour lecture at 3:30 or 4:00 PM. As discussed previously, these afternoon lectures were usually the *extraordinary* lectures and included those delivered by senior students as part of their degree training. There were, of course, no lectures on Sunday since this was officially the day of rest for Christian Europeans. However, the two day weekend was still many centuries away so, as with the rest of medieval society, Saturday was a work day for the students and masters.

The school years at the different universities all provided approximately the same number of class days: 130 to 150 days. The longest school year was at Bologna, where instruction began on 19 October and ended on 7 September. However, there was a 10 day holiday at Christmas, a 3 day (later 3 week) one for the pre–Lenten carnival, a 14 day holiday at Easter, and 2 days off in May or early June for Whitsuntide. (Whitsunday marked the end of the season of Pentecost and took place 7 weeks after Easter.) In addition, there were numerous one day holidays throughout the year for the myriad of saints' feasts and other holy days which were observed by all of medieval Christian society including scholars. And finally, during weeks that did not have a scheduled holy day, students at Bologna were given Thursday off. In England, the school year ran from 9 October to 20 July and was roughly divided into quarters with a 4 week Christmas holiday, a 3 week break at Easter, and a 10 day Whitsuntide holiday. The carnival before Lent was not a major event in England and so passed without a significant break in school routine. Again, all holy days were observed, but English students did not receive the extra day off which their Italian counterparts did when there was not a holy day that week.

Completion of Studies

Only a small fraction of the students who enrolled in universities in the Middle Ages completed their studies and were awarded degrees. Today, starting at a university but not earning a degree is usually seen as failure. Some of the students in the medieval universities who did not earn degrees were certainly academic failures. However, many appear to have studied successfully for some time and then left before completing a degree. One historian has estimated that approximately half of all scholars who enrolled as arts students left the universities without achieving a degree and that at the German universities, for example, the average stay for arts students was only about 19 months. Only ten to twenty percent of arts students are estimated to have stayed and studied for the entire six years required for a masters of arts degree. Yet, failing to complete a degree did not mean that the time spent at the university was wasted. For most of the Middle Ages, having studied at a university, even without obtaining a formal degree, provided many men with an education and credentials sufficient for successful and lucrative careers, both within the Church and in the secular world. Further, there were students who completed their studies but did not obtain their degrees. As explained later in this chapter, the awarding of degrees did not automatically follow the successful completion of a scholar's course work. And degrees were not always worth the additional expense and effort of securing them unless a scholar planned on teaching or undertaking advance studies. However, the value of degrees gradually increased outside the realm of the universities during the final centuries of the Middle Ages. For example, as noted in the previous chapter, some municipalities began requiring even secondary school teachers to have completed their degrees rather than simply to have studied at a university. Thus, by the end of the Middle Ages, merely having studied and learned was no longer sufficient. If a scholar wanted his educational qualifications to be accepted and respected by society at large, he had to obtain a certification of his academic achievements. He had to complete a degree.

Length of Studies

A student was expected to take six years to earn his master of arts degree but, in the later Middle Ages, the period of study was often reduced to four and a half years at many universities. In the six year course of studies which was common in the 13th century, the student attended lectures and disputations for the first two years. For the next two years, the student participated in disputations as well. Upon successful completion of his fourth year, the student could qualify for the degree of bachelor of arts. However, the title of bachelor of arts appears to have initially been conferred on any undergraduate student who had mastered his subjects well enough to be able to do at least some lecturing. Consequently, even new students were sometimes deemed to be bachelors since their pre-university education had trained them well in the trivium and quadrivium. Gradually, the status of bachelors became more formalized and became a recognized degree. In any event, the bachelor or fourth-year arts student was typically required to give lectures during the final two years of his studies. After completing his sixth year, the student could petition the masters of the university for his own master's degree.

For advanced studies, a master of arts degree or an equivalent level of knowledge was required. There was sometimes a minimum age requirement as well. For example, at Bologna, a student had to be at least twenty years old to be admitted to the doctorate program for medicine. Completing the course of study of medicine at Bologna was expected to take four years if a student already had completed his masters of arts degree and five years if he had not. In the 13th century, the university in Paris offered a bachelors degree in medicine as well as a master's degree. A medical student could qualify for this bachelor's degree after 32 months of study. To qualify for a license as a master or doctor of medicine at Paris required a total of five and a half years of study for a student who held a master of arts degree and six years for one who did not. While there were no formal age requirements for medical students at Paris, the de facto minimum age was twenty, since Paris required candidates for masters of arts degrees to be at least twenty years old. Montpellier, the most famed of the early university medical schools, required 42 months of study for a bachelor's degree in medicine for a student who did not hold a master of arts degree and 30 months for one who did. For the degree of doctor of medicine, Montpellier required five years of study for master of arts degree-holders and six years of study for those who did not hold an M.A. Montpellier imposed an additional requirement on all of its degree candidates which no other medieval medical school did: to qualify for a degree, whether as a bachelor or as a doctor, a student had to undergo a trial period of actually practicing medicine. For a bachelor's degree, the period was six months. A total of eight months' practice was required for the doctorate. While not specified, this trial practice was likely some form of internship with an experienced doctor.

Medicine is one of the longest courses of advanced study today, but it was the shortest one in the Middle Ages. Obtaining a degree in canon law, civil law, or theology took significantly longer. In 14th century Paris, attaining a bachelor's degree in canon law required 48 months of study over a six year period and a total of 88 months of study was needed for a master's degree. As for civil law, a scholar studying at Bologna could qualify for a bachelor's degree in civil law after five to six years of study. An additional one to two years of study were required for the master's degree, which was also referred to as a doctorate since the terms doctor and master were frequently used interchangeably in the Middle Ages.

Theology had the longest course of studies. In 1389 in Paris, after completing his arts education, a would-be theologian had to study for twelve years if he was a member of the regular clergy and fourteen years if he was secular clergy (see chapter 9). For the first five to seven years, he attended lectures on the Bible, the *Sentences* by Peter the Lombard, and various other works such as the writings of the early fathers of the Christian Church. He then delivered his own lectures on one book from the New Testament and one book from the Old Testament. After completing this work, he could qualify as a bachelor of theology after passing an examination administered by four doctors of theology. He then went on to give more advanced lectures on the Bible for two years and engage in disputations for another four years. Theology disputations appear to have been especially rigorous. Some were group projects and were conducted as marathon efforts, lasting from six in the morning until six at night without breaks. After successfully completing all these requirements, the scholar emerged a doctor or master of theology, provided that he also met the age requirement. The minimum age for a doctor of theology was 35, but this was likely not an impediment for most would-be theologians, given the length of the course of studies.

Examination and Graduation

Once a scholar had completed all the requirements for his degree, he could petition the governing masters, or regents, of the university for his degree. His petition stated the number of terms that he had attended the university and that he had attended a sufficient number of lectures, read all the required texts, and delivered all the requisite lectures to junior students. At some universities, there was an additional requirement that a number of masters, in addition to the master with whom the student was enrolled, testify that they personally knew the student to be qualified.

After the facts in the student's petition were verified, he was examined by a panel of masters. This was an oral examination. Many of these exams appear to have been pro forma. After all, universities in the Middle Ages were not the large and frequently impersonal institutions which they have become today. The masters examining the prospective graduate and any masters who testified on his behalf personally knew the master with whom the student was enrolled and likely knew the student personally as well. As a result, the examining masters presumably had a good understanding of the student's qualifications before the formal examination began. However, there appear to have been instances in which candidates who had not achieved adequate levels of academic competence begged or bribed the examiners to obtain their degrees. In any case, rather than being rigorous tests of a candidate's knowledge, the examinations appear to have simply verified that the candidate had completed his full course of studies and met all the formal requirements for graduation. The fact that those who applied for degrees were seldom rejected supports this conclusion. Further, at some universities, students from noble families were entirely excused from these public examinations, although such waivers may reflect the privileges of rank as much as the relative worth of the exams. However, not all examinations must have been cordial since at least one German university, Leipzig, required students to swear an oath not to exact revenge on any of their examiners. The few instances in which the reasons for refusing a degree are known suggest why such an oath was necessary. Rather than for any academic inadequacies, those degree candidates who were rejected were often cited for engaging in inappropriate personal behavior, including engaging in knife-fights and other violent acts.

After completing the examination, the would-be graduate had to await formal notification of the results. When the servant of the university arrived to deliver the news, the scholar was expected to reward this messenger with a dish of sweetmeats (candies). Assuming that the message was good news, the scholar then had to begin giving out many other gifts and payments as well. These gifts typically included a banquet for the examining masters and the rest of the faculty within the graduate's area of study. The new graduate was also frequently expected to give gowns, caps, gloves, knives, and other items to the masters as well to the chancellor and other university functionaries. In exchange, the masters presented the new graduate with a ring and a biretta as symbols of his academic achievement and his status as a member of the guild of university masters.

Gifts to the chancellor were necessary because, as the bishop's representative, he conferred the license to teach on the graduate. The license to teach was distinct from the degree conferred by the masters. The degree certified the scholar's education and admitted him into the guild of university masters. But the Church retained control over who was allowed to teach at the universities, and so any scholar who desired to stay on and teach at the university or was required to had to obtain a license to teach as well as a degree. In practice, this meant that most masters of arts and many masters of the higher arts obtained licenses to teach in addition to their degrees. There was no separate examination for the license and the Church prohibited charging a fee for the license, but chancellors appear to have always expected scholars to give them gifts in exchange for the licenses.

Over time, the banquets, gowns and other such "gifts" were increasingly commuted to monetary payments. At the English universities, payments to masters and other officials at graduation came to be a substantial part of university revenues. Occasionally, as an act of charity, wealthy students who were graduating would pay the costs for the feasts and gifts or of the cash payments for poor students so that they too would be able to graduate and receive their degrees.

In addition to the required gifts or payments, new graduates and their families sometimes spent lavishly on celebrations. Some of these medieval graduation parties were blowouts even by modern standards. In Italy, some graduating students from noble families held jousting tournaments as part of their celebrations. Some universities attempted to limit the extravagance of such festivities. A few tried to restrict the entertainment and music at them, even going so far as to ban dancing at these parties.

After the parties were over, new degree holders moved on in their careers. Some left the universities and took up positions in the Church or in civil governments. Others stayed on at the universities. Some stayed because they were required to do so. As mentioned previously, new degree holders at Oxford and Cambridge were often required to stay on and teach for a year or two. Clearly, this was an attempt to meet the demand for lecturers in times of chronic shortages. Even where there was not such a requirement, recent graduates appear to have frequently stayed at the universities and begun teaching immediately upon graduation. It is estimated that most of the masters of arts giving lectures at Paris in the 14th century were under the age of 25.

The Cost of a University Education

A university education has never been cheap. Fees for attending universities were not as clear defined in the Middle Ages as they are today. There were no course catalogs with schedules of tuition charges and lab fees. Combined with the difficulties of converting medieval currencies to modern values, it is impossible to establish a meaningful estimate of the total cost of a medieval university education. As discussed in this chapter, students' expenses included the cost of travel to the university and the necessities (room, food, and drink) while they were resident there. For their studies, they had to pay fees for lectures as well as for parchment, ink, and the rental or purchase of texts. Then there were also fees for joining a "nation" or other student group. These fees were often on a sliding scale based on a student's means. For example, at Bologna, the guild of German students charged new members from five to sixty solidi depending on their wealth and status. And, as discussed in the previous section, students who successfully completed their studies and took a degree had to pay still more fees or provide "gifts" to faculty members, university officials, and often to any student groups to which they belonged as well. At least in the early years of the universities, these fees and gifts, along with other obligations levied on new graduates, appear to have been sufficiently burdensome to deter some students from applying for their degrees despite their possession of all the necessary academic qualifications.

Another way in which some students minimized their expenses was to earn their masters of arts degree at one of the *studia* near their homes and then go abroad for higher study. Besides the convenience and savings of not having to travel far, earning one's master of arts degree at one of the *studia* was often cheaper since these less prestigious learning institutions appear to have had lower fees than the universities. Additionally, the cost of living was usually lower in the towns or small cities that were homes to the *studia* than in the larger cities that hosted the *studia generalia*, the universities.

Jews and the Universities

In addition to studying the Torah and the Talmud, educated Jews studied many of the same secular subjects as their Christian counterparts. As mentioned at the beginning of this chapter, Jews were generally not permitted to attend universities in medieval Europe. The few exceptions which have been found were all at universities in southern Europe such as at Montpellier in southern France and Padua in Italy. At Montpellier, for example, while there is no express mention of admitting non–Christian students to the university, the ruler of Montpellier and the surrounding area granted all expert instructors, regardless of their faith, the right to teach in Montpellier in 1181. Montpellier is near the Mediterranean coast and was a crossroads for trade for centuries. Peoples from around the Mediterranean, including both Jews and Muslims, were drawn to Montpellier as part of these commercial enterprises. It is quite possible that the university drew scholars and students from among all these groups, although some historians believe that there was a separate school of medicine in Montpellier run by Jewish masters and attended exclusively by Jewish students. Yet, even if there was a separate school, the faculties and students at both the Christian and Jewish schools likely had many occasions to meet and exchange ideas. Unfortunately, any intercultural contacts which existed at Montpellier and elsewhere in the south of France were severely reduced or entirely curtailed by the mid–13th century. This sudden change was a result of the Albigensian Crusade, the war fought by armies of northern France against the Cathar heretics who lived throughout this region. As part of this successful conquest of southern France, the Church instituted an inquisition and other measures to root out heresy. This increased scrutiny and regulation of people's conduct by the Church drove out most non–Christians and deterred Christians from having contact with those few who remained.

As for Padua, as discussed previously, Jewish masters sometimes taught there and university documents record a Jewish scholar graduating with a degree in medicine there in 1409. But apart from the limited evidence at Padua and Montpellier, there is little information on how Jewish scholars obtained advanced education in medieval Europe. Some likely went outside Christian Europe to schools in the Middle East or in the parts of Spain controlled by the Muslims. For those remaining in Europe, they probably learned from individual experts found in the larger Jewish communities. In a few instances, it is clear that sons learned from their fathers who were already experts in the field. In any event, the number of Jewish medical practitioners found throughout the Middle Ages, as well as the medical and other texts written by Jewish authors which have survived, prove that Jewish scholars were able to find teachers and learn advanced subjects despite being denied access to the universities.

8

Training for a Career and Earning a Living: Peasants, Craftsmen, and Merchants

Many medieval Europeans thought of their world as being organized into three orders of people: those who worked for all (the peasants), those who prayed for all (the clergy), and those who fought and ruled for all (the nobility). Since agriculture was the largest and most important enterprise in medieval Europe, the peasant who farmed the land to produce food for all of society was the accepted symbol of the working class. Merchants and craftsmen did not fit smoothly into this division of society but, in practice, were usually considered part of the last group since they were clearly neither nobles nor members of the clergy. In this chapter, we will see how children in medieval Europe learned to earn a living through agriculture, crafts, and trades. In the next chapter, we will turn to those children who entered the Church or were born into the nobility.

While there was some mobility within the classes, there was only very limited movement between the classes and most children remained within the same class as their parents. Children generally went into the same occupations as their parents. Some peasant families did manage to improve their children's prospects for the future by sending them out to learn a craft. And some peasant children even had successful careers within the Church. However, such improvement in social standing was usually only incremental. A few men of peasant or common background did become great successes. Still, such exceptions were extremely rare and most medieval Europeans lived out their lives within the class to which they born, doing the same sorts of work their parents did.

It should be noted that the Middle Ages was not an era of widespread child labor. Some children did go to work at difficult jobs at early ages, but most did not. Only with the Industrial Revolution and the mechanization of production was it economically effective to exploit child labor on a large scale. In the Middle Ages, which ended well before the introduction of steam- and even most forms of water-powered machinery, many jobs required physical strength which children lacked. This point appears to have been well recognized during the Middle Ages since children were seldom recorded as performing heavy labor. Further, in a 13th century text on raising children, the author noted that children should not do any heavy work before the age of twelve because such exertion was harmful to their physical development.

While a few children were put to work full-time at an early age, most medieval children appear to have had many years of childhood in which they were largely free of work before they began laboring in earnest.

As for the age that children started to work in the Middle Ages, twelve was usually considered a good age to choose a career and begin training. Many children did begin learning their vocations around this age, although some began much earlier. Training for younger children was not strenuous nor did it occupy their entire time. Children began by watching older children and adults work. When they were ready, children were given very simple and physically undemanding chores to perform. They were then eased into the adult world of work by being given increasingly more difficult chores until they were old enough to work on their own. This point appears to have been typically around the age of sixteen or eighteen but, depending in part upon the nature of the work, was reached by some as early as twelve or fourteen or as late as twenty or older. Thus, the age at which medieval children were consider to be adults for purposes of work was not significantly younger than that of children for many centuries after the Middle Ages. In fact, in Europe and America during the Industrial Revolution from the late 18th century through the 19th, the age at which many children first went to work was probably younger than during the Middle Ages. Only in the 20th century, with child labor laws and the expectation that every child should complete at least a high-school level education, did the age for entering the work force rise above medieval levels in industrialized countries.

Most children in the Middle Ages learned their future occupations through a combination of watching their parents and neighbors perform tasks and gradually carrying out more and more tasks until they had reached an adult level of proficiency. Through this method, children of peasants learned how to farm and maintain a household, and children of craftsmen and merchants learned their families' trades as well. Some children received training outside their families from established experts in a trade or craft. This vocational training also included giving the children increasingly more complex jobs to accomplish until they were capable of working independently. This form of job training was an *apprenticeship*. Apprenticeship is the type of career education most commonly associated with medieval Europe, and many children in the Middle Ages certainly served apprenticeships to learn their future trades. However, as explained in this chapter, far more children learned the jobs of adults through the process of watching, learning, and doing without serving formal apprenticeships.

Peasants

The largest segment of the population of medieval Europe was engaged in agriculture; growing crops and raising livestock were essential to the survival of society. Historians estimate that at least 90 percent of medieval Europeans were employed in agriculture. While this figure may seem high, the percentage of the population involved in food production did not begin to decrease significantly until the late 18th century. At that time, advances in horticulture and stockbreeding and the increased mechanization of food production enabled European countries to begin freeing larger and larger portions of their work forces from agricultural labor while still producing enough food to meet their needs. It was not until the closing decades of the 19th century that non-farm workers began to outnumber farmers in Europe and the United States.

As it was for centuries before the Middle Ages and would remain for centuries afterward, farming and stockbreeding were learned through experience. There were a few Roman texts on agriculture which survived and circulated in the Middle Ages, but these books were written for estate owners, not for the people who actually plowed the fields and tended the herds. There were also a handful of books on agriculture written during the Middle Ages. While these were largely based on the Roman examples, they did contain some new information that reflected current conditions and practices rather than those of the late Roman Empire. However, they were still directed at wealthy landowners and provided advice on managing their holdings rather than "how-to" instructions for growing crops.

For the landowners, many of whom were members of the nobility, keeping their lands productive and obtaining high yields was a matter of great importance. Besides providing sustenance for the owners of the land, their families, and everyone else who was dependent upon them, agricultural products were a source of wealth. While there were peasants who could barely tease enough food from the soil to feed their families, agriculture as a whole routinely operated well above the subsistence level in the Middle Ages. There were periods of famine caused by bad weather, wars, and other extreme conditions, but medieval Europeans typically produced sufficient harvests to feed themselves and provide enough excess so that foodstuffs were a major part of local and even international trade. Some regions took advantage of their particular climates and soils, specializing in growing certain types of crops. Wine from France, particularly from Bordeaux, is perhaps one of the best known examples, but other areas had their specialties as well. Sicily continued to be a major source of grain for all of the Italian peninsula, just as it had been in Roman times, while grains from lands that are now part of Poland were shipped to consumers across northern Europe. Even trade in grain in the form of beer formed part of international commerce by the late Middle Ages in northern Europe as well. All this trade produced revenue, and those who owned the lands that were the source of these commodities profited. But without the peasants plowing, planting, reaping, and tending the flocks, none of this would have been possible.

So how did the peasants learn the skills which, though seen as humble and inferior to those of the knight or priest, were vital to all of society? Like the children of farmers and livestock breeders before and since, they started learning their future occupation while they were still small children by watching their parents. Records of children's accidents found in coroner's reports and accounts of miraculous divine intervention show that boys as young as two or three were already falling in ditches while following their fathers as they went to till the fields. We also know that girls at this age were watching their mothers prepare food, since some came to grief when they tipped over pots of boiling pottage which they were stirring in imitation of their mothers. But farm girls' activities weren't confined to home and hearth. In one case, a little girl was playing on the threshing floor of a barn and inhaled a grain of wheat which then remained lodged in some part of her airway for two weeks. Fortunately for her, she coughed up the grain after being given holy water from a saint's shrine. Tragedies aside, these events show that children watched how fields were plowed and sown, how meals were prepared, and all the other routine tasks that were part of operating a farm.

As they grew, young children were still expected to primarily be observers rather than workers, but they were gradually given a few light chores, usually under the supervision of an adult or older sibling. However, some parents pressed their children to perform tasks that were beyond their strength or judgment. For example, children as young as four were recorded as being entrusted with supervising their younger siblings when their parents went off to work. But many members of medieval society appear to have recognized the danger of imposing such important responsibilities on young children. The language used in accounts of the accidents that resulted when one of these little babysitters wandered off and his younger brother or sister was injured or killed typically reflects recognition that the parents, not the children, were responsible for the tragedy.

Around the age of six, children were usually expected to start carrying out small, helpful chores suitable for their size, strength, and judgment. For example, children at this age began helping their families by collecting small dried sticks to use as kindling. They also picked berries and other fruits, gathered nuts, and helped weed vegetable gardens. While this last chore was undoubtedly tedious, collecting fruits and nuts sometimes provided an excuse for climbing trees. Similarly, boys and girls who lived near the shore and picked cockles and mussels at low tide to supplement their families' food supplies likely took the opportunity to play and explore a little as well. By the time they had reached the ages of six to eight, children were also expected to watch their younger brothers and sisters while their parents worked. Farm work, especially during the busy harvest season in the late summer and fall, often required both parents to be out in the fields, and so parents needed someone to watch their young children. And by this age, the children were usually able to carry out their babysitting duties without incident.

By age seven or a little older, children were considered ready to take care of any ducks or geese their families owned by guiding them to the nearest pond to feed during the day and watching out for hawks and others predators while they were there. They also ran errands, including carrying food and drink from home out to workers in the fields.

Starting at around the age of eight, tasks were increasingly divided between boys and girls, with girls being given more domestic chores while boys were given additional jobs out in the fields. However, wives and daughters of peasants often worked alongside their husbands and fathers in the fields while still cooking, cleaning, and carrying out all the other work needed to keep their families going.

Older Boys' Chores

At around the age of eight, as their strength and judgment developed, boys were often given the job of watching animals larger than fowl. Some were tasked with watching over pigs when they were let out of their pens during the day to forage for food. Others were given the job of watching sheep, which were raised in large numbers in many parts of Europe and needed constant supervision to keep them from straying too far and to protect them from predators. Sheep, like other livestock, had a high value. They yielded milk, meat and, most importantly, wool. Wool was often a major source of income for medieval farmers. Raw wool and woolen cloth were common commodities in international trade. Watching over and protecting the sheep was vital to many families' livelihoods.

A young boy might start his training to become a shepherd by accompanying an experienced shepherd such as his father, uncle, or brother. There is much more to being a shepherd than simply watching the sheep. From his mentor, the boy learned how to move the flock of sheep along and round up stray sheep without letting the others wander off. He learned how to drive off wolves, such as by using a sling to throw stones at them. A would-be shepherd also had to learn to identify diseased sheep and treat them or else cull them from the herd if they could not be cured. He also needed to learn how to care for injured sheep and to assist ewes in delivery during lambing season. The only way he learned these skills was from an experienced shepherd.

At the age of ten or eleven, a boy might be given a relatively small flock, perhaps a few dozen up but as many as eighty sheep, to watch over during the day when they were grazing and herd them back into their pens or *folds* before nightfall. As he grew and proved himself responsible, he would be given larger flocks to tend. By the age of fourteen or so, young shepherds were considered to be professionals and, according to at least one late medieval poem, were caring for flocks of two hundred or more sheep.

Also around the age of ten or eleven, boys were sometimes given the task of herding cattle out to pasture in the morning and back in again before nightfall. Unfortunately for the young cowherds, this appears to have been one of the most dangerous jobs for peasant children. Some were injured or permanently crippled when the large beasts stepped on their feet or kicked them in the legs. Still other boys were seriously injured or killed when they were gored by unruly cattle. One victim of such an accident was an eight year old boy, which again shows that some parents gave their children chores which they were too young to perform safely.

Not all peasants were shepherds or cowherds. Boys also learned how to plow fields, sow seeds, and harvest crops. For this type of farming, boys began by leading or goading the oxen which pulled the plow. Armed with a small whip or switch, a boy helped keep the team of oxen moving while his father trudged behind them, guiding the heavy plow. After the furrows were prepared, it was time to sow seeds, and boys helped again. They drove off the hungry crows and other birds that came to eat the seeds by throwing rocks at them. When the crops were ripe and ready to harvest, all available help was needed to bring in the crops before they spoiled or were damaged by the weather. Men and women, as well as boys and girls, all worked together in the frenzy of harvest activities. Children strong enough to work even served as hired labor during harvest time.

In areas which grew grapes for wine, boys were sometimes posted in small watchtowers in the vineyards. From such a vantage point, a boy could spot any birds that flew in to devour the juicy grapes and then throw rocks at them to drive them away. In some well-equipped vineyards, strings with bells were attached to the watchtower and to points around the vineyard. In these vineyards, the boy could simply grab and shake the strings to make noise to scare the birds away.

As can be seen, none of these activities were simply training exercises for the young peasant. While learning the skills needed to sustain him in adulthood, he was also making a material contribution to his family's welfare.

Older Girls' Tasks

In addition to learning how to reap grains and bind sheaves by helping with the harvest, girls learned many other skills by watching and helping their mothers. When they married, young peasant women were expected to be fully prepared to start their own households. Among the many skills which farm girls were expected to master were

- how to milk cows, goats, or sheep and transform the liquid milk into butter and cheese without having it spoil;
- how to care for the other animals which the family kept for its own food consumption, primarily pigs and chickens;
- how to grow herbs and vegetables;
- how to make a fire, bake bread, and cook a variety of dishes; and
- how to keep house and do everything else necessary to care for a family.

To learn all these skills, peasant girls slopped the hogs and collected eggs from the chickens and any other fowl the family raised. They helped their mothers weed and care for the kitchen garden where the families grew their herbs and vegetables. They cleaned the pots and dishes, swept the floors, and washed and mended the clothes. In northern Europe, girls were also expected to learn how to make barley into malt and then use it and other ingredients to brew ale and beer. By watching and imitating her mother and by taking care of her younger siblings or babysitting for neighbors, she learned how to care for children. Finally, in her free time, she was expected to card wool and spin into fine yarn for weaving into cloth. Girls in the early Middle Ages were expected to learn how to weave, and some households continued to weave their own fabric for their clothing throughout the period (fig. 12). However, most families gradually shifted to buying cloth made by professional weavers. Women continued to card and spin, but they typically sold the yarn instead of using it themselves.

A girl usually had many years to master all these skills, but a girl whose mother was disabled or dead was often expected to help with or completely take over the domestic responsibilities as quickly as possible. Such an unfortunate girl had her childhood cut short. While the magnitude of this problem cannot be established, given the high rates of mortality in the Middle Ages, it was probably not that uncommon.

As with older boys, girls too sometimes came to grief in the performance of their chores. One of the most dangerous but also the most vital and routine jobs was fetching water. Essential to cooking and cleaning, water in the countryside was drawn from springs, streams, or wells. Springs appear to have been generally safe, but streams and especially wells seem to have been the most common and risky sources of water. Drawing water from either of these two sources all too often resulted in drowning or near-drowning for girls sent to fetch a bucket of water. The risks of slipping and falling into a stream or small river while trying to stand on the bank and fill a container are fairly obvious, but wells in rural Europe in the Middle Ages presented similar risks. While we envision the wells of yesteryear as picturesque structures with low walls, a little peaked roof, and a bucket on a winch, many wells in the countryside of medieval Europe were little more than very deep, open holes in the ground. With edges worn down from use and the surrounding ground frequently slippery from the water, these wells were treacherous to use. One slip in the mud or wet grass and a girl could end up sliding or falling into the open mouth of the well. Girls were also at risk of injury in the home. Pots full of boiling soup were sometimes knocked over or slipped off their stands and scalded the unfortunate girls tending them.

Despite all these chores, children did not work from sunup to sundown. Boys and girls still had free time during the day to play, as described in chapter 3. But as they reached their mid-teens, they were expected to work more than they played until, by their late teens, they finally were part of the adult workforce. While we associate adulthood today with leaving home and establishing an existence separate from one's family, peasant children most often remained at home even after they were physically grown-up and working like adults. As we will see in chapter 10, some sons and even some daughters stayed at home and took over running the family farm from their ageing parents. Others lived with their parents until they accumulated enough resources to set up their own household.

Employment and Training Outside of the Family Farm

To improve their lot, most families needed all their children to help out at home and to work the land. Many needed all the help they could muster just to survive. Hiring out one's child would have brought in some money, but this compensation appears seldom to have been enough to offset the loss of the work the child was already performing at home. But there were exceptions. Some families were poor and landless. In these families, parents and their children eked out a living by hiring themselves out to work the land of others. There were also some families who had their own land but had more children than were needed to work it. Children from these families were sometimes sent out to work in the homes of others to perform the same sort of chores that they had learned to carry out at home. Boys were hired out to work in the fields of wealthier neighbors. Alternatively, a boy might become a house servant, but this type of employment was far more common for girls. Employment as a servant could range from simply working for neighbors during the day to becoming a live-in maidservant at a noble manor or other residence of the wealthy nearby. Some girls and boys even left the country and went to the city to find work. Children in the city sometimes entered service as well. This combination of employment and training will be discussed in more detail later in this chapter.

For children from prosperous peasant families, there was another option for vocational training: apprenticeship. Peasant families which had the necessary contacts and resources sometimes sought to advance their sons' financial and social standing by finding them an apprenticeship in a city. These formal apprenticeships are explained later in this chapter.

Craftsmen and Merchants

Like the children of peasants, many of the children of merchants and craftsmen followed their parents' professions. Most were taught the family business, whether dyeing cloth, making pottery, or engaging in international trade, by their parents or other close relatives. Again like the children of peasants, children of craftsmen and merchants began their job training while they were still quite young by observing their parents and other adults at work. Since craftsmen's workshops and merchants' offices and even storerooms were often a part of their homes, their children had constant opportunities to watch their parents and other adults at work, and many likely tried imitating what they saw just as children still do today. Thus, while as young as six or seven, these children had already begun learning their future occupations.

Learning a Craft

From watching, children progressed to doing simple chores. In craft families, these small jobs included sweeping up the work area and fetching tools and materials. One bit of evidence we have of such chores has been preserved at a site in France where pottery was made in the Middle Ages. Here, the footprints of the bare feet of the small helpers who gathered up kindling, carried heavy lumps of wet clay, and did other odd jobs for the potters have been preserved in the hardened clay. As they grew older, children in craft families began providing more assistance in producing goods and had more opportunities to closely observe how to do it themselves. Gradually, they began to participate in production, presumably first doing simple jobs which involved little risk of spoiling the materials if they made a few mistakes. As they gained experience, they were entrusted with more complex functions until they were finally able to produce an item from start to finish. For example, a shoemaker's son might have started out sweeping up the leather scraps from the workshop floor and sorting out the bits large enough to be reused. Meanwhile, he watched how his father worked in laying out the patterns, cutting the leather, and stitching the pieces together to make shoes. After a time, his father had him try his hand at these same tasks and, as the son's skills improved, had him do more of the work until he was producing goods entirely on his own.

Besides production, the shoemaker's son had to learn the other aspects of business. He learned how to judge the quality and the price of the leather which he bought from the tanners as well as how to bargain with these suppliers. He also learned how to take care of the retail operations. Children as young as ten were tasked by their parents to watch their families' shops or market stalls. In addition to simply keeping an eye on things, these older children were expected to be able to wait on customers, including making change for purchases.

If the son applied himself to his trade and learned it well, he could be a skilled craftsman by the time he reached his late teens. In the meantime, the work he performed often contributed significantly to his family's business.

Learning to Be a Merchant

Children of merchants underwent a period of training similar to that of craftsmen's children. Like the children of craftsmen, merchants' children learned to evaluate the quality of goods and the fairness of prices. But merchants were middlemen and retailers and so did not teach their children the manual skills needed for producing goods. Instead, merchants' children learned how to keep accounts of the expenses of buying and shipping goods, the prices charged when reselling them, and, depending upon where the goods were bought and sold, the exchange rates of the money issued by different governments. As this suggests, business in the Middle Ages was far more complex than is often pictured. Medieval merchants often traveled to many parts of Europe and beyond in pursuit of trade. Many maintained agents in the major trading centers scattered around the Continent and even beyond Europe in the Middle East and elsewhere.

Over the course of the Middle Ages, merchants created many financial tools to cope with the demands of international commerce. For example, to avoid having to ship large amounts of coins across long distances, they developed letters of credit. Here is a simplified example of how a letter of credit could be used:

An Italian merchant buying wool in England issued a letter of credit to the seller as payment for the wool. The letter was redeemable with any of the merchant's agents in Europe. So, the Englishman who sold the wool sent his own agent with the letter to one of the cities where the Italian merchant had a representative. The English agent traveled to the city of Bruges in the Low Countries, a noted hub of international trade. While the letter of credit could be exchanged for cash, it was far more common to use it to buy merchandise one needed instead. Per his master's instructions, the English agent then redeemed the letter of credit for finished cloth and other goods that the Italian merchant had in stock in Bruges and had all these items shipped back to his master in England. And all of this trade was accomplished without one silver penny ever changing hands.

In more complicated transactions, letters of credit were sold and purchased by other merchants before they were finally redeemed.

In addition to letters of credit, medieval merchants also developed early forms of insurance to help lessen the financial damage of the loss of goods in transit, whether from shipwreck or pirates at sea or from robbers on land. To secure supplies for the future, merchants, such as those in the wool trade, sometimes agreed to buy commodities a year or more in advance. Together with bankers, they developed various types of interest bearing loans and other financing agreements to pay for these and other purchases. Since the Church condemned charging interest as usury, these financial instruments required careful and creative formulation to avoid running afoul of canon law.

So, to be successful in international trade, a would-be merchant had to learn more than just to buy at low price and sell at a higher one. He needed to know how to read and perform basic arithmetic and learned these skills either at home or at one of the city schools described in chapter 6. But he also had to learn much that could not be taught in school. He had to develop the skill of assessing the quality and value of the merchandise he bought and sold and the ability to bargain effectively with both buyers and sellers. He had to understand the risks and estimate the costs involved in getting a cargo from one port to another, perhaps involving a long and treacherous voyage from a port on the Mediterranean coast to one on the Baltic Sea. He had to learn how to tell a real coin from a counterfeit one and calculate exchange rates. And he had to know how to use tools like letters of credit, including determining whether such a letter was worth the parchment it was written on. The best way to learn all these skills was through experience. As mentioned previously, a merchant's child began learning all these vital skills at home in his parents' offices and storehouses. Once a child displayed some understanding of the business world, he was given tasks such as helping log in goods as they were received, making entries into account books, and waiting on customers. As he matured, he was entrusted with some goods or money to manage, although his parents likely kept a close eye on matters. In the families of Italian merchants, sons as young as ten were sometimes given a small sum of money with which to speculate so that they could begin understanding how to make good business choices. By the age of fourteen, some of these boys were traveling across the seas with their fathers or other merchants to conduct trade. Some were even trading on their own accounts by this age as well, although many did not reach this level of independence until they were at least eighteen. Across Europe, sons of merchants of the Hanseatic League, the trading guild centered on the north German coast, underwent comparable training and began accompanying their fathers on the long annual sea voyages and trips to great market fairs when they were twelve. Eventually, these older boys and young men became sufficiently experienced that they were trusted to take voyages on their own or were placed as agents of the family business in cities far from home. Like those of peasants and craftsmen, the sons of merchants frequently became a valued part of their families' work forces well before their training was completed. Ultimately, these young men were prepared to become partners in the family business or, if they had acquired sufficient resources, to strike out on their own.

Daughters of Craftsmen and Merchants

So far, the focus has been on the sons of craftsmen and merchants, but their daughters received vocational training as well. Like their country counterparts, girls in urban families were trained by their mothers in the myriad housekeeping skills which they needed for their future roles as wives and mothers. These girls often received some training in the family business as well because, just as wives of peasants were expected to pitch in and help with whatever work needed to be done on the farm, wives of craftsmen and merchants frequently worked in the family business in addition to performing all the jobs expected of a wife and mother. Particularly among merchants, there are many examples scattered across medieval Europe of women who worked alongside their husbands in the family trade. Some even functioned independently of men, such as the widows of wool merchants who appear in records from 13th century London. These women were permitted to continue practicing the trade of their late husbands. And again as early as the 13th century, women were recorded as merchants importing and exporting goods in cities and towns in Germany. By the 14th century, female merchants appear in Cologne, Ghent, and other major cities trading in large quantities of a variety of essential goods such as iron, wine, and sugar. Some of these women were wives who had outlived their husbands and were continuing the family business like the London widows. Others were widows who had used their inheritances to set up new businesses of their own instead of simply continuing in their husbands' old ones. There were also many women who still had living husbands and were their business partners. Business contracts, wills, deeds, and other documents reveal that many wives were active business partners with their husbands. When a husband was traveling to trade fairs or away on other business, his wife typically managed the business in his absence. Even when husbands were at home, many appear to have relied on their wives' business skills in making decisions. In many of these marriages the husband was clearly the dominant partner, but records of business deals of some husband-wife teams indicate that wives were sometimes the heads of family businesses. And in some cases, such as for a business group headed by a mother-daughter team, the marital status of the businesswomen was considered irrelevant to the business at hand and so was not recorded.

Admittedly, some of these businesswomen may have learned their trade from their husbands rather than from their parents. However, many were clearly daughters of mercantile families and most had likely received some preparation for pursuing a trade before they were married. Besides this training, some of these women had been educated in reading, writing, and arithmetic while they were still girls living in their parents' homes (see chapter 6). The combination of education and vocational training, in addition to their often substantial dowries, made daughters of successful merchants and craftsmen very attractive wives. Prospective brides who had some personal wealth, business skills, and, presumably, social and business contacts appropriate to their status in society were highly sought after, especially by men who were already engaged in trade.

Just as in merchant businesses, wives also appear to have frequently worked alongside their husbands in craft trades. These women may have learned something about business from their parents as well as from their husbands. As we will see later in this chapter, guilds often permitted their members to teach their trades to their daughters and wives as well as to their sons, so many women from merchant and craft families had likely received at least some vocational training while growing up or after they married. These women were then capable of providing valuable assistance to their fathers or husbands in family businesses by both producing and selling goods.

As with boys, girls were sometimes placed as apprentices when their families wanted them to acquire skills which they could not learn at home. However, as explained in sections later in this chapter, formal apprenticeships were far less common for girls than for boys. Finally, like country girls, girls from merchant, craft, and other urban families were sometimes placed as servants in other households. For some girls, service became their occupation, but many used it as opportunity to earn money for a dowry and to improve their social status.

Guilds and Apprenticeships

By the 12th century, practitioners of some trades had begun organizing themselves into groups which came to be called *guilds*. Over the following centuries, many craftsmen and merchants in cities across Europe banded together with the other members of their trade and created guilds for most trades. The primary reason for practitioners of a trade to organize into a guild was to protect their economic interests. To accomplish this goal, guilds

- established and enforced quality standards for the goods produced and sold by their members. This created public trust in the quality of guild-made goods, which, in turn, helped create or maintain demand for these goods. It also helped justify the prices which the guilds set for their products;
- sought legal recognition from kings, city governments, and other political entities. This recognition included prohibiting people who were not members of a guild from competing with guild members;
- limited the number of guild members to maintain the profitability of their trades and to ensure that every guild member had a reasonable opportunity for making a living.
- fixed prices and, if necessary, limited production to maintain prices at levels favorable to guild members; and
- established qualifications and training requirements for would-be guild members.

Training for trades controlled by the guilds came to be called *apprenticeship*. Formal apprenticeships were only required when a guild member was training someone from outside the ranks of their immediate family. As mentioned previously, guilds permitted their members to teach their wives, sons, and daughters how to practice their trade. However, it must be noted that most guilds did not permit women to operate businesses on their own or to become guild members. Wives and daughters were permitted to work within a trade but typically only as part of their husband's or father's business. The regulation of female apprentices and workers by the guilds is addressed more fully later in this chapter. As for sons, they were routinely expected to take up the family trade and, after suitable training, become guild members just like their fathers. Guilds supported this practice and generally favored admitting men who already had a familial connection with someone in the trade over those who did not.

However, such in-house recruitment was often not sufficient. In London, for example, very few guild families are recorded as practicing their trades for more than two or three generations. Most appear to have survived only one or two generations before disappearing. High mortality and migration to other trades appear to have been the major causes of this high rate of turnover. To bring in new members, guildsmen were permitted to have apprentices; that is, they were allowed to take in boys who were not members of their immediate families and train them in their trade. But permitting apprentices was motivated by other factors besides the need for a supply of trained guild members. Apprentices were a source of cheap labor, and the fees their parents paid for their training was always a welcome source of income for the guild and its members. These two points are discussed in more detail later in this chapter.

Who Became an Apprentice?

Most apprentices appear to have been boys or young men from the country who were sent to the city to learn a trade from a master who had some association with their family or village. For example, a mercer (a merchant who traded in cloth) routinely dealt with men who ran cloth-making workshops in provincial towns. These cloth-makers could use their connections with the mercer to find apprenticeships for their sons within the mercery trade or other cloth-related trades in the city. Apprentices were also recruited from the country through the network of familial and social contacts. Although they had become city residents, many masters had started out as apprentices from the country themselves and so they still had many ties with their home villages and the surrounding areas. Family members or friends who knew of a boy who seem qualified would recommend him to the urban businessmen they knew. Similarly, merchants and craftsmen who needed apprentices could send word to their contacts in the country to keep an eye out for suitable candidates.

Within the cities, parents also used their familial, social, and commercial contacts to find apprenticeships for their children. Parents who were already in a trade guild but wanted their children to pursue more prestigious (and lucrative) trades used their contacts to secure apprenticeships for their children with higher-status guilds. For example, a successful fishmonger who had connections with a pepperer might have tried to place his son in an apprenticeship with that pepperer, since the international trade in spices was frequently profitable and led to contacts with wealthy consumers, including the nobility. At a humbler level, parents who worked as laborers in the city could try to help their children advance by finding them apprenticeships in one of the lesser trades such as pastry-making or one of the other food trades.

There was one group of urban children who often became apprentices: orphans. Orphans were frequently placed with merchants and craftsmen to learn a trade. Some parents, mostly fathers, made arrangements in their wills for their children to be apprenticed. In cases when a parent knew he was dying and still had time to act, he sometimes made the arrangements for his children's apprenticeships himself. These actions, whether accomplished through wills or deathbed requests, solved several problems. Since the apprentice's master provided food, shelter, and often clothing as well, apprenticeship provided a foster home for the orphan while also providing training which enabled the orphan to make a living upon reaching adulthood. When the parent had not arranged or left instructions regarding the upbringing of his surviving children, the decision was usually in the hands of the children's nearest surviving relatives. For these relatives, apprenticeship provided an easy and relatively inexpensive way to discharge their responsibilities. As with children whose parents were still alive, apprenticeships for orphans were determined by the social standing and connections of the child's parents and their wealth. Civic governments in London and other cities oversaw the treatment of orphans by their guardians and occasionally intervened to protect the orphans' interests, including ensuring that they were apprenticed appropriately.

While orphans and other children of city residents sometimes became apprentices, most apprentices appear to have been drawn from outside the city. Part of the reason for this was that children native to the cities seem to have often been in short supply. London and many other large cities appear to have had lower birth rates and higher mortality than the surrounding countryside. Part of the higher death rate is attributable to outbreaks of disease, including the Black Death, to which the crowded urban centers were particularly prone. Additionally, adults were usually better able to withstand the ravages of disease than children. Thus, medieval cities were consumers of people and required a constant influx of fresh immigrants, especially young ones, from the country to keep up and expand their populations. As a result, while some apprentices were natives to the city, most were likely newcomers.

Selecting an Apprenticeship

The child's own interests or talents rarely played a part in choosing an apprenticeship. His parents' contacts and wealth usually determined which trades were open to him. Still, it should be remembered that parents who placed their children in apprenticeships were trying to do what was in their children's best interest. Learning a trade, any trade, provided one of the few opportunities for social and economic advancement within the rigid class structure of medieval Europe. In trade, a person with skill and intelligence who worked hard could rise above his fellow commoners, although a family's wealth and connections still determined where one could start. A peasant family may well have had the social or family contacts and the money to find their son a place in one of the manual crafts such as carpentry, whereas placing him in a prestigious trade such as goldsmithing was simply out of the question. Even urban children whose parents were already members of a guild faced similar hurdles. For example, sons of lesser tradesmen such as those who sold frippery (secondhand clothes and other goods) might have been suitable as apprentices for one of the mid-level trades, like tailoring, but they had little if any chance of gaining entry to one of the higher-status trades. Only those from more privileged backgrounds, such as the son of a middling or wealthy landowner or a prosperous merchant or craftsmen whose trade had some measure of respectability, such as mercery or metalworking, were accepted into these more elite and more lucrative trades. Besides having the necessary social standing and connections with persons already engaged in the desired trade, these well-to-do families could also afford to pay all fees required for apprenticeship.

Those who were accepted into and were successful in one of the prestigious trades could rise quite high in medieval society. Some became councilmen or mayors of their cities and, through their wealth and social connections, had substantial political influence, even with their noble rulers. By the late Middle Ages, sons and daughters of these wealthy and powerful commoners were considered suitable spouses for at least some of the minor nobility. Some very successful merchants were given important government positions or even ennobled by their rulers in recognition of the services they rendered. These "services" typically took the form of making substantial loans or outright gifts of huge sums of money to the ruler.

Qualifying for an Apprenticeship

Children of friends, relatives, and business associates were preferred as apprentices since the master had some familiarity with their backgrounds. Additionally, from his own observations or from recommendations of people in whom he had some trust, the master had some measure of the character, intelligence, and abilities of apprentices drawn from this familial and social circle. He also had some assurance that if the apprentice turned out to be unruly or otherwise difficult that he would be able to get help from the parents in correcting their child's behavior or, if things had gone very badly, monetary compensation for losses or damages caused by the apprentice. In some apprenticeship contracts, masters went so far as to require the apprentice's parent or guardian to provide a surety, that is, to agree in advance to pay for any loss or damage the master suffered as a result of apprentice's action.

Prospective apprentices had to be sufficiently fit to perform all the work necessary for their future trades. Children with physical handicaps which could interfere with the performance of their duties were excluded from apprenticeships. Some guilds were more restrictive and barred children who were deformed or handicapped in any way from becoming apprentices, even if their handicap did not impact their ability to learn and work. By the end of the 15th century, many guilds in London made being "clean-limbed" and free of physical defects a requirement for all prospective apprentices. Some of the guilds which imposed these stringent requirements were among the more elite trades whose day-to-day business, such as the wholesale and retail selling of cloth, did not require much physical exertion. These guilds likely excluded would-be apprentices who had noticeable and severe deformities or disfigurements because permitting such a person to become a member of a trade was considered as bad for business or, at least, detrimental to the guild's public image.

Near the end of the Middle Ages, many guilds added the requirement that apprentices had to be educated. Previously, apprentices were not expected to have learned to read and write before starting their vocational training. In fact, apprenticeship contracts sometimes included provisions that the apprentices were to be allowed time off to attend school to learn these skills. But, as formal education became more available, people came to expect trained businessmen to be able to read and write their own correspondences and transactions rather than having to find a scribe to do it for them. Additionally, as discussed later in this chapter, the age at which apprentices started their job training generally increased over the course of the Middle Ages, and so would-be apprentices had more of an opportunity to learn to read and write before beginning their apprenticeships. As with the prohibition against handicapped children becoming apprentices, there was likely an element of elitism in the requirement for education as well. Guilds whose members were all literate from the very start of their careers may have claimed higher social status than those whose members generally lacked these skills. The fact that the most prestigious guilds, such as the goldsmiths, were the first to establish minimum education requirements for apprentices strongly suggests that this was the case.

Fees for Apprenticeships

The parents or guardians who placed a child into an apprenticeship had to pay the master for the cost of training the child. The master was also usually given money to cover the expenses of housing, feeding, and clothing the child since apprentices typically lived with their masters during their apprenticeships. Most of these amounts were paid at the beginning of the apprenticeship, although some contracts provided that they were paid in installments over the course of the apprenticeship. The value to the master of the work performed by the apprentice was factored into setting these fees. Masters sometimes paid apprentices for the work they performed but usually only as they neared the end of their contracts and were productive employees. Even then, they were usually paid only a fraction, often a third or less, of what an adult worker received for comparable work.

In some contracts, masters agreed to provide apprentices with certain tools upon completion of their apprenticeships. The tools were usually those which were essential to practice the trade which the apprentices had learned. For example, in one contract, a cooper (barrel maker) agreed to provide his apprentice with the compass the apprentice would need to draw large circles on the boards to make the ends of barrels. Fees paid by parents or guardians may have been used to defray the cost of these tools although the income generated by the skilled apprentice's labor also provided revenue to purchase these items.

The fees for training varied depending upon the trade being taught. Goldsmithing and other trades which involved precious materials cost much more to learn than weaving, reselling used clothing, and the like. In part, the higher fees were based on the complexity of the craft and the cost of the materials involved. However, the relative prestige of the trades was also a factor. Further, masters, even within the same trade, appear to have charged different fees, with very successful or very well-known masters charging higher rates than merely average ones. On the other hand, masters charged lower or even no fees when an apprentice was a nephew or other relative. For very desirable apprentices, such as those who were already well educated or were from prestigious families, masters sometimes drastically reduced their fees as well.

There were administrative costs for apprenticeships as well. Apprentices had to be formally enrolled with the appropriate guild, usually no later than the end of the first year of the contract. At enrollment, the apprentice appeared before the wardens of the guild, who verified that he was of free birth, of sound body, free of deformities, met the age requirements, and, if applicable, could read and write. The apprentice then took the guild's oath, which included a vow to keep secret all information he learned about the trade. As part of the enrollment, the guild collected a fee. Local government sometimes required payment as well. For example, in London, by the 14th century, apprenticeship contracts had to be recorded with the city government within a year and a day of being signed, and the city charged a fee for this service. Cities such as London required this formal recording of apprenticeship contracts because apprentices who successfully completed their contracts were granted citizenship. Citizenship in medieval cities was no small matter. Under charters granted by kings or other high nobility, citizens enjoyed many special privileges. These typically included exemption from tolls throughout the realm, and the right to carry out their trade within the city free of the taxes and other limitations which were imposed on outsiders who came to trade in the city. In some instances, non-citizens were prohibited from any trading within the city limits. They could still do business in the surrounding suburbs, but this was far less profitable since most business was conducted within the cities. Thus, this restriction ensured that the majority of trade was handled only by bonafide citizens. Despite the threat of fines imposed by their guilds, some unscrupulous masters avoided paying the enrollment fees by simply not enrolling their apprentices with the guild. Failure to enroll with the guild occasionally caused serious complications for unfortunate apprentices when they completed their terms of service and sought guild membership. However, this was not a problem for apprentices who did not plan to stay on in the city. In fact, these apprentices may have agreed with their masters to forego enrollment to avoid payment of all the required fees. Finally, when masters were training their own children, they were not required to pay any fees to the guild. Since their parents were citizens, masters' children were already citizens and so, when they were being trained by their own parents, there was also no need to register with the city or pay those registration fees.

As mentioned previously, apprenticeship contracts sometimes included provisions for the apprentice to learn how to read, write, and perform simple arithmetic in addition to receiving vocational training. This more formal education typically required additional payments to the master. Masters did not teach these skills themselves. Instead, apprentices were to be allowed time off to attend one of the small urban schools which provided such education (see chapter 6).

The Age of Apprentices

The age that children began apprenticeships varied greatly. In the case of orphans, the age could be quite young. One poor orphan girl in London was apprenticed to a used clothing dealer at the age of five. She was obviously not expected to begin vocational training until she was older, and her master likely served as a foster parent under this arrangement. For some very exacting trades, such as goldsmithing and surgery, apprentices were generally not accepted until they were at least eighteen, when they had presumably developed steady hands and some good judgment. More typically, apprentices appear to have been twelve or thirteen when they began their contracts and many were probably at least fifteen to sixteen when they started. The starting age for apprentices generally increased in the last two centuries of the Middle Ages so that, by the 15th century, few children appear to have started their apprenticeships before they turned sixteen. In fact, by that time, many did not start until they were eighteen. This increase in age may have had some connection with the minimum education requirements for apprentices which were first established in the 15th century.

The Length of Apprenticeships

The amount of time that an apprentice was required to serve under a master varied greatly. As one might expect, the duration of apprenticeships was based, in part, on the complexity of trade which was being learned. Mastering the craft of making jewelry required some of the longest apprenticeships. Learning goldsmithing typically required a ten year term and learning to make rosaries from coral took twelve years. On the other hand, there were some trades with fairly short apprenticeships. For example, becoming a cook in 13th century Paris required only a two year apprenticeship, although this short period of training was followed by becoming a journeyman cook rather than a master cook. The position of journeymen within the guilds will be discussed in more detail later in this chapter.

Higher prestige trades also tended to have longer apprenticeships than less distinguished ones. Some of these more prestigious trades were fairly complex and often involved international trade, such as dealing in cloth or spices, but the greater length of these apprenticeships may have also been driven by the desire of the guild members to maintain the reputation and exclusivity of their trade. Longer training implied that masters in these trades were better trained than those in lesser professions and that only the most suitable apprentices would complete the lengthy training process.

There also appear to have been significant regional variations in the length of apprenticeships. For example, in northern Italy, many apprenticeships lasted only three to five years, while in London the minimum length of apprenticeships for all trades was fixed at seven years beginning in the early 14th century. And the London regulations set no upper limit on the duration of apprenticeships.

The length of apprenticeships generally grew during the late Middle Ages, especially after the Black Death began ravaging Europe in the 14th century. In the wake of this plague, a few guilds found their ranks so seriously depleted that they allowed apprentices to complete their periods of service in less time to fill the vacancies. However, many guilds appear to have lengthened the duration of apprenticeships to cope with the labor shortage caused by the plague. Requiring boys to serve longer apprenticeships enabled masters to lock in an important source of cheap labor for a longer period. Further, apprentices improved their skills over time and so masters were getting not just more years of cheap labor but more years of *skilled* cheap labor when they increased the numbers of years apprentices were obligated to serve them.

As these examples suggest, adjusting the length of apprenticeships was another way that guilds protected the interests of their current members. Limiting the number of guild members maintained the profitability of their trades and ensured that every guild member had a reasonable opportunity for making a living. However, since market conditions could fluctuate wildly because of wars, plagues, famines, and other unforeseeable problems, guilds could not determine how many members the market would support even in the near future. As a result, they could not simply set a fixed number of guild memberships. Instead, they used other means to regulate the size of their membership such as lengthening or, more rarely, shortening the duration of apprenticeships so that the pool of qualified candidates met the guild's needs. As we will see, raising or lowering the fees apprentices paid for their admission to the guild at the end of their apprenticeships was another mechanism for regulating new guild memberships.

That the length of apprenticeships were not always determined by the amount of time actually needed to learn the trade is also proven by the practice of allowing apprentices to buy shorter terms of apprenticeship at the time of initial contract. In 13th century France, for example, it was possible to reduce the period of apprenticeship for a weaver from seven years down to four years if one was willing and able to pay the substantial sum of four *livres*. It also appears that some apprentices who were already under contract bargained with their masters to end the contract early in exchange for a sum of money. Presumably, these apprentices were sufficiently trained to begin working on their own and had the resources needed to set up their own businesses. Their possession of enough money to pay off their masters strongly suggests that they had ample funds. When released in exchange for a formal payment with the full agreement of their master, apprentices who bought their way out of their contracts were still eligible to become members of the guild, just as though they had served the entire term of their contracts.

Combined with the rising age at which boys began their apprenticeships, the lengthening of the duration of apprenticeships meant that boys in the 13th century would generally have completed their apprenticeships while they were still teenagers but that many boys in the 14th century were in their early twenties when they finished their contracts and many of those serving their apprenticeships in the 15th century were not free of their contracts until their mid- or even late twenties.

Numbers of Apprentices Permitted to Each Master

For the same reasons that they adjusted the length of apprenticeships, guilds limited the number of apprentices that a master could have at any one time. In many guilds, masters were permitted to have only one apprentice at a time. In other trades, typically those which required more manpower, masters were permitted two or more apprentices, but rarely more than four. Some guilds, such as the mercers (cloth merchants) in London, required their members to prove how many apprentices they needed. Under this rule, a few very successful mercers in late medieval London had ten or even twenty or more apprentices in their service. But such high numbers of apprentices were exceptional. Besides keeping the number of potential new masters in balance with the market for their products, an important reason for limiting the number of apprentices each master was allowed was to prevent a master from gaining an unfair advantage over his fellow guild members. A master who took on a large number of apprentices could use them as a cheap workforce and thereby produce more at a lower cost than his competing guild members. Masters who had large numbers of children may have had a similar advantage since, under guild regulations, the master's own children were not counted toward the cap on the number of apprentices. Masters were free to train and employ as many of their own children as they wished.

Limiting the number of apprentices also restricted the fees which masters collected for training apprentices. While this was less important than controlling the size of the masters' work forces, the apprenticeship fees collected by masters often provided an important source of ready cash. Masters were always in need of additional money for business investments.

Despite the efforts of the guilds, some guildsmen did not always honor the regulations and some particularly successful guildsmen broke these rules with impunity. Still, masters with large numbers of apprentices were a rarity. Most had only one at a time and many masters might have trained only a handful of apprentices during their entire careers.

The Training

The training apprentices received varied greatly. In late 13th century Paris, there were over 100 recognized trades. As might be expected, the apprentice of a moneychanger had a much less physically demanding course of training and probably a more pleasant experience in general than that of a boy who was apprenticed to a tanner and whose training included scraping off any hair or tissue that remained on cowhides that had been soaked in large troughs of stale urine. Similarly, a boy learning to be a cloth merchant or an accountant was likely a lot less sore and worn out at the end of the day than a weaver's apprentice who had been slaving over a huge loom for many long hours.

Regardless of the trade, masters trained apprentices the same way as they trained their own children, by letting them watch how the work was done and by giving them increasingly more complex tasks to perform until they were ready to work independently. An apprentice woodworker started out by sweeping up around the workshop and fetching boards. An apprentice barber, who learned the art of phlebotomy along with cutting hair, likely began his training with sweeping up too. He also held the bowl to catch customers' blood when his masters bled them (see appendix 1). Besides familiarizing him with the techniques used in bleeding, providing this assistance helped accustom the apprentice barber to the sight of blood. While performing these menial tasks, apprentices had plenty of opportunities to watch their masters at work.

After the apprentice had had a chance to learn a little by watching, he was given the opportunity to practice some of the skills he had observed. Little by little, he was given more to do as he became more competent. An apprentice surgeon, after seeing several operations, would be ready to help restrain a patient while his master manipulated dislocated bones back into their proper positions. An apprentice fishmonger could make or oversee deliveries without his master's direct supervision after having helped make deliveries for some time. Apprentices' responsibilities continued to be increased as their experience and judgment grew. Finally, after years of hard work and long hours, senior apprentices were trusted to perform their work with little or no supervision. Master merchants sent these older apprentices to distant fairs to buy and sell merchandise or, alternatively, take care of business while the master traveled abroad. Master craftsmen permitted experienced apprentices to handle expensive materials and perform work requiring artistic skill.

Over the course of the apprenticeship, masters were to teach their apprentices all the secrets of their trade. In manufacturing trades, these "secrets" likely included knowing how to assess the quality of raw materials and knowing which sources were the most reliable for providing good materials. The secrets also included all the steps in the processes needed to transform these materials into finished products that met the standards of the guild. For example, in ironworking, the trade secrets probably included information on how long to heat the metal and to what temperature (as indicated by the different colors which iron and steel turn when heated to extreme temperatures) to achieve the desired balance of hardness and flexibility or *temper*. In a few instances, masters who produced items noted for exceptional qualities were loath to disclose their manufacturing secrets and imparted them only to members of their own families. For merchant trades, the knowledge of how to assess the quality of goods was likely an important secret along with other inside information such as the best sources for various types of goods and the differences in the preferences and tastes of customers in different in regions. Merchants' trade secrets may have also included information on coping with import and export regulations of the jurisdictions through which their goods passed. As part of keeping one's shipments moving smoothly, this sort of information perhaps included guidance on which customs officials to bribe and with how much money. Finally, the trade secrets of both merchant and crafts trades likely included the inside scoop on how the guild set its prices.

Along with teaching them the skills needed to perform their future jobs, the merchant and craft guilds expected masters to encourage their apprentices to take pride in the quality of their work. In addition to this personal work ethic, masters were also to help their apprentices to develop a sense of pride in their guilds and encourage them to be loyal to their guilds as well. This fostering of a positive attitude towards their guilds was part of assimilating apprentices into the professional community.

During their apprenticeships, many boys received training in more than just their future careers. For the many apprentices who came to the cities from towns, villages, and farms, life in the big city was quite different than at home. Medieval cities were relatively small by modern standards. For example, during the last centuries of the Middle Ages, Florence, one of the largest cities in medieval Europe, had a population of approximately 100,000 while London had an estimated population of 60,000 to 80,000. However, the cities were still far more populous and crowded than any town most of the apprentices from the country had ever seen before. So, incidental to their formal training in their new line of work, many apprentices also had to learn the ways of the city from their masters and their masters' families. From how to dress and act to familiarizing themselves with the city's neighborhoods, apprentices gradually adapted to their new urban lives.

Relations Between Masters and Apprentices

Masters were more than just instructors and landlords for their apprentices. They were surrogate fathers as well. In fact, apprenticeship contracts typically specified that masters had the right to correct and discipline apprentices as a parent did and that the apprentices had to obey their masters. Many contracts went even further and detailed the behavior expected of the apprentices. The more common contract terms stated that the apprentice agreed that he would

- safeguard his master's home and belongings and not steal them;
- behave morally and not gamble, drink, hang around taverns, or frequent the company of prostitutes;

- not run away or otherwise leave his master's home without permission;
- not marry until after he had completed his term of apprenticeship, unless he had his master's permission; and
- not seduce any of the women in the household, including the master's wife, daughters, or maidservants.

As one would expect, there was often friction between the apprentices and their masters just as there was (and still is) friction between any teenagers and their parents. In some instances, these frictions became major disputes and ended up in court. These cases included those of apprentices who were accused of stealing money or other items from their master to pay for gambling, drinking, and whoring or who were alleged to have attacked their masters or other members of their household. But apprentices weren't the only ones accused of wrongdoing. Masters sometimes abused their apprentices. Like parents, masters were expected to use corporal punishment to discipline their apprentices, but some were alleged to have beaten their apprentices excessively, even to the point of blinding, crippling, or killing them. Still other masters were accused of not providing adequate food and clothing, to the point that their apprentices were starving and clad in rags. The records of these cases also reveal that parents routinely kept in touch with their children while they were serving their apprenticeships. A few apprentices, mostly older ones, did take legal action against their own masters. However, mother and fathers were more often the ones who brought suit against masters for the mistreatment of their apprentices.

In most cases, the court's goal was to reconcile the master and apprentice, but wrongdoers, whether apprentices or masters, were frequently punished. In those instances in which the accusations were proven, a variety of remedies and penalties were imposed by the courts. Courts awarded damages to the injured party and freed them from the contract as well. Apprentices found guilty of major thefts from masters were sent to prison, usually until their parents or guardian paid reparations to the aggrieved master. Masters who abused or neglected their apprentices were ordered to treat them properly. In severe cases, masters were fined or even jailed for their abuse of apprentices. Guilds also participated in arbitrating disputes between apprentices and masters. When mediation failed or the actions of a party were too egregious to go unpunished, guilds imposed punishments as well. Thieving apprentices were sometimes thrown out of the trade and barred from ever being readmitted, while apprentices who had attacked and injured their masters were subjected to whipping in the guildhall. In other cases, guilds required apprentices to publicly humble themselves and beg their masters for forgiveness. Guilds also took action against bad masters although the guilds appear to have more often admonished their members rather than truly punishing them for mistreating apprentices. For example, after finding that one of a master's apprentices had died and that another had fled to avoid being beaten by his wife, a London goldsmith was warned by his guild that he would be prohibited from taking in any more apprentices if there were any further problems. The guild appears to have taken no further action and let the master go with only a warning despite the evidence of his mistreatment of his apprentices. The fact that no punishment was imposed on the master suggests that guilds were loath to penalize their own members in such cases and left it to the courts.

Besides physically harming apprentices, some masters failed to provide the training as promised in the apprenticeship contract. Some cases involved masters who were simply lazy. In others, masters made their apprentices do routine household chores such as carrying water, cleaning the house, and running errands for the masters' wives instead of having them perform job-related tasks. Such misuse of apprentices was often specifically prohibited in apprenticeship contracts. Masters were supposed to have servants or other members of their households perform these tiresome chores. The apprentices were there to learn a trade and serve their masters in the workshop, not to be domestic servants. In other instances, apprentices were deprived of their training because their masters died, fled the city, were sent to prison for debts or crimes, or switched occupations. These unfortunate apprentices were frequently left with no money and no training. Masters were also usually permitted to sell apprenticeship contracts. While the consent of the apprentice was required for such transactions, some masters ignored their apprentices' concerns and sold them as bond servants to people who had no intention of teaching them a trade. Some poor apprentices had their contracts sold repeatedly, falling into ever worsening situations. Some of the victims of unscrupulous masters brought legal action to free themselves of their contracts and recover the money paid for their training and upkeep. Again, the parents or guardians of apprentices were quite often the ones who brought suit. While the court records are patchy, the victimized apprentices appear to have frequently been released from their contracts but were seldom able to obtain compensation. Even when the courts ordered masters to pay for their malfeasance, many masters appear to have fled or just refused to pay. As for the guilds, they routinely ordered offending masters to change their ways and provide the training required under the apprenticeship contract.

While there was likely some conflict between apprentices and masters in all apprenticeships, the cases above were extreme examples. Most apprentices appear to have successfully adapted to the rules of their new homes and their new masters and most masters seem to have taught them adequately while not mistreating them. Unfortunately, there is not much evidence regarding harmonious relations. Only when things went seriously wrong were people brought to the attention of authorities and their actions recorded for posterity. When things went right, they were unremarkable and passed with little or no notice. The primary evidence we have for situations in which relations between masters and apprentices went well are business agreements, wills, and records of marriages. In documents of business transactions, masters are shown to have entrusted their apprentices to travel abroad with valuable merchandise, sell it, and return with the proceeds. Wills of both masters and apprentices have been found to show very amiable and even affectionate relations between the two. Masters sometimes rewarded their apprentices, current as well as former, with bequests in their wills. For current apprentices, these included gifts of tools or remission of the remaining years of the term of their contracts, although this latter benefit was usually given only to apprentices who were within a year or two of finishing their period of service. Some masters remembered their former apprentices as well and gave them gifts of property or tools, and, in at least a few instances, these gifts were so substantial that the former apprentices received shares in the estate comparable to the masters' own children. In at least one case, a master appointed his former apprentice as the guardian of his children instead of his own wife. For their part, some former apprentices clearly thought fondly of their former masters. Some paid to have masses said for the benefit of the souls of their deceased masters, a charitable act which was most commonly commissioned by a person for his parents. On occasion, apprentices actually became members of their masters' families. Some former apprentices did so by marrying the daughters of their masters. Since marriages typically required the approval of the bride's father, such unions indicate that some masters were pleased to have their apprentices become family members. And at least a few former apprentices married the widows of their former masters. Some guilds actively encouraged this last practice. For example, shortly after the end of the Middle

Ages, the armorers' guild in Augsburg cut four years off the time required to become a master armorer for any trainee armorer who married the widow of a master.

Apprentices' Conduct Outside of the Workplace

Many apprentices appear to have violated the terms of their contracts, which prohibited them from drinking, gambling, and frequenting prostitutes. In fact, as a group, apprentices were quite well-noted by their contemporaries for engaging in just these activities. Apprentices also frequently entertained themselves with attending the theater and other public entertainments, buying fancy clothing, learning how to use a sword, committing acts of vandalism, violating curfews, and generally being annoyances to law-abiding citizens. In other words, like any large population composed solely of single guys, all in their late teens and early twenties with too much free time, they were a chronic problem for civic authorities. Whenever there was civil unrest or outright rioting, apprentices were typically recorded as participating to the fullest.

Interestingly, in London, the young men sent to learn the practice of law were considered to be among the worst behaved of the apprentices. These "apprentices of the King's Bench" were different from other apprentices in several ways. While they often had not completed a degree, they had studied at one of the universities before beginning their legal training. As mentioned in chapter 7, England was unique in this respect. Everywhere else in Europe, future lawyers received their training in civil, or *Roman*, law at a university. England, however, based its legal system on the common law, which was a mixture of the laws issued by the kings and the customary laws of the land. Common law was not taught at any of the universities in the Middle Ages. To learn it, a would-be lawyer had to first get a grounding in the liberal arts taught at the universities. Ideally, he would also have learned some canon or civil law, but that was not essential. He then moved to London so that he could watch lawyers at work in king's courts in London and receive instruction from some of these practicing lawyers.

As this training suggests, future lawyers were drawn only from among families who had the necessary wealth and prestige to secure both a university education for their sons and a place at one of the inns of court in London as well. Thus, all were from privileged backgrounds. Most were sons of wealthy commoners, but some came from the ranks of the nobility. These noble students had no intention of earning their livings by practicing law, but an understanding of the law was useful in their future careers, especially in the area of politics.

Besides their wealthy origins, apprentices of the King's Bench were unlike other apprentices in that they did not live in the homes of their masters. As result, their conduct outside the workplace of the law courts was largely unsupervised. Their studies and training also required far less physical effort than that of many other crafts and trades, leaving them plenty of energy for mischief and worse. This combination of privilege, wealth, and free time appears to have made them especially prone to participating in drinking and all the other vices the city had to offer.

Completion of Apprenticeship

Not all apprentices completed the full term of their contracts. In fact, figures from records of apprenticeships in London indicate that perhaps only about half of apprentices did so.

Some died. Some ran away from their masters. Some fugitive apprentices fled to escape abusive masters. Other runaways went to serve rival masters within the same city. This was done despite guild regulations that prohibited masters from luring apprentices away from their fellow guildsmen. In few extreme cases, masters were accused of outright kidnapping of apprentices. Such stealing of apprentices may have involved apprentices who were exceptionally talented but was most common when apprentices were simply in very short supply, such as after outbreaks of the Black Death. Others likely left their masters because they were bored with their training or unhappy with their future career prospects. And, finally, some had received enough training to be useful workers and left to take up their trade and begin earning a living. Since they had not become guild members, this last group of runaway apprentices had to flee to other cities or towns to find work or set up their businesses. Regardless of the reason for their fleeing, these fugitive apprentices were not free of their contracts. Masters had the right to have escaped apprentices hunted down and returned to them. However, surviving legal documents indicate that masters seldom enforced this right. Masters may have realized that they were unlikely to receive any useful labor out of such rebellious apprentices and that there was little point in going to the expense and trouble of having a runaway apprentice tracked down and returned.

In other instances, masters and apprentices, or their parents or guardians, appear to have reached mutual agreements to end contracts. While he lost the labor the apprentice would have provided during the remainder of his term, the master was freed from the expense of maintaining the apprentice. On the other side of the bargain, the apprentice was free to begin working on his own. However, he was usually ineligible to join a guild since he had not completed the full term of his contract. He could not set up his own business in the city, but he could go to work for a master who was a guild member or he could leave the city. There were many opportunities outside of the city, especially in the many towns which did not have guilds. For example, an apprentice in the grocery trade, which involved wholesale buying and selling a wide variety of foodstuffs, could practice this same trade in any large provincial town and make good use of the skills he had acquired and the business contacts he had made in the big city during his apprenticeship.

Those who did complete their full terms of apprenticeship then went on to be examined by the wardens of the guild to prove that they had learned their trade. The creation of special examples of the apprentice's work, sometimes referred to as "master pieces," does not appear to have been a common part of these examinations. After all, what masterpiece could a fishmonger or cloth trader produce? For such merchant trades, apprentices probably had to prove their business skills, such as evaluating and pricing merchandise. Admittedly, for those trades which did involve actually producing items, masters likely did inspect samples of the apprentice's work to confirm his skills. And apprentices and their masters would have chosen the best ones to put before the wardens. Additionally, for all trades, apprentices had to prove their knowledge of guild regulations and acceptable business practices. After successful completion of the examination, and the payment of more fees, the apprentice was initiated into the guild. The fees charged for examination and initiation were often quite substantial and bore no relation to the actual expenses incurred by the guild for performing these services. Instead, the high fees were another deterrent to keep numbers of guild members down and maintain the profitability of the trade for those who were already members. Again, guilds only charged lower fees for admission when guild membership was severely depleted and the economic conditions were good. At such times, some guilds in London charged as little as one-tenth of what they did in ordinary years, or even less.

Once they were allowed to complete their apprenticeships, many apprentices were still not able to begin their own businesses. Even initiation into a guild provided no guarantees that a person could then successfully embark on his trade. In theory, every apprentice who completed his full term of service and training was eligible to join the guild and become a master. He was then able to set up his own business, apply the skills he had learned, and begin making money in his chosen profession. The reality for many, if not most, apprentices was quite different. While the apprenticeship should have given them all the training needed for starting a successful career, only those apprentices who had the wealth and other resources needed to establish their own business could really expect to join the guild immediately and participate as a full-fledged master. For some trades, such as metalworking or one involving long distance, international commerce, the start-up costs were prohibitively high. On the other hand, some other occupations, such as shoemaking and woodworking, usually faced much lower economic barriers when first starting out. Thus, an apprentice needed more than completion of apprenticeship to start a career in the more prestigious and highly profitable trades, but for trades of lower social standing and lower monetary rewards, apprenticeship combined with a few tools and a fairly small amount of capital was often sufficient for embarking on one's career.

Throughout the Middle Ages, there were men who had completed their apprenticeships but were unable to start their own businesses. To make a living, they went to work for established masters within their trades. These hired workers were typically paid on a weekly or daily basis. This method of employment led to them being called *journeymen,* not because they had to travel around to find work but because they were paid by the day or, in French, *jour.* While fully trained in a craft, these young men were often only slightly better off than apprentices. Some journeymen eventually managed to accumulate enough money to become masters, but many remained employees of other craftsmen all their lives. Journeymen occasionally banded together and attempted to bargain collectively with their masters to obtain higher wages, but these early efforts routinely failed. While their attempts at collective bargaining failed, journeymen were eventually recognized as a formal class within many guilds and some guilds required a period of training as an apprentice followed by a period of service as a journeyman before a man could become a master. Still, such recognition did little to improve the standing or the income of the journeymen. Frustrated with their limited prospects of financial success, journeymen were often a volatile segment of medieval urban populations. They frequently appear alongside apprentices in accounts of urban unrest.

Apprenticeships for Girls

As mentioned previously, even in trades controlled by guilds, fathers were free to teach their daughters as well as their sons the family business. In fact, most girls who learned a trade appear to have been taught by their parents. Formal apprenticeship was far less common for girls than for boys. A review of one large group of apprenticeship contracts revealed that contracts for girls accounted for only 10 percent of the total number. The low number of formal apprenticeships for girls may be partially attributable to the fact that girls could learn many of the basic skills needed in the production of textiles, such as carding and spinning, from their own mothers at home. Apprenticeship in making cloth was needed only for specialized work like weaving silk ribbons. Similarly, girls who entered the food trades such as baking breads and meat-filled pies (the fast food of the Middle Ages) and roasting meats to sell were able to learn the skills needed at home. However, women did practice many trades outside of cloth and food production. As previously outlined, women engaged in a variety of craft and mercantile trades. Still, at least in medieval Paris and London, most women who were recorded as working on their own rather than in their husbands' or parents' businesses were involved in cloth or food related trades.

When girls were formally apprenticed, they were usually placed with female rather male masters. Similarly, boys were rarely trained by women. As with male masters, mistresses ranged from humane to abusive. Some were recorded as whipping their apprentices excessively or jabbing them with needles. Again, only the cases of extremely bad treatment were typically recorded, so it is quite possible that most female apprentices were not subjected to physical abuse during their years of training.

Girls appear to have typically begun their apprenticeships at about the same age as boys although some evidence suggests that many female apprentices started their training at a younger age than their male counterparts. This earlier entry into apprenticeship may have been intended to give these girls a better opportunity to develop marketable skills and to earn and some money for their dowries while they were still young. The possession of both a profitable skill and a relatively substantial dowry increased a young woman's chance of finding a suitable husband.

Apprenticeship contracts reveal some other differences in the treatment of male and female apprentices. One such difference was in education. None of the surviving contracts for apprenticeships for girls include any provision for formal education.

Another difference was in the size of the fees charged for apprenticeships. Fees for girls' apprenticeships were generally lower than those for boys. The lower fees were, in part, a consequence of the sort of trades in which girls were apprenticed. Embroidery, ribbon making, and the like were low prestige and low profit ones. Fees charged by masters and guilds for trades of this sort were always lower than for the more profitable and higher status ones. However, as we will see later in this section, at least one textile guild in a German city charged single women lower guild fees than it did for men.

While girls were often permitted to be trained in a trade, whether it was a craft or a mercantile enterprise, virtually all guilds prohibited women from becoming masters in their own right. This meant that husbands and fathers could teach their trade to their wives and daughters and these women could practice that trade but only as part of their husband's or father's business. They were often barred from setting up their own businesses and trade independently. However, there were some exceptions. As mentioned previously, widows of merchants and craftsmen were routinely permitted to continue practicing the family trade to support themselves. But, if a widow remarried, she lost this right if she married someone who was not a member of her deceased husband's guild.

Medieval guilds were usually only civic organizations and, with one exception, there were no reciprocal agreements between guilds in different cities. The exception was the Hanseatic League, the merchant league of northern Germany, which had members in most of major cities around the southern coast of the Baltic Sea. The lack of coordination and comity between guilds in different cities meant that, for example, when a master mercer traveled to trade in a foreign city such as Paris or Bruges, he was simply treated as another foreign merchant and not as a fellow mercer. Another aspect of the lack of unity between the guilds in different cities was that guild regulations, including those addressing the status of women, varied from region to region.

English guild regulations regarding women engaging in trade appear to have been the most restrictive. Many different trades in London granted the exception for widows to carry on the family business. As for women who were not widows, wives, or daughters of guildsmen, most London guilds prohibited such women from practicing a trade. Despite the guild regulations, there is clear evidence that women worked in a variety of trades. Tax and court records from London and elsewhere in England confirm that women routinely engaged in the business of brewing and selling ale as well as selling food items, especially fish and ready-to-eat foods such as bread and pastries. Women also appear in these records in a variety of textile trades including spinning and weaving. Some of these women may have been the wives or widows of men who were also engaged in these same trades, but the records indicate that their marital status was usually of no concern to the courts. The courts and tax officials treated *fishwives, bakeresses, brewsters* or *alewives,* spinsters, and weavers as independent business people and they were subject to the same laws and regulations on food and drink production and sales which applied to fishmongers, bakers, and brewers and to male spinners and weavers. When one of these women committed an infraction, the court held her personally liable and she, not her husband or other male relative, was responsible for paying the fines or making restitution. Some of these women were married, but their businesses were wholly independent from those of their husbands. In other cases, it appears that the women involved may have been unmarried.

In addition to the court and tax documents, there is also a royal statute issued in 1363 which provides proof of women's employment in a variety of trades in England. This statute was enacted after the Black Death had ravaged the country and was part of efforts to stabilize wages and employment in the face of the labor shortages created by the plague. Under this statute, women were permitted to continue practicing any trade in which they were already engaged. These trades included, but were not limited to, brewing, baking, carding wool, and spinning and weaving wool, linen, and silk.

As the statute and other records suggest, the food and textile trades were likely the most common businesses for women to practice. Women were drawn to these trades for a number of reasons. The most important was that both these trades relied on skills which girls were expected to learn while growing up. Every girl was expected to master baking bread and brewing ale or beer as well as the basics of spinning fibers into threads and then weaving those threads into cloth. Additionally, the food trades required few tools and most households already possessed them. Only a small investment was then needed to purchase the larger quantities of ingredients needed to produce a few extra loaves of bread or gallons of ale to sell to the neighbors.

Elsewhere in Europe, the surviving evidence also provides some answers about women engaging in trade. In Italy, women were recorded as working in some of the textile trades, and they were especially important in the production of silk cloth. The guilds which regulated these trades permitted women to work but denied them any formal standing within the guilds. Women were recorded as practicing 108 out of 321 trades listed in government documents in Paris in the late 13th and early 14th centuries. These women included wives who worked alongside their husbands. They also included widows of guild members who were permitted by many guilds to continue working in the same trades which their deceased spouses had practiced. Others were women who worked independently of men. Among these were proprietresses of public bathhouses as well as women who were masters, journeywomen, and apprentices in trades controlled by the guilds. In some trades, including the makers of gold ribbons, embroiderers, yarn makers, makers of hats adorned with pearls, and some of the other textile-related trades, women were accepted on an equal footing with men. There were also a few guilds for trades practiced exclusively by women. These guilds were for the crafts of spinning silk into thread, weaving silk thread into fabric or into silk kerchiefs and veils, and making purses. But even these guilds were not outside the control of men, since the city council appointed two or three men along with an equal number of mistresses of the craft to oversee each of these guilds. In both the exclusively female and the mixed sex guilds, girls were trained as apprentices and then frequently had to serve for a year or more as journeywomen before becoming masters. Finally, as with England, women appear in Paris and other cities in France in the victualling trades, although they were not accepted as masters in these guilds.

Guilds in cities in Germany and the Low Countries appear to have been the most liberal in their policies towards women practicing trades. Guilds in many cities across Germany and the Low Countries accepted women as well as men as members. Women were well represented in some of the textile production guilds. For example, in Strasbourg (now in France but then part of German-speaking Europe) the wool weaving and cloth making guild included a total of 39 single women and widows among its members in 1334. In another German city, the linen weaving guild granted single women a 50 percent discount on membership fees. However, because of varying economic conditions, there were significant differences between cities. In cities whose textiles were in high demand or had a shortage of labor, such as after outbreaks of the Black Death, the guilds needed every textile worker they could find and so were willing to accept women as members. But in cities with sluggish economies or sufficient numbers of male workers, guild regulations usually favored male masters over female ones and limited women's participation in trade. In the food trades, women appear to have been as active in Germany as they were in France and England. However, records from Strasbourg and other cities show that women were permitted to be guild members in their own right in the victualling trade guilds. In these cities, women appear in the bakers', fishmongers', and gardeners' guilds. Practitioners of this last trade grew vegetables and fruits in gardens in and around the city and sold the fresh produce to city residents. Women also participated in brewing and were accepted into the brewers' guilds in many cities. In one instance in the 15th century, a woman was considered to be such an expert in brewing that the city of Cologne contracted with her to instruct two men in her technique so that they could produce a similar superior beer. In addition to craft trades, women in many German cities were active as merchants. As previously mentioned, women in Cologne, Ghent, and other cities engaged in local and international trade, usually as part of their husbands' or fathers' business but sometimes on their own as well.

Other Training for Trades

Formal apprenticeships were not the only means by which children were trained for trades and crafts. As previously explained, while many children did undergo such formal training, many more were probably trained by their own parents. Additionally, some parents were likely able to find local craftsmen and others who were willing to train their children in a trade without all the fees and bureaucratic obstacles imposed by guilds and civic governments. Parents in rural areas were well placed for obtaining such informal training for their children since the guilds had far less control over trades outside of the cities. Admittedly, many of the trades practiced by country craftsmen were generally of low prestige, such as manufacturing ceramic goods including pots and tiles or wooden items like plates. Still, learning one of these crafts enabled a person to engage in small scale manufacturing which could be practiced either as one's full-time trade or as a seasonal business for those who were engaged primarily in agriculture. In either case, a child who learned such skills had an opportunity to earn more than a child who knew only how to perform agricultural jobs.

Some parents in rural areas also likely found construction workers to train their children. While the mention of construction in the Middle Ages usually brings to mind great castles and cathedrals, these buildings, magnificent as they are, constituted only a small percentage of the total structures built in medieval Europe. Far more common were the innumerable barns, houses, shops, and other buildings that once stood in farms, villages, and towns throughout medieval Europe. Constructing these humble but essential buildings required the labor of legions of specialized craftsmen and women over the course of the Middle Ages. Among these workers were the mortarers who mixed up the mortar used in stone construction, the thatchers and slaters who installed roof coverings, and the daubers who coated walls with various mixtures to make them more solid and draft-proof. And, of course, there were the carpenters and masons who were essential to constructing and maintaining buildings of all types. All of these workers had to have learned their trades and many, if not most, of them were trained completely outside the formal apprenticeship system of the guilds. Mortarers, thatchers, and other practitioners of the more minor construction trades were rarely, if ever, members of guilds even when they worked in the cities. As for the more prestigious construction trades of carpentry and masonry, while these trades required apprenticeship and guild membership within the cities, most rural carpenters and masons do not appear to have belonged to guilds.

So, away from the cities, workers in manufacturing and construction trades likely learned from persons who were already skilled in a trade but who were not members of any guild. Such training was similar to apprenticeship but without many of its fees and requirements, such as fixed terms lasting several years. Helpers were always needed to carry the materials and tools for the experienced workers, so the first step parents may have taken in having their children learn a trade was to arrange for their sons or daughters to lend the workers a hand in exchange for a little training. For providing prolonged training, workers likely required payments from the parents. However, some medieval building contracts show that construction workers often factored in wages for their assistants when billing their employers. Some of these assistants may have been trainees but that cannot be determined from the surviving documents. In any event, from that first step of watching and helping a little, boys and girls could work their way up by gradually doing more as they learned more until they were skilled in a trade. Unfortunately, such arrangements for training would have been very informal, and so there is no surviving documentary evidence, such as the records of contracts and disputes which survive for formal apprenticeships in the cities. However, in accounts of accidents, there are records of teenagers at work in a variety trades. For example, a teenage girl was part of a crew digging in a sand pit when the sides of the pit collapsed and buried her. Luckily, her fellow workers dug her out and she revived. The record does not specify whether the girl was considered a worker or a trainee, but the relative youth of the teenagers in these accidents seems to have been noteworthy to chroniclers at the time. This may indicate that they were younger than most of the people who were performing similar work and that they were still learning their jobs. Still, there is not sufficient evidence in these accounts to firmly establish whether the teenagers involved were in training or were simply paid help. We can only speculate.

As the preceding paragraphs suggest, gender was not always a barrier to learning a trade. Women as well as men appear in the contracts and payrolls for many medieval buildings both as full-fledged workers and as assistants. And, unfortunately, the evidence suggests that women were frequently paid less than men for comparable work.

Servants

Today, in much of Western society, being someone's personal servant is generally seen as an unappealing career unless the job involved is being the personal assistant to someone wealthy and famous. Apart from these "gofers" to the stars, being a servant is frequently thought to be a degrading, low paying line of work which is fit only for people with no other marketable skills. But in the Middle Ages, being a servant was a respectable and often desirable occupation and there was no shame attached to serving in another person's household. In fact, being a servant could improve one's social standing since servants shared somewhat in the prestige of their employers' household. This meant, for example, that a boy from a poor family could improve his lot not just financially but socially as well if he found employment as a servant in a rich man's house. Similarly, as we will see in later in this section, it was quite acceptable for sons of middling and wealthy non-noble families to become servants for the nobility (rather like being personal assistants to celebrities). In such cases, the social standing of the non-noble family was enhanced and in some instances the non-noble family was able to form strong and politically useful ties with their noble employer.

Becoming a servant was often an end in itself, but for many children it was a temporary position. As servants, older children and young adults had the opportunity to earn some money of their own which they could then use to buy land, to start a business, or to start a family. This last motive was particularly true for young women. Except among the lowest levels of society, a woman's prospects for a suitable husband were greatly handicapped unless she had an appropriate dowry. A period of service also often provided an opportunity to broaden one's contacts within society. As discussed previously, people in medieval Europe routinely made use of their social and other connections to improve their situations.

Who Employed Servants?

Today, a middle income family may hire someone to periodically mow their lawn or clean their house, but only the very wealthy have full-time servants. In medieval Europe, the nobility and other wealthy people certainly employed full-time servants, but many other people had full-time servants as well. Employing servants indicated one's wealth and standing in society. Noble households, depending upon their rank, might have anywhere from one or two servants for an impoverished country knight to well over a hundred in a royal household. In non-noble households, having servants was a matter of prestige as well, and many families, except those from the lowest and poorest levels of society, employed servants. But, as with the nobility, the numbers and types of servants varied greatly. A very successful merchant might have a dozen or more servants, including, among others, a cook, a laundress, several maidservants, and a groom for his horses. On the other hand, a craftsman barely making ends meet might still have employed a young girl or boy to help his wife around the house, especially if they had no children of their own to help them.

Besides the desire for social status which employing servants conferred, the need for servants was driven by the amount of work required to maintain a household in the Middle Ages. This is difficult to understand today since we have utilities like hot and cold running water, gas and other fuels for heating, and electricity for light and to run appliances to wash dishes, clean and dry clothes, heat our food, and perform many other tasks. But many of these amenities have only become available within the last century. In the Middle Ages, performing these chores required long hours of fetching heavy buckets of water, carrying kindling, making fires, doing laundry by hand, preparing meals, and all the other jobs that must be done to keep a family clean, fed, warm, and clothed. Not surprisingly, many families needed help to do this, and many were able to find boys and girls and even men and women who were willing to work in exchange for food, a place to sleep, and some small wages.

Becoming a Servant

As with apprenticeships, employers often hired servants based on referrals from friends, relatives, and business associates. Many urban children went into service, but young servants were frequently drawn from the country for the same reason as apprentices were: children and young men and women were generally in short supply in medieval cities. While both servants and apprentices often came from country families, servants typically came from families which were poorer than those of apprentices. A family which put their children out as servants usually lacked the resources needed to place them as apprentices. However, there were some exceptions. Girls, especially orphans, from families of middling wealth and social status occasionally went into service for a time before they married. This allowed the girls to further build up their dowries. Additionally, their employers were often of higher social standing and so the girls could improve their own status and contacts through their association with these more important families and possibly improve their prospects for marriage as well. Boys from middle and upper income families also became servants for their social superiors as part of their families' efforts to improve their social standing.

Some country children found employment near their homes in the country houses of the wealthy or the manors of the nobility, while others went further away from home to find work in the towns and cities. For this latter group of children, it was important to have employment arranged in advance or to have a relative or family friend residing in the town or city if at all possible. Even if their home village was a mere ten miles away, country children who went to the towns and cities were very vulnerable, and there was no shortage of unscrupulous adults to exploit them. Girls were especially at risk. Girls who went to the city seeking their fortune without advance arrangements or a trustworthy adult to protect them were all too often easily prey for pimps and procuresses. Children of city families were at less risk of exploitation since their parents or guardians were nearby and could easily check on how they were treated.

Children appear to have typically entered service at around the age of ten or twelve, but some were younger. In cities, girls are known to have entered service when they were as young as eight. However, even if these little maids resided with the families they served, they were not cut off from their families. Medieval cities were rather small by modern standards and, again, parents could easily remain in contact with their children elsewhere in the city.

As with apprentices, employers sometimes had trouble with their servants being lured away by offers of better employment in other households. Such poaching of servants was especially common in the aftermath of Black Death, when labor of all types was in short supply. During labor shortages, some people even stooped to enticing children away from their families to become servants. In one case, a man claimed that a seven-year-old girl had agreed to become his servant for the next seven years. Fortunately, a court did not believe the man and the little girl was returned to her mother. Children are known to have become servants at this young age, but only after their parents or guardians had found such employment for them. And older children were certainly preferred over such young ones since they could perform a greater range of tasks with less supervision.

Servants' Pay

Room, board, and a few pennies a week were the most basic compensation for servants. Relatively unskilled servants such as the boys who worked in the stables or kitchens received only minimal pay in addition to a daily ration of food. As for sleeping arrangements, servants such as these slept wherever there was space on the floor or, if they were lucky, in a bed shared with other servants. More skilled and more senior workers such as a cook or a steward (the chief servant who managed the other servants and other household matters for his employer) were paid as befitting their rank within the household. Their pay was several times greater than that of the lesser servants. They were given better food and a bed or possibly even a room of their own, depending on the space available. Personal servants such as a lady's maid or a man's valet frequently slept in the same room as their employers on mattresses or trundle beds pulled out from under their employers' beds and placed on the floor for the night. High ranking servants like these also frequently received clothing as part of their compensation. Some servants in noble households were given specially made clothing called *livery*, which was made of fabric that coordinated with the colors of their master's coat of arms. In some households, common as well as noble, servants were simply given ordinary new clothing once a year or were paid a small amount of cash as an annual clothing allowance. It was also common for employers at all levels of society to give some of their worn clothing to their servants. As with having to sleep on one's employer's floor, being given second-hand clothing to wear does not appear to modern eyes as very desirable. However, in medieval Europe, such compensation was valuable, and neither the employer nor the servant considered it to be the least bit demeaning. In fact, the practice of employers' giving servants hand-me-down clothing persisted in Europe for centuries after the Middle Ages.

Serving the Nobility

From minor lords to the great kings and emperors, the nobility of medieval Europe employed vast numbers of servants, children as well as adults. Children were considered suitable for a number of jobs. These included stable boys, boys who assisted in all the various aspects of food preparation, and assistants and helpers for the adult servants. Boys were also employed to help take care of the hunting dogs which were a fixture in all noble houses. Boys were also hired to serve as pages although, as explained in the next chapter, pages were typically drawn from the ranks of noble children. Pages carried out a variety of duties, from serving guests at meals to running whatever errands their lords or ladies commanded them to perform. Girls also served in noble households. Most appear to have been maids and assisted the older serving women in carrying out the innumerable tasks required to keep a household functioning. As these boys and girls grew up, many stayed on in service. Some even progressed into key positions within their masters' households. For example, a boy who started out caring for the hunting dogs could, with diligence and hard work, progress to being his lord's chief huntsman. Such a position was usually well compensated, since hunting was a popular pastime among the nobility. A girl who showed initiative and skill in performing her duties as a maid-of-all-work could advance to being the chief housekeeper or the personal maid of the lady of the house.

Service with the nobility was highly desirable. During the Middle Ages, government rested in the hands of hereditary nobility in virtually all of Europe. Having good connections with the noblemen and -women who were one's rulers provided a person with a measure of security not enjoyed by the general public. Servants often benefited from such connections, and anyone who offended or attacked a nobleman's servant ran the risk that these actions would be brought to the attention of that noble lord. A lord might then intervene on behalf of his servants when it was necessary to maintain the status and reputation of his household. He would also respond in order to protect his own political and economic interests when the circumstances indicated that the attack on his servant was actually an indirect attack on the lord himself. Even if a lord did not act, the threat of such action was always a deterrent to mistreating his servants. Unfortunately, servants of powerful nobles were well aware of this fact. Some were quite arrogant and attacked or otherwise abused ordinary citizens, secure in the knowledge that their connections would shield them from justice.

Employment by the nobility provided servants with other benefits as well. These typically included better quality food, clothing, and accommodations than those given to servants working for non-noble families. Admittedly, the quality and quantity of these perks varied depending upon the status of the noble employer: servants of a king or a duke enjoyed a higher standard of living than those of an impoverished knight.

The many advantages of employment in a noble household meant that even very prosperous families sometimes sought such employment for their children. In fact, some families willingly paid noblemen and -women to take their sons as servants. Boys who obtained such employment served as pages and not as scullery or stable boys. They usually had some education before entering service and, because of their families' wealth and standing within society, had a basic understanding of the manners and courteous behavior expected by their noble employers. During the course of their employment, these boys had the opportunity to further improve their social skills and their contacts. Above all, this employment gave a young man the chance to display his abilities and to be noticed by someone who could advance his career. One example of a boy who benefited greatly from such employment was Geoffrey Chaucer, author of the *Canterbury Tales*. His father, a successful London wine merchant, paid to have young Geoffrey accepted as a page in the household of the Countess of Ulster in 1357 when he was about fifteen years old. The countess's husband was Prince Lionel, son of Edward III, then king of England. Chaucer appears to have made the most of his opportunities, and his intelligence and wit were recognized and appreciated by his noble employers. He moved up in the world: he served in the king's household, carried out diplomatic missions, held other government posts, and became a member of parliament, all in addition to his brilliant literary career. While this success was certainly based on Chaucer's own merits, it is doubtful that he would have gone as far as he did without his early placement in a position where his talents were recognized and encouraged and where he was able to develop contacts with people who could further his career.

Servants' Relationships with Their Employers

As with apprentices, the relationships between employers and servants ran the gamut from good to bad. Some servants stole from their employers. Some employers beat their servants severely and without cause. And some employers sexually assaulted their female servants or failed to protect these girls from being assaulted by male servants in the household. Some female servants were even forced into prostitution by their depraved masters or mistresses. Orphans as well as children from the countryside who had no relatives in the city appear to have been the ones most vulnerable to abuse. Without a sympathetic adult to check on how they were being treated and, if necessary, intervene on their behalf, there was often little these victimized children could do to protect themselves. At the other extreme, some servants were loyal and devoted to their masters. A few suffered injury or death while defending their masters or their masters' families from attack, while some employers treated their servants as family members and gave them money and other items in their wills.

Training for Less Reputable Trades

Respectable trades such as those discussed above weren't the only ones practiced in the Middle Ages and taught to new practitioners. Not unlike apprentices, petty thieves, beggars, and prostitutes appear to have sometimes learned their trades from established experts. In the late Middle Ages, centuries before Dickens's "Artful Dodger," little boys as young as nine were surreptitiously cutting the purses from the belts of adults and making off with them. While it was not recorded how these children came by these skills, evidence from later times suggests that they were taught by older children and adults, perhaps even their own parents.

As for little beggars, some of these unfortunates were genuinely poor children who were trying to survive. Some may have learned begging from their parents, but many were likely orphaned or abandoned and instinctively turned to begging. The generosity of others was their only hope. But not all begging children were truly poor. From London to Florence, there are accounts of children who were kidnapped and forced to beg by their captors. These kidnappers stripped their little victims and dressed them in rags to make them look more pitiful so that passers-by were more likely to give them money. In one instance in London, a little girl had been seized by a woman, taken away, dressed in rags, and put out onto the street to beg. Miraculously, someone recognized her and returned her to her family. Unfortunately, such escapes appear to have been the exception. In the 15th century, some of these dreadful criminals were reported as engaging in even more terrible abuse of the children they had stolen. In Paris and northern Italy, adult beggars were accused of not only kidnapping children but also of blinding, crippling, and mutilating them so that those seeing them would be so moved by their suffering that they would give them alms. While the veracity of these particular accusations cannot be determined, evidence from post-medieval Europe and from other areas around the world indicates that such horrific exploitation of children may well have also occurred in medieval Europe.

Some young girls became prostitutes. Some took up this trade on their own but many appear to have been forced into prostitution by unscrupulous adults. In some cases, these pimps and procuresses were their own parents. In others, girls who had been sent to become maids or to learn a trade were forced into prostitution by their mistresses or masters, as mentioned previously. Again, orphans and country girls who had been sent into the city, far away from any relatives or friends, were particularly vulnerable to such exploitation. As with the wretched children who were kidnapped and made to beg, there is proof of these horrible practices in the records of prosecutions of the criminals involved and accounts of rare cases in which the victims escaped or were rescued.

Child Labor

At the beginning of this chapter, I said that it was rare for children to work or even begin their training for their future jobs in earnest before the age of twelve or so. But, as the previous section shows, children were not free from exploitation in the Middle Ages. While some poor families turned their children out to beg, others found employment for them. Even young children were capable of weeding fields and were sometimes hired out to do so. Other poor children were employed at even harder and more dangerous jobs. Because of their small size, young boys were sometimes employed in cleaning wells and in mining, although most miners were adults. Still, particularly in comparison with the heyday of the Industrial Revolution centuries later, when countless small children toiled for long hours in factories across Europe and the United States, child labor was a relatively uncommon practice in the Middle Ages.

Training for Jewish Children

Jewish children learned their future occupations like their Christian counterparts. Girls were expected to learn how to cook, clean, and keep house from their mothers. Boys often learned their crafts and trades from their fathers or other relatives, while some learned from established masters to whom they were not related. As with Christians, this extra-familial training could be an apprenticeship or other less formal training. While the evidence is very limited, it is very likely that Jewish boys were apprenticed only to Jewish masters and Christian children were apprenticed only to Christian masters. Despite this segregation, the contracts for Jewish apprentices appear to have conformed to the customs for apprenticeships found in the surrounding Christian communities.

Trades for Jewish Children

In the early Middle Ages, Jews in Europe engaged in the same range of trades as Christians, from farming to manufacturing and commerce, and Jewish children were taught all these trades. However, the actions of Christian rulers as well as growing antipathy towards Jews among the Christian population gradually reduced the number of trades which Jews could practice. By the late 12th century, Jews in northern Europe were largely confined to the larger towns and cities, and money-lending was one of the few trades left open to them. Still, there were Jewish physicians and craftsmen, although members of latter group were limited primarily to producing goods for their fellow Jews. For example, there were Jewish manuscript copyists and illuminators who produced texts in Hebrew, and there were Jewish butchers who slaughtered animals in accordance with their religion's dietary laws. In communities in southern France and elsewhere along the northern coast of the Mediterranean Sea, Jews enjoyed greater economic freedom than did the Jewish communities of northern Europe until much later in the Middle Ages. In these southern enclaves, Jews continued to farm and engage in a variety of trades until at least the end of the 13th century. However, a number of events, including the Albigensian Crusade, which concluded with the conquest of southern France by the nobility of northern France, and the reconquest of the Iberian Peninsula by Christians, drastically changed the political and religious situation in southern Europe. As part of these changes, restrictions like those long practiced in northern Europe were imposed on the Jews in this region as well. Thus, by the 14th century, the primary occupations left for Jews and their children were medicine, money-lending, and crafts and services catering to their own communities.

9

Training for a Career
and Earning a Living:
The Clergy and Nobility

Now we will examine the training for the clergy and the nobility. Under the three-part division of medieval society, these were two most important groups, since the clergy wielded authority over all religious matters within Christian Europe and the nobility held the reins of government and ruled over the physical world. Because of this division of authority, the nobility were sometimes referred to as *lords temporal* and the members of the higher clergy, such as bishops and archbishops, were called *lords spiritual*.

The Ties Between the Nobility and the Clergy

In real life, the distinction between these two groups and the division of the realms which they ruled was nowhere near as clear as their titles may suggest. As far back as the last centuries of the Roman Empire, beginning with the conversion of Emperor Constantine to Christianity, the Christian religion and temporal government became closely linked. These close relations survived the collapse of the empire in western Europe and, at the dawn of the Middle Ages, Christian missionaries were already at work seeking converts among the pagan peoples who had invaded the former lands of the empire and elsewhere in Europe. In many instances, the rulers were among the first to convert and they then ordered all their people to convert as well. This process usually involved the missionaries extending formal recognition of the rulers' temporal authority in return for their recognition of the Church as the sole and supreme authority on spiritual matters.

The ties between the Church and secular rulers were so close in the early Middle Ages that some secular rulers viewed the churches within their lands as being part of their property, and noble lords in many parts of Europe exercised considerable control over the clergy. For example, in some regions when a bishopric or other high-level Church position became vacant, the king claimed the right to name a cleric to fill the vacancy. Noblemen well below the rank of kings exercised similar control on a smaller scale and often dictated which priests would fill vacancies in the parishes within their jurisdictions. Some lords also collected a share of any revenue raised by the churches in their lands. However, by the end of the 12th century, the Church had succeeded in ending these practices, although kings were still able to levy taxes on the clergy from time to time.

For its part, the Church was frequently involved in worldly affairs. Cathedrals, churches, and monasteries received innumerable grants of land, rents from properties, and other valuable donations over the course of the Middle Ages. Through these gifts, some archbishops, bishops, and abbots became temporal lords as well as spiritual ones because possession of land under the feudal system typically entailed swearing fealty to the nobleman who had dominion over the land. The person who pledged his loyalty and support, including military service, to a lord in exchange for a grant of land was called a *vassal*. As a result, some clergymen became vassals of temporal lords. Some bishops even rendered the military support they owed their lords in person and were sometimes referred to as *warrior bishops*. Further, when lands were given to religious institutions, the lesser vassals who already resided on these lands were also transferred. These vassals then owed their fealty to their cleric-lords just as they would to an ordinary temporal lord. In parts of Germany and in one county in England, certain bishops were given the title of *prince-bishop* to reflect their dual roles. In addition to becoming entangled in worldly matters through land ownership under the feudal system, the Church also intervened in temporal politics to advance its interests. At times, popes faced off against kings and emperors and even resorted to excommunicating entire countries to force compliance with the Church's will.

As one can see, politics and religion freely mixed in medieval Europe. To function effectively as either a temporal or a spiritual lord, members of both the nobility and the clergy, especially those in the Church's higher ranks, had to understand politics in feudal world. Further, as with so many other areas of life in the Middle Ages, their family and social connections were also significant factors in their careers, whether within the Church or the courts of the nobility. Advancing from priest to bishop or from monk to abbot frequently required considerable support from both inside and outside the Church. Clerics who had influential friends or relatives among the secular nobility or in positions of authority within the Church had a far better chance of obtaining such advancement than those who did not. As a consequence, throughout the Middle Ages, most of the powerful positions within the Church were filled by the sons of noble or other wealthy families.

Who Became Clerics and Why

Many of the boys who trained to become clerics and the girls who became nuns in the Middle Ages did so for the same reasons that young men and women still go to seminaries and embark on religious careers: They had a genuine belief in their religion and they wanted to serve God and their fellow men and women. However, some men in medieval Europe, while their faith may have been genuine, appear to have entered the Church for more worldly reasons. As the previous section suggests, a clerical career could lead to great power, and some clergymen used this power to advance the interests of their own families or political factions. On a humbler level, some men who became priests or monks were likely motivated in part by the promise of a measure of economic and personal security in a very unstable world.

Others had no choice in the matter and were placed with the Church by their families for one of a number of reasons. Forcing a person to enter the clergy seems very peculiar and rather repellent when judged by today's standards. However, as we have seen with apprenticeships, it was not uncommon for parents or other relatives to dictate children's future careers and, for some, the Church was simply another way to earn a living. There were other economic reasons for compelling a child to enter the Church. Girls from noble families were sometimes encouraged or forced to enter nunneries when their families could not afford or were unwilling to pay suitable dowries for them. For most of the Middle Ages, the family of the bride had to give the groom a payment as part of the marriage arrangement. As explained in the next chapter, this payment, the dowry, was often quite substantial for wealthy and noble marriages. Placement in a nunnery usually required some "gift" but this was far less costly than a dowry.

Daughters were not the only ones placed in careers in the Church without regard to their own wishes. Some families gave their sons to the Church to be trained either as monks or priests as a sacrifice to God. Such placement was sometimes part of fulfilling a vow which a parent had made to God, such as promises made as part of prayers for deliverance from shipwrecks or other crises. Having a son become a cleric had additional spiritual benefits. Traditionally, Christians offered prayers for the souls of deceased loved ones in hopes that this act would somehow improve their fate in the afterlife. By the late Middle Ages, it was believed that souls of the deceased would go to heaven, hell, or purgatory. Purgatory was a place for the souls of those who had committed sins during their time on earth for which they had not atoned before their deaths. The sins of these souls were not so grave as to merit spending eternity in hell. Still, because of their sinfulness, they did not deserve to be immediately admitted to heaven. Instead, these souls went to purgatory where they underwent penitential punishment to purge their remaining sins. It was believed that this period of purification could be shortened if those still living offered prayers on behalf of these souls. Thus, besides the merit inherent in giving a child to the Church, parents whose son became a monk or priest enjoyed the added spiritual benefit of having a holy man in the family who would offer prayers or say masses for the benefit of their souls.

Youngest Sons and Careers in the Church

It is often thought that most of the boys from noble families who pursued careers within the Church were the youngest sons. This idea is supported by the fact that the nobility in many parts of Europe followed the practice of primogeniture in settling inheritances. In brief, primogeniture meant that the eldest son inherited all of his father's titles and lands while any younger brothers received very little or nothing. To provide paying occupations for their younger sons, noble parents sometimes sought suitable places for them within the Church. In practice, however, a family could not plan on who the oldest surviving heir would be until the actual moment of the father's death, because children so often predeceased their parents in the Middle Ages. Thus, a nobleman could not just place all of the sons from the second-born on down into the priesthood or in a monastery, since his first-born son might well die before he did. Having the next heir in line already committed by sacred vows to a lifetime in the Church could cause serious problems for a family. So, instead, many noble families raised all their sons as prospective heirs, although younger sons were also frequently given training for service within the Church.

In addition to training, some younger sons who were expected to enter the Church were even endowed with *benefices* while they were still only children. A benefice was the right to receive the income generated by a church and its property. This money was supposed to sup-

port the priest who was actually serving that church's parishioners but it was a common practice during the Middle to assign the revenue to someone else. The person receiving the income
hired a priest to serve at the church in his place but this substitute cleric was paid only a small
fraction of the church's revenue. Under this practice, the would-be cleric acquired a steady
stream of income and enjoyed the status of nominally being the priest of a church even though
he was not yet ordained.

While they were given religious training and received benefices, younger sons of the
nobility were often encouraged by their families to delay making any irrevocable vows to the
Church until their prospects for inheritance were more certain. For example, William Marshall, a famed English knight and earl of Pembroke in the late 12th and early 13th centuries,
had several sons. His third son, Gilbert, was intended for a career in the Church. However,
while Gilbert was in his early thirties, he became the primary heir after the deaths of his father
and elder brothers. He married and took up the life of a knight as the new earl of Pembroke.
Obviously, he had not undertaken his final vows to the Church. Additionally, his subsequent
performance at tournaments indicate that he had lived much like his secular brothers during
his prolonged time in minor orders.

As the case of Gilbert Marshall suggests, many clerics from noble families enjoyed a very
secular life before finally committing themselves to the Church. Even after taking their final
vows, clergymen from such backgrounds often indulged in very worldly tastes in food and
clothing and engaged in noble pursuits such as hunting, riding, and combat as well.

The Secular Clergy and the Regular Clergy

The Christian clergy in the medieval Europe was divided into two groups: the secular
clergy and the regular clergy. The secular clergy were those who were responsible for helping
lay people find salvation through Christ's teachings and the sacraments of the Christian church.
The most numerous members of the secular clergy were the priests found in churches in every
village, town, and city in medieval Europe. In addition to priests, the secular clergy included
the bishops, archbishops, and cardinals who formed the upper echelons of the Church. The
secular clergy also included the ostiaries, exorcists, lectors, acolytes, subdeacons, and deacons
who ranked below priests in the Church's hierarchy and, as explained later in this chapter,
were usually in training to become priests.

While the secular clergy were out among the people, the regular clergy were those who
lived communally in accordance with an order; that is, a set of rules designed to help in their
devotions toward God. Most orders required their adherents to turn away from the material
world so that they could better focus on spiritual matters. The most common member of the
regular clergy was the monk. Within his monastery, the monk was shut away from the distractions and temptations of the everyday world. He devoted himself to reading religious texts
and meditating upon them. He also attended and participated in numerous religious services
or *divine offices* each and every day. During these services, monks offered prayers for the souls
of their deceased relatives, benefactors of their monasteries and others. In some monastic
orders, monks were permitted to become priests, but their ministries were confined within
their cloisters. Their duty was to perform the divine offices and care for the souls of their
brethren rather than for those outside their monasteries.

Canons regular were priests who lived communally under rules somewhat comparable to
those of monastic orders. Duties of canons regular were similar to monk-priests in that,

unlike ordinary priests, they did not minister to lay people. Instead, they performed masses for the benefit of the souls of deceased.

While most of the regular clergy were secluded from the general public, there was one group whose mission was to go out into the world and preach. These were the friars. They lived under orders like monks or canons regular but they achieved their separation from the material world through strict vows of poverty. The early friars had to beg to support themselves while they served God as itinerant preachers.

Nuns constituted a special subset within the regular clergy. They too were cloistered and were to avoid all unnecessary contact with the material world so that they could devote themselves to meditation and prayer. Like the male monastic orders, orders of nuns also observed the divine offices but, since women could not become priests, nunneries had male chaplains who officiated at these and other religious services.

Simony

Before examining the training required for religious careers, there is one term which requires some explanation: simony. Placing children in religious careers sometimes involved making payments to officials of the Church. Parents and guardians often made such payments to abbots and abbesses when placing a boy in a monastic order or a girl in nunnery. People who entered orders later in life as adults commonly paid for their admission as well. Whether they were the parents or guardians of the would-be monk or nun or were candidates themselves, all who made these payments and the Church officials who accepted them were guilty of the sin of simony (fig. 33). Simony is the buying or selling of Christian sacraments or of positions within the Church, which the Church strongly condemned as a grave sin. The sacraments, such as baptism and communion, were seen as gifts from God, and the Church taught that no man should materially profit from them. However, as we saw in chapter 1, some priests insisted on payments for performing baptisms despite the express prohibition of that practice by the Church. Simony was also a problem when a person began a career in the Church. While it was quite acceptable to give donations to the Church when a son entered a monastery or a daughter was admitted to a nunnery, it was not permissible for parents and Church officials to negotiate payments for accepting a child into the clergy. Yet many did, under the rationale that the monastery or nunnery needed additional resources to cover the expenses of housing, clothing, and feeding the new monk or nun. Abbots and abbesses frequently demanded payments, sometimes rather substantial ones, in money or property in exchange for accepting a child into their communities. This was such a commonplace occurrence that parents understood from the start that such payments were to be made. They occasionally protested but most complied with the demands, although the amounts of the payments were a matter for hard bargaining.

As early as the 8th century, lay and Church officials had identified the practice of making payments upon entering a monastery as a form of simony and tried to prohibit it. To their credit, many reformers within the Church were genuinely disgusted with such blatant commercialism in permitting people to buy their way into the clergy. The Church made repeated efforts to stop this practice but could not completely stamp it out, and examples of simony can be found through the end of the Middle Ages.

One last point: Why was it called simony? As described in the Acts of the Apostles, a magician named Simon Magus saw the Apostles performing miracles in Christ's name. He

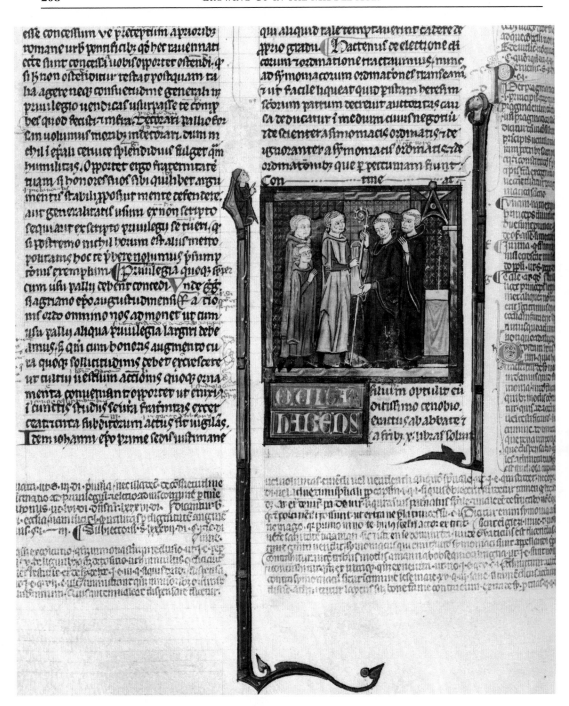

Fig. 33. In this detail taken from the page of Gratian's *Decretum* illustrated in fig. 31, one can see the act of simony taking place. One of the men on the left, who is likely the father of the boy standing next to him, hands a bag of money to the abbot on the right. In exchange for the money, the abbot accepts the boy into his monastery. While the placement of children in monasteries or nunneries was customarily preceded by a payment, this practice was condemned by the Church as simony. Men and women were to be admitted freely into the ranks of the church. Permitting them to buy their way in was sinful.

was impressed and wanted the Apostles to teach him so that he could perform them too. He saw the miracles as just another form of magic and not as something divine, and expected the Apostles to be willing to train him in exchange for payment. He approached St. Peter and offered him to pay him money for the secret of the Apostles' "magic." St. Peter refused, explaining that God's gifts were not for sale and condemning Simon for his impertinent proposition. So, Simon Magus became the first simoniac, giving his name to the sin which he was the first to commit.

Entry into the Secular Clergy

The clergy, both secular and regular, drew its members from across medieval society. In fact, as described in chapter 6, the Church made efforts to educate boys in part to increase the number of males who might become priests. As a result of these efforts, sons of peasants, merchants, and craftsmen entered the Church and became priests. However, as explained above, the Church was not an egalitarian body. While there were a number of men from non-noble families who, through their hard work and natural talents, rose through the ranks to become bishops, archbishops, and, in one instance, even pope, such advancement was an exception. It was always difficult to overcome the resistance of the nobility, both inside and outside of the Church, against promoting men from humble families to positions of authority. This prejudice was so common that a contemporary saying amongst the nobility advised that the son of one's lowest vassal was always a better choice for advancement to bishop than any son of a peasant. Thus, children from non-noble families could embark on the path to priesthood but seldom advanced beyond the rank of priest.

Besides the bias of the nobility, the Church itself imposed some restrictions on who could enter the priesthood. To the modern reader, these restrictions may appear unreasonable but, to the medieval mind, these requirements were rationally connected to a candidate's fitness for the priesthood. One of these restrictions was that a man who was deformed or suffered from any other major physical handicap could not become a priest. As discussed in chapter 1, such physical defects were not a bar to becoming a monk but they were an obstacle for anyone planning to enter the priesthood. The motive for this restriction may have been that the Church was concerned that such handicaps would interfere with the proper performance of a priest's duties. For example, a deformed or missing hand or arm could prevent a priest from making the sign of the Cross and other gestures required as part of Christian rituals. However, the restriction may have been based, at least in part, on the popular belief that physical handicaps which were birth defects were the result of diabolic action or were a mark of divine displeasure for some sin which the deformed man's parents had committed. Still, the Church's restriction was not absolute. Handicapped men could become priests if they obtained a dispensation from the pope. As part of obtaining such an exception, a candidate for priesthood may have had to prove that his physical defect would not interfere with the performance of his duties.

Another impediment to becoming a priest was illegitimacy. Men who had been born out of wedlock were barred from becoming priests. The carnal sin that attended their conception was somehow thought to taint them. However, it should be noted that illegitimacy of birth was usually not considered a handicap in one's adult career outside of the Church. As with the restriction for physical handicaps, this limitation was also subject to exceptions. A candidate could obtain a papal dispensation upon showing that he was otherwise of good character and qualified for the priesthood. While such dispensations appear to have been routinely granted to worthy candidates, it should be noted that obtaining this and any other dispensations from the pope required resources which most ordinary people lacked. A person seeking such a dispensation usually had to retain the services of a canon lawyer to draft the request to send to the pope. He also had to arrange for the request to be sent to Rome and be presented to the pope. All of this cost money. Not surprisingly, many of the men who were granted dispensations for illegitimate birth appear to have been bastard sons of noblemen.

Training to Become a Priest

Training to become a priest could start while a boy was still quite young. Children of all ages accompanied their parents to church services and, as mentioned in chapter 3, some children imitated what they had seen when they were playing, pretending to be priests saying mass. Still, to become a priest, a boy had to be literate. For many boys, training with their local priests was the only means for obtaining the requisite literacy. While the priests taught them how to read the necessary texts, these boys also learned how to perform the rituals of the Christian worship by assisting the priests in the performance of their duties. Boys in the larger towns and cities, especially those from middle and upper class families, learned to read at schools such as those found at the cathedrals. Like those in training with parish priests, boys at the cathedral schools performed minor roles in church services while learning how to read. They also usually served in the choir. In the Middle Ages, masses were sung or chanted by priests and a reply or response was required for certain passages during the services (fig. 26). Today, the congregation typically recites the response, but this was not the case in the Middle Ages. While they were supposed to watch and listen attentively, parishioners had little active role in the services. Further, most people lacked sufficient knowledge of Latin, the language in which all Christian services were performed, to permit them even to sing the responses. Instead, singing these responses was one of the functions of medieval choir boys.

The requirement for literacy posed no problem for the sons of the nobility since these boys were often tutored in reading and writing by chaplains and other literate men in their parents' households. Boys from these privileged backgrounds were placed in cathedral schools and in the households of bishops, who were sometimes their relatives. Here, they received further education as well as the training necessary to become priests. Additionally, those who were attached to a bishop's retinue gained valuable experience and insight into the workings of the higher levels of the Church and often of temporal politics as well. As members of a bishop's household, these boys had the opportunity to develop social contacts both within their own households and in the households of those spiritual and temporal lords whom the bishop visited or hosted. While of little use in performing routine priestly duties, such experience and contacts were very helpful for ambitious boys.

In the early stages of their training, boys were not required to make any irrevocable vows or otherwise permanently bind themselves to the Church. They were still free to leave the Church and go on to other careers at any time. One reason that they were not required to take such vows was their youth. Many of these boys were as young as seven when they began their training and were considered to be too young and immature to undertake such oaths. However, they could receive their first tonsure at this age. The tonsure was the distinctive haircut of all medieval clerics, both secular and regular. For a tonsure, the crown of the head is shaved bare, leaving a fringe of hair encircling the head (figs. 26 and 27).

The Minor and Major Orders

Those boys who truly planned on pursuing a career within the Church were expected to enter minor orders. The four minor orders were lector, ostiary, exorcist, and acolyte (fig. 34). The lector was responsible for performing the readings during mass. As with singing the responses, this task could only be performed by someone who could read Latin. The ostiary was the doorkeeper. The ostiary's duties included acting as an usher and maintaining order during services, ringing the bells, and taking care of the church building itself. The exorcist was tasked with casting out demons. Most commonly, this involved the routine exorcisms performed as part of baptism but could include cases of demonic possession as well. The exorcist was also responsible for seeing to the care of demoniacs within the parish, including giving them alms, clothing, and food donated by parishioners. Acolyte was the highest of the minor orders and was generally conferred only on boys who were at least 13 years old. An acolyte's duties were less narrowly defined than those of the other minor orders. He assisted the priest in the performance of his duties as needed.

Well before the end of the Middle Ages, priests had taken over the duties of the exorcist and most of those of the lector as well. As for the ostiary, his duties were often performed by laymen from the parish. Thus, apart from the acolyte, the minor orders appear to have been simply titles without real functions for much of the Middle Ages. This was likely just as well given the youth and inexperience of the boys who held these titles. Instead, while their duties were being carried out by others, boys in minor orders were free to learn to read and write. They still learned how to perform religious services, from baptisms to burials, by assisting the priest. In England, these boys training to become priests came to be called *holy water clerks* or just *clerks*.

After being ordained as an acolyte, the next step towards priesthood was to enter major orders. The major orders were subdeacon, deacon, and priest. Entering the major orders required taking solemn vows of poverty, chastity, and obedience. These vows were a promise to God and as such were irrevocable. Once a man had taken these vows and been ordained, he was bound to a lifetime of service within the Church. The minimum age for advancing from acolyte to subdeacon was seventeen or eighteen. The minimum age for deacons was nineteen and twenty-four or twenty-five for priests, although this was lowered to twenty in the early 14th century. However, because of irrevocability of the vows, some men put off entering major orders until they were at least twenty-four and fully prepared to commit themselves to being priests. In these cases, rather than gradually progressing from subdeacon to deacon to priest over several years, the men took their vows and were ordained as subdeacons, deacons, and priests in a single ceremony.

Before a candidate for priesthood was ordained, he underwent an examination. The examination was conducted four times a year by the bishop of the diocese or by his archdeacon. The archdeacon was the deacon for the cathedral and served as part of the bishop's administrative staff. At the time of examination, the candidate had to provide proof of his age and legitimate birth and presumably demonstrate that he was free of deformities. The bishop or his archdeacon then tested the candidate's knowledge of religion and his understanding of his duties. The questioning covered the Ten Commandments, the Seven Sacraments, and other fundamental aspects of the Christian faith. Those who passed the examination were then ordained by the bishop. Ordinations were usually on a Saturday, and the new priests then said their first masses the very next day.

Fig. 34. In this illumination, a bishop is ordaining men in minor orders. He is bestowing a set of keys to one of the kneeling clerics. The recipient of the keys is being ordained as an ostiary. As an ostiary, he is now responsible for maintaining and securing the church in which he serves.

The Higher Secular Clergy

For most secular clergy, priest was the highest rank they ever attained. For those with the right connections or for those with exceptional talent and virtue, bishop was the next step up. Thirty was the minimum age for bishops, although this limit was often disregarded when the candidate was the son of an influential family. Priesthood was not the only route to becoming a bishop. In some instances, members of the regular clergy such as abbots were effectively drafted from their cloistered lives and made bishops.

From their cathedrals, bishops governed their dioceses, which were also called *sees*. These were geographical areas into which the Church divided Christendom. The lowest subdivision was the individual parish. A bishop's see contained many parishes. He also often had oversight of any other religious institutions, such as monasteries and nunneries, within the area as well. However, there were sometimes struggles between heads of monastic orders and the bishops and archbishop over the responsibility for inspecting these institutions.

From bishop, a talented cleric could advance to archbishop. Archbishops were the next highest level of management within the Church. The area over which an archbishop had jurisdiction was called a *metropolitan*. Each archbishop's metropolitan contained several bishops' sees. The next step up from archbishop was cardinal. The term "cardinal" was originally an honorific title for the priests of certain important churches. Over the course of the Middle Ages, cardinal emerged as a position within the Church's hierarchy which ranked above that of bishop and even of archbishop. Cardinals functioned as part of the Church's central bureaucracy and gained considerable power and influence.

Entry into the Regular Clergy

In the early centuries of the Middle Ages, boys from common families, even poor ones, were accepted into the ranks of the monasteries. However, admission was increasingly limited to those boys whose families had sufficient wealth and social standing to persuade monasteries to accept their sons. Additionally, advancement within the monasteries, that is, progressing from being an ordinary monk to holding a position of responsibility, was often dependent upon the status and influence of the monk's family. As with advancement from priest to bishop and beyond, there were monks of common birth who advanced within the ranks of their orders, and a few even became abbots (the heads of individual monasteries). But, like those few sons of peasants who became archbishops, such abbots of base origins were rarities. Abbots and other monastic officials were far more often sons of the nobility. Further, those monks who reached the highest ranks and became heads of their entire orders appear to have always come from noble families.

Oblation

While many men joined monastic orders when they were old enough to make the decision for themselves, some boys were placed in monasteries when they were still quite young. Some were as young as five. As mentioned in chapter 1, some of these boys were handicapped or were from poor families, and their parents abandoned them to monasteries so that they could receive care which their parents either could not or would not provide. In other instances, parents offered their sons to the monastery as a sacrifice and part of their genuine religious devotion. In some cases, the parents were honoring promises they had made to God for answering their prayers or as a donation to show their sincere gratitude to God for some divine help. For others, such as noble parents who had so many sons that they could not provide adequate inheritances for all of them, giving a child to monastery served both worldly and spiritual ends. Regardless of the reason, the practice of giving young children to the Church was called *oblation*, and was most common in the early Middle Ages. In fact, many of the monks of first half of the Middle Ages had entered their monasteries while they were still children.

Up until the 8th century, the decision to remain permanently in the monastery rested with the oblate. He made this decision around the age of fourteen, when he became old enough to take his permanent vows. Unfortunately, there are no records which indicate how many boys opted out of monastic careers at this point. During the 8th century, oblates came to be bound entirely by their parents' decision. Oblates still could not undertake their vows until they were at least fourteen years old, but they were expected to comply with their parents' decision and commit themselves to a lifetime in the cloister at that time. A few oblates are known to have refused to take their vows, but all appear to have been ultimately compelled to stay within their monasteries. During the 12th century, some of the more prominent monastic orders began to impose minimum age limits for novices to curb the practice of oblation. These regulations were part of reforms aimed at restoring the spiritual zeal of the monasteries by preventing boys who had no genuine desire to become monks from being committed to a lifetime in the cloister by their parents or guardians. Instead, only men who had a true religious calling were to be permitted to enter the monastic orders. Additionally, the presence of young boys within monasteries had long been seen as disruptive to the peace and order which were such essential parts of the monastic life. By imposing these age limits, the number of boys within monasteries was reduced and, presumably, tranquility was increased. Officials within the Church also recognized that some parents and guardians were using oblation as a means to deprive children of their inheritances. Since monks took a vow of poverty and could not inherit anything from their families, unscrupulous parents, step-parents, and guardians who may have been the boy's siblings or his uncles, could deny a boy his rightful inheritance by placing him in a monastery. However, such placement of orphans was not always motivated by greed. Monasteries offered a secure place to live out one's life. It also improved one's chances of going to heaven after death since living piously and chastely in accordance with monastic rules was considered the ideal life for a Christian by many in the Middle Ages. Thus, some guardians were acting in what they thought were the best interests of the orphans in their care when they placed them in monasteries. Parents who were dying sometimes made arrangements for their surviving young children to enter monastic orders as well, just as some parents arranged for apprenticeships for their soon-to-be-orphaned sons and daughters. Still, whether because of the disruption children caused within the monasteries or because it forced persons who had no real vocation to undertake lifelong careers in the Church, many men within the Church considered oblation to be wrong and took action to end the practice. Thus, in the 12th century, one major monastic order set the minimum age at fifteen for novices and then raised it a few decades later to eighteen. In 1215, the Church abolished the practice of oblation and in 1234 officially set the minimum age for a boy to undertake vows that would irrevocably bind him to a lifetime in the cloister at fourteen while leaving it open for the monastic orders to set higher limits. Further, any boys who were admitted to the monasteries while they were still little children were to be allowed to leave upon reaching the age of fourteen if they did not chose to take vows. However, it cannot be determined how many boys ever availed themselves of this option to leave. With few, if any, friends on the outside and a family who would likely not welcome back a son whom they had expected to remain within the cloister, any boy who did leave the monastery at this point had little support for beginning a new life in the outside world. Still, the numbers of boys who may have faced such difficult circumstances was likely rather small since the Church's reforms appear to have succeeded in largely ended the practice of monastic child oblation among boys. However, girls continued to be placed in nunneries while they were still young children through end of the Middle Ages. This practice is discussed in more detail later in this chapter.

Other Boys in the Monasteries

At times, there were a few children who were placed in monasteries by their parents but who were not expected to stay there permanently. While it was contrary to monastic rules, some monasteries accepted boys as boarders. These boys were from prominent and influential families, often nobility. These families typically had some longstanding connection with the monasteries such as being related to the monasteries' founders or other major donors. Others were donors in their own right or already had relatives who were monks or even abbots at these institutions. Regardless of the exact nature of their relationship with the monasteries, the abbots involved presumably judged it wiser to bend the rules than to alienate their monasteries' wealthy and aristocratic neighbors. As part of their boarding, these boys usually received some education, although some brought their tutors with them rather than being taught by the monks. It also appears that many of these boys were actually attached to the abbot's own household rather than being placed in the monastery with the monks. Since the abbots were often from noble families themselves, the temporary placement of boys in their households was likely part of a practice which was common among medieval nobility. As explained in the second half of this chapter, sons of the nobility were frequently sent to live with other members of the aristocracy for a number of reasons, including to learn proper behavior and to broaden and develop their social contacts. Thus, while abbots were part of the clergy, it was their noble status and the power they wielded in the secular world that caused noble parents to send them their sons on a temporary basis. Other boys from noble families were placed with monasteries for safekeeping when their fathers went on long pilgrimages or to fight abroad. Still, these cases were exceptional and the numbers of such boarders was always very small. Most boys who were placed in monasteries were expected to become novices, take vows, and live the rest of their lives within the bosom of the Church.

Becoming a Monk

Boys and men who were in training to become monks were called *novices*. They were assigned to a master of novices, who was responsible for familiarizing them with the many rules which they now had to obey. The Rule of St. Benedict of Nursia (480–547 A.D.) was the basis for the regulations of all monastic orders. Under the Rule, the two most important personal qualities for the novice to develop were obedience and humility. Obedience included following all of God's commandments as well as carrying out all the orders given by superiors within the monastery. Novices and monks were to comply with all orders meekly and cheerfully. St. Benedict established twelve steps of humility. The first step towards achieving humility was to obey all of God's commandments. A monk reached the final step when he was truly humble in his heart as well as in his appearance and all his actions.

Silence was also prized by St. Benedict. Under the Rule of St. Benedict, monks were to speak only when necessary. Jokes and idle conversation were condemned under the rule. No talking or whispering was permitted during meals. Instead, all novices and monks were to listen to a single monk who read from a religious text during the meal. To comply with the requirement for silence, some orders developed sign language so that diners could communicate their needs, such as wanting the salt or bread passed to them, to one another. The novices learned these signals as part of their training.

Returning to the master of novices, he kept his charges under constant surveillance. During the day, he instructed them and accompanied them as they made their rounds. At night, the novices slept in individual beds in the open hall of the *dorter* (dormitory). The novices' dormitory was sometimes a separate room from the dorter for the monks but, as with the monks' room, a candle was kept burning in it at night. This enabled the master of the novices, or the abbot or other monastic official in the case of the monks, to see at any hour that all were in their beds and not engaged in any inappropriate activities. Additionally, under the Rule of St. Benedict, there was to be no talking after the monks had retired for the night.

One of the most fundamental things which the novices learned was the routine they were to follow each day for the rest of their lives. This routine included time for work, for meditation, and, most importantly, for observing religious services. Depending upon the monastic order to which a monk belonged, he may have been required to attend as many as seven services held around the clock. These services were *matins* or *lauds* at midnight, *prime* at 6:00 am, *terce* at 9:00 am, *sext* at 11:00 or noon, *nones* at 2:00 pm, *vespers* at 4:00 pm, and *compline* at 7:00 pm. Mechanical clocks were developed only near the end of the Middle Ages, so time was usually gauged by the position of the sun and stars. As a result, the exact time these services were observed varied with the seasons. It should also be noted that some of these services were often quite brief. For example, while matins, terce, and sext each lasted about an hour, prime, nones, vespers, and compline were only about a half-hour each. Further, judging by contemporary complaints about monasteries in which services were said so fast that verses were garbled or omitted, these services were sometimes even shorter.

In addition to learning the monastic routine, novices learned to read and sing. These skills were essential to performing their religious duties. As with the boys attending cathedral schools and those learning and working with parish priests, the novices learned to sing in Latin so that they could participate in the divine offices. They started out by learning to sing the responses, and their high, clear voices appear to have been as appreciated in the monasteries as those of the choirboys were in the cathedrals. Learning to read also enabled the novices to read religious texts and meditate upon their contents. Under the Rule of St. Benedict, each monk was to spend two hours reading each day. Monks were also allowed to read in bed after the midday meal. However, this time was supposed to be for rest, so they were permitted to read only if it did not disturb their fellow monks in the dorter.

Physical idleness was seen as inimical to spiritual well-being. Thus, monastic orders required their members to perform some manual labor in addition to their religious works. Under St. Benedict's Rule, monks were expected to perform manual labor for about five hours each day, three hours early in the morning and two hours in the mid-afternoon, during the late spring through early fall. In the late fall to early spring, they were still expected to work for five hours but, to allow for the limited hours of daylight, the time was shifted to the late morning and early afternoon.

The novices could have learned any number of skills within the cloister since the monasteries were often self-contained communities and needed most of the same services and products required by secular villages. A novice may have learned how to grow crops or grapes in the monastery's fields or vineyards or to prepare meals for his brother monks in the kitchen. He could also have learned metal-smithing in the monastery's forge. However, after the first few centuries of the Middle Ages, most monasteries appear to have increasingly relied on hired professionals to perform specialized work such as metal-working, building construction, and even cooking. Further, many monasteries came to recruit and use lay-brothers to carry out heavy agricultural work and day-to-day chores. (The lay-brothers and their roles are explained further later in this chapter.) So, instead of hard, physical labor, many novices learned how to perform more refined work such as healing, cultivating useful herbs, or producing the beautiful, illuminated copies of manuscripts so often associated with monasteries.

During their training, many monasteries made some allowances for the youth and lack of stamina of the novices and the needs of their still growing bodies. In some monasteries, they appear to have been permitted to sleep through the night instead of having to rise near midnight to trudge to the abbey church for matins. Novices were also given additional rations of meat and sometimes allowed exceptions from fasts so that their developing bodies would have adequate nutrition for growing. In a few instances, young novices were even allowed a little time to play so they could burn off some of their youthful energy, but these recesses appear to have been very short, perhaps amounting to no more than one hour over the course of a week. Such idle pursuits were not tolerated for very long and all these small mercies were only temporary. These little indulgences and others, such as being spared the duty of washing the corpses of deceased brothers to prepare them for burial, were phased out gradually as the novices grew and became more accustomed to their new lives. By the time they were fourteen to sixteen years old, they were expected to be full members of their communities and adhere strictly to all the rules of their order.

As part of their training, the novices had to learn to comply with the strict discipline required by their orders. As noted in chapter 5, disciplining of children in the Middle Ages was sometimes harsh and excessive. However, some abbots and masters of novices appear to have followed St. Anselm's guidance and corrected errant novices gently and in a way that was appropriate for their faults. Still, monks as well as novices were subject to physical as well as spiritual penances for their sins and any violations of their orders' rules. Flogging with wooden rods was mixed with penitential prayers and fasting.

Lay-Brothers

While the higher positions within the monastic orders were generally restricted to those of noble birth and even admission as an ordinary monk was increasingly limited to those from privileged backgrounds, sons of poorer families were still able to enter monastic orders as lay-brothers. Lay-brothers provided much of the labor required to keep the monasteries functioning. As one medieval abbot described them, lay-brothers were the "pious draft oxen of Christ."

Many of the lay-brothers joined the monasteries out of a genuine desire to serve God in any way they could. However, becoming a lay-brother also provided a man with a guarantee of food, clothing, housing, and even some medical care for as long as he served. Such security could be found nowhere else in medieval Europe and may have been more of a motive than religious devotion for some men.

Monastic orders originally did not have lay-brothers. Besides reading and meditating upon religious texts and attending and singing during the seven divine offices observed each day, all monks were supposed to work. Their laboring at the humble tasks necessary for their own upkeep was another part of their sacrifice and a sign of their devotion to God. However, as monasteries proliferated and grew in size, the demands of managing their estates and providing for the physical needs of all their members required more than part-time work. Additionally, many monks appear to have come to resent the requirement that they engage in manual labor. They still considered work such as tending an herb garden or copying and illuminating manuscripts as fitting employment, but many increasingly considered hard, sweaty work such as tending herds of sheep and toiling to grow and harvest crops as unsuitable for them. The growth of this opposition to performing hard labor may, in part, have been a consequence of the gradual shift to drawing monks only from noble, or at least wealthy and privileged, families.

During the 11th and 12th centuries, some of the major monastic orders began recruiting boys and men in large numbers to meet their need for laborers. These boys and men were drawn from among the lower ranks of medieval society and admitted as lay-brothers. They took vows of obedience, poverty, and chastity and became part of the monastic community. Like choir-monks, lay-brothers were subject to discipline for violation of the monastic rules, but they did not enjoy many of the privileges which the monks continued to enjoy. For example, many monks possessed some degree of literacy before entering the monastery, and additional education was provided to them as part of their training to ensure that they could execute their religious duties of reading religious texts and participating in all the divine offices observed each day. In contrast, most lay-brothers were illiterate when they were recruited and many remained so since education was not part of their monastic training. Further, unlike the monks who were often still children when they were first admitted to the monastery, most lay-brothers appear to have been grown men, ready and able to perform the jobs expected of them, when they came to the monasteries. And lay-brothers could not advance to become choir-monks. They remained laborers for their entire careers.

In recognition of the demands of their work and the fact that it frequently required them to be away from the monastery, lay-brothers were routinely excused from attending the endless rounds of religious services. When they did attend, the lay-brothers sat apart from the monks. Further, lay-brothers were not expected to participate in singing during the services. This practice contributed to the characterization of monks as *choir-monks* to distinguish them from the lay-brothers. In some monasteries, lay-brothers and monks were further segregated with each group having its own separate infirmary, latrines (for which 19th century historians coined the euphemism *reredorter)*, *refectory* or *frater* (dining hall), and dorter.

At some monasteries, the numbers of lay-brothers were quite large. For example, at Rievaulx Abbey, Yorkshire, there were 500 lay-brothers and only 150 choir-monks in the late 12th century. However, the number of lay-brothers appears to have decreased drastically in the last half of the 14th century, and lay-brothers virtually disappeared at many monasteries before the end of the Middle Ages. The Black Death was likely part of the cause for their disappearance. The sudden decrease in population caused by the plague in many parts of Europe created labor shortages. This meant that able-bodied persons were in demand and could readily find work, often at wages far above those available before the plague. As a result, men and boys who would have previously been willing to become lay-brothers in exchange for the guaranteed food, clothing, and housing such a position provided now had a greater range of far more rewarding opportunities from which to choose.

Canons Regular

While less numerous than monks, canons regular were another type of regular clergy. Canons regular were priests, but they lived communally under a rule similar to that observed by the monastic orders. Communities of canons, called *colleges*, were often attached to cathedrals. The canons said masses, but the masses they performed were not for the public to attend. These masses were said for the benefit of the souls of the dead. As explained previously, such masses were commonly believed to help shorten the time that souls would spend suffering in purgatory and hasten their acceptance into heaven. By the 14th century, wealthy people provided in their will for payments for masses to be said for the benefit of their souls. Some directed that the payments were to go existing churches, but some established special chapels where the masses were to be performed. These chapels were called *chantries*, and they existed solely for the purpose of chanting these masses for the dead.

Friars

The friars were another type of regular clergy. The first four orders of friars were the Dominicans (also called *Friars Preachers* or *Black Friars* since they wore a short black cape or mantle as part of their habit), the Franciscans (*Friars Minor* or *Grey Friars*), the Carmelites (*White Friars*), and the Augustinians (*Austin Friars*). All these orders were founded during the early 13th century and rapidly became very popular. One of the reasons for the popularity of the friars was their poverty. Rather than demanding tithes and accepting rich endowments of land, rents, and other valuable gifts as the monasteries and many other parts of Church did, the friars initially supported themselves solely through begging. Their lack of worldly wealth and their religious fervor appealed to medieval Europeans, who often saw the friars as being more suitable agents for God than many bishops, abbots, and monks who were seen as corrupted by their love of material wealth and the priests who were frequently perceived as ignorant and lacking in true spirituality.

The primary mission of the friars was preaching the word of God. The zeal and eloquence of many friars, particularly among the Dominicans and Franciscans, further enhanced these orders' popularity. Through their preaching and their exemplary lives of poverty and religious devotion, the friars attracted people to their orders. Young men seem to have been especially drawn to these new religious orders. Eighteen was the minimum age for a man to become a friar although, with their parents' approval, boys below this age could be accepted as well. However, in the 13th and 14th centuries, the Dominican and Franciscan friars had a reputation for luring boys as young as thirteen or fourteen into joining their orders. Some young men and boys even became friars against their parents' wishes. On occasion, this practice led parents to take their sons back from the friars by force.

Friars typically received schooling in oration as well as in theology. Talented friars were encouraged by their orders to attend university to study theology. By combining oratorical skill with a solid understanding of theology, some friars were very effective preachers and delivered very persuasive sermons on a wide variety of matters.

Nuns

Women were not permitted to become priests. Instead, girls and women who wished to formally devote themselves to a religious life became anchoresses or nuns. Anchoresses were female hermits. Before being allowed to become an anchoress, a woman had to convince her local clergy, usually the bishop of her diocese, of the sincerity of her devotion as well as her understanding of the hardships she would undergo. Girls do not appear to have been permitted to become anchoresses. While some anchoresses may have been only in their late teens when they embarked on their careers, girls younger than that age were likely deemed too young and immature to undertake such a rigorous lifelong commitment. However, as we will see, girls were permitted to make an irrevocable commitment to God and the Church at much younger ages when they became nuns.

Nuns were never as numerous as monks in medieval Europe. For example, by one estimate, there were likely only 2,000 nuns at most in England at any point in time between 1275 and 1535. During this time, the peak number of monks may have been at least five times that number. One reason for their relative scarcity was that nuns were drawn almost entirely from the ranks of the nobility and the wealthy commoners such as successful merchants and rural families with extensive landholdings. Part of the reason for this exclusivity was the cost of becoming a nun. As with men who wanted to become monks, girls and women who wished to become nuns were supposed to be accepted free of charge. In reality, they were expected to bring with them a substantial payment to cover the expense of feeding, housing, and clothing them, just as many monasteries expected prospective monks to do. This payment was often referred to as a dowry since the nuns became the spiritual brides of Christ when they took their vows. Many of the nunneries truly needed the extra funds to pay for the expenses they incurred in accepting new members. Despite their close affiliation with noble and wealthy families, nunneries typically received far fewer donations than monasteries and were chronically short of funds. Still, as with the comparable monastic practice, bishops and other Church officials repeatedly condemned this as simony and ordered nunneries to stop requiring novice nuns to bring a dowry with them. Yet despite these actions, the majority of nunneries appear to have continued the practice throughout the Middle Ages.

Why Girls Entered the Cloister

Girls entered nunneries for many of the same reasons that boys entered the monasteries. Some chose to forsake the world out of a genuine desire to serve God.

A few girls even became nuns over the strong opposition of their families and rejected their parents' pleas that they return home. For example, in 13th century Germany, one girl who was only nine years old sneaked into a neighboring nunnery and refused to leave. Her father and brothers broke into the nunnery to retrieve the girl despite her vehement protests that she wanted to stay. The local bishop intervened and returned the girl to the nunnery.

Other girls appear to have become nuns for less spiritual reasons, such as to avoid a marriage arranged by their families. However, girls appear to have more commonly become nuns because their families would *not* arrange a marriage for them. As mentioned previously, most nuns came from the elite families of medieval society. For noble families, a daughter was usually a drain on resources. While she was unmarried and remained at home, money had to be expended to maintain her in a style appropriate to her family's social status. Further, her marriage did not provide any financial relief for her family. In fact, it required even more outlays, since her family had to provide a dowry as part of the marriage arrangements. The dowry had to be commensurate with the status of the bride's family and large enough to attract a suitable husband of comparable or higher status. Some families, even those of considerable wealth, could not provide suitable dowries for all their daughters. In some instances, the dowries would have bankrupted the families. In others, the families could have afforded it but chose to conserve their resources for other purposes. In either case, the result was the same: the family had a daughter whom they could not allow to marry. This problem was not uncommon, and many noble families chose to resolve it by placing excess daughters in nunneries. While they were still expected to provide a dowry to the nunnery, the amounts of these dowries for the brides of Christ were substantially less than the cost of maintaining these girls at home or of the dowries which suitable grooms would have expected. This permitted the family to save its wealth while providing for their daughter in a manner which was socially acceptable.

Some girls from noble or prosperous families were sent to nunneries for another reason related to family finances: to deprive them of their inheritances. Upon the death of their fathers, unmarried daughters, especially young ones, were at risk that their brothers, uncles, or new stepfathers would send them to a nunnery. Like monks, nuns were bound by a vow of poverty and so were not eligible to inherit. Only a handful of girls are known to have successfully escaped and obtained their rightful inheritances after being sent to a nunnery. The combination of powerful relatives who wanted to keep their ill-gotten riches and the Church's policy against releasing anyone from their vows, regardless of how freely they were made, almost always kept these unfortunates behind the nunnery walls for life.

Some girls were sent to nunneries because they were handicapped, mentally or physically. As with some of the boys sent to monasteries, they were placed there by their families to receive care which their families could or would not provide. From accounts of bishops' inspections of nunneries, handicaps included, among others, deafness, deformed or crippled limbs, simple mindedness (which likely described many forms of mental retardation), and violent insanity. These girls typically came from noble or wealthy families since, once again, these were the only families that could afford such placement for their daughters.

Finally, some of the girls placed in nunneries were illegitimate daughters of the nobility. Like the male bastards sent to monasteries, their illegitimacy did not disqualify them from entering the Church. However, these girls were usually disqualified from advancing to the position of abbess of their community unless they obtained a dispensation from the pope.

In contrast to the elite, families of the middling and poorer classes, even if they had been able to afford to send their daughters to nunneries, did not have any strong economic incentives to encourage or force their daughters to become nuns. Having an unwed daughter at home was likely more often a benefit than a burden in the households of many peasants, merchants, or craftsmen. At the very least, such a girl could continue performing household chores and could care for other members of the household, including her aging parents. If she worked outside the home or had learned a craft, an unwed daughter could contribute to the family's resources. In this respect, the daughters of merchants and craftsmen had a distinct advantage over their noble counterparts. Noble girls were not trained to work and were prevented by the customs of their class from entering a trade even if they had wanted to. Besides paying for her own upkeep, being able to work also provided a means for non-noble girls to save up money for their own dowries. In this respect, the non-noble girls enjoyed another advantage over noble girls, who were entirely dependent on their families for dowries. Additionally, the dowries expected among the middling and poorer classes were substantially lower than those for even the poorest of the nobility. In many instances, the money which the daughter had earned herself or the promise of her future earnings in a trade sufficed for a dowry. Thus, there was far less chance that a daughter would go unmarried. Finally, unlike their wealthier counterparts, these less well-to-do girls were never placed in nunneries to deprive them of their inheritances since their inheritances were too small to inspire greedy relatives to take such despicable actions.

Other Girls in the Nunneries

Nunneries in medieval Europe were never established to be boarding schools, and being a governess or a teacher was not part of the nuns' vocation. But, just as some monasteries accepted boys on a temporary basis, there were many nunneries which accepted girls as temporary boarders. A few of these nunneries even accepted little boys. As with the boys who boarded at monasteries, the girls and little boys who stayed for a time in nunneries usually came from influential families. These families were typically wealthy neighbors of the nunneries and many appear to have been donors as well. When one of these families requested that a nunnery accept their daughter as a boarder, the abbess likely concluded that it was in the best interests of their nunneries to ignore the rules that prohibited admitting children rather than displease a powerful neighbor. In some cases, the girls were sent to the nunnery for safekeeping, such as when their fathers went off to war or abroad on lengthy pilgrimages. In such circumstances, fathers sometimes made it very clear in the written agreements with the nunneries that they had the right to retrieve their daughters if they returned home safely. However, only a few records have survived which give a reason for a girl's temporary placement in a nunnery.

As with the monasteries, the practice of admitting children into the cloister, other than oblates and novices, violated the rules that governed the nunneries. Across Europe, the bishops who conducted periodic inspections of the nunneries condemned this practice, especially when boys were involved, and repeatedly tried to end it. Despite these efforts, many nunneries continued this practice through the end of the Middle Ages. One historian has suggested that the nuns were so persistent in continuing to take in children because their nunneries were chronically short of cash and they needed the money which the parents paid for this service.

The nuns appear to have taught these children what they could but, as discussed in chapter 6, nuns were seldom distinguished for their scholarship. Still, the privileged upbringings of most nuns meant that they could at least read in the local vernacular and many likely knew how to write as well, and so they could teach these skills to girls or little boys in their care. Additionally, drawing on their own upbringing, the nuns could also have taught children the manners and behavior expected of members of their social class.

Becoming a Nun

The daughters of the aristocracy who were sent to the nunneries were often quite young. Sometimes they were as young as six or seven when they first entered the cloister. But there was often a friendly and familiar face waiting for them at their new home to comfort them and ease their transition into their new life. Whenever it was possible, families appear to have chosen to send their girls to nunneries in which a relative, such as an aunt, a cousin, or even an older sister, was already present. Additionally, the nunneries selected were often fairly near their former homes and families often visited their cloistered relatives. In fact, records of bishops' inspections in England reveal that many nuns left their nunneries to visit friends and relatives.

The training of novice nuns largely mirrored that of novice monks. Rules for orders of nuns were based on those for monks and so they were also based on the Rule of St. Benedict. The nuns-in-training were placed under the mistress of novices, who was responsible for teaching them.

As with novice monks, novice nuns also had to adapt to the discipline expected within their cloisters. Again, as in monasteries, penances for violations in nunneries included physical as well as spiritual correction. However, the young nuns were not always the victims. For example, in 13th century France, a bishop inspecting a nunnery noticed that the younger nuns entrusted with administering the corrective lashings beat some of their fellow nuns more severely than others. He questioned one of the older nuns who had received some of the heavier blows. This nun revealed that she couldn't really complain about the treatment since she had quite often beaten these same younger nuns herself when they were novices in her care.

As was typical for cloistered orders, nuns were expected to work along with meditating and observing religious services throughout each day. Nuns weren't expected to do any heavy manual labor. Instead, the work portion of their daily routines commonly involved embroidering and sewing vestments and cloths for use in their churches and for giving as gifts to members of the clergy. Some also made little embroidered and finely woven items such as purses, tassels, and even little silken bandages call *bloodbands* which were used to cover the incisions made as part of medicinal bleeding (see appendix 1). They gave these items to friends and relatives. Some nuns even appear to have sold their handiwork to raise a little pocket money for themselves. However, making personal gifts or crafts to sell was not permitted under the rules of their orders. Nuns, like monks, were not to possess any private property.

Novice nuns received the tonsure but it appears to have been different from that given to monks and priests. No illustrations of a nun's tonsure survive, since nuns were always depicted wearing the veils that were part of their uniform dress. However, there are records of complaints about those nuns who failed to adhere to their order's dress codes. These complaints include charges that some nuns were letting their hair grow so long that it reached below their ears, even down to the base of their necks or longer. This suggests that the nun's tonsure involved cropping their hair very short but probably not shaving the top of the head completely bald as was required for clergymen. In a set of rules written for anchoresses, an unidentified cleric of the 13th century recommended that these female hermits have their hair cut quarterly. He also wrote that they should wash themselves whenever necessary and "as often as ye please." Although these rules were written for anchoresses, they were likely similar to the rules followed by nuns on such matters.

Lay-Sisters

While girls from poor and middling families appear to have seldom become nuns, a few did become lay-sisters. Like lay-brothers, lay-sisters proved their devotion to God through the labor that they performed at the nunneries. However, lay-sisters were never as numerous as lay-brothers. As with monasteries, many nunneries seem to have relied on paid employees, from maidservants to cooks, to perform the many menial chores needed to keep their institutions functioning.

Runaway Monks and Nuns

Over the course of the Middle Ages, a few of the girls and boys who were placed in nunneries and monasteries against their wills did try to rebel. Some stayed within their cloisters but refused to take vows. Others ran away. Their success in escaping varied. Many appear to have been unable to bear the guilt of breaking their vows and returned contritely to accept their punishment. Others could not withstand the pressure the Church was able to apply to them and to any friends and relatives who aided them. Persons who abetted these runaways were subject to excommunication just as the runaways themselves were. When spiritual coercion failed, the Church sometimes called on secular authorities to seize the offenders and return them to Church authorities. Unrepentant and repeat offenders were subject to being imprisoned within nunneries or monasteries to prevent further escapes. Some were even sent off to remote institutions, far away from any friends or family who might aid or shelter them in any future escapes.

The Nobility

While feudal lords occasionally bestowed noble status on commoners to reward them for their services, most members of the nobility in medieval Europe were born into their class. Further, although the lands and titles held by a vassal were supposed to revert to his lord when the vassal died, titles and lands were routinely passed down to the male descendants of the vassal. Thus, noble status was largely hereditary and children of the nobility were trained to be lords and ladies.

Training for the Nobility

As with children of ordinary people, children of the nobility began their training by observing the actions of their parents and other adults. And, like other children, they imitated adult activities. As part of this imitative play, as explained in chapter 3, sons of the nobility played with wooden swords and other toy weapons. At around the age of seven, they were expected to move from watching and playing to beginning their training for their adult careers.

Up to the age of seven, sons and daughters of noble families were raised together, often under the supervision of their mother or a governess. At around the age of seven, boys and girls were typically separated. Girls continued to be taught by the ladies of the household, while boys were placed under male masters to begin learning more about their future roles. This change was likely gradual so that many little boys were not just suddenly carried off from the care of the women in the nursery and thrust into the world of men. However, the lives of some boys did undergo drastic changes at this early age since many members of the nobility throughout medieval Europe engaged in the practice of sending their sons to households of other nobles around the age of seven.

Placement in Other Noble Households

The children of the nobility, especially boys, were far more likely than those of commoners to be separated from their parents at an early age. Besides the placement of boys as oblates in religious institutions, as discussed in the first half of this chapter, many noble families engaged in the practice of placing their young sons in other noble households, occasionally even including those of clerics such as bishops and abbots. Parents did not send their sons away because they wanted to be rid of them. Rather, parents did so with the genuine hope that such placement would provide their sons with opportunities to better themselves and advance their careers. These boys would certainly have had some opportunities for improving themselves had they remained at home, but placement in another household usually provided much greater range and number of opportunities both for self-improvement and for career advancement.

Placing sons in other households was done by all levels of medieval nobility, from the poorest lords to the greatest kings. At all levels of the nobility except the highest, parents usually sought to place their sons in households of nobles who were superior to them in rank. When possible, many noble families chose to place their sons with uncles or other relatives whose rank was equal to or greater than their own. For example, in the tale *Beowulf*, at the age of seven, the hero had been placed in the household of his maternal grandfather, who was a king. In real life, William Marshall, a famous English knight of the 12th and early 13th centuries, was sent to the household of his father's cousin when he was eleven or twelve. This distant relative was a noble official in Normandy. Since there were no households superior to those of their own family, princes were often sent to an uncle or other close relative of noble blood. Noble families also often placed their sons with other families with whom they had some social or political connections such as the lords to whom they owed fealty. This was to foster stronger and better relations between the two families while giving their sons the opportunity to develop important contacts with their peers and their superiors. Boys might find these early relationships very useful later in life when dealing with each other as grown men. Still, such "old boy" connections were not an absolute guarantee of lasting friendship or loyalty since later political developments could cause men to turn on even those with whom they had trained in boyhood.

In some instances, noble parents placed their children with families with whom they had no direct familial or feudal relationship. For example, Christine de Pisan, the noted French author of the late 14th and early 15th centuries, placed her thirteen-year-old son with the household of the earl of Derby. Christine had no formal ties to the English earl or his family, but the earl had a noted reputation as a fine and chivalrous man and so was considered a very worthy mentor for any sons of the nobility, even those from abroad such as Christine's son. Households of noted men such as the earl attracted boys from a number of noble families, and these boys mingled and formed connections just as boys who served in the households of their feudal superiors did.

Besides providing them with the opportunity to develop contacts with one's peers and immediate social superiors, boys who were placed in noble households were able to see how such a great household functioned. They could apply this knowledge later in life both in managing their households and in their dealings with other nobles. During their period of service, noble boys also watched and learned how their peers and superiors interacted with each other and with their inferiors. This reinforced the training these boys had received in their own home but, given the higher status of the household in which they were placed, likely included a broader range of situations than they would have been exposed to at home. Through observing and participating in functions such as receptions of visitors or being received as a guest when traveling with one's foster household, boys better understood their own place in society as well as that of others. Through these activities, the boys learned etiquette and how to conduct themselves in a manner appropriate to their place in the social order. And this was more than just a matter of learning good manners. The relationships within feudal society were complex, and these boys had to learn the respect and deference they either owed or should expect to receive from other members of society. Failure to master these skills could seriously harm one's standing and chances for advancement.

Placement in a noble household gave noble boys the opportunity to display their skills and expertise in front of adults who could aid their careers. Boys who displayed intelligence as well good social skills might make a lasting impression on their own mentors as well as on any visiting nobility. Further, having an entourage of witty and sophisticated young men was an asset for any nobleman.

While sons were sent to other families to learn and to make contacts, daughters of the nobility were generally kept at home until they were married off or entered a nunnery. It was essential for maintaining a family's good reputation that its daughters were kept virgins until marriage or entry into the Church. Placement with another noble family usually carried too great a risk that a girl's virtue would be compromised, because she would be away from the direct supervision of her own parents. Even for boys, families sometimes recognized that placement in another household was a mixed blessing and that their sons might be exposed to bad influences by new companions and others they would meet during their time away from home. This was particularly a concern when the son was a royal heir. Royal families sometimes screened the boys and servants who had close and continuing contact with their princes. Those who proved unsuitable were removed.

Further evidence of family concern about sons who were placed in other households can be found in the few descriptions we have of the moments when noble boys left their homes and families. This was a highly emotional time. The mothers and sisters of these boys were sometimes recorded as shedding many tears over their departures. As for the boys themselves, it was a time of mixed feelings as they left the comfort and security of their families' homes to embark on the path to adulthood in strange households some distance away. Many must have felt a longing for their parents and siblings, but this was likely balanced by their excitement at being in a new place.

Before moving on to discussing the types of training young nobles received, there was another reason why noble children, particularly boys, were placed in the households of other noble families, especially those of families to whom their parents owed allegiance. Parents sometimes sent their sons to other noble households as part of political settlements. For example, to guarantee the continued loyalty of his vassals, a lord could demand that his vassals send their sons to his court. At court, the boys would receive training, but they were also hostages. If their parents betrayed the lord, the lord could have these boys executed. Similarly, when concluding a peace treaty, the former belligerents could arrange to exchange some of their sons with each other. Under such diplomatic arrangements, anyone who failed to keep the peace risked the immediate execution of his own son. Alternatively, when one side had been decisively beaten, the victors routinely rounded up the children of their defeated noble foes. The victors often sent some of these children off to careers in the Church while others, usually the principal heirs, were sometimes kept at the victor's court as his wards. On a happier note, sending one's son to the court of another noble appears to have been performed most often as part of maintaining friendly relations and was a sign of the parties' good faith in each other.

Training for Noble Boys

Whether they were educated at home or sent to another family, noble boys were often taught how to read either by the household's chaplain or by a teacher hired by their family (see chapter 6). In the late Middle Ages, some of the noble households that attracted large numbers of boys even retained grammar teachers on a permanent basis to instruct all the boys. In addition to this education, noble families also had their sons tutored by other men in their households in the skills expected of nobility, such as riding and combat. In England, this practice was first documented in the 12th century, but it likely existed in England and on the Continent for some time before it was recorded. These men were referred to as masters and were sometimes knights themselves but of lesser social standing than the lords they served. For noble families of low rank, masters were often not knights but were squires or other men of the household who were trusted and respected for their skills and judgment. At the opposite end of the social ladder, by the late Middle Ages, masters in the households of kings and other high nobility were sometimes selected from among some very powerful men. For example, the first master chosen for the future Henry VI of England was his uncle, the duke of Exeter. When the duke died, he was replaced by the earl of Warwick. However, very few boys had such prestigious masters to teach them how to be a nobleman.

Training by a master was rarely done on a one-on-one basis. Even among royal families, masters typically had several boys in their care at any given time. In addition to the sons of his own lord, a master was also responsible for training any other boys who had been sent to his lord's household, including any orphaned noble boys who were wards of the lord. Further, while boys were usually about seven when they began such training, the ages of the members of these groups could range from five up to sixteen. The size of these groups varied as well. While the surviving records give no firm figures, they appear to have ranged from two or three boys up to perhaps a dozen or more in large and prestigious households. Further, family servants often accompanied boys when they went to another household. As a result, the boys and their entourages sometimes formed their own household within the lord's home. Near the end of the Middle Ages, groups of boys and their servants in the royal household in England were sometimes quite large. For example, in 1454, the household of the one-year-old Prince Edward, son of Henry VI of England, had a complement of thirty-eight servants.

Discipline

As described in the previous chapters, children in the Middle Ages were routinely subjected to corporal punishment as part of their education and training. This was true for the nobility as well as for commoners. Noble parents, even kings, were known to authorize masters to act as their surrogates and to chastise their sons verbally and physically just as the parents themselves would have done to correct the boys' behavior. However, some allowances were made for the boys' noble standing. While boys among the lesser nobility seem to have been subjected to corporal punishments like ordinary children, boys from middling and higher nobility seem to have been struck or spanked less often. When they were corrected in this manner, it appears that the punishments were administered in private rather than in front of other members of the household. Humiliating a royal prince, a future king, in front of his peers and servants was likely considered contrary to the good order of society.

Courtesy

Throughout their training, noble boys learned how to behave courteously. "Courtesy" had a different meaning in the Middle Ages than it does today. Rather than simply meaning behaving politely, it meant knowing how to behave in a noble court. This required more than just good manners. A noble boy had to learn how to speak, dress, and behave in ways that were appropriate for his rank in society. A boy learned much of this by watching how adults, including his parents and his master, acted. By developing sophisticated manners, a boy could impress his peers and superiors. While it is difficult to understand the importance of this today, boys who grew into men famed for their courtesy stood out in noble society and were often marked for advancement.

Besides watching and imitating others, boys gained experience in courtesy through performing specialized tasks. For example, when he was deemed ready by his master and his lord, a noble boy might be given the honor of personally serving his lord or lady. Most commonly, boys served as pages. Some pages were hired help, but many were noble boys in training. Pages were "gofers." They ran whatever errands their lords or ladies assigned them. Occasionally, pages were given enjoyable tasks. For example, because of their small size and weight, lords sometimes used their pages as jockeys in horse races.

As the boys grew older and more competent, they could advance to other positions. For example, for most of the Middle Ages, lords ate together with their households and, even when it was not a formal feast, meals were occasions for everyone to display their courtly manners. Waiting on one's lord at a meal was a signal honor, and some noble boys were given the privilege of serving as cupbearers or carvers to their lords. The cupbearer was responsible for pouring drinks. The carver's job was to carefully cut up the meat dishes into suitable portions and serve them up. Another task suitable for young boys was to assist with the pre-meal hand washing. Guests washed their hands as they entered the hall. For important feasts, the lord sometimes poured the water for his guests personally from a special pitcher called an *aquamanile* but more commonly a servant called a *ewerer* did the pouring. A boy helped in this ritual by holding a bowl to catch the water as it ran off the guests' hands. He or another boy also held a towel for the guests to use in drying their hands. By performing these tasks, boys had many opportunities to study their elders and their behavior while dining and socializing. As early as the 12th century, in addition to serving guests at the table, noble boys also learned proper conduct at mealtimes by reading books on etiquette. These books contained such useful advice as

- Wash your hand before eating.
- Chew with your mouth closed.
- Don't talk with your mouth full.
- Don't eat too much.
- Don't pick your teeth, fingernails, or nose.
- Don't fidget, slouch, or rest your arms and elbows on the table.
- Don't pet dogs and cats during the meal.

When they became adult lords themselves, they could apply this knowledge of etiquette and proper ceremonial conduct in their own households and when being entertained by others.

In addition to jobs such as page, cupbearer, and carver, noble boys served their lords in other small but symbolically important tasks. Some were recorded as being their lord's helmet-bearers, while others served as the grooms for his horse. While this latter job sounds like it involved menial work, it was actually a ceremonial position and appears to have entailed overseeing the hired grooms to ensure that the lord's horse was properly groomed and equipped for the occasion. The noble groom also led the horse to his lord when he was ready to ride.

As part of courtly behavior, many boys also learned how to be entertaining. In an age before television, radio, or even recorded music, the ability to amuse and entertain one's companions was highly valued at all levels of society. Knowing how to sing well or play an instrument helped pass the long hours, whether traveling or at home. Even warriors famed for their martial skills were sometimes noted for their musical abilities as well. For example, Henry V of England knew how to play the harp, while William Marshall, considered by many of his 12th century contemporaries to be an ideal knight, is known to have sung to entertain ladies during tournaments. Along with being able to produce music, the ability to dance well gradually became another desirable skill for medieval noblemen to possess. Besides music-making and dancing, being a good conversationalist or having a large repertoire of tales was also valued among the nobility. Regardless of whether his stories were new or classic, a skilled storyteller was always welcome company, as the characters in Chaucer's *Canterbury Tales* and Boccaccio's *Decameron* demonstrate. As with music, time spent traveling or at home in the long evening hours passed more quickly and more pleasantly when there were exciting and engaging tales to hear. Finally, as mentioned in chapter 3, noble boys also learned to play games, including chess and backgammon. They also learned to play dice and, beginning in the late 14th century when playing cards were first produced in Europe, card games, despite the fact that the gambling which usually accompanied these games was condemned by the Church as well as by secular moralists. Possessing any of these skills, whether singing, chess-playing, or any of the others, put a further shine on a nobleman's reputation for being courteous.

Skills such as singing or playing an instrument may have been learned from professional musicians, such as itinerant minstrels, hired to teach noble youths, but there is little evidence of this practice. Members of the household who possessed these skills may have also instructed the boys in these arts. For dancing, skilled amateurs appear to have provided the instruction in this art for most of the Middle Ages. Professional dancing masters first appear in noble courts in the late 14th century. As for storytelling, there was no formal training available for this skill, although those who were able to read certainly had an advantage in having a stock of recorded examples with which to work. Still, most storytellers likely relied on having a good memory to recall stories which they had heard previously and on having a good imagination, which enabled them to create new stories or embellish and update old ones.

Riding

The most important and most basic physical skill for any member of the medieval aristocracy to learn was how to ride a horse. As we will see, besides being the primary form of transportation, horseback riding was essential to two other noble pastimes: hunting and warfare. Noble boys were introduced to riding at a very young age. The popular view was that one had to learn young if one was to ride well. One 13th century writer on education wrote that any boy who had not learned to ride a horse by the age of twelve would be fit only for a career in the clergy.

Boys were introduced to horses and riding gradually. The first step was to become comfortable being around horses and then to become accustomed to the feel of sitting atop one in a saddle. For little boys under the age of four, it was recommended to first place them in the saddle on the back of a horse that was tethered in its stall. The boy was then taught how to speak to the horse and keep it calm. The next step was for the boy to stay in the saddle while the horse was led around by an adult. In all likelihood, little boys also spent some time riding on horses with adults, either sitting in front of them or holding on to their backs as they rode. From this stage, the boys eventually progressed to riding on their own. Many noble boys appear to have been competent riders by the age of eight. By the time they reached the age of sixteen, they were expected to be skilled horsemen.

During this time, the boys also learned how to care for horses and the saddles and other riding tack. While nobles employed grooms and other servants to care for their horses, it was important for noble boys to learn how to care for horses properly. This knowledge helped them later in life in evaluating the condition of horses they were buying. It also gave them the expertise needed to supervise their own grooms to ensure that their horses and their equipment were well cared for and would be in good condition whenever they were needed. Horses were also expensive, and a wise nobleman would want to ensure that valuable investments were well taken care of. Finally, when on campaign as knights, noblemen might find themselves without grooms, and they had to be able to keep their horses in fit condition on their own. In the age of the automobile, it is difficult to appreciate all the knowledge and skill that was required to keep a horse healthy and in shape. But in the Middle Ages, if a person didn't have some basic expertise in these matters, he could easily end up walking on his own two feet instead of riding. As well as being a very tiring mode of transportation, it was one which no nobleman considered acceptable.

Hunting

Once they could ride, boys joined in another pastime popular with medieval nobility: hunting. They learned how to hunt birds using trained falcons and how to pursue deer with dogs and to slay them with a bow and arrow or with a sword. Noble hunters condemned the use of traps and snares and any means of taking game by stealth. Such techniques were fit only for poachers in their view. Ideally, a noble hunter took his prey *par force,* by pursuing it and killing it face-to-face. However, most noble hunting was not a one-on-one struggle of man against beast. Hunting for deer, hart, or any other large game involved teams of well-trained dogs, numerous servants, and several hunters. In some hunts, servants and dogs even herded the deer past prepared positions where the noble sportsmen shot them down with arrows.

Along with the skills actually needed to track and to kill prey, noble boys also learned the social rituals which surrounded the hunt in medieval Europe. Protocol had to be followed during all stages of the hunt. For example, at the end of the hunt for an animal such as a hart, its body was *broken* or *undone* by the hunters. As part of this ritual, some pieces were presented to the hunter who slew the animal, while the choicest cuts were reserved for important guests. Further, since hunting was most often a group activity, it provided another opportunity for the boys to develop social bonds with each other as well as with the adults in the hunting party as they shared the thrill of the chase.

In addition to the social lessons taught during a hunt, hunting large game also provided noble boys and men with training for combat. The pursuit of game across a variety of terrain required skill. This same skill was needed for mounted combat. Further, while they were sometimes slightly modified for bringing down game instead of men, spears, swords, and arrows were employed in hunting as well as in warfare and the same physical strengths and expertise were required for their use. Hunting of large game often involved the placement of many servants and hunters along the expected path of the prey, and such hunting provided opportunities to learn how to deploy and coordinate the activities of small groups of armed men. This tactical experience had clear military applications as did mastering the skills of understanding how to use the terrain to one's best advantage and tracking one's prey (or enemy) by the marks left by their movements. Finally, hunting was recognized as accustoming boys to many of the same hardships that they would endure later when they were men on campaign, such as sleeping rough and having to carry out their duties in all kinds of weather.

Physical Fitness and Combat

Most, if not all, noble boys received some training in combat. Aristocrats in medieval Europe were seldom so secure in their positions that they could risk not being capable of defending themselves. The Middle Ages in Europe was a time of conflicts and, from minor skirmishes to major campaigns, noblemen were usually expected to lead their men into combat personally. Unless they were aged or infirm, they were expected to fight alongside their men and not simply direct the action from a safe position at the rear. Even kings were expected to subject themselves to such risks, and many, including such noted warrior kings as Edward I and Henry V of England, did so. By providing such active leadership, noblemen lived up to the standards of personal honor and courage expected of them. Their appearance on the battlefield usually boosted the morale and resolve of their forces as well.

Many noble parents encouraged their sons to be aggressive from an early age. While they were still very young, they were given wooden swords and small sets of bows and arrows to play with to encourage an interest in warfare. Some very privileged boys such as young princes were sometimes given miniature metal swords as playthings. To toughen them and help develop the skills they would need on the battlefield, noble boys engaged in a number of games and sports that developed their strength, agility, and coordination. These included running, jumping, and various ball games, not that little boys need much encouragement to do these things. Several medieval writers advised that exercise should be limited to such relatively light activities until the boys reached the age of twelve or fourteen. These writers recognized that too much strenuous exercise at too early an age could harm rather than help a boy's growth and development. However, age was no guarantee against being hurt during training. Throughout the Middle Ages, in activities ranging from hunting and practicing the use of the lance to wrestling and throwing stones, noble boys of all ages suffered grievous injuries and even death during their training.

When they had reached a suitable age, noble boys began more strenuous training which appears to have often included wrestling, gymnastics, and lifting heavy stones and sometimes throwing them as well. They also began their formal military training. From wooden swords and other toy weapons, they graduated to their first metal swords and real spears. To further improve their stamina and strength, some authors on military training recommended that boys practice with special swords that were twice the weight of real swords or with clubs of similar heavy weight. Sword practice likely began with practicing blows on large wooden stakes set upright in the ground. After becoming accustomed to the weight and feel of the weapons, the boys moved to practicing against live opponents using blunted weapons to lessen the risk of serious injury. While the sword was the preferred weapon of the noble warrior, the masters trained the boys in the use of a variety of weapons, including the spear, mace, and axe. The masters advised on whether it was better to cut or thrust and where it was best to hit on an opponent's body.

Noble boys also had to learn mounted combat and the use of the lance. As part of his training in horsemanship, a noble boy had to master holding the reins and controlling his horse using only one hand, the left. This was essential in combat since the right hand needed to be free for holding and wielding a weapon, whether a sword or a lance. However, mastering the use of the lance was somewhat difficult and dangerous, and so the initial training for this skill was not taught on horseback. Instead, to lessen the risks to both horse and rider, boys began their training with the lance on foot. In the early Middle Ages, the lance was simply a form of spear. It was used for throwing as well as for thrusting. Lances gradually developed into specialized weapons designed exclusively for thrusting. In training to use this type of lance, noble boys first learned to hold it in the correct position, couched high under the right arm with the tip aimed slightly to the left. The next step was to practice holding the lance while running at a target (fig. 35). The target was often in the form of a *quintain* (fig. 36). The quintain was a pivoting practice dummy which held a shield on its left side and a club on its right. The object was to hit the shield solidly. This caused the quintain to spin. Any boy who failed to move out of the way in time received a blow to his head from the quintain's club as it spun around. Practice then advanced to riding towards a target while holding the lance, but this was sometimes accomplished using a wooden horse instead of a live one. Wooden practice horses looked like large versions of modern sawhorses mounted on wheels and fitted with a saddle. One boy rode the horse while other boys pushed him towards the target (fig. 36). After practicing this way for some time, a boy would be ready to mount a live horse and try charging the quintain. Once he had mastered hitting the target without being hit by the quintain's club, he was finally ready to practice with live opponents.

Such practice sessions were not the same as tournaments. Tournaments were organized competitions in which knights fought one another to prove their strength and skill in arms.

Fig. 35. In this unique picture, a boy is practicing the use of the lance by running at a shield by a knight. The boy has the lance couched under his left arm instead of in the correct position under his right arm. This error suggests that the boy may be just beginning his training. While the boy on the right seems shocked or dismayed that the knight is allowing the other boy to charge straight at him, the knight is likely indulging in this exercise since he knows the boy is inexperienced and won't deliver a heavy blow.

Fig. 36. These boys are learning how to use a lance. On the left, one boy couches a lance under his right arm and charges on foot at a quintain. On the right, a boy with a lance is riding a wheeled sawhorse which is being pulled by a pair of boys. The boy riding on the wooden horse is aiming his lance at a fixed target.

Boys training to become knights could not enter these games, because they were open only to warriors who were already knights. Still, the boys could attend as spectators and watch their masters and other mature warriors compete at these events.

In addition to becoming skilled in using a variety of weapons, the warrior-in-training had to become accustomed to wearing armor. Very wealthy and powerful nobles, such as kings, sometimes had miniature suits of armor made for their sons, but most noble boys had to do without such luxuries (fig. 16). Carrying weights was one alternative method for developing the strength, endurance, and calluses needed for wearing armor. Another may have been to wear pieces of adult armor. Mail was the predominant form of body armor until well into the 13th century. It was flexible and form fitting, so boys may have gotten used to its weight and feel simply by putting on *hauberks* (shirts of mail) made for adults. Even after plate armor began to supplement and later supplant mail as the preferred form of armor, mail shirts were still quite common and so continued to be available for training young warriors to help accustom them to wearing any type of armor in combat. Part of learning how to wear armor was developing the skill and coordination needed to mount and dismount a horse while wearing full armor. Despite depictions in movies and other works of fiction, knights were never lifted onto their warhorses by cranes or other devices. Noble boys had to be able to climb or even jump onto their horses while fully burdened with armor.

Along with learning how to use weapons and wear armor, boys who were training to become warriors had to learn to care for the tools of their future trade. As part of their apprenticeship, they, along with valets who routinely performed these chores, kept the weapons and armor of their masters and lords polished and free of rust. They inspected the leather fittings on these items and had them replaced as needed. As with caring for horses and their equipment, these noble boys would have valets or other servants to perform these tasks for them when they were grown, but the condition of their arms and armor were, with no exaggeration, a matter of life and death. They had to be able to oversee the quality of their valets' work at maintaining them and to perform the task themselves in emergencies. They also needed these skills to determine when equipment needed to be repaired or replaced and to assess the products of armorers and weaponsmiths when purchasing new items.

As mentioned previously, noble boys were usually trained in groups. This ensured that there were always partners available for sparring. Learning together also gave them an opportunity to bond, not unlike the experience of modern military trainees in boot camp. They also appear to have been taught to fight together as an organized unit. Such experience could prove invaluable in battle.

At least up until the 12th century, some boys applied their military training by raiding the lands of neighboring lords. While accounts of these war games survive primarily in contemporary fiction, such small-scale raiding and pillaging was common in many parts of Europe at the time, so it is quite likely that some families used them as opportunities to test their sons' abilities. The goal of these raids was to carry off as much of their neighbors' livestock as possible but without engaging in an open attack. These raids appear to have been performed under the cover of darkness, and the successful raider was one who accomplished his mission without being detected by the livestock's owners.

By the time a boy who was training for knighthood reached the age of seventeen or eighteen, he was usually well prepared to embark on his career. However, there was no fixed age requirement for knighthood or for simply becoming a warrior without the formality of being knighted. For example, the Carolingian kings in early medieval France had their sons knighted when they were as young as thirteen or fifteen, while Edward, the Black Prince of England, fought at the famous battle of Crecy in 1346 when he was only sixteen.

Based on excavations of battlefield gravesites and other evidence, fourteen appears to have been the youngest age at which a boy could be an effective combatant in the Middle Ages. Today, in Third-World countries, children even younger than fourteen are pressed into service and forced to kill. But the reason that younger boys did not usually fight in medieval Europe had more to do with technology than with any sensitivity about having children kill one another. Pulling the trigger on an automatic rifle requires little physical strength, but wielding a sword, axe, or a bow did. Thus, young boys were spared the horrors of combat. In fact, even older boys were scarce on medieval battlefields. While boys training to be knight sometimes accompanied their masters and other warriors on campaign, they mostly remained out of the action, and the fighting was left to more mature men. For example, excavations of graves from the 15th century English dynastic struggle, known as the War of the Roses, indicate that the minimum age for fighters at that time was sixteen and that most were significantly older, with those between the ages of twenty-six and thirty-five forming the largest single age grouping. At another medieval battle site, however, numerous remains of teenage boys were found. This was at the site of the battle of Wisby on the Swedish island of Gotland. Danish forces invaded the island in 1361 and defeated a hastily prepared group of local defenders, most of whom were peasants and who were not trained for combat. All the teenagers were among the defenders who were slaughtered by the Danish warriors. Thus, in some situations, boys in their mid-teens and younger did enter combat but they did not constitute a regular part of any military force in medieval Europe.

The Ideal Progression to Knighthood and the Reality

Ideally, a boy destined for knighthood began the training discussed above at around the age of seven. For the next seven years, he would serve as a page and learn courteous behavior. He would also begin preparing his body for the rigors of his future career and learn how to ride if he did not already possess this skill. At the age of fourteen, he would advance to being a squire. As a squire, he would continue improving his courtliness, including possibly learning to singing or to play an instrument. He would also begin his military training in earnest and serve as an apprentice to a knight. While learning to care for a knight's weapons, armor, and horse, he was taught how to use all these items. Finally, somewhere between the ages of seventeen and twenty-one, he would be ready to be a knight. After ritual purification, his mentor would present him to his lord. The knight-to-be would then kneel before his lord.

The lord would lightly strike him on the shoulders and, with that dubbing, he would arise a knight. He would then conduct himself in a chivalrous manner. He would be courageous, generous, and loyal to his companions and especially to his lord. He would also be just, honest, modest, and merciful. He would always defend the Church and the Christian faith and protect the weak and the helpless. This was the ideal.

In reality, most knights did undergo some period of training under more experienced masters such as described at the beginning of this section. However, this training was never carried out according to any fixed timetable. Additionally, the nature of knighthood evolved over the course of the Middle Ages. Originally, knights were simply warriors who served the nobility. They appear to have developed in the early Middle Ages as a fusion of two different types of warriors. One had its roots in the various groups of Germanic peoples who invaded western Europe in the early centuries of the first millennium A.D. Among these peoples, warriors were organized into bands, and they were fiercely loyal to their leaders and to each other. The other type of warrior was the heavily armed and armored cavalryman of the late Roman Empire. At some time in the 8th century, these two martial traditions seem to have merged in the land of the Franks which is now parts of Germany, France, and several adjoining countries. These mounted warriors served the Frankish kings. In French, such a warrior came to be called a *chevalier* (horseman). Similarly, in Italy, he was called a *cavaliere* and, in Spain, a *caballero*. In German, he was known as a *ritter* (rider). However, in the Anglo-Saxon language of England, he was called a *cniht*. This term denoted a servant or retainer of a noble lord and reflects the knight's Germanic origin as a select warrior who served as part of a lord's household.

In the early centuries of the Middle Ages, any warrior who distinguished himself in combat may have been referred to as a knight. However, use of this title came to be restricted to only those warriors who had proven themselves in battle and were recognized and acclaimed by other fighters as worthy of the title. Gradually, the bestowing of the title of knight was further restricted so that only those who were already acclaimed as knights could extend this honor to others who were worthy of it. At some point, the nobility assumed the role of bestowing knighthood, and "knight" became the lowest rank within the nobility. Finally, by the 12th century, a candidate for knighthood had to be of *gentle birth*; that is, he had to be the descendant of a knight or other member of the nobility.

The nobility were not the only part of medieval society which sought to control the warrior class. Knights were certainly expected to be good Christians, but the Church recognized that they were men of violence whose actions often threatened social order. During the 11th and 12th centuries, as part of efforts to exert additional control over the secular lords and their followers, the Church succeeded in adding a religious element to knighthood and the dubbing ceremony. As part the Christianization of knighthood, the Church injected many of the values we now associate with the ideal of knighthood. Christian knights were to be defenders of the faith and of the clergy as well as of the poor and the weak. Further, they were to be just and merciful. The Church's co-opting of knighthood was part of larger efforts to rein in the warrior class's violent behavior and channel it into projects that caused less harm to fellow Christians and, when possible, that advanced the goals of the Church. It was no coincidence that the concept of ideal Christian knight was created at around the same time as the Church attempted to restrict warfare within Europe by various agreements such as the *Truce of God*, which forbade acts of violence at certain times of year and on certain days of the week as well as prohibiting attacks on non-combatants. Further, it was during these same years that the Church began preaching crusades to retake the Holy Lands from the Saracens. The crusades provided the Church with an opportunity to redirect the bellicose warriors away from Christians and towards the enemies of Christendom.

As for the personal qualities a knight was expected to possess, the qualities which were most valued among the knights themselves were skill in arms, personal courage and honor, and a strong loyalty to his lord and his brothers in arms. Chivalry, in the medieval sense of courtesy and all it entailed, only gradually became part of the concept of knighthood. As far as being a protector of the weak and innocent, in practice this protection was only extended to noblewomen and other members of the aristocracy of which the knights were part. Peasants and others outside the noble class appear to have been protected only to the extent that they were considered to have some value. For example, a knight would protect the peasants and other commoners who lived on his estates because their labor, payments of rent, and other revenues they generated contributed to the knight's own wealth and status. On the other hand, a knight would seldom hesitate to loot and burn farms and kill the peasants on the lands of his enemies. Such looting filled the knight's treasury and the devastation helped weaken his enemies. The only exceptions to this practice occurred when a knight was hoping to occupy and permanently annex the lands he conquered. One example of this was during Henry V's campaigns in France, when he prohibited pillaging because he hoped to win the French people over to his side. Thus, knights were rarely upholders of the peace and protectors of the weak, except when it was in their own interest.

While the reality of becoming a knight did not match the ideal, attaining knighthood was still an important event in a young nobleman's life, although it did not confer adult status. Generally, a man could become a vassal and hold lands and titles only after he reached the age of twenty-one. It was possible to become a vassal at a younger age but such young vassals were usually in the care of guardians. However, even turning twenty-one did not usually provide any advancement for young noblemen within medieval society. Although some fathers granted lands and titles to their sons, most did not, and so lands and titles were typically received only by inheritance after the father had died. This meant that even many eldest sons remained landless until their fathers died. Some oldest sons remained in their fathers' households, but it was not uncommon for them to strike out on their own to make their own fortune, although they would, of course, return to their ancestral home when it was time to inherit.

For younger sons who had little or no chance of inheriting from their fathers, knighthood and turning twenty-one seldom provided advancement in themselves. Thus, it comes as no surprise that the next step after knighthood for many landless young nobles was to prove themselves in combat, whether on the battlefield or in tournaments. By distinguishing themselves, they hoped to gain the attention of some worthy lord who would take them into his household. In exchange for upkeep, they would serve their new lord in any capacity for which they were suited, whether fighting by his side or acting as his emissary to other noble courts. If they were lucky and skilled, they might then advance further and be rewarded for their loyal service with a title and some land. This aspect of the progression to adulthood is discussed further in the next chapter.

One peculiar development concerning knighthood in the last centuries of the Middle Ages was that squires often refused to be knighted. By this time, the position of knight had come to be burdened with numerous legal and fiscal responsibilities. As a consequence, many squires, although they were skilled, armored combatants and provided the military service expected of a knight, declined to be dubbed since they would then have had to pay more taxes. Some kings had to resort to ordering squires to accept dubbing.

Training for Noble Girls

While the boys were learning proper behavior, manners, and combat skills, noble girls trained for their future roles as well. Contemporary moralists advised that mothers at all levels of society should educate their daughters, and many mothers certainly did. However, among the nobility, some mothers entrusted much of their daughters' care and training to servants, a practice condemned by some of the moralists. Still, even when serving women were the ones providing the day-to-day care, noble mothers appear to have retained a large degree of oversight over their daughters' upbringing.

Some noble daughters remained under the guidance of the governesses who had cared for them as young children. Often these governesses had, in fact, originally served as their wet-nurses. In other instances, the governess was replaced by a mistress. This practice was most common among royalty and the high nobility. Mistresses were chosen from women of noble birth who were noted for their good judgment and model behavior. As a result, mistresses were usually mature women rather than young maids. As with masters for boys, mistresses were responsible for training all the girls of suitable age within the household.

While it was preferable for a mistress to be educated so that she could teach her charges how to read and write, such learned women were in short supply, and so family chaplains likely provided any education noble girls received in those areas. But mistresses did teach subjects that were considered as important, or even more important, than mere literacy. They taught the girls how to behave as noblewomen should. This training included etiquette and how to conduct one's self in a manner befitting one's place in society. As with boys, this latter issue was more than simply learning good manners and politeness. Noble girls too had to absorb the complexities of feudal society and learned to identify their superiors, inferiors, and peers within the nobility. They also learned the respect and obligations they either owed or should expect to receive from other members of nobility.

Unlike the training for boys, it was uncommon for noble girls to be sent to other households to learn how to behave in courtly society and to make useful social contacts. As mentioned previously, parents seldom risked placing their daughters in the homes of others because of the risk that their chastity might be compromised. Even within their own homes, mothers and fathers kept a watchful eye on their daughters and sought to prevent them from becoming overly familiar with male servants. Sometimes these efforts failed. For example, in the late 15th century, Margery Paston, whose family was among the landed gentry in England, fell in love with her family's bailiff. Although the bailiff was a senior servant and enjoyed a position of trust and responsibility within the household, the Pastons considered him a completely unsuitable match for their daughter. This star-crossed pair will be discussed further in the next chapter.

It should be noted that there were a few exceptions to the general practice of keeping girls at home until they were either married or embarked on a career as a nun. One group of noble girls who were placed in households outside their own families were orphans. Lacking parents, these girls had no choice but to be placed with other families. Still, their guardians usually had the same concerns as parents with regards to protecting the virtue and honor of these girls. Additionally, by the late 15th century in England, some girls from the minor nobility were placed with other noble families, although such placement does not appear to have been common even at this time.

Learning to Be a Virtuous Woman

Besides learning about their roles within society, girls, noble as well as common, were expected to learn to be good, virtuous women. As good, moral women, they would be prepared to perform their future roles within the family as wives and mothers. In medieval Europe, the ideal qualities for a woman to possess were piety, chastity, modesty, and submissiveness. A good woman was one who shunned vanity and extravagance while embracing all Christian virtues. Francesco da Barberino and other writers provided guidelines to help women achieve this goal. First, a well-behaved, upright girl did not simply walk around town on her own. She was always to be accompanied by a chaperone. She was also never to be left alone in the company of men or boys who were not her immediate relatives. When she was allowed out in public, it was only for some specific purpose, such as going to church. When in public, she was to keep her eyes downcast. At all times, she was to speak only when absolutely necessary, except when she was alone in her room. She was then free to talk all she liked! For her amusement, she was allowed to sing one song, one with decent content, each day. As for her personal appearance, she was prohibited from plucking her eyebrows, wearing makeup, and curling or dying her hair. She was not to wear expensive jewelry, extravagantly styled shoes, or other ostentatious and costly items of dress. Finally and most importantly, she was to attend church frequently and pray often.

It is likely that very few girls were subjected to all the requirements of this strict routine. Parents used their own judgment and typically allowed their little girls and boys to play together freely. However, as the children reached puberty, parents became concerned about protecting their daughters' chastity and their reputations. As a consequence, many families among the nobility and the upper classes of urban Italy and elsewhere appear to have followed some of the guidance on chaperoning and keeping girls at home. Not surprisingly, many girls appear to have resented being shadowed by an adult whenever they ventured out of the house and being confined to their homes the rest of the time. In Italy, some girls are known to have complied with the letter but not the spirit of these restrictions. They resorted to hanging out in the doorways and windows of their houses so that could chat with passersby and see and be seen by members of the opposite sex.

Men were expected to be virtuous as well, but women appear to have been held to higher standard. Further, men were usually judged by their accomplishments as well as their personal virtues, while good morals and character were generally the most important factors when judging a woman. Noble girls were expected to develop their virtues by modeling their behavior on that of their mothers, their governesses or mistresses, and other women in the household. Additionally, a few noble parents placed their daughters temporarily in nunneries so that the girls could learn these traits from the nuns, as discussed previously.

Along with learning to be a virtuous woman and an obedient and faithful mate, noble girls, like girls from non-noble families, learned to care for children. Like commoners, little noble girls imitated the actions of their mothers, nurses, and governesses. As they grew older, they likely helped take care of their younger siblings. Additionally, not all of the nobility were wealthy and powerful. Most noble families could afford servants to perform every chore necessary to maintain their homes and estates, and many could afford to employ stewards, bailiffs, and other higher ranking servants to oversee the other servants. However, for the lesser nobility, daughters may have assisted their mothers in supervising and possibly even performing some of the domestic duties.

Managing a Household

Noble girls needed to learn how to run a household, including managing servants as well as the properties their families held. In the early 15th century, the renowned female author Christine de Pisan wrote a book of advice for noblewomen which addressed these matters. She observed that noble ladies were often left on their own when their husbands went away on political or military business and that these absences were sometimes quite prolonged. Therefore, Christine wrote, a noblewoman had to know how to manage her family's estates, including knowing the total income their properties generated and controlling expenditure to avoid going into debt. The noble lady also had to know the legal rights of her husband and herself to ensure that she could exercise and defend these rights to the fullest and not be cheated by any tenants or vassals who did not live up to their legal obligations. She also needed to know what support her husband's lord could rightfully demand. Further, a noblewoman had to be able to screen employees and supervise them to prevent losses through theft or carelessness. Ideally, she should also have a basic understanding of agriculture and any other revenue producing activities on her family's estates. While Christine's book provided some guidance on all these matters, there was never any formal training available for noble girls in any of these matters. The best means for them to learn all these skills was to watch how their mothers ran their households. From observing these women direct their servants, manage their households, and work with their husbands, noble girls began to learn their future roles as valued helpmates to their own husbands.

Defense of the Home and Children

The wife of a nobleman had to be prepared organize and manage the defense of her home during her husband's absence. While noblewomen were never trained for combat and did not actually take up arms, some did walk the battlements and direct their forces. Additionally, should her husband be captured while away on campaign, she was usually the one who gathered the funds needed to pay the ransom for his freedom. If her husband was killed, the noble wife also took up the legal defense of her children to safeguard their rights and ensure that they succeeded their fallen fathers in all their rights and estates. Again, girls were never given training in military or legal matters, so whatever skills they possessed in these areas came from observing their mothers and other noblewomen.

Courtesy

As with noble boys, noble girls had to learn how to conduct themselves within feudal society in a manner befitting their rank. As mentioned previously, girls learned courtly behavior from their mothers, governesses, and mistresses. From these women, they learned how guests were received and entertained. Like boys, they also learned to dance, to sing, and to play musical instruments such as harps and lutes. As the presence of female participants in the *Canterbury Tales* and the *Decameron* suggests, they learned to tell amusing stories as well. Many learned to play chess, backgammon, and other games as well. Noblewomen who conducted themselves flawlessly and entertained their peers with any of the arts just described were noted and praised for such talents just as noblemen were. While today we might merely consider such a person to be well-rounded and fun to be around, for the medieval nobility, such a woman was highly desirable and brought fame and honor to her family. In feudal Europe, such fame and honor could be parlayed into social and political gain.

Riding and Hunting

Boys weren't the only noble children who learned to ride and hunt. Riding was an essential skill for girls as well. Noblewomen were sometimes depicted in medieval illustrations as riding in covered wagons specially designed for passengers, but this mode of transportation appears to have been used primarily for long-distance travel and ceremonial occasions. Riding on horseback was much more common. While there are no depiction or records that describe how girls learned how to ride, they likely learned the same way that boys did. Thus, they started at an early age and were gradually introduced to horseback riding. One significant difference was, however, the way that girls and women sat upon their horses. In illustrations, medieval women were always shown riding sidesaddle; that is with both legs placed to one side of the horse rather than straddling the horse as men did. They rode in this manner whether they were riding on a horse alone or on a *pillion*. A pillion was an extra seat placed behind the saddle to accommodate an extra rider. There appear to have been two reasons why women and girls rode in this fashion. First, spreading their legs wide to straddle the horse seems to have been deemed an unsuitable posture for any decent woman. In other words, it was unladylike. Second, while the exact designs of their clothing varied, women in the Middle Ages always wore garments with full, long skirts. These long dresses and other garments were wholly unsuited for riding while straddling horses. Additionally, unlike men who wore braies (underpants), women in medieval Europe do not appear to have worn any form of underpants, so sitting on a saddle like a man was simply out of the question.

As for hunting, girls did learn to hunt with hawks, and women were often shown enjoying the sport on horseback, sitting sidesaddle of course, with other fashionable noble men and women. For other types of hunting, such the *par force* hunting of deer and other large game, women were spectators rather than participants. They attended to watch and admire the activities of the men.

Embroidery and Other Cloth-Work

Like most other women in medieval society, noble girls learned how to do cloth work such as spinning, weaving and embroidery. While the items they made were used around their homes and given as gifts, they did this work as a hobby rather than to produce items that were essential for their families. The primary reason for doing such work was to keep themselves occupied. Idleness was considered a sin and was known to lead to worse ones. Attending religious services filled only an hour or two a day, so many noble girls and women spent part of their free time working with cloth. Such work was seldom performed alone. The women and girls of the family gathered together to do weaving and needlework. The young children of the household, both boys and girls, appear to often have been part of these gatherings as well. The women and girls often whiled away the time by singing or telling stories to entertain themselves while performing their handiwork. Enjoying music was considered better than engaging in idle gossip, although many popular songs were about love affairs, hardly a suitable topic for virtuous ears.

10

Coming of Age

At what point in their lives did children in medieval Europe become adults? There is no single answer to this question. For some purposes, boys and girls were treated as adults when they were as young as twelve or fourteen but, for other purposes, some men and women were not considered to be adults even when they were in their twenties. Marrying usually conferred or affirmed adult status, but medieval Europeans married at a wide range of ages. Further, some brides and grooms were still young children and were certainly not considered adults simply because they were married. Before we examine the various ages at which one became an adult under Church and secular laws, let us first examine a more universal measure of adulthood: the completion of physical growth.

Physical Maturity

The ages at which the bodies of boys and girls in medieval Europe stopped growing were the same as today. For example, in the 12th century, Hildegard of Bingen, a famous nun who composed works on religion and a variety of other topics including medicine, stated that women completed their physical growth at the age of twenty. Men, too, appear to have been fully grown by some time around the age of twenty as well.

So how big were youths in the Middle Ages when they were finally "all grown up"? To answer this question, we can turn to information gleaned from the actual physical remains of medieval Europeans. Medieval cemeteries, particularly mass graves found near sites of major medieval battles, have provided large numbers of skeletons from which physiological facts, such as height, can be determined. By comparing the length of bones from these skeletons to known standards and applying various algorithms, experts are able to estimate the height of these people when they were alive.

People in the Middle Ages are commonly imagined as being substantially shorter than people today, but measurements of skeletons of medieval people reveal a different picture. Based on remains found in the London metropolitan area, experts at the Museum of London estimate that the height of men in medieval London averaged around 5 feet, 7½ inches, while women's average height was around 5 feet, 3 inches. Skeletons excavated from mass graves near Towton, England, which was the site of a fierce battle during the Wars of the Roses in 1461, have yielded similar results. The heights of these men ranged from 5 feet, 3 inches, up to six feet, with a mean height of 5 feet, 8 inches. Comparable figures were produced by the remains recovered from the mass burial sites on the island of Gotland, Sweden, for the battle of Wisby, which was fought a hundred years earlier than the battle of Towton. The Gotlander men who fell in 1361 had an average height of around 5 feet, 7 inches. Research on populations elsewhere in Europe has produced similar figures with average heights of 5 feet, 8 inches, for men and 5 feet, 3 inches, for women.

Interestingly, these figures are only slightly shorter than those for modern Europeans and Americans of European ancestry. In 2002, the average height for an adult male from these populations was 5 feet 9 inches and 5 feet 4 inches for an adult female. We've all heard that, on the average, people today are substantially taller than their ancestors, due in large part to improvements in diet and health care. How can this be true if people today are only an inch taller than people who lived five hundred years ago? In fact, people today are taller than their more immediate ancestors. Figures from London and elsewhere reveal that Europeans became shorter in the centuries following the Middle Ages. From the 16th through the 19th centuries, disease and other factors caused the height of the average European male to shrink to 5 feet 5½ inches, while the average height of women declined to 5 feet 1¼ inches. It has only been in the last 100 to 150 years that this trend has been reversed.

Comparisons of the skeletal remains of different classes of medieval society indicate that height sometimes varied significantly between the classes. Specifically, the skeletons indicate that the nobility and other members of the upper classes were generally taller than average, while people from the poorer classes were shorter than average. No genetic cause has been discovered to account for this difference in physical development. Differences in diet appear to have been the cause. Diet played as an important role in determining height in the Middle Ages as it does today. The children of the nobility and wealthier classes had access to plentiful and nutritious food during their years of growing. Children from poor families, on the other hand, often suffered from inadequate nutrition during their critical growth years and so had their growth stunted.

As for the weight of medieval Europeans, there can only be speculation. Skeletons have not revealed any significant information on this matter nor have the few items of clothing and other objects which have survived. Contemporary illustrations and descriptions of people both in tales of fiction and in factual accounts suggest that relatively few men and women were overweight. Those who were overweight led sedentary lives such as choir monks and some members of the nobility. These same groups were also noted for suffering from diseases associated with rich diets, such as gout. However, most people led active and physically demanding lives, whether they were farmers engaged in the myriad tasks of growing and harvesting crops or were nobles engaged in warfare or in pastimes such as hunting. Additionally, even when harvests were good and food was plentiful, fattening foods were far less available during the Middle Ages than they are today. Sugar, whether in the form of honey or the rarer and more expensive cane sugar, was used sparingly and considered a treat even among the nobility. While an essential part of most diets, oils too, whether from animal fats or from vegetable sources such as olives, were relatively expensive and were used far less in food preparation than they are today. Most medieval Europeans appear to have eaten diets which consisted primarily of grains, vegetables, fruits, and some meat and fish with little fat and sugar. As a consequence of this diet and the physical demands of their occupations, most medieval Europeans were likely quite lean, especially when judged by modern standards.

Weight or, at least, diet likely played a role in the uniquely female physical measure of maturity: the onset of menstruation. Girls in the Middle Ages typically began menstruating between the ages of twelve and fifteen, with the daughters of nobility tending to start menstruation at a younger age than daughters of peasants and other commoners. The better diet enjoyed by the nobility and the resulting accumulation of body fat appears to have been cause for the earlier fertility of noble girls. As we will see later in this chapter, girls from noble and other wealthy families were often married when they were still quite young and some became mothers at the age of twelve.

As for the life expectancy of medieval Europeans, it was definitely shorter than that of modern Europeans, but how much shorter cannot be determined with a high degree of certainty. The documentary record is far too patchy to provide anything like a complete picture for the entire Middle Ages for all of Europe, so historians have had to rely on those scattered instances where records have survived, such as in Italian cities from the late Middle Ages. From the limited evidence available, it is estimated that the average life expectancy was 35 to 40 years in the period preceding the Black Death and dropped to 17 to 18 during the plague years. In the 15th century, Europeans had recovered somewhat and the average was up to 30 years. It must be remembered that these figures are averages, and so the high death rate among infants and children brings down the overall averages. Many people lived much longer than the averages. By one estimate, 20 percent of medieval Europeans survived to age 50 or beyond. This estimate is supported by records such as those from 15th century Florence which reveal that many citizens lived past 50, with some living into their 70s and at least a few who made it to 90. Even in the hazardous occupation of man-at-arms, there were men who lived far above the average lifespan. These include Sir John Talbot, who served on the English side of the Hundred Years' War for 50 years. He died on the battlefield when he was in his 70s.

Adulthood Under the Law

Today, there are several different legal milestones in a person's life. For example, in the United States, one can obtain a driver's license at the age of sixteen, vote at age eighteen, and buy alcohol at the age of twenty-one. As this progression shows, modern society has determined that a person is capable of exercising different levels of judgment at different ages and entrusts people with increasing rights and responsibilities as they grow older. This is not a new concept and, in the Middle Ages, boys and girls were similarly admitted into adult society in a gradual fashion.

Criminal Liability

The age of a child determined whether he would be prosecuted for a crime. Age also limited the range of punishments imposed by the law. Below the age of six, children in medieval Europe were deemed to lack the intent to commit criminal acts. For actions ranging from petty theft to accidentally blinding or even killing a playmate, young children were generally not considered guilty of crimes since they were thought to be too young to have intended any harm. If anyone was held responsible, it was the children's parents, and they were the ones who were admonished by public authorities for their children's misdeeds. Under the laws of Anglo-Saxon England, for example, children became culpable for some of their misdeeds at the age of six. By the time an Anglo-Saxon child reached the age of twelve, he was treated as fully adult under the criminal laws and could be executed for his crimes. However, at least one king thought the laws were too harsh and attempted to raise the minimum age for the death penalty to fifteen. While his efforts were ultimately unsuccessful, it appears that the death penalty was only imposed on those below the age of fifteen when they were repeat offenders, had fled, or had resisted arrest.

Later in the Middle Ages, children between the ages of six and twelve were still being tried and punished for their crimes, but English examples indicate that such young children were usually tried only when their crimes involved causing serious injury or death. Further, by the 13th century, even when found guilty of a crime such as killing a playmate by hitting him with a rock, children this young were routinely pardoned. The basis for pardoning was that the child was still too young to have intended the harm and to understand that his actions could cause such harm. For example, a ten-year-old boy practicing archery shot an arrow which struck and killed a five-year-old girl who was standing nearby. A jury accepted that the death was an accident, so the boy was not punished. On the other hand, in a few extremely griev-ous cases, children were found to have intentionally caused serious harm and were executed for their crimes. In one case, an eleven-year-old boy was executed for the murder of a five-year-old girl. When he was ten, the boy had broken into the girl's house. She had attempted to stop him from stealing bread, and he hit her in the head with an axe. The judge in the case considered the death penalty appropriate because the boy had immediately attempted to hide his victim's body. To the judge, this proved that the boy was aware of the evil nature of his act.

Boys were not the only ones who ran afoul of the law. In the 14th century, a thirteen-year-old serving girl killed her mistress. She was executed by being burnt. (Killing one's mas-ter or mistress was held to be comparable to treason and so the punishment was the same as for treason.) However, cases such as these appear to have been exceptional and were consid-ered noteworthy even at the time. More commonly, until they were fifteen, boys and girls were generally not deemed old enough to be tried as adults and subjected to the full range of punishments meted out to adults, including execution.

Adulthood Under Civil Law

For civil law and purposes of government administration, the ages of twelve and four-teen were common thresholds. For example, in the early Middle Ages boys became subject to paying taxes as an adult male at the age of twelve. This age was eventually raised to fourteen or older in many parts of Europe. Boys could make valid wills when they were fourteen, while girls could do so at twelve. In the early Middle Ages, boys could make binding oaths when they were as young as twelve, but this age was later raised to fourteen. In 12th century England, boys had to be at least fifteen to sit on a jury or bring a suit before the court.

To come into one's inheritance and be free of guardianship, boys often had to wait until they were twenty-one, although there were many exceptions. For example, under the English common law, a nobleman had to be at least twenty-one to hold a feudal tenure (property and rights held in exchange for service to a lord) when that tenure required military service. On the other hand, for tenures which did not entail military service, the minimum age was only fourteen or fifteen. Additionally, in the cities, twenty-one was a common age for an orphan to be released from guardianship and inherit property in their own right. However, boys and girls as young as fifteen were sometimes permitted to come into their inheritances if they could prove that they were capable of handling adult responsibilities. Tests for such maturity included being able to count money, tell counterfeit coins from real ones, measure cloth, and other skills which medieval citizens were commonly expected to perform. For girls, the tests also included showing that they were capable of running a household, including knowing how to properly secure valuable items.

In theory, girls were often permitted to inherit at an earlier age than boys. A noblewoman in England, for example, could inherit and hold a military tenure when she was only sixteen. However, she was likely expected to be under the control of her father or else married and subject to the guidance of her husband. At the other end of feudal society, a lord would not accept a serf as a tenant until he was at least twenty.

Adulthood Under the Laws of the Church

Under canon law, the law of the Church, fourteen was also the earliest age at which a boy could ordinarily marry. For girls, this age was twelve. However, as discussed later in this chapter, the Church permitted exceptions to these minimum age requirements. Church courts ordinarily did not let children testify until they were sixteen. As for the sacraments, up through the 12th century, children could receive communion, but in 1215 the Church required that a child had reached "the age of discernment." This requirement was part of the Church's efforts to ensure that persons receiving communion fully understood that the bread and wine had been transubstantiated into the actual body and blood of Christ. By the 14th century, this was interpreted as meaning twelve for girls and fourteen for boys. For confession, in 1215, the Church imposed the same age requirement as for communion. Even before this date, young children were generally held not to need confession except in rare cases such as when it appeared that they were engaging in sinful sexual activity.

Confirmation

In the rite of confirmation, a baptized Christian was confirmed in his religious beliefs by a bishop. The confirmation ceremony began with the Christian to be confirmed being presented to the bishop by a sponsor, another Christian of the same sex. Further, the sponsor was to be unrelated to the person being confirmed. The bishop blessed the person being confirmed and prayed that the Holy Spirit descend upon him and help strengthen and perfect his faith. The bishops then made the sign of the Cross on his forward using chrism, the same blessed mixture of oil and balsam used at baptisms.

While the origins of this sacrament are unclear, confirmation was a well established practice by the beginning of the Middle Ages. In the early Middle Ages, infants were often confirmed immediately after they were baptized or not long afterwards. However, over the following centuries, the Church determined that it was more appropriate to confirm children at a later age. A council held in Cologne in 1280 decreed that seven was the minimum age for confirmation, but others in the Church held that twelve was the correct age. One 14th century religious writer advised that confirmation should be delayed until a child reached the age of discernment. In any event, confirmation of infants became increasingly rare and appears to have stopped before the end of the Middle Ages.

Since confirmations were performed only by bishops rather than by priests, many parents, especially those living in small rural communities, had difficulty in having their children confirmed. It was often a hardship for them to travel all the way to the nearest cathedral. Even if parents brought their child to a cathedral, there was no guarantee that the bishop would be available to perform the confirmation, since bishops were very busy men with many secular as well as sacred duties to perform. Further, while bishops often traveled around their dioceses, they seldom visited every parish on anything approaching a regular basis. In recognition of the limited availability of bishops, the Church ordered parents to bring their children for confirmation whenever a bishop passed within seven miles of their homes. In some instances, this practice purportedly resulted in some bishops performing confirmations in the road without even dismounting from their horses. As a consequence of the irregularity of bishops' visits and other difficulties, children were confirmed at a variety of ages, ranging from infancy on up. It is also likely that many children were never confirmed.

Emancipation

As part of the revival of Roman civil law in southern Europe, formal emancipation reemerged as a means of declaring that a person had reached adulthood. The practice was most common among the urban classes in Italy, where daughters as well as sons were emancipated. To emancipate a daughter or son, a father drafted a document which stated that he was no longer responsible for his child's actions or debts. Reciprocally, the document provided that the daughter or son was not responsible for any debts incurred by her or his father. The document also often gave the son or daughter some of the family's property. This property was usually treated as an advance against the inheritance the daughter or son was expected to receive upon the death of his father. The document and act of emancipating the child was then recorded by a notary or a judge and became effective.

There were several motives for a father to formally emancipate his children. Prior to emancipation, sons could not own property in their own nor could they enter into contracts in their own right. Emancipation gave them the independent legal standing and resources to embark on their own business careers. Emancipation was also frequently a prelude to a son's marriage, since it gave him the property needed to attract a spouse and establish a household of his own. In fact, some negotiations for arranging marriages made emancipation of the prospective groom a requirement. However, not all emancipated sons married and moved out of their parents' homes. Records show that many stayed on for years after emancipation. In one case, a son was still single and living at home when he was forty and had been emancipated for nearly twenty-five years. In other cases, the children who remained at home were still quite young at the time of their emancipation. While most sons were emancipated when they were in their late teens through their late twenties, some were emancipated when they were only twelve or even younger. In cases of such early emancipation, the father's motive was not to give his child independence but to protect the family's assets. By transferring ownership of property to a child and then emancipating him, the property was then considered the child's and so the creditors of the father could not take it to settle their debts.

Marriage

Marriage was one of the most common actions which led to public acceptance of a person, male or female, as an adult. Husbands and wives were usually free of most, if not all, of the controls of their respective parents and were responsible for their own actions in the eyes of the law. However, before we examine how couples married during the Middle Ages, we need to examine the institution of marriage itself, since it evolved over the course of the period and involved some requirements and prohibitions which have long since been eliminated.

Marriage and the Church

For the first several centuries of the Middle Ages, marriage was primarily a civil and secular matter, just as it had been in the days of the Roman Empire. Families arranged the marriages of their children as they saw fit and the Church played little, if any, role in either the wedding or the subsequent marriage. The lack of Church involvement was due in part to the Church's ambiguous position on marriage. Many of the early Christian theologians, or "Church Fathers" as they are often called, held celibacy to be the ideal state for Christians. By being celibate, Christians could free themselves from carnal desire and other distractions of the material world. Having a spouse and children were included among these earthly distractions. With one's fleshly desires under control and one's worldly ties kept to a minimum, the Church Fathers believed that it was far easier for Christians to lead lives free of sin and focus on attaining spiritual salvation. However, other Church Fathers, including Saints Paul and Augustine, recognized that most Christians could not lead such ideal lives. They concluded that, while celibacy was still the ideal, it was better for men and women who could not control their lusts to marry rather than commit the sin of fornication. This position was sometimes summed up in the aphorism that "it is better to marry than burn" (in hell). According to these theologians, only sex within marriage was not inherently sinful. They further specified that sex within marriage was not sinful only when it was done for purposes of procreation and not simply to satisfy lust. Some of these theologians also held that marriage was for the purpose of building familial relations between groups of people who were previously unrelated. By building such relations, marriage promoted the uniting of society and the spread of familial love.

Church Regulation of Marriage

Under Pope Gregory VII in the late 11th century, the Church aggressively sought to bring marriage under its control. During the 12th century, the Church finally displaced secular authority in the matter of marriages and succeeded in enforcing a number of conditions on those who wished to be married. One of the most important of these was the provision that all that was required for a valid marriage was for the couple to freely give their consent to being married. In theory, this requirement freed men and women from coercion by parents and others to accept arranged marriages. However, as explained in this chapter, free consent was often compromised. Still, some couples were able to take advantage of having free consent as the only precondition for a valid marriage but, as we will see later in this chapter, such ease and freedom in creating a binding union sometimes caused problems.

Another part of the Church's regulation of marriage was the establishment of conditions which prevented a couple from lawfully marrying. These impediments to marriage included

- Force: If either the man or woman was forced to enter into the marriage, their union was invalid. However, as discussed later in this chapter, Church courts rarely invalidated marriages for this reason.

- Age: The bride had to be at least twelve years old and the groom fourteen years old, but there were exceptions to these minimum age requirements.
- Pre-contract: Someone who was already married could not marry again while his or her first spouse was still alive.
- Impotence or barrenness: A man or woman who was known to be infertile could not marry. If the condition was discovered after the wedding, the marriage could be annulled.
- Incest and consanguinity: The bride and groom could not be closely related to each other.

At first glance, this last impediment appears to have been quite a reasonable requirement. After all, incest is not condoned in civilized societies. Initially, the Church followed the Roman law on incest and forbade marriages within four degrees of kinship. As illustrated below, this prohibition simply meant that a person could not marry his siblings, parents, aunts, uncles, and first cousins.

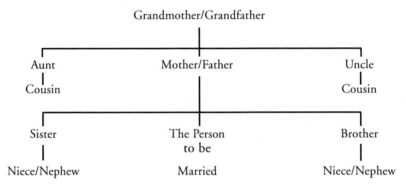

Roman Four Degrees of Kinship

Under the Roman method of calculating degrees of kinship, parents are within the first degree of kinship to the person for whom the kinship is being calculated. Siblings and grandparents are within the second degree. Aunts, uncles, nieces, and nephews are kin in the third degree and first cousins are related to the person in the fourth degree. Marriages between any of these closely related people were morally repugnant. Further, it was generally recognized that such incestuous unions rarely resulted in healthy children. The Church, however, extended the prohibition to cover relatives by marriage as well as by blood. Applying the idea that married people became of one body, a person's widowed stepmother fell within the first degree of kinship since she was considered as being part of a person's father. Similarly, a man was prohibited from marrying his sister-in-law or daughter-in-law after she was widowed. Eventually, all of a person's in-laws fell within the prohibition. For example, up through the 6th century, two brothers from one family could marry two sisters from another family, but later such pair unions were prohibited because each brother would be marrying the sister-in-law of the other.

As though this expansion of the prohibitions against incest were not enough, by the 8th century, the Church added spiritual relatives to a person's kinship group as well. Spiritual relatives were godparents, confirmation sponsors, and their relatives. This addition meant that godparents were treated the same as a person's biological parents so that their children, siblings, and cousins also fell with the prohibited degrees of kinship. This creation of spiritual kinship appears to have been the primary reason that parents could not serve as the godparents of their own children. If a mother served as the godmother of her own child, she became spiritually related to her husband and, under strict application of the laws of the Church, she then had to separate from him even if their marriage was otherwise valid. Similarly, a woman who sponsored her own child at his confirmation became impermissibly related to her own husband. Some women allegedly used this bizarre bit of Church law to obtain separations from their husbands. The Church closed this loophole in the early 9th century, but spiritual kinship remained an impediment to marriage throughout the Middle Ages.

The Church also held that sexual intercourse created an affinity between persons. For example, if an unmarried man had sexual intercourse with a woman, he was subsequently barred from marrying any of her sisters or any other of her close female relatives, since the act of intercourse was deemed to create a relationship between the man and the woman just as though they had married.

In addition to expanding kinship from blood relatives to include those to whom a person had an affinity by marriage, spiritual means or sexual intercourse, the Church changed the method by which degrees of kinship were calculated. By the early 8th century, the Church had replaced the Roman method with the one used by the Germanic peoples who had invaded and began settling in western Europe during the final centuries of the Roman Empire. Under the Germanic method, degrees of kinship were calculated by counting the generations back to a common ancestor. Thus, four degrees of kinship now extended to everyone who shared one of the same great-great-grandparents. But the Church did not stop there. It expanded the prohibited degrees of kinship and affinity to seven (fig. 37). This meant that a person could not marry anyone who shared one of his 128 great-great-great-great-great-grandparents. In an age when there were no birth certificates, it was difficult for anyone to firmly establish what their lineage was for the past seven generations, a span of generations which stretched back over one hundred years.

There are no solid explanations of the Church's motives for expanding the definition of incest and consanguinity to cover such a vast variety of relationships. The only contemporary reason is found in the writings of St. Augustine. He indicates that the purpose behind forcing men and women to marry outside of their immediate social circles was to spread and tighten the bonds of kindred affection throughout the Christian community. Through this means, Christians would be united into one large, loving family. While this was a noble goal, the Church's regulations appear to have resulted in more confusion for laymen and more work for canon lawyers rather than in a more peaceful and affectionate society.

It is difficult to determine just how much the average medieval European adhered to the Church's strictures on incestuous unions. The complexity and breadth of the impediments caused even saints to have difficulty in interpreting and applying the Church's regulations. For example, St. Boniface permitted a man to marry a widow who was the mother of the man's godson. St. Boniface did not see the couple's spiritual kinship as a valid obstacle to their marriage, but other Church officials did and chastised him for his error.

For many people, particularly those who lived in small villages which had only limited influxes of newcomers, it was likely nearly impossible to find any suitable prospective spouse who did not fall within the prohibited degrees. The best documented cases of people trying to locate spouses to whom they were not related come from among the nobility.

The prohibition against marrying anyone with such a broadly defined group particularly affected the nobility. In the early Middle Ages, noble marriages frequently involved partners

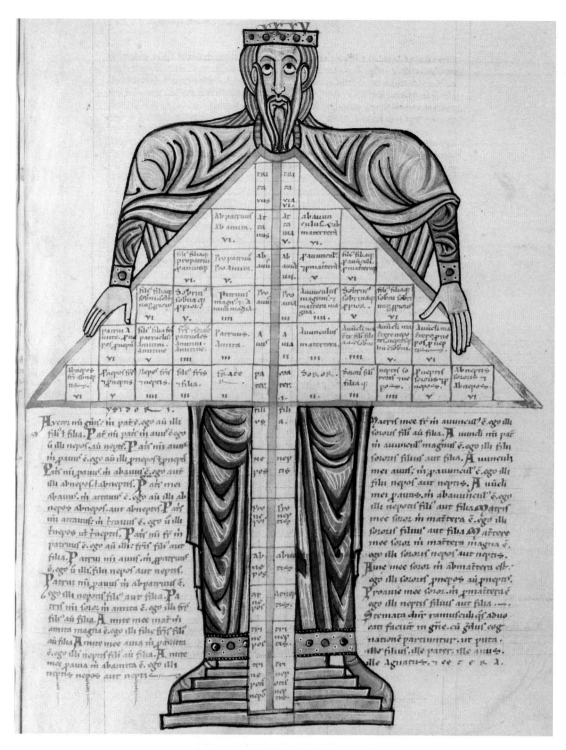

Fig. 37. This is a diagram of the degrees of consanguinity from a 12th century copy of Gratian's *Decretum*. While this chart was intended to make it easier to determine whether a potential marriage partner was related within the prohibited seven degrees of consanguinity, it shows just how confusing this process was. In 1215, the Church reduced the prohibited degrees to four but retained a broad definition of what constituted consanguineous relations. As a consequence, consanguinity remained a potential pitfall for couples seeking to marry.

who were related somewhere beyond the old four degrees of kinship but within the newer seven degrees of kinship. There were a number of reasons why noblemen and women often married people to whom they were related in some degree. One reason was the limited number of noble families. While it is impossible to determine the total numbers of the nobility, they certainly constituted a small minority of the total population of medieval Europe. Combined with the prevailing attitude that it was unacceptable for a member of the nobility to marry someone from outside their class, in other words a commoner, this meant that the available pool of suitable spouses was quite limited. Further, the pool of acceptable noble spouses became more and more restricted as one went higher and higher in the ranks of the nobility. This was due to the noble ideal that a nobleman or woman should not marry beneath their station. This meant, at the highest level, that the only suitable match for a royal prince was a princess from another royal family. While Europe was far more fragmented in the Middle Ages than it is today and had many more independent regions governed by their own kings, there was only a finite number of princes and princesses to go around. As a consequence, princesses from outside western Europe were sought out for brides for kings in France and elsewhere. A few of these brides came from Byzantium, while others were drawn from the newly Christianized areas at the eastern fringes of Europe. As for noble women, less effort was given to find them spouses of suitable rank and so many were married to men of lesser social standing but who were outside the prohibited degrees of consanguinity. Despite these efforts, by as early as the 10th century, it was extremely difficult for the higher nobility to arrange marriages which did not violate the Church's strictures on incest and prohibited kinship.

The Church did permit some exceptions. Persons who wished to marry within the prohibited degrees were sometimes able to obtain papal dispensations which allowed them to marry. Such dispensations were costly to obtain and typically required some political influence as well. As a consequence, dispensations were granted only to the nobility and the wealthy. In a few instances, members of the nobility simply ignored the Church's prohibition. For example, when Aethelwulf, the Anglo-Saxon king of Wessex in England, died in 857, his widow, Judith, a Frankish princess, married one of his sons. While this may sound like a clear-cut case of incest, in the widow's defense, it should be noted that she had only been married to Aethelwulf for two years before his death and that she was just fourteen years old when he died. Further, the stepson she married was already a grown man. Still, even at the time, this marriage created a scandal and drew strong criticism from the Church, although the Church did not take any action to invalidate it.

The prohibition against consanguinity had one outcome the Church did not desire: it provided grounds for annulment. In some instances, the "discovery" that the husband and wife were related was only a pretext for annulment. This was the case in 1152 when King Louis VII of France suddenly discovered that his wife, Eleanor of Aquitaine, was related to him within the fourth or fifth degree. Some noblemen even used consanguinity as grounds for annulment, despite having previously obtained a papal dispensation to waive that impediment.

Since many marriages in the early Middle Ages were conducted in the presence of friends and family who witnessed the union rather than being solemnized by a priest, many couples were able to avoid having to prove that they were not related within the prohibited degrees.

In 1215, the Church finally revised its rules on consanguinity and affinity as impediments to marriage. In part to make the rules easier to follow and administer, the Fourth Lateran Council revised the rules to reduce the prohibited degrees back down to four. However, the

Germanic method of calculating degrees of kinship was retained so that the sharing of a common great-great-grandparent was still a bar to being wed. Further, affinity by marriage, sexual intercourse, and spiritual means were also retained.

Polygyny and Concubinage

At the beginning of the Middle Ages, it was not uncommon for the male aristocrats of Europe to have multiple wives and to openly retain mistresses as well. Polygyny and concubinage appear to have been exclusively practiced by the nobility, since only they possessed the resources needed to attract and maintain multiple partners. Perhaps for this reason, these practices were particularly common among the higher nobility.

Despite the increasing Christianization of Europe, both polygyny and concubinage persisted for several centuries. By the 9th century, the Church had made significant progress in imposing its model of monogamous marriage in most of Europe, but it took until some time in the 11th or 12th century before the Church was fully successful. While some members of the nobility continued to keep mistresses throughout the remainder of the Middle Ages, such conduct was subject to criticism from secular society as well as the Church.

The Ages of Brides and Grooms

Many people in medieval Europe married at young ages. Today, it is generally accepted and, indeed, enforced by law that men and women should not marry until they are mature enough to understand the consequences of their actions. When looking back at the early ages at which many people in the Middle Ages married and at which women began bearing children, a modern person is often shocked. Yet, these practices were quite acceptable to medieval Europeans. On average, lifespans were much shorter then and the odds of a sudden death far higher than today. Further, parents commonly wished to see their children married while they were still alive and so encouraged them or arranged for them to marry at young ages.

As part of its regulation of marriage, the Church set minimum ages for brides and grooms. Under canon law, boys could marry at the age of fourteen and girls at the age of twelve. Again, while these ages are quite young by modern standards, they reflect the views of medieval society about the mental and moral development of boys and girls. By these ages, boys and girls were thought to have developed sufficiently so that it was reasonable to hold them responsible for their decisions and actions. However, the Church permitted exceptions to these age limits, and parents could promise their children in marriage when they were only seven. While such betrothal was not the same as marriage, children were expected to ratify their parents' promises and marry when they reached the appropriate age. Further, the Church did allow some children to marry below the minimum ages set in canon law. When the marriage was in the interest of public peace, children could be married at the age of seven. This exception applied only to the nobility and was intended to facilitate marriage that secured political alliances and peace treaties such as when former enemies agreed that their children would marry as part of ending hostilities. However, the Church assumed that the marriage could not be consummated until the bride and groom had reached the ages specified in canon law and so it permitted the dissolution of these child marriages before either the bride or groom reached the age for consummation. Once the bride and groom had reached the minimum ages, they were expected to give their consent to their union. In practice, this usually required no action on their part. A man and woman who were wed as children were presumed to have consented to their childhood marriage and their union was deemed valid and binding unless they acted to formally repudiate it. There must have been considerable parental pressure against escaping a marriage this way; yet in at least a few instances, men and women who had been wed as children did successfully repudiate their marriages. While it is not clear from Church court records, some of these repudiations may have been obtained with the consent of the parents of at least one of the parties. Changes in the political or economic fortunes of either the bride's or groom's family between the time of the childhood marriage and the time of consummation could lead one of the families to seek to free itself so that it could make a better match for its son or daughter.

Ages for Noble Marriages

Marrying at very early ages was most common among the nobility. Besides the reasons just discussed, noble fathers had a strong incentive in wanting to have their children's marriages arranged before they, the fathers, died. If a nobleman delayed too long and death intervened before he could arrange marriages for his children, his children usually became the wards of his lord. As explained later in this chapter, lords arranged the marriages of their wards to suit their interests. The best interests of wards and their families might be completely ignored as a lord advanced his own ambitions. This was an outcome which every noble father sought to avoid. Thus, by arranging their children's marriages although they were still quite young, many noble fathers were simply trying to do what was best for their families including their children.

At times, the nobility sometimes ignored the Church's restrictions and exceptions entirely. Noble children were sometimes married at ages much younger than seven. Some were married while they were still infants. Their parents acted as their proxies in the wedding ceremonies. The extreme youth of some noble boys and girls at the time of their first marriage is reflected in medieval laws and records of marriages. In England, for example, a widow who was nine years old was permitted to claim her share of her deceased husband's estate. Some of these little noble brides were so young that they were recorded as still playing games such as dressing up in costume jewelry, dancing with other little girls, and playing with dolls even after they married. A girl's physical immaturity at the time of her marriage and her subsequent development was also sometimes remarked upon, such as in cases where a wedding ring suitable for a child's finger had become cripplingly tight by the time the girl was a fully grown woman.

Child brides and grooms often continued to live with their own parents until they reached a suitable age to live with their spouses, although child brides were occasionally taken into the household of the grooms' families and raised their along with their husbands. For example, in 1211, Elizabeth, a princess of Hungary (later recognized as a saint), married at the age of four. She moved into the home of her eleven-year-old husband immediately after the wedding. While the Church denounced the practice of marrying such young children, it does not appear to have ever declared such a marriage invalid except when one of the families sought to dissolve the union before it was consummated.

While many young noble boys and girls were married to partners close to their own ages, many were not. Most instances in which a much younger person was married to someone many years their senior involved young girls being wedded to men who were much older. For example, in England in 1455, Edmund, the earl of Richmond, married the daughter of the duke of Somerset when he was twenty-five and she was twelve. Keen to secure the marriage and rights in the rich estates she had as her dowry, Edmund successfully impregnated his young bride that same year.

Despite the numerous instances of marriages at very young ages, most of the nobility were married when both the bride and groom were more mature. Many noblemen first married when they were in their mid- to late twenties. Noble brides were usually younger than their husbands and were often in their late teens or early twenties when they first married.

Ages for the Marriage of City-Dwellers

Marriages in medieval cities appear to have commonly been between younger women and older men, not unlike many of the marriages of the nobility. Urban women were usually in their late teens or early twenties when they first married. Men in the cities typically married when they were at some age between their early twenties and mid-thirties. The largest discrepancies in ages have been documented in the city-states of northern Italy, where men often married women who were eight or more years their junior. In fact, in late medieval Florence, grooms entering their first marriages were typically in their thirties and were twelve years older than their brides.

There were a number of factors which led to men in the cities to wait to marry until they were in their twenties or older. Those learning trades and crafts, the apprentices, typically lacked the material resources needed to attract a suitable mate and establish a household of their own. Further, their apprenticeship contracts usually forbade them from marrying until they had complete the full term of their training. And, as explained in chapter 8, some had to serve as journeymen after their apprenticeships before they could accumulate the resources needed to attract a mate and establish a household. As a consequence, many urban craftsmen and merchants had to wait until their mid- to late twenties or even early thirties before they could seriously consider marriage.

Compared to men, there were fewer incentives for women to delay their marriages. In fact, it was often in a family's interest to marry off their daughters at as early an age as possible. In the marriage market, younger women were simply more desirable than older ones and so, the younger a woman was, the easier it was to find a spouse for her. Additionally, while some worked in their families' businesses, daughters could be a drain on families' resources. Put bluntly, the expense of maintaining them sometimes outweighed their economic value. Finally, a woman's virtue, her chastity, was highly valued in medieval society. Protecting a daughter's virtue and reputation was an important matter for most families. If a daughter's virtue was compromised, whether by actually losing her virginity, by being reputed to have done so, or simply by keeping bad company, it became much more difficult, if not impossible, for a family to find a suitable match for her. By marrying her off early, a family could lessen the risk that a daughter's reputation might be sullied before a spouse was found for her.

Some city-dwellers rarely married regardless of their age. The working poor, such as day laborers, had difficulty in earning enough on which to live, let alone enough to afford to marry and raise a family. As a consequence, many men and women in medieval cities appear to have remained single for their entire lives. Similarly, there were people in the countryside who were unable to marry because of their poverty.

Ages for the Marriage for Peasants

While the records of marriages of peasants are even less extensive than those of the nobility and for the urban classes, it is still possible to discern some general patterns in the ages at which peasants first married. Peasants, men and women alike, appear to have frequently married when they were in their late teens and early twenties. Although the grooms were typically at least a few years older than their brides, peasant brides and grooms were usually closer in age to each other than were those of the nobility and the cities.

In part, the differences between the urban and rural economies account for the relatively young age at which many male peasants married. Before they could marry, young men in the cities had to undergo apprenticeship or other training and then establish themselves in a trade. In contrast, peasant men were ready to take up their families' trade and begin farming on their own when they reached their late teens. Further, to run a productive farm, they needed wives, and, ultimately children, to help them. Thus, they had a strong incentive to marry as soon as possible.

Arranged Marriages

Arranged marriages were common among the nobility and wealthy in medieval Europe. While parents were usually not entirely insensitive to the desires of their children, the interests of sons or daughters were often subordinated to what the parents thought was best for the entire family. Through carefully planned marriages, parents, primarily fathers, sought to perpetuate their lineages. They also strove to make matches that improved their families' social and political standing. And, of course, gaining land and other resources was always desirable as part of enhancing a family's security and prestige.

Merchants and craftsmen in the cities sought suitable partners for their sons and daughters from among the children of their business associates and fellow guild members. The goal was to find a husband or wife who would bring some measure of wealth and prestige to family. Wealth included money and property, but intangibles such as business or political contacts were also valued. Such unions benefited not just the child being married but his or her entire family as well.

Peasants engaged in arranging their children's marriages as well. Wealthy peasants who owned land often used the marriages of their children to enlarge or consolidate landholdings. By marrying a son or daughter into another family which held property and then repeating that process over generations, some rural families amassed large estates and advanced up the social ladder to landed gentry. Even among the poorer peasantry, marriages were sometimes arranged simply to gain an acre or two for a family's patrimony.

Noble parents, like any others, sought to perpetuate their families by having their children marry and become parents themselves and arranged marriages to help accomplish this goal. There were other reasons for marriage among the aristocracy which were more unique to this class. Marriages of noble men and women were affairs of state and were too important to be left up to the whims of the individuals involved. Noble marriages were often arranged as part of building political alliances and so often involved careful planning by the parents as well as their advisors. Marrying one's son or daughter into a family that was more powerful or held key castles was desirable as part of a larger strategy to secure and enhance a family's own political position. Not surprisingly, negotiations of noble marriages were sometimes quite protracted as each side struggled to get the best deal.

In many instances, records of marriage negotiations reveal just how cold and calculating fathers could be when arranging marriages. In many marriage contracts, it is quite clear that the goal was to unite the two families without any regard to the desires of the sons and daughters involved. For example, one 15th century contract for the marriage of a six-year-old girl to a teenage boy provided that the girl was to marry his younger brother if the boy died. This did, in fact, occur, and the girl, then ten, was married to the younger brother. In another marriage contract, the name of the bride was left blank because the family had several daughters and the father had not yet decided which one to marry off.

Arranged marriages for young noble boys and girls were not always loveless affairs. Records of negotiations reveal that some brides- and grooms-to-be exchanged love notes and gifts along with letters discussing contract terms. Thus, even in arranged marriages there was a place for courtship and trying to win the affections of one's future spouse.

In some cases, love sometimes blossomed after the wedding. For example, Prince Edward of England, the future King Edward I, married Eleanor of Castile in 1254. He was fifteen at the time. She was about fourteen. Their respective parents arranged the marriage as part of forming political alliances. Over their thirty-six-year marriage, Edward and Eleanor traveled almost constantly together. Eleanor accompanied Edward even when he went on crusade in the Holy Land from 1270 to 1273. In the Holy Land, she helped nurse him back to health after he was nearly killed by a Muslim in an assassination attempt. In some accounts of the attack, the assassin was said to have used a poisoned blade, and Eleanor was reported as saving Edward's life by sucking the poison from his wound. Besides being his constant companion, Eleanor bore Edward sixteen children over the course of their marriage, although only seven survived past infancy. When she died in 1290, Edward was grief-stricken. Eleanor died at Nottingham and Edward had memorials erected at the twelve places at which the bier containing her body stopped on its long trip to Westminster Abbey (fig. 38). Although Edward married again in 1298 as part of another politically advantageous arrangement, Eleanor was clearly the love of his life. Many arranged marriages were likely not as happy as that of Edward and Eleanor, but their example shows that it was possible to find love in such a relationship.

Family Approval for Marriages

Even when a marriage was not wholly arranged by the parents, the approval of the fathers of the bride and groom was still usually essential. In fact, secular laws in some German cities and elsewhere even stated that parents had the right to choose the spouses of their children. Children who married without their parents' permission were subject to fines, banishment, and disinheritance. And, despite its position that the free consent of the bride and groom was all that was required for a valid marriage, the Church generally sympathized with parents, and few unions appear to have made in face of parental opposition.

Parents had a variety of tools for pressuring their children to accept the spouses cho-

Opposite: Fig. 38. This is one of twelve such monuments commissioned by Edward I of England as memorials to his beloved wife after her death in 1290. Eleanor died in Lincolnshire and her body was carried back to London for burial. The crosses were built in each town in which her funeral cortege stopped on its progress to London. While their marriage had been arranged to further political ends, as was common among the nobility, Edward and Eleanor clearly developed genuine love for each other.

sen for them or to give up plans of marrying someone to whom the parents objected. The most common means were economic. Parents were always able to use the threat of disinheritance to try to force a wayward son or daughter into acceptance of the parents' choice of spouses. Parents could also deny dowries to daughters that refused to marry their chosen grooms. As explained later in this chapter, except among the poorer classes, a woman without a dowry was unlikely to attract a suitable husband. Only those women who did not need to rely on their parents for their dowry could marry free of their parents' economic influence. Sons were subject to the same sorts of coercion. For example, among the peasantry, fathers often divided up the family lands and gave a portion to a son who was marrying. This land was vital for the son since it provided him with the means to support himself. Without this land, he would not be able to survive, let alone marry. As a consequence, a father could influence a son's choice of bride simply by refusing to allot him any land unless the bride was considered suitable. Similarly, among merchants and craftsmen, sons were often given some money or property, sometimes as an advance on their inheritances, to provide them with the resources needed to support themselves and their new brides. Again, by withholding such support, a father could quash any plans for marriage his son had if his choice of bride was unacceptable. A man was truly free to select his own bride only if he was already established in his own trade and no longer needed any financial support from his parents.

There were also cases in which parents resorted to cruder, more direct methods of forcing their children, particularly their daughters, into marriage. To force them to consent to marrying the husbands selected for them, fathers threatened their daughters with violence, including throwing them into ponds or breaking their necks. One particularly well-documented case of such coercion is found in late medieval England. Elizabeth Paston was the nineteen-year-old daughter of minor country nobility. Her father had died and in his will had requested that Elizabeth be married to someone close to her own age. Instead of following his wishes, Elizabeth's mother and brother arranged for her to marry a fifty-year-old widower. Elizabeth refused to marry the man. Her brother and mother put her under house arrest and beat her. A cousin intervened and persuaded the mother and brother to give up their plans. It then took more than ten years to find a husband whom Elizabeth would accept.

Some women were less strong-willed than Elizabeth and less successful in fighting plans for their marriages, and gave in to pressure from their families. Some of these woman subsequently attempted to have their marriages annulled on the grounds that they had been coerced into consenting. However, despite free consent being essential for a valid marriage, the Church courts rarely granted annulments in cases of coercion. The courts deemed the assertion of coercion to be negated if the woman lived peacefully with her husband after the wedding. By cohabiting with her new spouse, the courts held that the woman had given her consent to the marriage.

While the choices of spouses for most men and women were heavily influenced, if not dictated outright, by their relatives, there were some people who enjoyed a greater degree of freedom in selecting their partners. The boys and girls who migrated from the country to the cities and towns and became apprentices or servants were subject to far less parental control than those who remained at home. Those who stayed on in the cities and towns and created new lives for themselves likely made their own marriage matches without any interference from their families. Even the men and women who returned to the country may have had more of a say in who their spouses would be since they had accumulated money of their own and so were not wholly dependent on their families for dowries or dowers.

Other Approval for Marriages

Interestingly, for much of the Middle Ages, both those at the top of medieval society, the nobility, and those at the bottom, the serfs who were bound to the land, had to obtain the approval of their feudal lords before they could marry. In many parts of Europe, up until the middle of the 13th century, the daughter or widow of a nobleman could not marry unless her family's choice of husband had been reviewed and approved by the lord to whom they owed fealty. The reason for this requirement was that the husband would usually have control over the land which his wife brought into the marriage. This land, like all other land held by the wife's family, was held in exchange for their being the vassals of their lord and serving him. One of the most basic rights of feudal lord was the right to choose whom he would accept as a vassal, and so the lord had the right to decide if the prospective husband would be an acceptable vassal. This requirement was also often used as an excuse for the lord to collect a payment from his vassal by requiring the purchase of a license to marry. However, many lords recognized the ill-will this process generated and waived or limited this right. For example, in the 12th century, King Henry I of England required his chief vassals, the highest of the nobility such as earls and dukes, to consult him before they arranged marriages for their female relatives, but Henry did not levy any fees for his approval of their arrangements. Further, he stated that he would intervene only if a marriage was to any of his enemies.

As for men, kings and other lords sometimes played a role in arranging the marriages of their male vassals, but such marriages were not usually subject to the same review and potential veto as those of noblewomen were. The reason for this disparity was these men were already vassals of their lords, and their marriages did not alter the terms by which they held their lands from their lords. As for the lands brought into their marriages by their wives, it was up to the lord of the wife's lands to ensure that his rights were adequately protected.

At the opposite end of the social scale, lords had the right to require their serfs to obtain their approval before they could marry. As with noble marriages, this requirement applied only to women. The motive was the same in part. Any land or other property which the bride brought into the marriage was held from the lord in exchange for service. The lord had the right to assure himself that the husband was capable of rendering the service, such as cultivation and other farm work, that was due in exchange for the land. Lords appear to have rarely rejected their serfs' choices of spouses. It was in the lord's best interest to promote marriage among his serfs to ensure a settled and stable community to work his lands. These unions also helped secure the lord's future labor force, since the children produced by these marriages were serfs, just like their parents, and would work for their lord when they grew up.

Lords typically collected a fee or fine when the daughter of one of their serfs married. In England, this was called *merchet* and was assessed only against the bride and her family, although the groom was not precluded from paying it on behalf of his bride and many grooms did make the payment. The amounts paid for merchet varied widely and appear to have been based on the wealth of the bride's family as reflected in the size of the bride's dowry. Brides from poor families seem to have been largely exempt from merchet, likely because their lords knew they lacked the resources to pay. Toward the end of the Middle Ages, merchet payments were often token amounts and seem to have been levied more to remind the bride and her family of their servile status than to generate revenue for the lord.

Unlike some other fees which the lord claimed, merchet was not a cash payment in lieu of payment in kind. Feudal lords never had the right to have intercourse with the bride on her wedding night. This right, the so-called "Lord's First Night" or *jus primi nocti*, was an invention of opponents of the aristocracy in 18th century France. They created this legend to further blacken the image of the nobility as part of efforts to justify the overthrow of the monarchy.

Instead of paying merchet, some women purchased general licenses to marry from their lords. Such a license permitted a woman to marry any man she wished at any time in the future. The charges for these licenses were generally lower than those for merchet. This lower charge may have reflected the limited wealth possessed by a woman who was taking the arrangements of her marriage into her own hands. Women who took such action were likely from families which were too poor to furnish a dowry. These women had to rely instead on their own meager earnings to attract a husband and finance a marriage. One positive aspect of this situation, at least to modern eyes, is that these women were presumably free from parental influence in selecting their husbands. Without the economic leverage of the dowry, parents had few means of imposing their wills on their daughters' choice of husbands. As previously discussed, men as well as women from the poorer ranks of medieval European society enjoyed the greatest freedom from parental and economic pressures when selecting a spouse, although their selection was limited to other members of their class.

Serfs and noble weren't the only ones whose right to marry was subject to authorities other than their parents. As mentioned earlier in this chapter, apprentices were prohibited from marrying during the term of their apprenticeships. Apprentices who married without their masters' approval were subject to fines and other punishments for violating the terms of their contract. Wards were another group who could not marry freely. As explained later in this chapter, their guardians acted as surrogate parents and usually dictated whom they would marry.

Courtship

Although many marriages were arranged by parents or guardians, there was still a place for romance and courtship in medieval Europe. Even those men and women who had their marriages arranged for them often exchanged notes and tokens of affection during the negotiations. Further, outside of the nobility and the wealthy classes, there was greater freedom for men and women to choose their future spouses. This freedom was most apparent among the peasantry.

In the rural areas in which most of the population lived, there were festivals throughout the course of the year at which boys and girls as well as young men and women met and mingled. These included May Day, St. John the Baptist's Day (June 24), and harvest celebrations. Some of these festivals had their roots in pagan fertility rites, such as St. John the Baptist's Day, which fell close to the date for the summer solstice, a traditional time for celebrations in pre–Christian Europe. Not surprisingly, the Church condemned many of these celebrations but was unable to overcome the popular support for them. Singing and dancing were a common part of all these festivals. And, just as dances and other gatherings with music give men and women the chance to meet and flirt with each other today, medieval men and women certainly used these opportunities to find partners, whether for short-term dalliances or for marriage.

Betrothal

After a couple (or their parents on their behalf) had decided to marry, the next step was betrothal. To become betrothed, a couple exchanged vows in which they stated their intent to marry each other. This was sometimes done as a ceremony before a priest. In Italy, betrothals usually took place before a notary who formally recorded betrothal. At the very least, the betrothal was to take place before several reliable witnesses. The couple also sometimes exchanged rings at this time as tokens of their promises. Betrothal created a binding contract between the parties. Betrothals could be ended with the mutual consent of both parties, but if a party unilaterally withdrew from the contract, the other party had a legal right to sue for damages.

After the betrothal came the announcement of the wedding. By the 12th century, the Church required that the priest of the couple's parish make a formal announcement of the forthcoming wedding for three consecutive Sundays. If the couple resided in two different parishes, the announcements had to be made at both parishes' churches. These announcements were called *banns*. The priest read out the banns at some point during the Sunday church services when all of the residents of the parish were supposed to be in attendance. The purpose of the banns was to put the entire community on notice that the couple intended to be married and that anyone who knew of any reason why the couple should not be allowed to marry was to notify the priest immediately. Through these means, the priest could make a more informed decision as to whether there were any impediments to the proposed marriage.

Priests were generally prohibited from marrying couples who were not members of their parishes. Couples who sought to be married in parishes where their identities were unknown were presumed to be attempting to evade valid objections to their unions, such as their being related within the prohibited degrees. Couples who did this were subject to excommunication. Priests who performed weddings for such couples were also subject to severe punishment by the Church.

The Financial Arrangements for Marriages

Marriages in medieval Europe, particularly those of the nobility and the wealthy, were often preceded by bargaining between the bride's and groom's families over what assets each party would bring with them into their new household. In many instances, these negotiations were carried out before the formal betrothal of the couple. The bride and groom usually did not bargain on their own behalves but were represented by their fathers or guardians instead. The negotiations were sometimes quite protracted and the terms agreed upon were frequently recorded in written contracts. These contracts detailed the land and other property, such as livestock, which each party was bringing into the marriage, including the bride's dowry and the groom's dower or marriage portion. Some contracts went on to specify what rights each party had in the property, such as whether the property could be sold and whether such a sale required the consent of both spouses.

While elaborate arrangements of dowry, dower, and other financial provisions were primarily matters for the nobility and the wealthy, prenuptial negotiations occurred even among middling and poorer families. Although the assets of these families were quite modest, especially when compared with those of the nobility, a few acres of land or a small amount of money frequently constituted a substantial investment and were often the product of long years of working and saving. These valuables were not bestowed lightly on the new couple. Hard bargaining was often a part of arranging marriages and financial settlements even among peasants who held only enough land to support themselves.

Dowry and Dower

Following the customs of the Romans, it was a common practice in medieval Europe for the bride's family to give gifts to the groom and his family as part of the marriage arrangements. These gifts were the wife's dowry. The dowry was intended to provide for the wife's support both during her marriage and during her widowhood, should her husband predecease her. The husband held the dowry in trust for his wife and so he could not sell it or encumber it for any longer than his own lifetime without his wife's consent. However, the husband did have the authority to manage his wife's dowry in any way he saw fit. When a husband died, the wife reclaimed her dowry as well as inheriting part of her husband's estate. If their marriage was annulled, the wife reclaimed her dowry unless the annulment was based on her being an adulterer. If the wife predeceased her husband, her dowry passed to her children.

In contrast to the Roman practice of dowry, the custom among the Germanic peoples who invaded western Europe was for the groom to give gifts to the bride's family in exchange for being given the bride. These gifts were sometimes referred to as *brideprice* or *bridewealth*. Initially, brideprice rather than dowry was predominant in Europe. However, after the first few centuries of the Middle Ages, the practice waned in most of Europe, except Spain where it lasted through the 13th century. In the rest of Europe, by the 12th century, families were generally required to furnish dowries in order to attract husbands for their daughters. However, grooms still had to provide something for their brides. The groom's financial contribution towards the marriage was most commonly referred to as *dower*. Dower was a portion of the groom's property designated for the support of his bride both during their marriage and, should the groom predecease his bride, during her widowhood as well. Like dowries, dowers grew in size during the Middle Ages. To prevent dowers from becoming excessive, they were capped at one-quarter of the value of the dowry in some Italian cities. In other parts of Europe, the limit was one-third of the groom's total property at the time of the marriage. Upon the wife's death, her dower passed to any children she and her husband may have had. If there were no children, the dower reverted to the husband's family. In Germanic countries, the groom also presented his new wife with the *Morgengabe*. This was an additional gift to the bride and was traditionally given on the morning after the wedding in recognition of the consummation of the marriage.

The dowry provided parents with substantial leverage over their daughters when selecting a husband. Some fathers made their provision of a dowry conditional on their daughter's marrying a suitable man, likely one of their father's choosing. Even if a father did not state it outright, such a condition likely existed in most, if not all, instances. Fathers had *de facto* control over whom their daughters married since they controlled their dowries. If a daughter wished to marry someone of whom her father did not approve, her father could simply withhold the dowry.

Even death did not stop some parents from dictating whom their daughters would marry. In some instances, parents wrote conditions in their wills which required their daughter to either marry the man whom they had selected for her or forfeit her inheritance.

The items which made up a dowry depended upon the bride's position within society. A noble bride's dowry sometimes included vast areas of land as well as noble titles. For example, in 12th century France, the dowry of Eleanor of Aquitaine included the entire duchy of Aquitaine and the title of duke. Among the lesser nobility, dowries also included estates and titles. In the cities, dowries of daughters of successful merchants and craftsmen included large sums of cash as well as revenue from rental properties. Lesser businessmen gave their daughters correspondingly smaller amounts of money. In the countryside, peasants usually sought to give their daughters parcels of land as dowries, but only the wealthier peasants could afford such grants. Families were cautious about breaking their landholdings into pieces that were too small to support anyone. As consequence, peasants often gave their daughters livestock, small amounts of cash, and other more portable valuables as dowries. Some peasant dowries included a combination of tangible items and services such as the promise to build the couple a new house. Even among those who were moderately well off, dowries were sometimes paid in installments or as annuities so that a family could avoid the economic hardship of having to find the money needed for a single, huge, lump sum payment.

The amount of the dowry varied according to a number of factors. These included the scarcity of marriageable males. In fact, surveys of the aristocratic population of medieval Europe indicate that men of marriageable age were less numerous than comparable women. The risks of warfare appear to have taken their toll on the number of noblemen. When there were few suitable men, a large dowry was needed to attract a desirable mate. Besides being alive and of marriageable age, what made a man desirable? Among both the nobility and the wealthy, a man's social status and political influence were very important. Ideally, he should be equal or superior to his wife in social standing and political power. Parents always tried to avoid marrying their daughters to men who were beneath their class, but many either had to accept a social inferior or else have their daughter become a nun. If a daughter had to marry a social inferior, her family at least tried to find a husband who was the eldest son of his family. It was always desirable for a prospective husband to be the eldest son of his family since, among the nobility, the eldest son usually inherited the family's land and titles. Younger sons typically received little. Younger sons were desirable mates only if they were from a higher social class and so could enhance the bride's status or if they had made a fortune of their own, such as through success in warfare. An example of the former were royal princes. Even if they had little property, their high social standing conferred great prestige and political power. Further, there was always the chance that they might inherit property and titles if their older siblings died prematurely. Wealth was always a positive attribute for a man. Possession of large estates and other sources of revenue, whether inherited or earned, always made a man attractive. Age was sometimes a factor as well. While marriages of young women to men who were many years their senior were not uncommon, prospective husbands who were close in age were generally more desirable. In some instances, tenderhearted fathers tried to please their beloved daughters by selecting young men for them. More practically, younger men had a better chance of living long enough to sire children and continue the family line. There was also less chance that the bride would be left a young widow.

Over time, dowries among the urban classes grew to be quite large in some parts of Europe, especially in Italy. One location in which this phenomenon is well documented is late medieval Florence. Florence also provides a unique example of an attempt to cope with this problem. In 1425, the government of Florence took action to help parents with the high costs of dowries and established the *Monte delle doti*. This was a fund in which parents could invest money and receive a guaranteed return to use as their daughter's dowry. In some ways, it resembled modern state-run funds for college tuition which permit parents to lock in tuition rates. Similarly, just as many parents today begin saving for their children's college tuition when their children are still quite young, records of the *Monte delle doti* reveal that parents planned far ahead for their daughters' dowries. Daughters were typically about five years old when their parents opened up an account with the *Monte*.

By providing a source for the increasingly large amounts of cash required for dowries, the *Monte* allowed families to provide adequate dowries for their daughters while keeping family property intact. Without large cash reserves, families usually had to sell off parts of their property to provide dowries. This led to the fragmentation of estates, sometimes even to the point where the remaining estate was no longer sufficient to support the remaining family members. This economic problem discouraged families from allowing their daughters to marry. By providing an alternative source for dowry funds, the *Monte* also encouraged marriages at a time when Florence's population was still recovering from the depredations of the plague.

Even among the middling classes in the cities, there were some families with many daughters who could simply not afford adequate dowries for them all. Daughters without dowries had very poor prospects for marriage. Some remained at home and unmarried. Some accepted marriages to men who were willing to accept the little dowry they had, although such men were likely from lower social classes. Other remained at home and unmarried. Remaining unmarried for lack of a dowry was seen as a tragedy and it became an act of Christian charity to donate money to provide dowries for poor girls so that they could marry. For example, one of the legends about St. Nicholas which was popular in the Middle Ages was about his surreptitiously providing money to a poor father who could not afford dowries for his three daughters. In everyday life, donations for the dowries of poor girls were made as part of the charitable bequests in wills. This practice was particularly common in Italy.

Trousseaus

Brides also brought their trousseaus with them. The content of the trousseau varied depending on the social class of the bride. Among the nobility and other wealthy families, trousseaus included jewelry, fine gowns, and other luxury goods. As mentioned in chapter 4, in 1406, the trousseau of Princess Philippa, the twelve-year-old daughter of King Henry IV of England, included a wedding dress composed of a tunic and mantle of velvet and miniver (an expensive white fur). The dress and its sleeves were edged with the dark ermine fur. Among other luxurious clothes, she had five gowns, including three made of cloth of gold (a rich cloth with fine strands of gold woven in). Some of these were also edged in miniver and ermine. This finery was in addition to the jewelry and other riches she brought to her marriage.

In Italy, it was a common practice in the cities for the delivery of the trousseau to precede the bride's arrival at her new home. It was sometimes paraded through the street with some fanfare as it journeyed from the home of the bride's parents to the newlywed's home. Among middling and poorer families, trousseaus contained more utilitarian items, such as pots, pans, and bed linens. While much of the trousseau was for the bride's personal use, it was legally considered to be the property of her husband. Additionally, the value of the bride's trousseau was often included when calculating the amount of her dowry.

The Development of the Wedding Ceremony

As mentioned previously, weddings in the early Middle Ages were secular affairs. At the appointed time, the two families met at a convenient, public location and assured themselves that all the property settlements for the marriage were in order. These financial arrangements were also publicly announced at this point. The bride's father then gave her to the groom. This was more than just a figure of speech. In the Middle Ages, women were generally subordinated to men and, at the wedding, the authority over the wife was transferred from her father to her new husband. From that point on, he was responsible for her and she was subject to his discipline.

The first Christian wedding rituals appeared near the end of the 4th century. In these rituals, a priest blessed the couple after the completion of the secular ceremony. This blessing was commonly imparted when the couple was in their marital bed. As Christianity exerted more influence over marriage, the site of weddings shifted to the local churches. However, the focus long remained on the worldly transactions of the exchange of property and the transfer of authority over the bride rather than on the spiritual union of the bride and groom. Perhaps as a reflection of the Church's continuing ambiguous attitude towards marriage, weddings took place outside the church rather than inside. The usual location for weddings was in front of the church's main door, which was often sheltered by a porch (figs. 3, 4, and 39). Priests officiated at these services. In addition to executing their religious duty of verifying that there were no impediments to the marriage and that the couple freely consented to their marriage, priests also performed the secular function of announcing the arrangements for dowry and dower. By the late 12th century, the service at the church door was followed by a mass inside the church. With this addition, the Christian wedding ritual had reached the form it would follow for the rest of the Middle Ages.

Even after the Church succeeded in regulating marriage, there were still people who continued to wed in ceremonies outside of the Church. At these weddings, the exchange of vows was typically accompanied by the exchange of rings or clasping together of bride's and groom's hands to symbolize their union. These marriages were usually considered valid by the local community but, as discussed later in this chapter, the Church and secular authorities came to oppose any marriage which was not solemnized by a priest.

The Wedding Ceremony

Wedding ceremonies were usually performed on Sundays. Weddings could not take place during Advent (the four weeks preceding Christmas), Lent (the forty days before Easter), or Rogationtide (the days between Pentecost Sunday and the Feast of the Ascension). The timing of Rogationtide depended upon the date of Easter, and so it fell at varying times from late May to early June. January, October, November, and the summer months, except during Rogationtide, appear to have been the most popular times of the year for weddings. In part, the choice of these times for weddings reflects the predominantly rural culture of medieval Europe. Peasants were busy preparing the fields, plowing, planting, and tending their crops during the spring months. For those that raised livestock, spring was the time to oversee the births of their animals' young and care for these valuable but vulnerable additions to their flocks. At the other end of the agricultural cycle, late August through September were the busiest time of the year as peasants struggled to bring the harvests in as quickly as possible to prevent loss or spoilage. In contrast, January, October, and November were times of relatively little activity on farms, apart from the traditional slaughter of livestock in November. October and November were particularly suitable months to marry and celebrate, since the harvest was in and people could relax a little and enjoy the fruits of their labor. Summer, while the crops were growing and ripening but before any were ready

for harvest, also had periods of comparative idleness as well as pleasant weather for wedding celebrations.

At this time, there was no special wedding clothing for either the bride or groom. They likely just wore their best clothing for the occasion.

The wedding party and their friends and relatives proceeded to the porch of the church. The Church also encouraged all local residents to turn out as well to act as witnesses to the wedding. Witnesses were essential if the validity of a marriage was ever called into question, since Church courts required a minimum of two witnesses in order to prove that a union was binding. At the porch, the wedding party was greeted by the priest (fig. 39). He announced to those assembled that the purpose of the ceremony was to unite the bride and groom in marriage and that anyone who knew of any reason that the couple should not be allowed to marry should speak up and state that reason now. Assuming that there were no objections, the priest then conferred with the couple to determine that they were both of age and were not concealing any impediment to marriage such as being related to one another within the prohibited degrees. He also confirmed that they were entering into the marriage freely and were not being forced to do so. In many regions, the priest continued to verify that the financial arrangements for the marriage, including the endowment of bride with her dower, had been concluded.

The couple then exchanged vows (figs. 40 and 41). These vows were very similar to those still used at Christian weddings today. Each promised to have and to hold the other in sickness and in health, for better, for worse, for richer, for poorer, until death did they part. However, unlike the groom, the bride also had to vow to be obedient and cheerful. This requirement reflects the attitude of the time about the relations between men and women. Men were supposed to be the masters of their wives while wives were to be humble and submissive to their husbands. The Church supported the view that women were inherently inferior to men and that they should be subject to guidance and correction by men. Further, besides verbal chastisement, it was quite acceptable for a husband to correct his wife's behavior by physical punishment.

After the vows, the groom placed a ring on a book or a dish. In England, those who could afford it placed pieces of gold or silver along with the ring. The priest blessed the ring. The groom then picked up the ring and, following the priest's instruction, he then recited:

> With this ring I thee wed, and this gold and silver I thee give, and with my body I thee worship, and with all my worldly goods I thee honor.

The groom then placed the ring on the thumb, index finger, middle finger, and finally the ring fingers of the bride's left hand. While doing this, the groom recited:

> In the name of the Father [placing the ring on her thumb],
> And of the Son [ring on her index finger],
> And of the Holy Ghost [ring on her middle finger],
> Amen [ring on her ring finger].

In some accounts, the groom placed the ring on the thumb, index, and middle fingers of the bride's right hand and then placed the ring on the ring finger of her left hand. The placement

Fig. 39. The open arch framing the landscape beyond and the vegetation on the ground indicates that this wedding is taking place in a church porch rather than inside the church itself. The tonsured priest in the center of the picture is joining the bride's and groom's hands while the rest of the wedding party looks on. The bride is kneeling slightly, which reflects her submission to her new husband and her acceptance of him as her lord and master.

Fig. 40. This is another wedding ceremony. It appears to be taking place in a church but not in front of the altar, as became common after the Middle Ages.

of the ring on the fourth finger of the left hand continued the Roman practice, which was based on the belief that a vein ran directly from this finger to the heart. The practice of brides giving rings to their grooms did not appear until the 16th century.

The couple was now married and the priest gave the couple several more blessings. As mentioned previously, beginning in the 12th century, the wedding ceremony was followed by a special mass in the church for the new couple and the rest of the wedding party. For this service, the couple entered the church and knelt or prostrated themselves in the main aisle of the church. Here, the priest bestowed more blessing upon them. The couple then rose and advanced closer to the altar, where they heard mass. During the service, they again knelt or

Fig. 41. This depicts the marriage of King Juan I of Portugal to the sister of Henry IV of England in 1406. A bishop officiates instead of mere priest because of the high rank of the bride and groom. Still, the ceremony involves the same joining of the bride's and groom's hands that was a part of every wedding.

prostrated themselves (fig. 42). At this point, it was customary for a large veil to be placed over the couple by four members of the wedding party. A routine part of every mass was the *Pax*, a rite in which the congregation shared the kiss of peace. At a wedding mass, the priest gave the groom the kiss of peace who, in turn, gave it to the bride. After communion, the service then concluded with the priest bestowing additional blessings on the bride and groom. These included requests that God help the new wife to be modest, obedient, faithful, and fertile.

The wedding ceremony sometimes included an additional ritual to legitimate any children which the couple had had prior being married. Generally, any child conceived after the betrothal was considered legitimate. In most cases, the time between betrothal and marriage was not lengthy, so children conceived during this time were usually not born until after the wedding and so there was no question as to the legitimacy of these children. As for children born before the wedding, one 13th century account which claims to describe an old custom states that such children were legitimized at the point in the mass in which the veil was placed on the couple. The children were taken up and placed under the veil as well and, by this action, were legitimized.

Continuing the ancient practice, the service at the church was often followed by having the priest proceed to the new couple's home and bless their bed and bed chamber. With the couple in their bed, the priest prayed that the couple would have a long, happy, and loving

Fig. 42. By the late Middle Ages, after the wedding ceremony, newlyweds typically entered the church and attended mass. Here, the couple kneels before the priest as he bestows blessings upon them.

marriage and that their union would be blessed with children. This included dispelling any curses of impotence or barrenness which may have been placed on the couple. The priest also asked God to watch over the bed chamber and guard the couple. He concluded by sprinkling holy water on them.

Wedding Celebrations

Then as now, weddings were an occasion for celebration, and the families celebrated according to their means. For the nobility, weddings were marked with feasts and entertainment, including tournaments. For those further down the social scale, feasting and drinking in the home of either the bride's or groom's family was common. Drunkenness at wedding celebrations was a common occurrence, and the Church decried the fact that such scandalous and impious behavior so often followed what was supposed to be a serious occasion.

In addition to the general feasting, wedding celebrations in medieval Europe sometimes included a custom which was called *charivari* in England and France. In the charivari, neighbors and other members of the community donned masks and gathered up improvised musical instruments. They then "serenaded" the couple with raucous music. Bribes of wine or money to buy drinks at a nearby tavern were usually needed to persuade these musicians to stop and leave the couple alone.

Abduction

Sometimes the uniting of a man and a woman was done in a manner that was not condoned by society. In the records of criminal courts and other documents from across medieval Europe, there are references to the abduction of girls and women by men. In some instances, these abductions were genuinely violent crimes and frequently involved the rape of the unfortunate girls and women. The goal of some of these crimes was to force the victim into marrying her attacker. In such cases, after being kidnapped and raped, the unfortunate victim was held captive until she consented to the marriage. Rape often caused such disgrace and damage to the reputations of the victims that they were unable to find suitable men who were willing to marry them. Faced with these prospects and intimidated by their attackers, miserable victims sometimes gave in and married the men who raped them.

Some men made such attacks simply to obtain a wife. However, in many of these crimes, the victims were heiresses and the men's motive was to gain access to their fortunes by means of such coerced marriages. Not just young girls were subject to such attacks. Mature widows were also sometimes targets since they held estates inherited from their late husbands. In theory, such attackers were subject to the severe penalties including death, but they appear to have seldom suffered any punishments for their crimes.

The infrequency with which abductions were punished and the apparently high number of abductions which were followed by the marriages of the attackers and victims suggests that many abductions may have actually been elopements carried out with the consent of the girls involved. In these abductions, the girl's lover, sometimes with the aid of their friends, spirited her away from the house of her parents or guardian and then consummated their love. Faced with actions of their children and the public attention which seems to have often accompanied such unions, many parents appear to have acquiesced and allowed the couples to marry. Abductions such as these were sometimes featured in the romantic fiction of the day and involved noble lovers. Unfortunately, not all of these elopements were simply romantic adventures for two young lovers. In some cases, the girls involved were young heiresses who were seduced by men who only wanted to marry them for their wealth.

Regardless of the motives and circumstances behind the abduction, the Church opposed such actions and sought to end the practice. Through Church and secular pressure, abduction for the purpose of forcing a woman to marry against her will was largely suppressed by the late Middle Ages. As for elopement, this practice has survived to the present.

Clandestine Marriages

Despite the increasing role of the Church in marriages, many couples throughout the Middle Ages continued to marry without their unions being solemnized by the Church. Regardless of how public such a wedding and marriage were, the Church and held them to be "clandestine." However, the Church's own position that the only requirement for a valid marriage was the free consent of both parties facilitated marrying in this manner. As stated previously, in the early Middle Ages, there was no requirement under the law of the Church that couples had to express their mutual consent before a priest. Only the expression of consent was needed. Further, even after solemnization by a priest was required, the Church was still forced to find many clandestine marriages to be valid, although it denounced the circumstances surrounding these weddings as sinful.

Despite the opposition of the Church, many couples continued to marry without the benefit of a priest. Some may have married this way because they were poor and could not afford the expense of a church wedding. Others married without a priest simply because they saw no need for one. They felt themselves to be adequately bound to one another simply by exchanging vows. When any of these couples were brought before a Church court, the usual punishment was simply to order them to have their union formally solemnized by a priest. However, if they refused to do this, the courts sometimes ordered the couple to separate. If they failed to do so, they were subject to excommunication. Similarly, if a couple's union violated one of the prohibitions against marrying, such as consanguinity, the courts could order their marriage dissolved and forced them to separate unless the couple could obtain a dispensation for their impediment.

Many so-called clandestine marriages were formal and serious affairs in which the bride and groom publicly exchanged their vows and rings or other tokens of their intent to bind themselves together in matrimony. Friends, relatives, and others often witnessed these unions and celebrated them afterwards. However, not all clandestine marriages were so honorable and open. For example, records of Church courts reveal many cases in which women were seduced by men who had exchanged vows with them but which the men later denied were valid. Figures for Church courts around Europe prove that such cases were not uncommon. For example, in 1350, half the two hundred cases brought before the Church court in Augsburg were suits seeking the recognition of a clandestine marriage. Unless there were witnesses to the event, it was a matter of one's words against the other's, and so such cases were difficult to prove. Additionally, in some of these cases, the men involved were already married. Since polygyny was prohibited, these men knew that the court could not find their second marriage to be valid. However, these men were still subject to punishment by the Church. In some areas, bishops required that any man who had exchanged wedding vows with a woman for purposes of seducing her was to be punished by walking around the parish church three times while being whipped. The same punishment was also imposed on any man who exchanged vows with a woman in a tavern since it was presumed that the man was not sincere and was simply trying to seduce her. Sometimes harsher punishments such as excommunication were meted out by the Church as well.

Some couples resorted to clandestine marriage because there was some impediment to their being married, such as being related to each other within the prohibited degrees of kinship or because one of the parties was already married. These latter cases often involved people who had separated from their spouses without the sanction of the Church. In many of these cases, it appears that the first marriages were truly ended with the consent of both parties. Examples of such separation are found in legal records from the city of Ghent and other cities which reveal cases of separating spouses who documented their division of property and their resolution of child custody and support. Like many other types of contracts, these separation agreements were formally recorded by the cities' notaries. However, in some instances, the first marriages had not been ended and this fact was being concealed. Records from various courts reveal instances in which a person, usually a wife who had been abandoned, came forward after discovering that his or her spouse had married again without having obtained a legal separation. Not surprisingly, clandestine marriages generated work and fees for many canon lawyers.

Some of the couples who were prohibited from marrying simply exchanged their vows privately and then began living together as man and wife; others still wanted their unions to be blessed by a priest. To accomplish this, such couples went to parishes away from their home parishes to marry so that the priest would not be aware of their problem. The Church treated such attempts to bypass the impediments seriously and excommunicated couples who took such action. Further, any priest who married a couple whom he did not know personally risked serious punishment if it was discovered that the couple was prohibited from marrying.

Besides the religious issues surrounding clandestine marriages, such marriages also created problems for secular authorities. Unless there were adequate witnesses to a clandestine marriage, great legal difficulties could arise in determining whether children were a man's legitimate heirs. Further, only a validly married woman could reclaim her dowry and be granted her dower interest in her husband's estate upon his death. As a consequence, secular authorities deterred clandestine marriages by fiscal means. The primary deterrent was to deny clandestinely married couples the property and inheritance rights which legitimate couples enjoyed. Faced with these consequences, it was not unusual for a couple to formalize their marriage with a church service at some time after their original clandestine marriage.

Some couples who married clandestinely did not do so to avoid the Church's regulations. Some secretly exchanged wedding vows with their beloveds to escape parental control over their marriages. This is precisely what was done by Margery Paston and her lover, Richard Calle, her family's bailiff, in the mid–15th century. Incidentally, Margery was the niece of Elizabeth Paston, the woman who refused to marry the man chosen for her, whom we have previously discussed.

Margery and Richard fell in love and privately exchanged vows. When the seventeen-year-old Margery announced what she had done, her mother and her brother, who was the head of the family since his father was dead, were furious. The Pastons were minor nobility and so were outraged that Margery would dare to disgrace the family by marrying a mere servant. They immediately had the couple separated and began pressuring Margery to recant. Margery refused. The matter was finally brought before the local bishop to determine whether Margery and Richard's marriage was valid. The bishop heard the case, including examining Richard and Margery separately. During this process, the bishop strongly admonished Margery that she was bringing shame to her family and that her actions were alienating her from her friends and family, but Margery held to her conviction. Reluctantly, the bishop found that her marriage was valid. After nearly two years of separation, Margery was free to live with her husband. The Pastons virtually disowned Margery, ordering the servants that she was never to be admitted to any of the family properties again. Richard, on the other hand, continued to be the Paston's bailiff. One can only surmise that good servants were hard to find.

Love

Despite the fact that many marriages in medieval Europe were arranged by parties other than the couple, there was still courtship and romance in both arranged marriages and, of course, in love matches made by the couples themselves. Courting couples often exchanged of tokens of their affection, such as rings. Women sometimes sent scarves as keepsakes. For the nobility, some gifts for fiancées included quite costly items of jewelry and other luxury goods.

Couples also sent love letters to each other. Surviving correspondence reveals that, even in the midst of nuptial negotiations over finances, some couples wrote love notes along with statements of their bargaining positions. Notes such as these suggest that men and women who were facing arranged marriages frequently tried to make the best of their situations and endeavored to kindle some affection with their future mates.

Within marriage, the relations between husband and wife appear to have been as varied as they are today. But there were some fundamental differences between medieval and modern marriages. The most important was the relative position of the husband and wife in the view of secular and Church authorities as well as within society in general: a wife was to be subordinate to her husband. He was her lord and master. She was to obey him and be meek and humble. She was to accept his correction of her behavior even if this meant being struck. From legal records, we know that some husbands took such "correction" to extremes and abused their wives to the point of causing serious injury and death. However, these records also indicate that such abuse was not always tolerated. Relatives of the wife, neighbors, and sometimes even complete strangers intervened to stop a husband from beating his wife. It cannot be determined how common such intervention was since the records only reveal those cases which were serious enough to reach the courts, but these cases do show that unbridled abuse was not considered acceptable by much of medieval society.

While there were certainly marriages marked by violence, many marriages appear to have been amicable and some were certainly loving. While more scattered than the records of domestic violence, there is documentary evidence for such fortunate marriages. The lengthy lists of miraculous cures at shrines around Europe include many accounts of husbands and wives who made pilgrimages to seek help for their ill spouses. In wills, some spouses, especially husbands, included statements of praise and love for their partners. Thus, it should not be presumed that all marriages were loveless and that all wives lived in constant fear of their husbands.

The Indissolubility of Marriage

In the late Roman Empire, both husbands and wives had the right to separate from their spouses and end their marriages. Among the Germanic peoples who migrated into western Europe, only husbands were permitted to initiate the separation. Any wife who presumed to do so was subject to the death penalty. By the beginning of the Middle Ages, separations were permitted under secular law across Europe. Either a husband or wife could take action to end their marriage but, in practice, women appear to have seldom instituted such proceedings. Besides the general view that women should be submissive to their husbands, economics likely played a role in women's decisions about separation. A woman who separated from her husband lost his economic support. Admittedly, the wife's dowry was returned to her after separation, except in cases where the wife was an adulterer. However, unless her own dowry and any other resources she possess were sufficient to support her or she had relatives willing to take her in, a woman could easily sink into poverty after separation.

Under secular law, both parties were free to remarry regardless of who initiated the separation. The Church, on the other hand, condemned separation and remarriage but, as with other matrimonial matters, the Church had little influence over these issues until the late 11th century. As part of the reforms of Pope Gregory VII, the Church restricted the grounds for the dissolution of a marriage to coercion, consanguinity and affinity, impotence, adultery, and entry into the religious life.

Since the Church required that both parties freely consent to their union, the discovery that one of the parties had been coerced into the marriage was a reason to permit the couple to separate. However, as explained previously, Church courts were usually able to interpret the subsequent cohabitation of the parties as evidence of their mutual consent. As a consequence, the courts seldom dissolved marriages on the grounds of coercion.

Even in cases of consanguinity, the Church was loath to separate otherwise lawfully married couples. Instead of separating couples who discovered that they were related by consanguinity or affinity, the Church preferred that they obtain papal dispensation to permit their unions to stand. This was considered especially preferable if the marriage had already been consummated, but some couples were granted annulments even after they had had children.

Annulment was routinely granted when a husband was found to be impotent. In such cases, it was presumed that his handicap had prevented the couple from consummating their union. Further, impotence meant that the couple would not produce children, which was one of the central purposes of marriages in the view of the Church. Women freed from such fruitless unions were free to remarry. In contrast, annulment was usually more difficult to obtain in cases in which the wife was infertile. The Church courts may have been influenced by numerous biblical examples of women who became pregnant after long years of infertility.

As for adultery, in practice, only husbands appear to have acted as accusers. Wives had little recourse but to tolerate any extramarital affairs of their spouses. Husbands who were victims of adultery were urged to keep their repentant spouses. If the husband did choose to separate, he was barred from remarrying for as long as his ex-wife remained alive. The ex-wife was generally barred from over remarrying.

Finally, entry into the religious life was favored by the Church, and it carried with it the presumption that the husband or wife who became a cleric or a nun would be celibate for the rest of his or her life. However, marriage was still a sacrament and involved both vows to God and to one's spouse. The Church took both these vows seriously and did not let husbands or wives unilaterally break their vows. Before a husband or a wife could leave their marriage and embark on a life within the Church, both parties had to give their consent. Under such a separation, the spouse who did not enter the Church was usually barred from remarrying as long as the other spouse lived.

Obtaining an annulment was usually expensive. These fees and the costs of employing a canon lawyer to formulate and present the case to the court as well as fees levied by the courts themselves were often substantial. As a consequence, formal annulment was usually a matter for the nobility and the wealthy. Additionally, even after payment of these sums, there was no guarantee that the annulment would be granted. Church courts usually took these matters quite seriously and required genuine proof of the grounds and the need for the separation. The courts did not simply approve every request which was accompanied by the payment of requisite fees.

Annulment was not the only means for a couple to separate under the laws of Church. Legal separation was also permitted under canon law but it, too, was only granted for limited reasons, such as life-threatening physical abuse of one party by the other. Additionally, unlike in an annulment, legally separated men and women were not free to remarry. Faced with these limitations, some couples with marital problems took matters into their own hands and agreed to separate and live apart without having obtained any approval from the Church. By separating informally, couples avoided the burden of presenting and proving their cases to Church courts. They also avoided the fees and other costs of having their cases heard by the Church courts. While they lacked the approval of the Church, some of these separations did involve secular legal formalities. In city of Ghent, for example, some separating couples negotiated and formally recorded the division of their properties and debts as well as custody and support of their children. Although informal separations did not permit them to remarry, this did not prevent men and women who had separated from having lovers and living with them as though they were husband and wife. In some instances, these liaisons did provoke some scandal, but local society appears to have accepted the couples' actions in many cases.

Orphans and Wardship

One consequence of the relatively low life expectancy during the Middle Ages was that children frequently lost one or both parents before reaching adulthood. If only one parent died, children usually remained in the family home in the care of the surviving parent. There were exceptions, however, especially among the nobility. As explained later in this section, when a noble father died, his children often became wards of someone other than their mother.

The coming of age of orphans was often subject to many legal constraints which did not apply to those whose parents were still alive. Additionally, their marriages sometimes involved issues which were unique to orphans. Because of these differences from the general population, the entry into adulthood and marriage of orphans are addressed in this separate section.

Middling and Poor Orphans

When both parents died, someone had to be found to care for their surviving children. Among the middling and poorer classes, these unfortunate children were usually taken in by their relatives or neighbors. Such fostering was usually done on an informal basis without approval by any authorities, secular or lay. The only exception was for children of serfs. These children had the right to hold and work the land which their parents had held, but they were too young to perform the work needed to keep the land in production. In these cases, lords often appointed a guardian to work the land and care for the children. This guardianship lasted until the children reached an age when they could work the land themselves and become tenants in their own right.

Wealthy Orphans and Wardship

Orphans from wealthy urban families frequently underwent formal wardship. In many instances, fathers specified in their wills who the guardians of their children should be. Many made their wives the guardian, but other relatives such as their brothers or business associates such as fellow members of the father's trade or craft guild were also named as guardians. When no guardian was named, local authorities such as the city council or mayor determined who should fill this role. While being a guardian might seem like an undesirable burden, being a guardian of a wealthy orphan was sometimes quite profitable. The guardian managed the orphan's estate until he reached adulthood. Guardians were entitled to recoup their expenses for this service as well as for payments to support the orphan. In addition, many guardians appear to have often managed the estates in their care in their own best interests rather than that of their wards. Further, guardians had the authority to arrange the marriages of their wards, and there was profit to be made in arranging the marriage of a wealthy ward. As explained previously, arranged marriages were quite common in the Middle Ages and people were quite willing to pay for the privilege of having their child marry a ward who was heir to a large estate.

To guard against exploitation of wealthy orphans, some cities oversaw their wardships. The best documented examples of such civic care took place in London. The mayor and city council of London saw to the protection of the orphans' economic interests by having their inheritances inventoried and then keeping accounts of any charges made by their guardians. The mayor of London also had the right to arrange and approve the marriages of wards. In part, the mayoral oversight of marriages of wards helped ensure that the wards were being married to people of appropriate social standing. The goal was to protect wards from being forced to marry people who were of lower social standing than they were. Marrying someone of lower social standing was called *disparagement* and was considered a serious problem in a society which placed so much importance on social status. By maintaining control over the marriages of wards, the mayor sought to prevent greedy guardians from profiting by arranging disparaging matches. However, the mayor's actions were not entirely altruistic. He was entitled to a fee for every ward's marriage.

The age at which a wardship ended was sometimes set by the father in his will. When the time for terminating a wardship was not specified in a will, a wardship frequently lasted until the ward achieved the skills needed to fully function as an adult. In many cases, then, the wardships of male wards lasted until they completed their apprenticeships. For female wards, their wardships often lasted until they were married.

When a ward finally reached adulthood, his guardian was required to render accounts and return all of the ward's property along with the profits which the property had generated during the period of wardship. A former ward could sue his guardian if he believed that the guardian had defrauded him. This right was not limited just to the wealthy urban classes. Out in the country, peasant wards were able to sue their guardians in manorial courts once they had reached adulthood.

Noble Orphans and Wardship

Among noble families, when a father died while his children were still young and unmarried, his children often became the wards of his feudal lord. Even if their mother was still alive, they still became wards of their father's lord. In medieval Europe, it was generally believed that, when she remarried, the mother would be under pressure from her new husband to put the interests of any children she had in her second marriage ahead of the interests of her children from her first marriage. Despite this perception, in their wills, some husbands still made their wives the guardian of their children. On the other hand, laws in some parts of Europe forbade wives from becoming guardians of their children. Thus, mothers were often not permitted to become the legal guardians of their children because of this potential conflict of interest, and so the lord of the first husband became the guardian of the orphaned children. However, becoming a ward did not always result in being wrenched away from one's surviving family members and thrust into a strange household. Many wards continued to live with their mothers in the family home although they were legally the responsibility of someone else.

The lord or the guardian to whom the lord assigned the wardship was supposed to look after the ward's future inheritance and manage it in the ward's best interest. A guardian was needed since, without adult supervision, an estate could easily fall out of productive use. If this happened, the ward lost revenue and the lord was deprived of taxes and other income which he derived from his vassals' estates. As with wardships for wealthy commoners, when a ward reached the age of majority, the guardian had to render accounts and was supposed to turn over the entire inheritance along with the revenue which had accrued over the years of the ward's minority. The guardian was allowed to offset the expenses he had incurred in managing the ward's inheritance as well as his expenditures in feeding, clothing, and otherwise maintaining the ward. However, many guardians appear to have put their own interests ahead of the wards and used their wards' estates for their own benefit. Some kept all or part of the profits that had accrued during the wardship despite being required to render accounts to their wards when the wardships ended. Again like wardships for commoners, a noble ward had the right to take legal action against his former guardian if he suspected that he had been cheated. However, a noble ward had to weigh whether it was politically advisable to make such accusations against his equally noble guardian.

The fact that wardships were expected to be profitable for guardians is borne out by the common practice of trading and selling wardships. Kings and other higher nobility frequently bestowed wardships on favorite courtiers or other vassals as rewards for their services. These vassals often then sold these wardships to other members of the nobility. The value of the wardship depended upon the size of the inheritance and the prestige of ward's family. For example, the wardship of the son of an earl who stood to inherit vast landholdings, large annual revenues, a prestigious title, and the political influence that went along with these assets was obviously a very valuable commodity. On the other hand, the wardship of the son of a knight who held only a little property had a correspondingly lower value. There appears to have been a fairly active market in wardships, and some were sold repeatedly as guardians sought to turn a quick profit. In a few instances, mothers purchased the wardships of their own children, but this appears to have been done for economic rather than sentimental reasons since many of these mothers subsequently resold the wardships for gain.

Along with revenue from the estate for the duration of the wardship, guardians profited from arranging the marriage of the ward. As with marriages of wealthy non-noble wards, a noble ward who was destined to inherit a valuable estate was a very desirable match and many people were quite willing to pay a fee or commission to a guardian to secure a marriage for one of their children to such an heir or heiress. As a result, the right to arrange the marriage for a noble orphan was often a sought after commodity.

Marriages of wards were often arranged while the ward was still young. This was done for a number of reasons. Wardships for males usually expired when the ward reached the age of twenty-one and was eligible to assume his father's lands and titles, so any guardian who wished to profit from arranging the marriage of his male ward had to do so before the ward attained the age of twenty-one and passed out of his control. Female wards, on the other hand, were sometimes permitted to end their wardships when they were as young as fourteen, but girls usually remained wards until they married. Thus, there was usually less of a time constraint for arranging their marriages. However, because of the generally high mortality rates experienced in medieval Europe, there was also a significant risk that a ward might die and thereby deprive the guardian of his profit from any marriage. Consequently, the possibility of an early death provided motivation for marrying off both male and female wards at a young age.

The high rate of mortality during the Middle Ages also led to some wards being married repeatedly before they reached adulthood. This appears to have been especially common for heiresses. These girls, some only seven or eight years old, were sometimes married to noblemen who were many years their seniors. In some instances, these men died within a short time of their marriages and girls as young as nine were sometimes widows. While marriage often freed a girl from wardship, ones who were still so young when their husbands died became wards again and were again subject to being married off by their guardians. Even mature widows were not free from pressure to remarry. Noble widows who held valuable estates were frequently pressed to remarry by their lords as well as by male relatives who stood to gain by brokering their marriages.

Among the nobility, just as among the wealthy urban classes, unscrupulous guardians were sometimes willing to marry off their wards to persons who were beneath them in social standing but who were able to pay a high fee. As mentioned before, this practice was referred to as *disparagement*. Disparagement was so repugnant to the nobility that wards were permitted to bring suits to stop their guardians from marrying them to their social inferiors. Additionally, kings and other high nobility sometimes intervened or enacted laws to stop the practice. For example, in 13th century England, a provision barring disparagement was included in the Magna Carta. But apart from cases of disparagement, wards had little power to protest, let alone reject, their guardians' arrangements of their marriages. While the Church required the free consent of both the bride and groom, the guardian was the ward's surrogate father and as such wielded the same parental power to coerce the ward to marry the spouse selected for him or her.

In some instances, guardians were able to keep the ward's fortune within their own family by arranging for their wards to marry one of the guardian's own sons or daughters. However, not all of these marriages appear to have been contrary to ward's own interest. Guardians were usually of the same or higher social standing as the ward and so their children were appropriate matches. Further, since they were sometimes kept and raised within the guardians' households, wards may have grown up with their guardians' children and developed some affection for them during that time.

Given the value of the right to arrange their marriages, it is no surprise that a ward who managed to marry someone of his or her own choosing had to pay for that privilege. If a ward married without having first obtained the approval of his or her guardian, he or she was subject to a substantial fine. This fine was paid to the guardian as restitution for the loss of the fee he would have otherwise collected. In a few cases, the wards were sufficiently sophisticated to negotiate with their guardians and to purchase the right to arrange their own marriages in advance. Some wards did this when it appeared that their guardians were going to marry them off to persons they found unacceptable.

As mentioned previously, female wards typically remained under guardianship until they married. This led to another form of abuse of wardship. Despite the risk that their female wards might die young, some guardians delayed the marriage of their female wards for as long as possible so that they could continue to enjoy the revenue generated by the wards' inheritances. Other greedy guardians went further and, as mentioned in chapter 9, forced their wards into nunneries to deprive them of their inheritances. Some rulers recognized these abuses and took action to protect the interests of female wards. For example, an English law enacted in 1275 required guardians to arrange marriages for their female wards by the age of sixteen or else forfeit their rights over the wards' marriages.

Coming of Age in the Jewish Community

Jewish children were accepted into adult society in the same ways as Christian children were. Within their own communities, they were not held responsible for any misdeeds they may have committed before they reached the age of thirteen. Instead, their fathers were punished. The freeing of fathers of such responsibility for their sons' actions came to be celebrated in the rite of bar mitzvah. It is uncertain when and where this ritual first developed. Some 14th century German references attribute its development to the south of France in the preceding century. In any event, it was clearly being practiced in Germany in the 14th century. From northern Europe and southern France, it slowly spread south to the Jewish communities in Italy and Spain. The ceremony itself was not regularized throughout western Europe until the late 16th or early 17th century. Bat mitzvah, the coming of age ceremony for girls, did not appear until the 19th century.

Comparable to emancipation under Roman law, bar mitzvah came to mark a boy's entry into adulthood. However, also like emancipation, simply undergoing bar mitzvah did not actually result in a thirteen-year-old boy becoming a fully fledged adult. As with many emancipated Christian youths, Jewish boys typically continued to live in the home of the parents and were subject to their guidance and received their support. Instead, bar mitzvah marked a boy's progress towards adulthood and provided formal recognition that he was now mature enough to participate in religious services. This latter aspect was reflected in the practice of having the boy recite a blessing and read a passage from the Torah as part of a Sabbath service in the synagogue.

Bar mitzvahs were an occasion for a family to celebrate. From as early as the 15th century, bar mitzvahs were followed by large parties. The size of these celebrations grew over the centuries. By the 17th century, they had become so lavish that some Jewish communities in Europe enacted regulations to rein in the extravagance of bar mitzvah parties.

Jewish Marriages

As with Christians, some Jews practiced polygyny in the early Middle Ages. Among European Jews, the practice was formally ended in the 11th century. However, Jews in Muslim Spain continued to permit it until some time in the 14th century since it was an acceptable custom under the Muslims.

Jewish marriages in medieval Europe shared some common elements with Christian ones. For example, like Christian marriages, Jewish marriages required the free consent of both the bride and groom. However, as with Christian marriages, the fathers of the bride and groom exerted considerable control over the selection of spouses, and arranged marriages were quite common. While eighteen was considered the proper minimum age for a boy to marry and sixteen for a girl, many boys and girls were married at younger ages. At the age of twelve, girls were legally no longer minors and so were eligible to marry. Even so, some were still married below that age despite the disapproval of the rabbis. Boys appear to have rarely been wed before the age of twelve and most were in their mid- to late teens. Grooms were typically at least a few years older than brides. Within the Jewish community, the practice of child marriages was defended on the grounds that the position of Jews in medieval Europe was tenuous and disaster could strike at any time. Thus, fathers were justified in arranging their children's marriages while they possessed the necessary resources for dowries and other wedding expenses since they might lose their fortunes before their children reached adulthood. In contrast to the Christian practice, a Jewish boy who married as a child typically lived with his wife's family instead of having the bride live with the groom's family.

Because the Jewish population was thinly scattered across Europe and Jewish communities were often separated from each by considerable distances, medieval Jews sometimes had to go considerable effort to find suitable spouses. In eastern Europe, fathers sometimes arranged marriages for their children at trade fairs such as the one held at Lublin, which is located in modern day Poland. In other instances, traveling matchmakers helped arrange matches between men and women from different towns. These matchmakers were men who charged a fee for their services. In still other cases rabbis assisted in finding spouses. Since religious education was highly valued within the Jewish community, rabbis were particularly suited to recommend young men who were good scholars.

As with Christian marriages, Jewish marriages were preceded by negotiations between the two families to determine the financial contributions and any other support each family was to provide to the new couple. The financial arrangements and other conditions for the marriage were some times recorded in a contract called a *ketubah*. The negotiation of these contracts was usually conducted by the fathers of the prospective spouses. As part of these arrangements, the future groom designated a share of his property for the support of his wife which was comparable to the Christian dower. According to the noted 12th century Spanish rabbi, Maimonides, the husband was also obligated to provide his wife with nine other things. These were

- food,
- clothing, household furnishings including furniture and cooking utensils, cosmetics to keep her attractive to her husband,
- conjugal rights,
- medical treatment when she was ill,
- ransom if she was captured,
- burial when she died,
- the right to continue living in the couple's home after her husband died, until such time as she remarried,
- maintenance for their daughters from his estate when the husband died, and
- the right for their sons to inherit the wife's dower.

At some point during or after the negotiations, the couple was formally betrothed. Like Christian betrothals, this created a binding contract between the two parties, and any party which broke the contract was subject to monetary penalties. The betrothal was usually accompanied by a banquet. However, by the 11th century, this was often combined with the wedding feast since it was not uncommon for couples to become betrothed and marry on the same day.

The Wedding Ceremony

Not unlike Christians, Jews did not perform weddings during certain times of the year. For the Jews, no weddings were to take place between Passover and Pentecost. The Jewish

Pentecost covered the seven weeks after Passover. The fiftieth day after Passover was celebrated as the day that God gave the Ten Commandments to Moses. As for the preferred days for weddings, weddings could not be performed on the Sabbath. Despite the fact that celebrations carried over through the Sabbath, Friday was the most popular day for Jewish weddings in the Middle Ages. In observance of the Sabbath, Christian musicians were sometimes employed to perform for wedding banquets on that day.

The wedding clothing of the bride and groom reflected the mixture of joy and mourning common to many Jewish celebrations. In Germany, in addition to wearing their best clothes, grooms typically wore hoods or cowls that were worn for mourning. Brides sometimes wore fur-trimmed gowns over their white dresses as a sign of grief as well. Similarly, at the wedding feasts, laments over the loss of Zion were sung but these were balanced by songs about love.

At dawn on the day of wedding, the rabbi went to the house of the groom and led him to the courtyard of synagogue. People bearing torches and playing musical instruments often accompanied them. Having delivered the groom, the rabbi stayed at the synagogue while the torch-bearers and musicians escorted the bride from her home. With the courtyard filled with the entire wedding party, the rabbi brought the bride to the groom, who then took her hand. As the rabbi blessed them, the assembled group threw grains of wheat over the couple while calling out, "Be fruitful and multiply," three times.

The couple then proceeded into the synagogue for wedding ceremony although, when large numbers of people turned out, the ceremony was sometimes performed in the courtyard of the synagogue rather than crowding everyone inside. As with Christian weddings, these ceremonies were important social occasions and the entire community were encouraged to come and witness the union. Under the Talmud, a congregation, or *minyan*, of at least ten men had to be gathered to witness a wedding for the marriage to be valid.

The rabbi led first the groom and then the bride to the platform in the center of the synagogue. During the service, the bride and groom stood side by side with the bride on the groom's right. They were covered with a cloth of some type. At many weddings, the cloth took the form of a canopy supported by a pole at each of its four corners. Boys held the poles. In other instances, a veil was placed over their heads. In others, the groom's hood or the bride's veil was draped so that it covered both their heads.

The rabbi then blessed the couple. The wedding ring was then presented. Wedding rings had become part of the Jewish ceremony in 7th or 8th century.

The groom then recited: Behold thou art consecrated unto me by this ring, according to the Laws of Moses and Israel.

He placed the ring of the index finger of the bride's right hand. Two witnesses were then called up to testify that the ketubah and any other financial arrangements pertaining to the marriage had been settled. The rabbi then blessed the couple with seven benedictions.

At the conclusion of the blessing, the rabbi presented the couple with a cup filled with wine. The rabbi held the cup while the couple drank from it. When they were done, he handed it to the groom who threw it at a wall. This tradition of breaking a glass at the conclusion of the wedding ceremony was recorded as occurring in Ashkenazi Jewish communities in western Europe as early as the 12th century and appears to have already been a well established custom by that time. Later in the Middle Ages, it advanced from being customary to being a prescribed part of the ceremony. The origins of this practice are unclear and are still a matter of considerable debate. In some accounts, unmarried girls picked up pieces of the broken glass as tokens of good luck for their future marriages in the same way that bridesmaids today try to catch the bride's bouquet.

With the ceremony ended, the celebrations began. Traditionally, these lasted a full week, and all members of the community were invited. As with Christian wedding celebrations, music, food, and drinking were important parts of these lavish festivities and they were enjoyed even on the Sabbath although, as noted previously, Christian musicians substituted for Jewish ones on that day. These banquets took place either in the groom's home or at a public hall maintained by the community for such occasions.

Appendices

Appendix 1: The Humoral Theory

In several sections of this book, I mention the humoral theory of medicine. Here is a brief summary of the humoral theory. If the reader would like a fuller explanation, please consult the chapter on medicine in my book *Daily Life in the Middle Ages* or the books on medieval medicine listed in the bibliography for this book.

University students and others who studied medicine in the Middle Ages relied heavily on the surviving works of Galen, Hippocrates, and a handful of other medical experts of ancient Greece and Rome. While the true authorship of many of these texts remains dubious, they remained the standards for medical education and practice for centuries. The underpinning for much of these medical texts was the theory of bodily humors. This theory held that every person's health and temperament was governed by four bodily fluids or *humors*. These humors were blood, phlegm, yellow bile, and black bile. People whose balance of humors was dominated by blood were expected to have ruddy, healthy complexions and be cheerful, warm, and generous, while those with excessive phlegm were thought to be cautious, sluggish, dull, and slow to act for any reason. Excessive yellow bile would make a person thin, irritable and prone to anger, and too much black bile made one gloomy and depressed and possibly cowardly, pale, envious of others, and covetous of their possessions as well.

Under the humoral theory, everyone had some of each of the four humors and, while blood gave the most desirable characteristics, all four were needed for good physical and mental health. The key was that they had to be balanced in the right proportions. Imbalances would result in illness. The physician's task was to analyze a patient's humoral balance and devise a regimen to adjust the balance to maintain or restore the patient's well being. The regimen usually contained guidance on suitable exercises and improvements to diet. Virtually all regimens seem to have included bleeding as well. Bleeding, also called venesection or phlebotomy, typically involved making a small incision in a vein in the patient's arm and draining off some of the patient's blood, though veins on the forehead and elsewhere were sometimes tapped for particular ailments. Occasionally, leeches were used to suck out the blood, but the most common technique was to simply have a barber pierce or slit the vein open with a small knife.

Cupping was an alternative technique for bleeding. A number of small, shallow slashes were made in the patient's flesh at the appropriate location and then a little glass or metal cup was pressed over the scarified flesh. The cup was heated over an open flame immediately before being applied and created a slight vacuum as it sealed against the patient's soft flesh. Despite its requiring both slashing the patient's skin and sticking hot glass or metal on to the bleeding flesh, contemporary practitioners appear to have considered cupping to have been less hazardous or discomforting than venesection for drawing blood since they thought that cupping was especially suitable for women, children, and the elderly.

Regardless of which technique was used to remove the blood, the theory behind the practice of bleeding was the same: that the balance of bodily humors could be adjusted and corrected by drawing off small quantities of blood that contained excessively high levels of humors.

Appendix 2: Medieval Math Problems

1. Six workers were hired to build a house. Five were master builders and one was an apprentice. At the end of the day, the five masters were paid a total of 25 deniers. The masters divide their pay equally. From their pay, the master builders must pay the apprentice and each master must pay the same amount. The apprentice is paid half as much as a master. How much did each man receive?

    First, they divided 25 deniers equally between the five masters and each received 5 deniers. At half a master's pay, the apprentice's pay is 2½ deniers, so each master chipped in half of a denier, leaving each master with 4½ deniers.

2. A boy chased a boar and killed it but then stepped on a poisonous snake and received a fatal bite. While he is dying, his mother tells him, "If you had lived for as long as you have and yet that long again and then half as much plus a year, you would have lived to be a hundred years old, my son." How old was the boy?

    The boy lived for x years before he was bitten by the snake. *Starting on the day he was bitten*, if he had lived for as long as he had already (x+x=2x) and yet that long again (2x+2x=4x) and then half as much (4x+2x=6x) plus a year (6x+1=100), he would have been one hundred years old. 100–1=99. 6x=99. x=99/6x.=16½. He was 16½ years old when he died.

Appendix 3: The Children's Crusade

There is one episode in the history of childhood and growing up in medieval Europe which is so unusual that it does not fit into any of the topics discussed in the body of this book. That event is the Children's Crusade. This synopsis is drawn from the account in Sir Steven Runciman's *A History of the Crusades*.

There were two parts to the Children's Crusade. The first began in May 1212 in France, when Stephen, a twelve-year-old shepherd, claimed that he had been given a letter by Christ. The boy went to court of the French king to present the letter, but the king told him to go home. Undeterred, the boy decided to preach a crusade and rally the people to go to the Holy Land and retake it from the Muslims. (The Kingdom of Jerusalem and most of the other crusader states in the Middle East had been wiped out in 1187 after Saladin's victory at Hattin.) Despite his youth, Stephen was an effective and charismatic speaker and impressed many adults as well as children. He traveled around France and preached his crusade. He claimed that God would part the Mediterranean for them to reach the Holy Land just as He had parted the Red Sea for Moses. He told all who heard him to meet at the city of Vendôme, at the end of June. Vendôme, which is about 100 miles southwest of Paris, was near Stephen's home.

At the June, Vendôme was flooded with people, many of them children. One medieval account estimated the number at thirty thousand, but this was certainly an exaggeration. In any event, while their numbers cannot be established, Stephen had certainly attracted at least several thousand people to his cause. These were primarily peasant boys but there were also some of noble birth. There were some girls and adults as well, including some young priests. From Vendôme, they began their march to Marseilles, hundreds of miles to the south, where they planned to make their crossing to the Holy Land. Virtually all of them were on foot except for the noble boys and Stephen. The journey was long and the summer was reported to be exceptionally hot. Despite the charity they received along the way, many died, while others left and tried to make their way back home.

A much diminished group, still led by Stephen, finally did reach Marseilles. They went down to the harbor, expecting the sea to part so that they could continue their march directly to the Holy Land. When the sea failed to do so, some despaired and left to return home, but many others stayed and waited. Each day they expected to the sea to open. After several days, two merchants claimed that they were so moved by the children's piety and resolve that they would arrange their transportation to the Holy Land for free. According to tradition, these two merchants bore the inauspicious names of William the Pig and Hugh the Iron. Stephen and his followers gladly accepted the merchants' offer. The merchants hired seven ships and loaded the children on board.

Nothing was heard from these children for eighteen years. In 1230, a priest returned to France claiming to have been one of the young priests who had accompanied the children on their voyage. He said that two of the ships had sunk with all aboard in bad weather a few days after they had set out. The other five ships made it to the coast of Algeria. Once there, the children were handed over to local slave traders to be sold. Again according to tradition, this perfidious arrangement had been set up in advance by the two merchants. Most were sold in Algeria, but some, including the priest, had been shipped east to Egypt to be sold there. Some were shipped further east to Baghdad. This transshipment was in expectation that these slaves would fetch even higher prices in Egypt or Baghdad, where western Europeans were highly prized as slaves. The priest said that about seven hundred of the children were still alive in Egypt, while he had heard that eighteen of those sent to Baghdad had chosen to be martyred rather than convert to Islam. The priest claimed that he and the few other members of the crusade who were literate had been bought by the Muslim governor of Egypt and kept as translators, secretaries, and teachers. After years in the governor's service, the priest explained, he had been released and allowed to return home. There are no further records about the priest. This account is the only one which ever came to light to explain the fates of Stephen and his companions.

The second part of the Children's Crusade began in Germany, also in 1212. Stories about Stephen traveled east to the Rhineland. Here, a boy named Nicholas was inspired to follow Stephen's example but, instead of reconquering the Holy Land, he would convert the Muslims to Christianity. As for reaching their destination, Nicholas took a page from Stephen's book and promised that the sea would open up to permit his followers to walk to the Holy Land. Nicholas preached his crusade in the city of Cologne and attracted a large number of children, although contemporary accounts suggest that these were older children than those who followed Stephen. Additionally, Nicholas's group included more boys from the nobility as well as more girls. Further, while Nicholas also attracted some adult followers, they were prostitutes and beggars, unlike the priests that accompanied Stephen.

The contemporary accounts again place the number of children in the tens of thousands. Their numbers were so large that they split into two groups. One group, said to number twenty thousand, led by Nicholas, continued from Cologne, up the Rhine to Switzerland, then around the western part of Switzerland, through a pass in the Alps, and then down into Italy. The second group also traveled to Switzerland but took a more easterly route through the Alps and into Italy. Regardless of the route, both groups suffered heavy casualties, particularly on their climb through the Alps. The first group reached Genoa on the northwest coast of Italy in late August and was estimated to have lost more than two-thirds of its members. As for the second group, it came to Ancona on Italy's east coast and was likely similarly depleted.

The sea failed to open up at either Genoa or Ancona. The Genoese invited the children to stay on in Genoa permanently but any who did not had to move on. Many took them up on the offer and settled in Genoa. Nicholas led the rest further south to Pisa. There found two ships that were leaving for the Holy Land. The ships' masters agreed to take a few of the children on the voyage. The rest proceeded to Rome and were received by the pope. The pope was impressed with their piety but knew their expedition was doomed to failure. He told them all to go home and fulfill their vows of going on crusade when they were grown up. Few made it home. Many appear to have settled in Italy, while others died on the trek back north. The same fate befell those at Ancona. They had gone slightly further south to Brindisi where they found ships sailing for the Holy Land. A handful were able to book passage. The rest disbanded. Some stayed in Italy, and others tried to make it back to their homes, but many of them died on en route. Nothing is known about the fates any of the children who sailed from either Pisa or Brindisi.

Like Stephen, Nicholas disappeared. To avenge the loss of their children, some parents had Nicholas's father arrested. He was hanged for his son's actions.

Now, having said all this, considerable doubt has been cast on this version of the events. The primary medieval account on which the above synopsis is based was written at some time between twenty to sixty years after the events supposedly took place. The only contemporary record was in a chronicle written in Cologne in 1213. It describes a spontaneous gathering of thousands of children and adults, primarily peasants, who suddenly decided to go on crusade to Jerusalem in 1212. This group then proceeded east to Metz, a city which is now in northeast France on the border with Germany. The crusaders then turned south to march toward the Mediterranean. Some turned back along the way, but others traveled into Italy and reached Piacenza, which is a little over eighty miles from Genoa. Other proceeded on to Rome. Some others reached Marseilles. The chronicler wrote that it was unknown whether any reached the Holy Land. The entry concludes by noting that very few returned to their homes.

For the French portion of the crusade, there are no records in any of the areas in which the crusaders supposedly gathered or passed through on their way south. It seems highly unlikely that such an extraordinary event could have occurred without there being some contemporary accounts written in the cities along the route of the crusaders. As for the account written some decades after the events supposedly occurred, it appears likely that this version took the events described in the chronicle and embellished them. Still, there may have been a movement in France comparable to the German one but not on the grand scale in the later account. In any event, the Children's Crusade appears to have included many adults in its numbers and so was not the army of little children which the name evokes.

Bibliography

Abrahams, Israel. *Jewish Life in the Middle Ages.* Philadelphia: Jewish Publication Society, 1896.

Alexandre-Bidon, Daniele, and Lett, Didier. *Children in the Middle Ages.* Trans. by Jody Gladding from the French. Notre Dame, Ind.: University of Notre Dame Press, 1999.

Amt, Emilie, ed. *Women's Lives in Medieval Europe: A Sourcebook.* New York: Routledge, 1993.

Amundson, D. and Diers, Carol Jean. "The Age of Menarche in Medieval Europe." *Human Biology* 45, no. 3 (1973): 363–369.

Aries, Philippe, and Duby, Georges, general editors. *Revelations of the Medieval World: A History of Private Life.* Vol. 2. Trans. by Arthur Goldhammer from the French. Cambridge, Mass.: Belknap Press. 1988.

Benbassa, Esther. *The Jews of France.* Trans. by M.B. DeBevoise from the French. Princeton: Princeton University Press, 1999.

Benedict, Saint. *The Rule of St. Benedict.* Trans. by Anthony C. Meisel and M.L. del Mastro from the Latin. Garden City, N.Y.: Image Books, 1975.

Bennett, Judith M. "The Tie That Binds: Peasant Marriages and Families in Late Medieval England." In Neel, pp. 214–233.

Bonner, Stanley F. *Education in Ancient Rome.* Berkeley: University of California Press, 1977.

Bouchard, Constance B. "Consanguinity and Noble Marriages in the Tenth and Eleventh Centuries." *Speculum* 56 (1981): 268–287.

Boureau, Alain. *The Lord's First Night: The Myth of Droit de Cuissage.* Trans. by Lydia G. Cochrane from the French. Chicago: University of Chicago Press, 1998.

Bowen, James, and Bowen, M.J. *A History of Western Education.* London: Methuen, 1972.

Bradfield, Nancy. *900 Years of English Costume.* London: Peerage Books, 1987.

Braunstein, Phillipe. "Toward Intimacy: The Fourteenth and Fifteenth Centuries." In Aries and Duby, pp. 535–630.

Brundage, James. *The Crusades: A Documentary History.* Milwaukee: Marquette University Press, 1962.

Bullough, Vern L. *Universities, Medicine and Science in the Medieval West.* Aldershot, Hampshire: Ashgate Publishing Ltd., 2004.

_____ and Campbell, Cameron. "Female Longevity and Diet in the Middle Ages." *Speculum* 55 (1980): 317–325.

Camille, Michael. *The Medieval Art of Love.* New York: Abrams, 1998.

Cobban, Alan. *English University Life in the Middle Ages.* Columbus: Ohio State University Press, 1999.

_____. *Medieval Universities.* London: Methuen and Co., 1975.

Cooper, John. *The Child in Jewish History.* Northvale, N.J.: Jason Aronson, 1996.

Coppack, Glyn. *Fountains Abbey.* London: B.T. Batsford, 1993.

Courtenay, William J. and Miethke, Jurgen, eds. *Universities and Schooling in Medieval Society.* Leiden: Brill, 2000.

Crawford, Sally. *Childhood in Anglo-Saxon England.* Stroud, Gloucestershire: Stroud, 1999.

Cunnington, C. William and Phillis. *The History of Underclothes.* New York: Dover, 1992.

Cunnington, Phillis. *Children's Costume in England, from the Fourteenth to the End of the Nineteenth Century.* London: Black, 1966.

Davis, Isabel, Miriam Muller, and Rees Jones, Sarah, eds. *Love, Marriage and Family Ties in the Later Middle Ages.* Turnhout, Belgium: Brepols, 2003.

DeMause, Lloyd, ed. *The History of Childhood.* New York: Psychohistory Press, 1974.

Dronzek, Anna. "Gender Roles and the Marriage Market in Fifteenth-Century England: Ideals and Practices." In Davis et al., pp. 63–76.

Edge, David, and Paddock, John Miles. *Arms and Armour of the Medieval Knight.* London: Guild Publishing, 1988.

Fildes, Valerie. *Wet Nursing: A History from Antiquity to the Present.* Oxford: Basil Blackwell, 1988.

Fiorato, Veronica, Boylston, Anthea, and Knusel, Christopher, eds. *Blood Red Roses.* Oxford: Oxbow Books, 2000.

Fitz Stephen, William. *Norman London.* New York: Italica Press, 1990.

Fleming, Peter. *Family and Household in Medieval England.* New York: Palgrave, 2001.

Gidal, Nachum T. *Jews in Germany from Roman Times to the Weimar Republic.* Trans. by Helen Atkins, et al., from the German. Cologne: Konemann Verlag, 1998.

Gies, Frances, and Gies, Joseph. *Marriage and the Family in the Middle Ages.* New York: Harper and Row, 1987.

Goldberg, Harvey E. *Jewish Passages: Cycles of Jewish Life.* Berkeley: University of California Press, 2003.

Gordon, Eleanora C. "Accidents Among Medieval Children as Seen from the Miracles of Six English Saints and Martyrs." *Journal of Medical History* 35 (1991): 145–163.

Hanawalt, Barbara A. *Growing Up in Medieval London.* New York: Oxford University Press, 1993.

_____. *The Ties That Bound.* New York: Oxford University Press, 1993.

Herlihy, David. *Medieval Households.* Cambridge, Mass.: Harvard University Press, 1985.

_____. *Women, Family, and Society in Medieval Europe.* Providence: Berghahn Books, 1995.

Hildebrandt, M.M. *The External School in Carolingian Society.* Leiden: Brill, 1992.

Howell, Martha. "The Properties of Marriage in Late Medieval Europe: Commercial Wealth and the Creation of Modern Marriage." In Davis, et al., pp. 17–61.

Ifrah, Georges. *The Universal History of Numbers.* Trans. by David Bellos, E.F. Harding, Sophie Wood, and Ian Monk from the French. New York: John Wiley and Sons, 2000.

Jones, Peter Murray. *Medieval Medicine in Illuminated Manuscripts.* London: The British Library, 1998.

Kanarfogel, Ephraim. *Jewish Education and Society in the High Middle Ages.* Detroit: Wayne State University Press, 1992.

Kintzinger, Martin. "A Profession but Not a Career? Schoolmasters and the Arts in Late Medieval Europe." In Courtenay and Miethke.

Kirshner, Julius, and Molho, Anthony. "The Dowry Fund and the Marriage Market in Early Quattrocento Florence." *The Journal of Modern History* 50, no. 3 (1978): 403–438.

Leff, Gordon. *Paris and Oxford Universities in the Thirteenth and Fourteenth Centuries.* New York: Wiley, 1968.

Lynch, Joseph H. *Simoniacal Entry into Religious Life from 1000 to 1260.* Columbus: Ohio State University Press, 1976.

Marcus, Ivan G. *Rituals of Childhood.* New Haven: Yale University Press, 1996.

McCarthy, Conor, ed. *Love, Sex, and Marriage in the Middle Ages: A Sourcebook.* New York: Routledge, 2004.

McKee, Sally. "Households in Fourteenth-Century Venetian Crete." In Neel, pp. 347–404.

McLaughlin, Mary Martin. "Survivors and Surrogates: Children and Parents from the Ninth to Thirteenth Centuries." In deMause, pp. 101–181.

Mitchell, Piers D. *Medicine in the Crusades.* Cambridge, England: Cambridge University Press, 2004.

Montagu, Jeremy. *The World of Medieval and Renaissance Musical Instruments.* Woodstock, N.Y.: Overlook Press, 1980.

Neel, Carol, ed. *Medieval Families: Perspectives on Marriage, Household, and Children.* Toronto: University of Toronto Press, 2004.

Newman, Paul B. *Daily Life in the Middle Ages.* Jefferson, N.C.: McFarland, 2001.

Nicholas, David. *The Domestic Life of a Medieval City: Women, Children, and the Family in Fourteenth-Century Ghent.* Lincoln: University of Nebraska Press, 1985.

Nightingale, Pamela. *A Medieval Mercantile Community, the Grocers' Company and the Politics and Trade of London 1000–1485.* New Haven: Yale University Press, 1995.

Orme, Nicholas. *English Schools in the Middle Ages.* New York: n.p., 1973.

_____. *From Childhood to Chivalry: The Education of the English Kings and Aristocracy from 1066–1530.* London: Methuen, 1984.

_____. *Medieval Children.* New Haven: Yale University Press, 2001.

Owen-Crocker, Gale R. *Dress in Anglo-Saxon England.* Manchester: Manchester University Press, 1986.

Paterson, Linda M. *The World of the Troubadours: Medieval Occitan Society, c. 1100–c. 1300.* Cambridge, England: Cambridge University Press, 1993.

Pederson, Olaf. *The First Universities.* Trans. by Richard North from the Danish. Cambridge England, Cambridge University Press, 1997.

Piponnier, Françoise, and Mane, Perrine. *Dress in the Middle Ages.* Trans. by Caroline Beamish from the French. New Haven: Yale University Press, 1997.

Platt, Colin. *The Abbeys and Priories of Medieval England.* New York: Fordham University Press, 1984.

_____. *The Parish Churches of Medieval England.* London: Chancellor Press, 1995.

Power, Eileen. *Medieval English Nunneries.* Cambridge, England: Cambridge University Press, 1922.

_____. *Medieval Women.* Ed. by M.M. Postan. Cambridge, England: Cambridge University Press, 1975.

Rashdall, Hastings. *The Universities of Europe in the Middle Ages* (3 volumes). Ed. by F.M. Powicke and A.B. Emden. Oxford: Oxford University Press, 1936.

Reeves, Compton. *Pleasures and Pastimes in Medieval England*. New York: Oxford University Press, 1995.

Riche, Pierre. *Daily Life in the World of Charlemagne*. Trans. by Jo Ann McNamara from the French. Philadelphia: University of Pennsylvania Press, 1978.

de La Roncière, Charles. "Tuscan Notable on the Eve of Renaissance." In Aries and Duby, pp. 157–309.

Ross, James Bruce. "The Middle-Class Child in Urban Italy, Fourteenth to Early Sixteenth Century." In deMause, pp. 183–228.

Ruegg, Walter, and De Ridder-Symeons, H., eds. *Universities in the Middle Ages*. Vol. 1 of *A History of the University in Europe*. Cambridge, England: Cambridge University Press, 1992.

Runciman, Steven. *The Kingdom of Acre and the Later Crusades*. Vol. 3 of *A History of the Crusades*. London: Penguin Books, 1978.

Schwinges, Rainer Christoph. "Admission." In Ruegg and De Ridder-Symeons, pp. 171–194.

_____. "Student Education, Student Life." In Ruegg and De Ridder-Symeons, pp. 195–243.

Shahar, Shulamith. *Childhood in the Middle Ages*. Trans. by Chaya Galai from the Hebrew. New York: Routledge, 1992.

Sheehan, Michael M. "Choice of Marriage Partners in the Middle Ages: Development and Mode of Application of a Theory of Marriage." In Neel, pp. 157–191.

Sherman, Claire Richter. *Writing on Hands: Memory and Knowledge in Early Modern Europe*. Carlisle, Pa.: Dickinson College, 2000.

Siraisi, Nancy. "The Faculty of Medicine." In Ruegg and De Ridder-Symeons, pp. 360–387.

Soranus of Ephesus. *Gynecology*. Trans. by Owsei Temkin, et al., from the Greek. Baltimore: Johns Hopkins University Press, 1956.

Thordeman, Bengt. *Armour from the Battle of Wisby 1361*. Stockholm: Almqvist and Wiksells, 1939.

Thorndike, Lynn. "Elementary and Secondary Education in the Middle Ages." *Speculum* 15 (1940): 400–408.

_____. *University Records and Life in the Middle Ages*. New York: Columbia University Press, 1944.

Uitz, Erika. *The Legend of Good Women: Medieval Women in Towns and Cities*. Trans. by Sheila Marnie from the German. Mt. Kisco, N.Y.: Moyer Bell, 1990.

Verger, Jacques. "Patterns." In Ruegg and De Ridder-Symeons, pp. 35–74.

Vleeschouwers-Van Melkebeek, Monique. "Incestuous Marriages: Formal Rules and Social Practice in Southern Burgundian Netherlands." In Davis, et al., pp. 77–95.

Vorhringer, Christian. *Pieter Bruegel*. Cologne: Konemann Verlagsgesellschaft, 1999.

Werner, Alex, ed. *London Bodies*. London: Museum of London, 1998.

Index

Numbers in *bold italic* indicate pages with illustrations.